Heloise®
AROUND
the
HOUSE

2,647 Household Problems Solved from Basement to Attic

RODALE

Portions of this book were originally published in *All-New Hints from Heloise* copyright © 1989 King Features Syndicate, Inc. and *Heloise from A to Z: An Indispensable Home Reference Guide by America's Most Trusted Household-Hints Advisor* copyright © 1992 King Features Syndicate, Inc. by Perigee Books.

© 2003 by King Features Syndicate, Inc.

Reprint by arrangement with Perigee, a member of Penguin Groups (USA) Inc.

Printed in the United States of America
Rodale Inc. makes every effort to use acid-free ∞, recycled paper ♻ .

Photograph by Michael Keel Photography. Courtesy of King Features Syndicate, Inc.
Photograph © Michael Keel Photography. Courtesy of King Features Syndicate, Inc.
Illustration by Sandra Bruce
Illustration © Sandra Bruce

Book design by Tara Long

Library of Congress Cataloging-in-Publication Data

Heloise.
    Heloise around the house : 2,647 household problems solved from basement to attic.
        p.   cm.
    ISBN 1–57954–696–X hardcover
    1. Home economics.   I. Title.
TX158.H439   2003
640—dc21   2003001209

   4 6 8 10 9 7 5   hardcover

Acknowledgments

Thanks to my fabulous crew at Heloise Central—Ruth, Kelly, Jane, Joyce, Marcy, Brucette, and the ever-capable Merry, Editorial Director of Heloise, Inc. You help make everything I do connected to "Hints from Heloise" possible.

Many thanks to Mr. John Duff, who gently reminds me about deadlines! After 10 years of working together, you would think he wouldn't have to nudge me, but he does sometimes—and, oh, so pleasantly.

Especially thanks to the Heloise fans over the years who have submitted questions and great hints!

And, as always, thanks to my husband, David, who just smiles and says, "Oh, another book?" You are the glue that keeps me together.

introduction

When the "Hints from Heloise" newspaper column began in 1959, one mention of using cocoa butter to help heal a minor burn or using boric acid to rid your house of roaches caused a run on these items in drugstores. The reaction is the same today. Every time I mention white iodine to strengthen fingernails, my pharmacist asks me to please let him know about it ahead of time because he just can't keep it on the shelves.

So, although the column has spanned several decades, Heloise fans are still as loyal and numerous as ever, if not more so. And while the fan of 40 years ago was a "housewife," today's fan is anyone—young or old, male or female—whose lifestyle demands saving time, money, and energy. While things naturally change over time, some things remain the same—and the need for hints is greater than ever before.

Which brings me to the reason for this new Heloise hints book. I realize that Heloise hints can't solve all the world's problems, but they can help to make each person's individual world and daily life less stressed by the little things that are so aggravating.

And that's why I'm hoping that whoever is in charge of running the household can use this book to find all kinds of ways to make their household run more smoothly. But that's not to say they should do everything themselves.

Rather, this book is designed to be a practical reference guide for everyone in the house. In addition to tips on how to do things better, more quickly, and more economically, you'll find that some of the information in this book is very basic, such as how to iron or exactly what to do when cleaning a room. Perhaps the person in charge can use it when leaving notes to their household helpers—for example, "Please start [the laundry, supper, cleaning the bathrooms, etc.]. See page _____ in *Heloise Around the*

House." The pages to use for a particular job can be tabbed, and the specific way of doing a chore can be highlighted so that the helper knows exactly what to do. Another strategy would be to make a copy of the stain-removal section and thumbtack it to the wall above the washer so that everyone in the household can get their own stains out before the stains have set. The idea is to have the information where it's needed most.

Hopefully, strategies like these will help everyone in the house achieve the priorities they set for themselves. In a sense, my hints have always been about priorities. Do you want to spend time cleaning the bathroom tiles with a toothbrush? Or would you rather visit a friend or read a book? You make the choice; you set your own priorities.

For example, when it comes to housekeeping priorities, *clean* to some people means uncluttered; to others, it's totally antiseptically spotless and shining. To still others, *clean* is a "four-letter word," something to be avoided whenever possible. The point is that each person's level of what *clean* means is different, and one benefit of this book is that everyone can take exactly what he or she needs—and skip what doesn't fit into today's busy schedule.

In order to help you do just that, I've made this new book as easy to use as possible in several ways. For starters, it's arranged in an A-to-Z format with plenty of cross-references to help you find the information you're looking for quickly. Plus, you'll find symbols next to some of the hints. They cover a wide range of situations and will help you know at a glance how the hint can help you.

Need to find a faster way to do things? Hints that can save you valuable time have a picture of a clock beside them.

Looking for hints to help you remember things better? Look for memory-boosting hints next to the picture of a finger with a string tied around it.

Need to repair or replace something quickly? Hints marked with a lightbulb can shed light on ingenious ways to substitute one thing for another and fix problems fast.

Want to stretch your dollar? Follow the advice in the hints marked with a money sign, and you'll see the savings start to add up.

Looking for the best way to clean everything from alabaster to wicker? Just keep an eye out for the hints marked with a bucket, and you'll find the information you need fast.

 Searching for a new cooking idea? Look for hints that follow the small picture of a stove.

 Would you prefer to use Earth-friendly hints to help save our environment? Look for the hints marked with a picture of the Earth—they favor mild cleaning solutions over harsh chemicals.

 Are you passionate about recycling? Hints to help you recycle everything from old socks to window shades are marked with a recycling symbol, naturally.

Just for fun, I thought you would also enjoy the "Letters of Laughter" sent to me by readers. Take for example the reader who wrote to tell me she'd overheard a young woman at the grocery store asking for help to find the "elbow grease" she'd read about in Heloise's column. If only it really were a new product we could buy on the shelves!

Of course, if you have any hints you'd like to share, please send them to me at Heloise, PO Box 795000, San Antonio, TX 78279-5000. Or you can visit my Web site at www.Heloise.com or simply e-mail me at Heloise@Heloise.com.

As always, hugs,

ABRASIVE CLEANERS

Avoid them to protect sinks and tubs. Here are some reasons why I recommend cleaning with baking soda and vinegar instead of abrasive cleaners. Baking soda and vinegar are both simple, gentle, environmentally safe cleaners. I should note that my mother and I both recommended them because they are cheap and safe, long before I even met my husband, David, a plumbing contractor. David and I joke about having a premarital agreement that if he finds a can of scratchy stuff stashed away anywhere in our new home, it could be justifiable grounds for divorce.

It's a scary fact that most powdered cleansers on the market will scratch your sinks and tubs and can cut the life of a new fixture by 10 to 15 years. They also scratch kitchen fixtures and plastic-like surfaces such as laminated countertops, fiberglass sinks, and shower stalls. Surfaces lose their shine once these cleaners scratch them, and they become dull, porous, and more easily stained.

If you prefer commercial products to plain, cheap baking soda and vinegar, clean with spray-on, foamy-type bathroom cleaners. Also, powdered dishwasher detergent has enough chlorine bleach in it to clean like powdered cleansers, but protect your hands if they are chlorine-sensitive.

Sometimes just a squirt of liquid dishwashing detergent and a little extra elbow grease will do the job.

See also BATHROOMS and KITCHENS.

ACRYLIC PLASTIC DOOR PANES

Restore storm doors. Despite careful cleaning with various commercial products, one reader said that her storm door's acrylic panes stayed dull and cloudy most of the time. Then she applied liquid furniture polish with a soft, lint-free cloth and was amazed at how easily they became sparkling clean and clear.

ADDRESS BOOKS AND LABELS

Safeguard your losses. Because losing an address book is an incredible inconvenience, I keep a duplicate in my safe in case of fire—the addresses are as important to me as any other valuable!

Keep them neat. Write the names in ink and the address and phone number in pencil. Then you can correct them if the people move.

Add instant addresses. Cut the return address labels from envelopes and tape them to file cards or in address books.

Create change-of-address postcards. When you have a large family and circle of friends and move a lot, notifying everyone about your latest move is a chore. Here's how to make it easier. One reader gets one change of address form from the post office and fills it in appropriately. Then she has a local print shop copy the filled-out address form onto blank, plain 4- by 6-inch index cards—much faster and easier than writing in the information over and over! Don't forget to mail the cards!

Consider a file format. Instead of an address book, keep track of your mailing list in a 3- by 5-inch index card file. You can then simply replace the cards of people who move a lot. Add notes on birthdays, anniversaries, home and work phone numbers, and other helpful information such as a couple's children's names, their food preferences or allergies, and directions to their homes. (My family was military and I remember how hard it was to keep track of such information when you have a large circle of friends who stay on the move.)

Seven Smart Ways to Use Address Labels

Address labels are so inexpensive that I love to find new uses for them. Here are some of my favorites.

♥ Give extra address labels (like those you get from organizations soliciting donations) to college students or elderly relatives to use when they write to you. (And in the case of students, hope they use them!)

♥ If addressing envelopes is a bother, have labels printed for the people to whom you write most, get labels duplicated at a copy shop (ask for a "master" on which to put addresses), or ask people for their extra labels! Then, don't forget to write!

♥ When you move, send a label with your new address to your friends and business contacts so they can just put the new label over your old address.

   Hint: Look for labels that will hold four lines so that the first line can be "We've Moved to:" or "Note New Address." If you can get five lines, have your new phone number printed on the label, too. To make sure there's no way to miss it, have them printed on yellow green or other bright "Day-Glo" paper.

♥ Stick an address label on your note or tablet paper for "custom-printed" stationery. Your address will always be legible.

♥ For identification for joggers and walkers, put an address label on the tongue of each walking or jogging shoe so that you can be identified in case of an accident on the road.

♥ Stick your address labels on the Halloween treats that you give away so parents know who gave them and that they are safe.

♥ Stick a label on your casserole dish or serving utensils so that when you take them to potluck affairs, you'll always get them back.

ADHESIVE BANDAGES

Remove without pain. Soak a cotton ball with baby oil and apply it to the sides of the bandage. In about 10 minutes, the adhesive will be softened so much that the bandage will come off automatically and painlessly!

ADVENT CALENDARS

 Unwrap holiday decorations at turkey time. If your family practices the tradition of using an Advent calendar or wreath but forgets to get them started on time, pack the Advent things with Thanksgiving decorations as a reminder. Save by buying Advent calendars at post-Christmas half-price sales.

AIR-CONDITIONING

It's hard to imagine how people survived in hot climates before air-conditioning made comfortable life as we know it possible. How our ancestors must have sweltered! Since air-conditioning can be 50 percent of your utility bill in a hot climate, it's important to choose an air-conditioning system wisely, making sure that it is neither too big nor too small. Here are some things to keep in mind when buying and using air conditioners.

Find out the square footage to be cooled. According to the Department of Energy, an air conditioner usually needs 20 Btu's for each square foot of living space. If a room is 20 feet long by 15 feet wide, calculate 20 feet $\times$ 15 feet $\times$ 20 Btus = 6,000. The room needs an air conditioner with a 6,000-Btu capacity. Buy a unit within 5 percent of this capacity. (When calculating Btu capacity for central units, you also have to take into consideration your home's individual needs, such as ceiling heights, floor plans, and number of stories. For example, the Btu can be lowered if you have the benefit of trees and shrubs to cool the house, but if you use a lot of heat-producing appliances, the Btus will increase. Sometimes, more than one central unit is needed in a home.)

Compare the ratings. Energy efficiency is probably the most important consideration when you are buying an air conditioner. All new air conditioners have yellow "Energy Guide" labels that show their efficiency ratings, and help consumers choose an appropriate model for their needs. Units with a rating of "9" or more are very efficient.

Check your fan speed. Set the fan speed at high, except in very humid weather, when it should be set at low. Although you'll get less cooling, more moisture will be taken from the air, and this will make you feel cooler.

Set the temperature that you want. When you first turn on the air conditioner, don't set the thermostat lower than the temperature you want. If you set it too low, it won't cool any faster, but it will cool to a lower temperature, wasting energy and increasing your utility bill.

Keep filters clean. Check filters monthly and clean or replace them as needed. This can cut your utility bill by 5 to 15 percent.

Note: If you have a long-haired pet, you'll be surprised at how quickly your filter becomes full of hair! You may have to check it more than once a month. My service technician told me that if a dirty filter allows pet hairs to get to the AC heating unit's coils, the damage caused is considered "lack of maintenance" and may not be covered by appliance insurance.

Don't confuse the thermostat. If you place heat-producing appliances near the thermostat, it becomes "confused" and runs longer than necessary.

Provide some cover. Most central air-conditioning and heat pump units are placed a distance from the outside wall of your house to help muffle the fan's noise, which means the unit may be deprived of shade from the building. Heat from summer sun increases air-conditioning energy use by about 5 percent. In winter, sun exposure increases the heat pump's heating capacity. It is generally recommended that you provide some sort of portable shade for the unit that can be removed in the winter, such as a collapsible lath-covered frame made from 2- by 2-foot laths or an awning if the unit is close enough to the house. Awnings can also shade window air-conditioning units in the summertime.

See also HEATING AND COOLING.

ALABASTER

 Clean it like marble. Alabaster is similar to marble in that both are very soft, so you can clean it with some marble-cleaning kits. Read the instructions on the label.

Or try this gentle method. You can also wipe alabaster items gently with mild detergent suds, and then rinse and dry with a clean, soft cloth. Use this general cleaning method only occasionally; cleaning too frequently can damage alabaster. Commercial cleaning kits are also available.

ALARM CLOCKS

Use a snooze tag strategy. You can find the snooze button with your eyes closed and one hand still gripping your pillow if you stick a self-gripping fabric dot on the snooze button.

ALBUMS AND SCRAPBOOKS

Protect old pages. If the pages of your favorite scrapbook begin to crumble with age, place them between clear plastic protector sheets. Use clear protective covering from hobby shops to protect odd-size pages.

See also MEMORY BOOKS.

ALLERGIES

Those of us who suffer from allergies are the darlings of the advertising world. We consume antihistamines and decongestants, and nobody knows how many forests have been destroyed to produce the paper pulp for our tissues. Here are some hints for allergy sufferers.

See a doctor. Your allergist has a whole new battery of tests and medications to help you. Using some of the new inhalants before going where the pollen flies will help a lot, and some of the new antihistamines won't make you drowsy.

Get rid of the allergens when you can. Cut your grass before it goes to pollination and seed. Wear a mask when you mow the lawn to keep from inhaling the dust and pollen the mower is throwing into the air. Find out when your town's peak pollen times are and stay indoors during those times. Shower and shampoo immediately after working or playing outdoors to get pollen off your skin and out of your hair.

Hang up the clothesline. When bedding is hung outside to air, pollen flying around in the breeze clings to it and is brought indoors with it—irritating you when you try to sleep in that "fresh" bed. Use a clothes dryer instead of hanging clothes and bedding outside, even if you have to miss that fresh air scent!

Replace your pillows. Often, when people have a chance to sleep away from home on polyester-filled or foam rubber pillows, they find out that they are allergic to feathers. Don't wait—replace feather-filled pillows now.

Control the mites. It's not uncommon to be allergic to dust mites, which live in carpets and furniture. Dry air from winter heat and summer air-conditioning controls these mites.

Clean the air conditioner. If you are sensitive to molds, you may be aggravating your allergies when you turn on your car air conditioner. Many car air conditioners are contaminated with mold spores, and most of them blast out at you when you turn on the air conditioner. If you run the air conditioner with the vent closed and your car windows open for a short time (better with you out of the car), you may get relief. You can have your air conditioner cleaned out at some car dealers and service centers.

Say "goodbye" to real houseplants. If you are allergic to molds, avoid houseplants because molds grow in their soil and on their pots. If you replace your real plants with fake silk ones, don't forget to dust them, because you may be allergic to dust, too.

Use the vacuum. If you have allergy sufferers in the house, it's better to vacuum up dust and pollen and all the other stuff floating around and landing on the furniture. A feather duster just throws the dust someplace else, where the poor allergic soul can breathe it in.

Clean regularly. Of particular note, bathroom mold and mildew can cause allergy symptoms. Scrub sinks and fixtures regularly and mop hard-surface floors at least once weekly.

Be informed about pets. Yes, you can be allergic to pet dander, and yes, pets bring pollen into the house on their fur. But, like other animal lovers, I don't want to even think about getting rid of pets! First, try restricting them to certain areas of your home. If someone living in the house becomes seriously ill with asthma or has other major allergy problems from animals, however, you may have to consider parting with your pets.

Get to the bottom of it. If you have skin allergies, work with your doctor to find out if you're allergic to fabrics, metals in jewelry, plants, dyes or whatever—then eliminate what you can from your wardrobe. I know lots of people who are allergic to fabrics that contain even small percentages of wool, linen, or ramie.

ALMONDS

"Roast" them in the microwave. Here's an easy way to get that roasted flavor. Toss the almonds with oil to coat them lightly. Arrange them in a single layer on a microwave-safe plate. Heat them on full power for 2 minutes. Toss again and let rest 1 minute. Heat 2 minutes longer, until almonds are golden brown. Drain and cool on paper towels.

ALUMINUM

Cash in on cans. Pick up aluminum cans when you walk. You'll be exercising and helping the environment at the same time. If you don't want to turn the cans in yourself, give them to a church or other fund-raising group.

Reuse aluminum foil. If you line cookie sheets with aluminum foil, use that same foil, unwashed, to cover up the plate of cookies or between layers of cookies if you store them in a tin. If you'd rather save it for another use, clean it with a damp sponge, wiping the foil from the center out to the edges, smoothing as you clean.

Hint: If everybody could use every disposable thing at least twice, we'd cut our daily trash output by half. That's not really realistic, but we can try to use as many disposables as possible at least twice to decrease trash output and save landfill space in our environment.

ANIMALS

Help stray cats and dogs. Strays lead a hard life, fighting disease, each other, and traffic on dark streets. Unfortunately, they usually lose the fight. So call your local animal rescue organization if a stray animal finds you. Even if you don't plan to adopt the animal permanently, get it neutered and make sure it has its immunizations; it's really the kind thing to do. Also, the animal you're feeding may be registered as lost with the shelter, and its owner may be anxiously waiting for word about it.

Keep cats and dogs from shrubbery and porches. Sprinkle hot pepper powder or flakes on the area that needs protection. Flakes will settle into the grass and last for several days so that you need apply them only twice a week or so (only once a week after a while). The animals may eventually avoid that place even if you don't put out flakes anymore.

Note: Flakes will definitely last longer in the grass and soil, but hot pepper powder (also called powdered red pepper) will do the job, too.

Feed wild animals with ease. If you feed your pets outside or feed birds, squirrels, and other creatures, it's convenient to store the food outdoors. Keep uninvited animal guests from eating it by storing it in a self-locking trash can.

See also PETS.

ANSWERING MACHINES

Test it out. We take these machines for granted, but they do wear out, and you may be missing your messages due to malfunctions. Most machines have a setting that allows you to check your outgoing message periodically to see if it's working properly.

Leave reminders. When you think of "must do's" at work, call your home answering machine to leave yourself a message—no more lost self-notes!

Announce good news. Not all messages have to be straightforward and businesslike. For example, if you have a new baby, put a message on the machine that gives the baby's weight and other vital statistics. Then say that you and the baby are napping, and you'll call back later.

Provide information—cautiously. Give an alternative number that the caller can use to reach you if there is one. It's never wise, though, to have your message say that nobody's home.

Screen your calls. If you've been having too many telephone sales calls or calls from anyone else that you don't want to talk to, let your machine answer all calls for you. Turn up the volume so you can hear the message being given on your machine; then decide if you need to call back immediately.

Avoid harassment. If you have been struggling with a series of obscene or just annoying callers, it's better not to put your name or any other identification on the machine. Just say, "Leave your message at the beep, and I'll call you back" until the harassing calls stop. Most of the time, the caller will hang up. If not, you have a record of what was said if you report the call. Don't return calls to any name or number that you don't recognize. Look in your phone book for instructions on what to do about annoying or harassing calls. And don't hesitate to call your local phone company for help with this problem.

ANTIFREEZE

Keep it contained. Animals, especially dogs and cats, love the sweet taste of antifreeze, and only 2 ounces is enough to kill a pet. Once ingested, there is little to be done for the animal. Keep all antifreeze containers away from pets and wipe up all spills thoroughly.

ANTS

Powder their trails. Sprinkle boric acid or borax powder along the ant trails and entrances. Keep crumbs vacuumed and any other ant "treats" wiped up so you don't attract more.

Caution: Boric acid can be toxic to children and small pets. Keep it out of their reach.

Keep them from Fido's feast. If ants regularly dine on your pet's outdoor feeding dish, make a moat! Partially fill a shallow dish with water and place the pet's food dish in the center of it.

See also PEST CONTROL.

APPLES AND APPLESAUCE

Grate it. If you can't bite apple chunks because of dental problems, grate apple for adding to salads or fruit compotes.

Freeze with ease. Peel, core, and slice apples. Sprinkle with lemon juice or ascorbic acid (sold at supermarkets) to keep them from turning brown. Store in freezer containers or plastic freezer bags in specific-use quantities like 1-, 2- or 3-cup packs so they'll be ready for recipes.

Keep them from the carrots. Apples give off ethylene gas and will make carrots bitter if stored in the same crisper drawer with them.

Make homemade sauce rosy pink. To make a lovely pink applesauce, don't pare the skins of red-skinned apples, such as Cortland or McIntosh, before you cook them. Wash apples, cook them with the skins on, and then press them through a sieve or run them through a food mill (sold in cookware departments or shops), which will mash the cooked apples and remove their skins and seeds.

See also PRODUCE.

APPLIANCES

They slice, dice, chop, stir, wash, dry, clean, cool, and heat. And, like the human helpers in our lives, appliances need some TLC (tender loving care). Often the problems we have with appliances result from misuse or lack of cleaning.

Maintaining Appliances

We keep our human helpers going by saying "please" and "thank you" and "You sure did a good job." We keep our appliances going with maintenance. And, just as some humans need more encouragement than others, some appliances need more pleases and thank-yous than others and a bit more TLC. Here then are some hints for the best appliance maintenance, use, and care.

Save service contracts and booklets. Manufacturers spend a lot of money researching and developing their products, and they provide printed materials with them so that you will know how to properly use and troubleshoot these products. You paid for the research and development and the resulting booklets when you paid for the appliance, so you might as well get your money's worth by keeping the instruction booklets, guarantees, and warranties in one place so that you can get them easily when you need them. Put them in a three-ring binder or accordion folder, assign one special drawer in the kitchen for them, or keep them in a filing cabinet. Or you can put them in a large envelope and tape the envelope to the back (or side, if inconspicuous) of the appliance.

If you've lost your appliance booklet, it can usually be replaced if the product is still on the market. Dial information, (800) 555-1212, or check on-line, to get the manufacturer's consumer information number. Most have 800 numbers or call your local public library's business information number and get the address and phone number.

Unplug appliances when not in use. This safety warning is often given but seldom heeded as we leave toasters, automatic shut-off irons, sewing machines, hair dryers, and other appliances plugged in, feeling confident that they are not on. Readers have sent me examples of near-disasters caused by leaving appliances plugged in between uses. The "toast" button on one family's toaster oven accidentally got pushed down and wasn't noticed until the smoke detector went off just in time to prevent an electrical fire. A roll of paper towels fell on a toaster oven; the oven went on and then the towels overheated to the point of catching fire. A rolled-up rug was placed on the foot treadle of a sewing machine, which was threaded and plugged in. The machine caught fire after running for hours with the thread tangled in the bobbin case. The family woke up to a smoke-filled house.

It takes only a few seconds to unplug an appliance. Those are precious seconds that could save your life or property! *Always* unplug unused appliances, and check smoke alarms frequently to be sure the batteries are working.

Don't rely on extension cords. Some appliances such as electric fry pans or roasters may not heat properly when plugged into extension cords. Try plugging such appliances directly into the wall socket.

Cleaning Appliances

Always unplug appliances for cleaning or servicing. Never immerse a whole appliance or its electrical components in water unless the manufacturer's booklet specifically states you can do so. This safety information is so important.

Clean your blender or food processor correctly. Quick-clean your blender or food processor by filling it halfway with water and adding a drop or two of liquid dishwashing detergent; run it a few seconds to wash away all the built-on particles, rinse, and let dry.

Don't fill it up. Blenders operate best if only two-thirds full. A blender that is too full may not operate at all.

Appliance Reliance

In the following table, I've listed the average number of years an appliance can be expected to function. I've also detailed the typical minimum and maximum life expectancies for these products. These life expectancies are based on the first owner's length of use and don't necessarily mean that the appliance is worn out.

Use this information to plan your next appliance purchase. If your appliance conks out at an age that is near the maximum, it may be more economical to buy a new one than to have it repaired—most likely over and over again, until you've spent the equivalent of a new appliance.

And naturally, if your brand has lasted longer than the average, you'll surely want to buy the same brand next time.

Here are the average, minimum, and maximum life expectancies (in years) of many household appliances.

Appliance	Average	Minimum	Maximum
Air conditioner	11	8	14
Blanket, electric	8	7	10
Can opener, electric	7	5	10
Charcoal grill, outdoor	6	3	9
Clock, electric	8	5	10
Clothes washer	12	9	14
Compact stereo system	6	5	7
Corn popper	5	4	7
Desk calculator	7	5	10
Dishwasher	11	8	14
Dryer, electric	13	11	16
Dryer, gas	14	12	16
Electric fan	16	11	22
Fax machine	8	7	10
Floor polisher	11	4	13

Appliance	Average	Minimum	Maximum
Furnace, electric	18	15	22
Furnace, gas	16	13	20
Garbage disposal	10	7	12
Hair dryer	4	2	6
Home-security alarm system	14	10	17
Humidifier	8	6	11
Ice-cream maker, electric	9	7	10
Iron	9	6	12
Lawn mower, power	8	5	10
Microwave	11	10	14
Personal computer	6	5	10
Range, electric	15	13	19
Range, gas	15	11	18
Refrigerator	13	11	18
Shaver, electric	4	3	5
Smoke detector	10	8	15
Snow thrower	10	6	12
Styling comb, electric	4	3	5
Telephone answering machine	5	3	5
Television, black and white	7	5	7
Television, color	8	6	10
Toaster	8	5	9
Toothbrush, electric	3	1	3
Trash compactor	10	8	13
Typewriter, electric	8	7	9
Vacuum cleaner	11	4	12
Videocassette recorder	7	6	8
Waffle iron	10	5	11
Water heater, electric	12	8	17
Water heater, gas	10	5	13

Clean your electric can openers. In order for them to work well, clean the blade with a scouring pad, scrubber, or an old toothbrush. Clean blades help your opener work efficiently and are more sanitary.

Don't neglect your toaster trays. If the tray in the bottom of your toaster is covered with crumbs, the thermostat won't work properly to give your toast the shade of brown you want. Also, crumbs at the bottom of the toaster can catch fire. Usually there is a latch on the bottom of the toaster that releases the tray so that you can clean it. Open the tray over the trash can and dump the crumbs right in. Or turn the toaster upside down and give it a few gentle shakes to release stuck-on crumbs.

Troubleshoot a malfunctioning vacuum cleaner. If your vacuum cleaner has lost suction, check to see if the bag is too full or if objects are caught in the intake mechanism. Use a seam ripper or a single-edged razor blade to cut across the hairs and threads that get wound around a vacuum cleaner's or carpet sweeper's rotating brush.

Use waffle irons right. New or recently cleaned grids can stick. Before using them, grease with unsalted fat and preheat thoroughly before pouring on batter. To clean metal grids that have accumulated burned-on grease, place an ammonia-soaked paper towel or napkin between them, and leave it overnight. Then clean with steel wool and rinse well. If you have nonstick grids, follow the manufacturer's instructions.

See also DISHWASHERS, DRYERS, FANS, FREEZERS, HUMIDIFIERS, IRONING, MICROWAVES, OVENS, REFRIGERATORS, TELEVISIONS, VAPORIZERS, WAFFLE IRONS, and WASHING MACHINES.

AQUARIUMS

A well-balanced aquarium with bottom-feeding and top-feeding fish and a properly functioning filter system needs less maintenance than most people think. In fact, too much fussing and water changing can disturb the pH and the bacteria balance in a tank—not to mention disturbing the fish, which become disoriented when you change their scenery too often. These tips will keep your aquarium in tip-top shape (not to mention crystal clear) and lessen maintenance chores for you.

Don't buy your aquarium and fish at the same time. Even if you don't have to allow the water to season, as you do for saltwater fish, having the tank set up for a few days gives you a chance to make sure the filters and motors work properly and that the tank doesn't leak. It's no fun to move fish around when you find defects in your aquarium setup, and it can harm the fish.

Check water temperature regularly. If the room in which you keep your aquarium has a constant temperature, you may not need to heat your aquarium and, in fact, you may tend to overheat the water. Check water temperature frequently with an aquarium thermometer. Most fish live well at 68° to 72°F. Fish are healthier if they aren't submitted to too many changes of water and temperature, and they will be most active at moderate temperatures. Too cold or too warm water makes them sluggish and can stress your fish; it can also encourage growth of bacteria in the tank.

Use only store-bought decorations. Souvenir shells from the ocean may be contaminated with bacteria or parasites. Shells from a dime store could be lacquered, and some decorations could have poisonous paints or other chemicals on them.

Make your own decorations. The one exception to store-bought-only rule concerns the plastic backdrop decorations you can buy from the store. If you'd rather make your own, tape a sheet of wrapping paper to the outside back of the aquarium.

Don't mix sun and water. Putting a fish tank in front of a window may seem like a good decorating idea, but sunlight makes algae grow. Aquarium stores keep their tanks in the dark and use the tank lights to display fish. If left on too long, even aquarium lights will encourage algae growth, so experiment to find the timing that works best for your tank's lighting.

Save some seasoned water. Always dechlorinate water before adding it to a fish tank, and always return some of the "seasoned water" to the tank when you clean it. Dechlorinate water by letting it stand for several hours or by using commercial preparations that dechlorinate water with a certain number of drops per gallon.

Don't throw away the "used" water from your aquarium. If you have a fresh water tank, not a saltwater one, when you clean out your fish aquarium, water your plants with this free nonchemical fertilizer solution.

Mix saltwater separately. If you maintain a saltwater aquarium, use a large plastic wastebasket or small plastic garbage can to mix up your saltwater or dechlorinated water for the aquarium. If you don't keep a container specifically for this purpose, avoid getting harmful substances into the tank by lining the wastebasket or garbage can with a clean, sturdy plastic garbage bag, which you can use for garbage after you've mixed the water and put it into the tank.

Use salad tongs. Move aquarium decorations, such as shells and ceramics, with plastic salad tongs instead of contaminating the water with your hands. A plastic spaghetti grabber also helps you to move things around in the tank.

Or try shish kebab sticks. Unplug mineral deposits from aquarium tubing with wooden shish kebab sticks. They are also useful for cleaning algae out of a tube. Make a long-handled cotton swab by wetting the end of a shish kebab stick and twirling the wet end in an appropriately sized wad of cotton.

Feed them green. Allow some of the green algae that form under your tank lid to fall to the bottom and feed invertebrates in a saltwater tank. Then you won't have to buy green algae from the pet store freezer compartment.

Keep algae under control. Excessive algae can turn white coral or other tank decorations murky gray, but you don't have to throw these expensive decorations away. Make them white again by soaking them overnight in a solution of 1 part liquid chlorine bleach to 4 parts water.

Caution: You must remove the bleach before returning the decorations to the tank. Do this by soaking the items in water to which you've added at least 5 times the normal amount of dechlorinating chemicals. Soak them until you can't smell any chlorine in them.

Clean with salt. Because detergents may leave harmful residue, scrub an empty aquarium with noniodized salt and a heavy-duty plastic pot scrubber (one without any soap in it).

"Baste" the bottom. A kitchen baster makes a good vacuum for the bottom of the tank. Don't wave it around as you remove the gunk, or you'll splatter it everywhere. And use this baster only for the fish tank!

Keep the lid on. Always have a lid on the aquarium to keep things from falling in and to keep the fish from jumping out. Yes, even some very small fish are "jumpers" and will land belly-up on the floor!

Listen to the motor. When your usually quiet aquarium motor starts to hum loudly, it's probably getting ready to die. Better buy a spare.

Give gravel a new life. Put used aquarium gravel in a terrarium or the bottom of flower pots before planting; substitute it for florist foam in flower arrangements; or layer different colors in an apothecary jar.

Note: Not all fish tanks require gravel, and some newer filter systems are not under gravel. Also, some fish, such as African Chiclids, dig so much that you're better off placing appropriately colored pebbles at the bottom of your aquarium.

See also FISH.

ASPARAGUS

Keep it on ice. The fresher asparagus is, the better it tastes. But if you have to store asparagus for a day or so, here's what to do. Put the uncooked asparagus stalks in a deep pot with the cut ends down. (Trim a little off the hard bottoms so the stalks can take up water.) Pour ice water into the bottom of the pot, and cover it with a plastic bag. Keep the pot in the fridge until you're ready to cook.

Microwave easily. For variety, place asparagus in a shallow microwave-safe dish and pour chicken broth over it. Sprinkle cut-up shallots and a bit of lemon juice on top, and then microwave for a few minutes (see your microwave book for times per amount) until the asparagus is hot.

See also PRODUCE.

AUTOMOBILES

Some years ago, my column had a hint to put a plastic flower or bicycle safety flag on your radio antenna to make it easier to find your car in mall parking lots. Afterward, I received lots of "Letters of Laughter" telling me that the best way to find your car in the lot was *not* to follow the hint. It seems that almost everyone attached something to their radio antennae, and it was easier to spot an undecorated car in mall parking lots.

If only every aspect of having and maintaining a car was so simple! Nonetheless, I've tried to make it as simple and straightforward as possible. Here are some of the best automobile hints for making life on the open road a bit easier.

Battery care

Clean corrosion with carbonated colas. If the battery terminals are heavily corroded, the easiest way to solve the problem is to pour a can of carbonated soft drink over them; it will eat away all the corrosion.

Try baking soda. Or, you can mix 1 or 2 tablespoons of baking soda with water and pour over battery terminals. It will bubble away the corrosion.

Keep corrosion from coming back. After removing the connections to the terminals and cleaning them well, rub a little petroleum jelly around the posts and the inside of the terminals; then reconnect. This will help prevent corrosion, which is the major obstacle to recharging a battery.

See "Jump Starts" on page 262 for more information.

Cleaning

Keeping your car in tip-top shape will get you a better price when you trade it in and make it more pleasant to ride in while you own the car.

Keep it clean. Wash your car only with soap formulated especially for car washing, never dishwashing soap or other such products. The car-cleaning pros use soaps with a neutral pH factor—the pH of water. (The pH factor is the amount of acidity or alkalinity in a solution: Low pH signifies high acid, and high pH signifies a very alkaline solution. Both are bad for your car's finish.) And if you live where road salts are sprinkled to deter ice, wash your vehicle as often as possible to prevent damage and corrosion, or you'll find yourself dealing with lots of rust.

STEP ♥ BY ♥ STEP

Summer Driving

Overheated cars can spoil summer travel. When the temperature-warning light flashes or the heat gauge registers in the hot zone, try the following hints.

1. Turn off the air conditioner to give your car's cooling system a rest. Turn on the heater to drain some of the heat away from your engine.

2. If your car continues to overheat, pull out of traffic to a safe parking place. Put the transmission into neutral and race the engine for a minute or two. This increases the fan speed and moves more air through the engine compartment.

3. If the temperature gauge still says hot, turn off the ignition, raise the hood, and wait for the engine to cool off. Then get to a repair facility.

Don't forget to dry. The chlorine in city water will leave droplet marks if you don't towel dry your car. So if you wash your car at home, wipe it down afterward with old, terry-cloth towels. (Terry cloth is better than chamois for washing and is good for drying, too.)

Note: Make sure the towels are clean. It takes only a bit of grit to scratch a line across the finish.

Protect the paint job. Waxing your car at least three times a year protects against grime and sunlight and keeps the paint shiny. As a rule, a good heavy-duty paste wax will last 6 months or more and will give the finish better protection than liquid waxes. Remember to always apply wax in a shady area. Car wax applied in full sunlight gets "baked on" and is hard to remove.

Keep on top of touch-ups. Keep a small bottle of matching color touch-up paint (bought at auto supply stores or dealers) to cover up small scratches, chips, and minor nicks before they become rust spots.

Wash off road tar. Spray spots with an oil-based prewash spray. Let it set for a few minutes, then scrub with nylon net or a plastic scrubber. Reapply to stubborn areas. Rinse and buff with a soft cloth.

Don't forget the inside. In the car interior, protect vinyl with a cleaner/protector to keep it from drying out and cracking. This also helps prevent color fading. Vinyl car tops are especially prone to these problems. Maintain cloth upholstery by removing dirt and dust before it gets ground into the fabric. A quick brush or vacuum will do the trick. Foam upholstery cleaner will remove the dirt from cloth seats.

Insurance

Get the best rate. Make sure you get the best rate for the amount of coverage that you need. Newer cars purchased with a car loan are required to have full coverage. Older cars can get by with liability coverage alone.

Ask for discounts. Check your insurance to see if you'll qualify for a reduction in rate by installing an antitheft device or for having certain safety features like antilock brakes. Don't just pay without asking questions.

Don't loan a rental. If you lend a rental car to anyone, the collision damage waiver agreement may be invalidated if a driver who's not listed

Auto Safety Checklist

Having an accident or car breakdown is bad news, but a little preparation can make it less terrible. Keep the following items handy in your trunk or glove compartment, and you'll be well prepared for most roadside emergencies.

- ♥ Flashlight with extra batteries
- ♥ Ice scraper
- ♥ Road salt or cat litter
- ♥ Extra windshield-washer fluid
- ♥ Set of jumper cables
- ♥ Duct tape (for minor repairs)
- ♥ Flares or reflective devices
- ♥ Extra container of antifreeze
- ♥ Blanket
- ♥ Sweatshirt or jacket
- ♥ Pair of gloves and hat
- ♥ Sandpaper to clean corroded battery terminals
- ♥ Plastic sheeting or garbage bag to kneel on in case you have to fix a flat on wet ground
- ♥ Spare change
- ♥ Emergency phone numbers (including one for road services)
- ♥ Cell phone

on the rental agreement causes damage, if the accident doesn't occur on a highway, or if the rental company believes you were the careless driver in an accident (even if the other driver is clearly at fault). The deductible for most collision damage waivers is $100 to $250, to be paid by the auto renter if the car is in an accident.

Roadside Emergencies

Make it easy to get help. Place an envelope in your glove compartment marked "In Case of Accident" that contains the name and phone number of a person to notify in case of emergency, your doctor's name, your blood type, and any allergies you may have.

Keep a "throw-away" camera in your glove compartment. It's easier to remember details if you photograph damages, license-plate numbers, street signs, construction work or other obstacles, and anything else that gives you information for filing and proving an insurance claim.

Don't stray in the snow. If you're stranded in a car during a snowstorm, above all stay calm and stay put. Don't leave your car unless you can see another shelter close by. While you wait for help, alert passing vehicles with flares, reflective triangles, or even a brightly colored piece of cloth tied to your car antenna. Keep warm in the car by running the heater once an hour or every half hour in extreme cold.

Caution: To avoid carbon monoxide poisoning, check around your car to be sure the exhaust pipe and heater vents are not obstructed by snow or anything else.

Safety

Say "hands up." Get into the habit of saying "hands up" to child passengers before you close the door to avoid hand injuries, and make "Hands Up" a standing rule.

Color code your seat belts. When there are three seat belts in the backseat, it's hard to figure out which parts go together. An easy way to keep them straight is to color code the belts. Use colored Christmas tape or colored "dots" so that riders can match the buckle parts according to color.

Be safe with your car keys. Keep car keys separate from house keys. Don't put your name and address on key chains. Don't leave house keys in your car. If you leave keys with a valet, leave only the car key—never house keys—and don't tell when you will return.

Practice safe parking. Park your car with the front end toward the street and as close to a building as possible. This makes it easier to spot anyone tampering with it. At night, always park in well-lighted areas. If parking on the street, always turn the wheels sharply to the curb; it makes towing difficult. Put the emergency brake on.

Install an antitheft device. You can install an alarm system that turns on lights, car horn, or siren if someone tampers with the car or a locking gas cap or fuel switch that cuts off the fuel supply when the car is parked. Or you can buy a "crook lock" or "club lock," which either locks the steering column to the brake pedal or prevents the steering wheel from being turned without breaking the windshield. These devices make stealing a car so difficult that they are excellent deterrents—thieves won't bother with them.

See also BUMPER STICKERS, GARAGES, and TRAVEL.

BABIES

Try out these uses for a baby-bottle brush. The pointed tip and flexibility make these brushes ideal for cleaning crevices and corners, like the holes of cheese graters or the space around faucets.

Reuse the baby gate. Expandable doorway gates used to keep children and pets out of rooms can be stretched widthwise across the bathtub for sweater drying. (Be sure the gate is plastic-coated or has no metal parts to put rust marks on the sweaters.) When your toddler grows up, nail two wood strips inside a closet to support the tension of the gate and make a "closet dam" to hold out-of-season blankets, comforters, extra pillows, and children's sleeping bags for overnight guests.

Open baby-food jars easily. Instead of wrestling with vacuum-sealed jar lids, place the end of a spoon handle under the rim of the jar lid. Pry it open just enough to break the seal and pop the "safety button." The lid comes off more easily, and the bonus is that you make sure the safety button was down on each jar and the food is safe for your precious little one.

Make blankets available around-the-clock. Because her first child suffered so much when her favorite "blankie" was in the washer, one mother made a point of having two identical "blankies" for her second child. One could be cuddled while the other was in the wash. Some children are comforted by a cotton gauze diaper, which all look the same, so any one of them is a comfort and laundry time isn't a time of anxiety.

Decorate with snap beads. Snap together a circle big enough to frame a clock, mirror, or picture, and glue it in place for a baby room decoration.

Keep the cat out of Baby's room. Replace the bedroom door with a light wooden screen door. You can see and hear anything that goes on in the room, but the cat can't get in to snooze with the baby or on his bed.

See STAINS for hints to remove baby formula from fabric.

BACK SCRUBBERS

Make your own back washer. Get a strip of nylon net the length of a bath towel. Look for bridal illusion, it's softer than plain netting. Put a bar of soap in the middle, wrap the net around it a few times, and then tie a knot at both ends to keep it in place. When showering, pull the net "towel" back and forth across your back as if you were drying off with it.

BACON

Store it in the freezer. If you don't use up a package quickly, try freezing individual strips. The bacon stays fresh, and you can take out as many slices as you need. Place individual slices on a cookie sheet and freeze quickly. Then stack the frozen strips in a freezer-safe container with waxed paper between layers. Or to recycle, use the waxed paper from cereal boxes instead of store-bought waxed paper.

Make a BLT without the "B." Substitute imitation bacon bits for real bacon when you make a bacon, lettuce, and tomato sandwich, and you'll get the flavor without the fat.

BAGS

 Use your own. Carry your own mesh or other bags to the store when shopping to avoid collecting grocery bags at home. Europeans have done it for years. We can, too!

See also DRY-CLEANER'S BAGS.

BAKING

Make measuring cup cleanup easy. Before measuring honey, corn syrup, molasses, and other sticky things, spray cups and spoons with non-stick spray. Cleanup will be a breeze.

Use scissors with dried fruit. When a recipe requires cutting dried fruit, it's faster and easier to spray scissor blades with nonstick cooking spray and snip the fruit into small pieces.

Measure your baking dishes. When you can't tell if a new dish will hold as much as your old one did, pour water to the level your recipe filled in the old dish. Pour it into the new one to test for overflow. Or, if you know the quantity your recipe makes, measure that quantity in water and pour it into the new dish to make sure there'll be no overflow. (For example, a 9-inch pie plate holds exactly 4 cups of liquid.)

Bake crispier fish sticks and potato nuggets. When baking, place food on a wire rack, then place the rack on a foil-covered cookie sheet so that extra grease drips out while the food cooks. The sticks and nuggets will be crisper, too, and there's no need to turn them over.

BAKING SODA

Clean with baking soda. This all-purpose household cleaner safely cleans many things around the house. Just sprinkle baking soda, wipe or scrub with a damp sponge, and rinse well. Sinks, countertops, you-name-it will sparkle. For easy access, keep baking soda in an empty plastic jar with a shaker top, like those that hold dried herbs.

See also ABRASIVE CLEANERS.

BALCONIES

Childproof your view. Buy the widest available heavy plastic webbing (for lawn chairs) and then weave it in and out of the balcony's railing bars until all spaces are completely closed. Secure the ends and make sure the webbing is close together and strung tightly. Test by pushing on it. This doesn't replace adult supervision because a determined child can get through any barrier. This method can also help confine pets or give a bit of privacy if you like to sunbathe on your balcony.

BALLPOINT PENS

See STAINS for hints to remove ballpoint pen ink from fabric.

BANANAS

Store them right. To hasten ripening, store bananas in a plastic bag. Once they're at the proper state of ripeness, you can place bananas in the fridge. The skins will darken, but the fruit will be good for about 2 weeks.

Make your own banana treats. Bananas frozen on a stick or in chunks make delicious and nutritious treats. They're especially good for dieters, because they take longer to eat. If you can afford the calories, cut peeled bananas into quarters and put peanut butter on the cut sides, wrap in plastic wrap and freeze. Or dip them in chocolate syrup and refreeze until the syrup hardens.

See also PRODUCE.

BARBECUES

Make your own fire starters. Half-fill each section of a cardboard egg carton with dryer lint; pour melted wax over it and allow to harden. Cut apart segments for fire starting.

Caution: Do not use plastic foam egg cartons; they won't burn away, and they give off toxic fumes!

Sanitize before storing. Before storing your grill for the winter, be sure to wash the grate well. An unwashed grate sitting all winter can build up bacteria that can contaminate your food and make you sick when you cook on it in the spring.

Cut campfire start time with a chimney. Buy a new, empty 1-gallon paint can with a wire handle. Then, take the triangular end of a can opener and make about a dozen triangular openings around the bottom of the outer side of the paint can. (That's the side, not the flat bottom end!) Then

Barbecue Auto-Grill

I get lots of barbecue hints, but this one's ingenious! On a camping trip to the mountains, a family discovered that they'd forgotten their barbecue grill. They took the metal hubcap off their spare tire, cleaned it, covered it with foil, punched holes in the foil for grease to run out, and used it for a grill. The heavy metal worked so well that now they always use the spare tire hubcap for a camping grill! Perhaps a used hubcap from a wrecker yard would do, too.

cut off the flat bottom with a manual can opener so that both ends are open. Now, it's a "chimney."

To light a campfire, place the can in the bottom of the barbecue pit and ball up about six half-sheets of newspaper; put them at the bottom of the can. Fill the rest of the can with charcoal. Light the newspaper in several places through the holes in the bottom of the can. Because everything is contained in the can, there will be very little flame, just smoldering paper to light the coals. The chimney effect of the can decreases the fire starting time.

Before you grill over your campfire, when the coals are good and hot, use metal tongs to lift the can out of the grill by the wire handle.

Caution: Protect your hands and arms with fireproof barbecue mitts and be very cautious when removing the hot can. The can will cool quickly once it's removed from the fire. You can reuse it many times.

Cook ahead. When you grill something that cooks for only a short time, like fish, have portions of another meat ready to cook on the coals to make use of the heat. You can reheat the second meal in your microwave the next day.

Make a barbecue grill planter. Drill a few holes in the bottom of an old barbecue grill, remove rust with a wire brush, and then spray inside and out with rust-retarding paint. After the paint dries, put a layer of stones or broken pot pieces on the bottom, fill with potting soil and peat moss, and add ornamental plants.

BARRETTES

Store them neatly. When you have long hair, usually the combs, barrettes, and other accessories are a mess in the bathroom. One reader tacked 8 separate lengths of 1-inch ribbon horizontally with fancy tacks to the back of her bathroom cupboard door. She attaches all combs, barrettes, and other hair care items to the ribbons and can tell at a glance where each of them is.

See also HAIR.

BASEBALL

Repair your caps. If the plastic adjustable strip on the back breaks, sew a piece of ¾-inch elastic on one side, measure for the right fit, and then sew the other end in place. Often these baseball caps are one of a kind and are as precious to their wearers as a blanket or teddy bear is to a toddler—so repairing them is an absolute necessity!

Switch-hit a baseball gift. If you want to disguise a baseball bat so that it's a surprise gift, buy a florist's box, the kind that is normally used for long-stemmed flowers. You won't even have to wrap it.

BATHING

Soak in a lemon bath. A reader suggests that you shower first, then fill the tub with lukewarm water, squeeze juice from sliced lemons into the water, and throw the slices in, too. Then soak in refreshing, lemon-scented, natural astringent water. I like to put lemon juice in my hair rinse water. It removes all the soap film and oil and smells great all day.

Make your own bath salts. Pour 3 cups of Epsom salts into a metal or glass bowl. In a separate cup, mix 1 tablespoon of glycerin (available at drugstores), a few drops of food coloring (optional), and some of your favorite perfume. Blend well and slowly add it to the Epsom salts, stirring until thoroughly mixed. Store in a sealed decorative container and add it to your bath water for a treat.

Enjoy a warm bath towel. Just before you get out of the tub, ask a nice person to warm your towel in the clothes dryer so that you can jump into a warm "cozy" when you get out. (Check out discount linen stores for bargains on "bath sheets" to wrap in.)

See also SKIN.

BATHROOMS

Cleaning the bathroom is a terrible chore to most people. But think about this. The bathroom is usually the smallest room in the house, so there is really less total area to clean, whether you measure it in cubic feet or square feet of surfaces. Isn't that a nice thought?

Also, we have to accept the fact that no matter how spotless we make them, bathrooms don't stay pristine unless they are locked shut. But there are ways of making this chore less tedious. Read on.

Making Your Own Cleansers for Tiles and Fixtures

Make your own all-purpose cleaner and shiner. Mix and store the following in an empty plastic quart bottle: 2 tablespoons of vinegar or 2 tablespoons of sudsy ammonia and enough water to make 1 quart. Be sure to label this clearly as your homemade cleaner so it doesn't get used for other purposes.

Make your own ceramic-tile cleaner. This recipe uses several common household ingredients. Mix ¼ cup of baking soda, ½ cup of white vinegar, and 1 cup of ammonia in a bucket. Add 1 gallon of warm water and stir until the baking soda dissolves. Apply with a sponge or scrub brush. You'll need to mix a fresh batch for each cleaning, because this is not a "keeper."

Caution: Wear rubber gloves, because this is a bit unkind to your skin and nails.

Quick-Clean the Bathroom

Here's one of the easiest ways I know to quick-clean a bathroom, especially one with tile walls and floor.

1. Get a bunch of paper towels and a spray bottle of commercial window cleaner or the homemade all-purpose mix described on page 34.

2. Clean from the top down, changing paper towels as you go and saving all the wet ones to do the floor. Do mirrors, sink area, wall tiles, the outside and rim of the bathtub, toilet tank and seat, and finally the floor. (Most plastic and painted wood toilet seats and many wall paints can be cleaned with liquid window cleaner. Test an inconspicuous place first to make sure.)

3. Wash the floor with the used towels and more sprays of cleaner, wiping it with dry towels as you back out of the room to avoid putting footprints on the wet floor. It helps if you get dust and hair off the floor first, but it's not absolutely necessary.

4. Close the shower curtain to cover the tub, throw a rug over the heavy traffic patch of the floor, and you have a shiny, clean bathroom. (Clean the tub or shower stall some other day, when you aren't in such a rush.)

Make a heavy-duty cleaning paste. A variation of the ceramic-tile cleaner, which can be used for serious scrubbing or heavy-duty grout cleaning, is the following paste. In a medium-size bowl, mix 3 cups of baking soda and 1 cup of warm water to a smooth paste, and then scrub it into the grout with a damp sponge or toothbrush. Rinse thoroughly afterward. Always mix a fresh batch for each cleaning.

Make your own glass cleaner. This glass-cleaning solution is good for cleaning glass and mirrors in any room. Mix 2 cups of water with 1 cup of

Quick Décor Change

Sometimes, such as in the middle of a dreary February, we just need a quick change to perk us up. These are a few of my quick décor changes.

Try decals on bathroom walls. They can be applied to gloss or semigloss paint. I applied three butterflies so that they looked as if they were fluttering across my bathroom toward the window.

Draw a mural. If you have artistic talent (or artistic friends), use acrylic paints or waterproof markers to draw murals or decorations on your walls. Just be sure the paints or markers are waterproof, or you'll have some really "drippy" designs when you wipe off the walls! I took several colored waterproof markers and drew wispy willow trees on my bathroom walls rather than repainting the whole thing. When I get tired of this, I'll simply spray it with a sealer and paint over it.

isopropyl rubbing alcohol (70 percent) and 1 tablespoon of household ammonia. Pour into a clean pump-spray bottle.

Cleaning the Toilet Bowl

Try an extra-heavy-duty cleanser. If you find yourself living in an apartment or house that was previously inhabited by someone with toilet-cleanophobia (the fear of cleaning toilets), sprinkle ¼ cup of sodium bisulfate (sodium acid sulfate from the hardware store or drugstore) into the wet toilet bowl for a single scrubbing and flushing. Let it stand for 15 minutes; then scrub and flush as usual.

Caution: Wear rubber gloves. Also, don't use this acid with chlorine bleach because the resulting fumes are toxic.

Remove rust stains. In some parts of the United States, the only way to completely avoid rust-stained toilet bowls is to not have toilet bowls, and who could live with that!

That said, rust stains under a toilet bowl rim will sometimes yield to chlorine bleach, but be sure to protect your hands with rubber gloves, even when you use a long-handled brush—even small splashes of bleach can hurt your skin. This is also true for strong commercial preparations for toilet bowl cleaning.

The best way is to get a good commercial rust remover made specifically for porcelain. Be sure to read the directions carefully.

Caution: Never combine bleach with toilet bowl cleaners; the mix can release toxic gases.

Never misuse a toilet cleanser. Chemical toilet bowl cleaners, commercial or homemade, should never be used to clean the bathtub or sink because the chemicals will etch and ruin their finishes.

Cleaning the Bathtub

Let soft water help. You can enjoy your bath without leaving a tub ring if you add water-softener bath crystals or bubble bath to the water. If you are out of anything fancy, try a capful of mild liquid dishwashing (not dishwasher!) detergent in the bathwater. Of course, this is if you have no allergies, and it is not recommended for young children.

Rub away ring-around-the-tub. Roll an old nylon stocking into a ball and use it as a nonscratch scrub pad for cleaning the sink and tub. You can also use old skin-cleaning pads once they become too worn and abrasive for your skin.

Deal with a stubborn bathtub ring. Try covering it with a paste of cream of tartar and hydrogen peroxide. When the paste dries, wipe it off along with the ring.

Get rid of bathtub rust stains. Try rubbing them with a paste of borax powder and lemon juice. (You will also find commercial preparations for this chore; follow the directions exactly as they appear on the label, and be sure to rinse the bathtub well after cleaning it.)

Don't forget the rubber or vinyl bathtub mat. Clean your bathtub mat regularly by tossing it into the washer with bath towels. Terry cloth towels scrub the mat, all come out clean at the same time, and you avoid the risk of mildew buildup. Another quick way to clean the bath mat is to spray it with a foamy spray bathroom cleaner, let it sit a few moments, scrub, and rinse well with very hot water.

Remove the bathtub decal residue. Apply prewash spray and scrub with a nylon scrubber; or, when the tub is dry, sprinkle the residue with dry cornmeal and apply elbow grease with a nylon-net scrubbie.

Protect the finish. Once the glaze finish is removed from a bathtub, it will stain gray even with normal daily use and will be difficult to brighten with ordinary cleaning. Certain epoxy finishes or reglazing can be applied by professionals, or you can use finishing kits available at some hardware stores. This is a major project, and prevention is a better idea.

If you haven't been lucky enough to preserve the glaze on your tub, you can find someone to reglaze it by looking in the Yellow Pages under "Bathtub Refinishers" or "Bathtub Reglazers." Ask how long the company has been in the business. Be sure to ask to see references and talk to these people to see if they were happy with the job. Once this has been done, you must be sure never, ever to use abrasive cleansers on that finish, or you will have wasted your money.

Cleaning the Shower

Wipe down regularly. Shower enclosures are a chore to keep clean. Teach the people who live and shower in your house to wipe down the shower walls and glass doors with a rubber window wand wiper—or the towel they've just used—while they're still standing in the tub. Then you can stretch the intervals between vigorous, thorough cleanings.

STORAGE SOLUTIONS

Eliminate Bathroom Counter Clutter

Hang a three-tier wire "egg basket" near your shower or tub, where you can reach without getting out. This solution gives you a perfect holder for shampoos, conditioners, bath oil, washcloths, and extra soap. Or you might want to attach a wicker hanging basket from the ceiling about 10 inches above the countertop to hold brushes, toothpaste, combs, and other bits and pieces. There's no rule against using baskets in the bath.

Be gentle. Never use harsh abrasive powders or steel wool pads because they'll scratch porcelain or fiberglass.

Give a spritz of prewash spray. Here's another quickie cleaner for tiles and shower doors. Spray tiles or glass shower doors liberally with any brand of prewash spray. Wait a few minutes, and then rub the scum away with a damp sponge. Rinse the area thoroughly and dry with a towel.

Caution: If you use a petroleum- or oil-based prewash spray, be sure to rinse or wash out the bottom of the tub or shower stall carefully, as it can be slippery.

Use your shower to clean the walls. When the walls need a thorough cleaning, run the shower water at its hottest temperature so the steam will loosen the dirt before you start to scrub.

Caution: Don't stay in the tub for this.

Keep your hands dry. To clean the shower in a jiffy, without even getting your hands wet, use a sponge mop dipped into a mixture of ½ cup of vinegar, 1 cup of clear ammonia, and ¼ cup of baking soda in 1 gallon of warm water. (Yes, yes—vinegar, ammonia, baking soda—aren't they great?) After cleaning, rinse with clear water.

Remove mineral deposits from the showerhead. Remove the showerhead, take it apart, and soak it in vinegar. Then brush deposits loose with an old toothbrush. Clean the holes by poking them with a wire, pin, toothpick, or ice pick. If the showerhead cannot be removed, take a plastic sandwich bag, fill it with vinegar, wrap it around the showerhead, and attach it tightly with a thick rubber band. Let it sit overnight. Proceed with the cleaning.

Make glass shower doors sparkle. Clean them once a week with a sponge dipped in white vinegar. This is a good tip; regular cleaning of any part of the bathroom will help you avoid having to use strong chemicals and lots of energy (yours) to clean it.

Wash plastic shower curtains in the washer. Wash them with towels to get some automatic scrubbing action. Put them in the washing machine with ½ cup of detergent and ½ cup of baking soda, along with 2 large bath towels. Add a cup of vinegar to the rinse cycle.

You can hang the shower curtain to dry. If you want to get wrinkles out of plastic shower curtains and soften them at the same time, toss them into the dryer with the towels for a few minutes. Shower curtains can't go through the whole drying cycle; some will all but melt! Just let them spin for 2 to 4 minutes, depending upon the heat of your dryer, then remove them from the dryer and hang them immediately.

Clean the grout. You can remove most mildew from the grout between tiles by rubbing it with an old toothbrush or nail brush dipped in liquid chlorine bleach or powdered cleanser. (Don't use abrasive powders or steel wool pads, because they'll scratch the tile.) Rinse with clear water after cleaning.

Camouflage the stains. If some brown spots remain no matter what you do, you can disguise stained grout with a white fingernail pencil or white typewriter correction fluid.

Keep tiles and shower doors looking shiny. Spray them with your favorite oil-based furniture spray and shine with a soft cloth or paper towels. Of course, the tiles must be clean before you use this, or you'll just end up with a mucky mess. And again, be sure that you've cleaned spray residue from the floor of the tub or shower, as it can be slippery.

Protect the drains. Place a 1½-inch-diameter kitchen sink strainer cup upside down over your bathtub drain to catch bobby pins and other dropped things that can go into the drain. You can still open and shut the drain.

Remove hair gunk from a bathroom drain. Hate to stick your fingers into the hairy drain? Whisk it clean with a swish of a cotton swab. You touch only the other end of the swab!

Cleaning Mirrors

Make them sparkle. Try polishing your bathroom mirrors with a cloth dipped in a borax-and-water solution or in denatured alcohol. Wipe dry to a shine with a lint-free cloth, newspapers, paper toweling, or panty hose.

Use rubbing alcohol. This is one of my favorite hints. For a quick swipe, dab a little rubbing alcohol or even vinegar on a facial tissue, wipe the mirror, and it will sparkle and shine. Rubbing alcohol will also wipe away that dull hair spray haze from a mirror.

Stop the steam. Bathroom mirrors won't steam up if you run an inch of cold water in the bathtub before you add the hot water. And if you need to defog a bathroom mirror in a jiffy, try "spraying" it with hot air from your hair dryer.

To help prevent the mirror from getting foggy, wipe it with an antifog product that is sold for automobiles. You can also use a bit of shampoo on a dry cloth and wipe the mirror with it before you bathe. Or, if you have a medicine cabinet where the mirrors slide over each other, close them so that one mirror is covered while you're taking a shower. Then, when you're ready to use the mirror, simply slide the door back and there will be an un-fogged mirror to use.

See also COUNTERTOPS, FIBERGLASS, KITCHENS, MIRRORS, SHOWER CURTAINS, SINKS, SOAP AND SOAP DISHES, and TOILETS.

BATTERIES

Store them safely. It's no longer advised to store batteries in the refrig-erator. Store them instead in a dry place at room temperature. Exposure to extreme heat, such as in attics or garages, can reduce battery life. If kept loose in a purse, coins or keys could cause them to short out.

See AUTOMOBILES for information on car batteries.

BEANS

Cook dry beans right. Perplexed about changing cooking times for dry beans? The higher the mineral level in your water, the longer it takes to cook beans. Since the mineral content varies from day to day, your cooking times also vary. And, the older the beans, the longer the cooking time; that's why it's not a good idea to mix bags of beans.

Reduce the gas. Dried beans are less likely to produce gas if you soak them overnight, discard the water in which they've soaked, and then cook them in fresh water. Or, add a pinch of ginger to remove the "gaseousness" of home-cooked or reheated canned beans.

BEDDING

Revive faded sheets for kids. Tie a strip of old fabric around the center of a bed sheet and keep wrapping it around and around until you get to the outside edges. Fasten it tightly, then dye it in the washing machine with fabric dye.

Make your pillowcases fit for a king. If you can't find matching pillowcases at a sale, or if you want to save some money and sew, one twin flat sheet has enough fabric for at least two king-size pillowcases and usually costs less than a set. So buy top and bottom fitted sheets plus one twin.

Use suspenders and look for deep pockets. Newer mattresses are thicker than many old ones. Look for "deep pockets" or those that give the depth in inches on the package. Some queen-size fitted bottom sheets only fit thick double-bed mattresses. Suspenders can help, too. Adjust the suspenders to fit the bed width, slide them between mattress and box spring about ¼ of the way from each end, and then clip an end to each side of the sheet. Several catalogs offer elastic "garters" to place on each corner.

Return pilling sheets. Sometimes defects in milling cause pilling on sheets, and shaving with a fabric shaver is usually not satisfactory. The best idea is to return the sheets to the store along with the receipt that proves purchase, or contact the manufacturer. Readers have reported getting replacement sheets.

($) **Save money on water bed sheets.** King-size or queen-size flat sheets will fit on a water bed mattress if you tie each corner of the flat sheet into a knot and slip it under the mattress corner, securely tucking in the sides. If you sew, create corners using your sewing machine. Then use a second king- or queen-size flat sheet as the top sheet.

See also BLANKETS and QUILTS.

BEDROOMS

Organize your dresser drawers. Shoe boxes that fit inside drawers make great dividers for underwear, stockings, and jewelry. "Divide to conquer" is the motto for drawer organizing.

Keep a hall tree handy. Use it to air clothing that doesn't get washed after each wearing. A hall tree is a good "guest closet," too.

Make your bed easily. Attach two safety pins on the underside of the bedspread at the end of the mattress—one on each side to indicate its width. Feel for the pin, and line it up with the edge to save yourself from walking back and forth, from one side of the bed to the other, lining up the spread. You can line up sheets the same way, except instead of using safety pins, sew a couple of colored stitches on each side. (This saves a lot of steps if you have a king-size bed.)

Make your bed before your feet hit the floor. Unless you are one of those sleepers who completely pulls apart the bedding each night (or you have a bed partner who does), you can make your bed before you get out of it, like I do. When you're ready to get out of bed, sit in the middle of the bed and pull up the sheets, blanket, and spread. Smooth out any folds, then slide out the side. Finish off the head of the bed in whatever way you keep it.

If you use a quilt or coverlet instead of a bedspread and blanket, and your pillows show, just fold a little of the top sheet over the edge of the quilt before you slide out, and the bed is made.

Weigh down one side. Having one side of the bed close to a wall is a problem when you're making the bed. If you have a lightweight spread, you can pin nuts and bolts for weight to the underside of the spread's edge. Then the spread will slide right down into place on the wall side.

Reuse the tablecloth. A lace or cut-work tablecloth spread over a colored sheet can be a pretty guest-room spread and a way to store and get more use from the tablecloth.

Get the most from a guest room. If you're short on bedding storage space, keep guest-room beds made up and toss a fabric softener sheet or a mildly scented bar of soap under the blanket to keep the linens smelling fresh.

If you have a daybed with a pull-out twin bed underneath and only one guest, have the guest sleep on the pull-out bed instead of the top one. Then, instead of having to arrange pillows and spreads on the daybed every day, you can just slide the bottom bed into its usual place each morning.

Store extra pillows on beds and sofas. Cover them with zippered corduroy or other room color-coordinating pillowcases.

Consider using sheets and towels fresh from the dryer. This is one of my father's favorite hints. It's his way of solving the how-do-you-fold-the-fitted-sheet problem—he doesn't. In fact, it may make more sense for many people to use only one set at a time.

You just use the same color-coordinated sheets and towels over and over right from the dryer, without ever folding or putting them away, until they are worn out. Then you can choose a new color scheme without having a closet cluttered with half-worn-out things that don't match your rooms anymore. Plus, if you make your bed with sheets still warm from the dryer, they will "iron" themselves on the bed.

See also BEDDING, BUNK BEDS, and CLOSETS.

BEEF JERKY

 Make your own jerky without preservatives. Jerky is best made with lean beef flank steak and cuts easily when partially frozen. Here's an easy way to make it.

1. Cut off visible fat, then cut into thin strips across the grain, making the strips as thin and uniform as possible for even drying. The steak can be dried as is or marinated overnight in a shallow baking dish in the fridge. If you marinate it, drain it well before you start the drying process.

2. To dry, lay strips close together but not touching on a cookie-cooling rack and place in the oven. If you have a gas oven, the pilot light will give off enough heat to dry them; but if your oven is electric, turn it on to the lowest setting. Prop the door open for good air circulation. Dry the jerky for 12 to 48 hours, testing it every so often. It's done when a piece snaps in half when you bend it.

The drier the jerky, the longer it keeps without refrigeration, but if you don't like it too dry, store it in the freezer until you're ready to eat it.

BELTS

Hold the tab securely. When a belt is too long and sticks out in front, a single pierced earring will secure the end in place. Coordinate the earring stud with buttons or other decorations on the outfit so it's an extra accessory as well as functional.

BICYCLES

Ensure the right fit for a child. Riding a poorly fitted bike can result in an accident. Have your child stand barefoot and measure her or his inseam from crotch to floor. From this measurement, subtract 10 inches for a boy's bike and 9 inches for a girl's model to get the proper frame size. (Adult bicycles generally measure from 19 to 26 inches.)

Buy a bicycle helmet when you buy a bike. Consider the helmet and bike as going together like seat belts and cars. Thousands of deaths and head injuries from bike falls could be prevented if bikers wore properly fitted helmets. They should protect without obscuring vision.

Foil the thieves. Most bicycles have serial numbers. Record this number and keep it in a safe place along with a picture of the bike and the sales receipt. This information will help the police if your bike is stolen. When you leave your bike at a destination, lock it with a heavy-duty bike lock to a solid object, such as a telephone pole.

At home, never leave your bike on the front lawn or porch. Keep it in a safe, locked place like your garage.

Hint: A door-to-door salespeson gave me this other reason to store your bike out of sight. A house with lots of bikes is a house with many children and parents who may be good sales targets for encyclopedias, insurance, and other family-oriented items!

Make a bike rack. Tripping over children's bikes lying askew on the front lawn? Make a bike rack from a large uniform log. Treat the wood with wood preservative and then dig a shallow ditch and place the log in it. Using a saw, cut equally spaced grooves in the log—one for each bike—and make each groove the proper width to hold the front tire of a bicycle.

Pick safe colors. Hot pink clothing, even if you hate the color, is the safest, most visible color to get you noticed by motorists. You can also sew bands of fluorescent material around the sleeves and legs of your biking outfit. Fluorescent bands sewn on hot pink would be double safety and a good idea if you ride in heavy traffic.

BILLS

Keep your financial balance. You don't have to own your own business to have a business account. If your company reimburses you for business expenses that you put on your credit card, such as like lunches or trips, deposit your reimbursement checks into a separate account. Then the right amount of money is always available when your credit card bills come in. Pocketing the reimbursement money could lead to spending it and being "short" at the month's end. You'll have better records for tax preparation, too.

Pay on time. Since paying your bills on time gets you lower rates, or at least avoids penalties for overdue payments, you need to have a bill-paying system. Some people pay their bills as soon as they arrive; others pay on the first and fifteenth of the month. Some people throw their bills into a drawer and forget about them entirely. These people are called "the defendant" when they are summoned to small claims court!

Keep track of the deadlines. Note payment due days on a monthly or yearly calendar throughout the year. Another way to keep track of bills is to fill a three-ring binder with pocket folders. Each month place all your bills and receipts in designated pockets (car, insurance, house payments, and utilities) and write the check number on the bill it was written for. You can also note interest paid, income, and payments on the pocket folders so that at tax time you have all the information handy. After you have paid your taxes, you can tie up the notebook, clearly marked with the contents and the year, and store it in a safe place.

Keep all unpaid bills in one folder. It would make sense to also keep a list of each bill, the due date, and amount. As each bill is paid, cross it off the list. File the receipts, marked with check numbers and any other important information, in folders designated for specific categories, like utilities, house payments, and car.

Keep phone numbers handy. Enter the phone number of the billing company into your check register. If you have to call about a payment problem, the number is right where you need it.

Don't put messages on the outside of envelopes. Many businesses open envelopes with automated systems, so if you write messages on the outside of envelopes, they are not likely to be seen. Put messages on the bill or on a separate piece of paper. Write address changes in bold letters or highlight them. Along the same lines, never wrap your checks in blank paper. It may slow the processing in automated systems because it's assumed that there is correspondence in the envelope, and it will be sent to a different location.

Don't send cash. Since automated envelope-opening systems process as many as 40 or 45 letters per minute, coins or cash can actually fly out of the envelopes as they go through the opening machines. Checks or money orders are much safer.

Make sure the right information is on the check. If someone else is paying a bill for you with their personal check, be sure *your* name and account number are included on the check for proper crediting. Similarly, when you place a mail order or pay for magazine subscriptions, put your code number (found on the mailing label, usually above your name) on your check for added identification.

Make photocopies of all your credit cards. Put one copy in a safe place, like a bank safety deposit box, keep one at home, and take one with you when you travel for quick reference in case you lose your wallet. (Obviously, you shouldn't keep the copy in your wallet!) Keep a photocopy of all your credit cards and their numbers in your desk drawer for handy catalog phone ordering and other bill paying.

Memorize your credit card numbers. I'm so organized that I even have one of my major credit card numbers memorized, which means that I don't have to go searching for it when I find something in a mail-order catalog with an 800 number!

See also TAXES.

BIRDS

Birds are such beautiful creatures. They are a delight to keep as pets and an amazing source of delight if you watch them out the window. Read on for hints on how to care for them responsibly.

Pet Birds

Buy birds only from a reputable dealer. All imported birds must have stainless steel leg bands, which are put on when they enter quarantine.

Many birds are smuggled in illegally without the benefit of quarantine, a practice that endangers birds in the United States. Outbreaks of Newcastle disease, a devastating bird ailment, have occurred in the past because of illegal importation of pet birds.

Line the bottom of the cage. Stack 7 or 8 pages of an old phone book or catalog in the bottom of your bird's cage and remove one at a time as they get soiled.

Buy the right size cage. Your bird should have a cage large enough so that it can fly from one perch to another. Place the cage away from air-conditioning and heating ducts, out of drafts, and away from direct sunshine. Keep your bird out of the kitchen and clear of kitchen fumes, which can be deadly to birds. Also, cooking oil and grease settling on birds' feathers can destroy their natural insulation. Birds are sensitive to fumes of any kind, such as insecticides, paint and varnish, deodorants, and hair spray, so protect your bird from them.

Keep them company. All birds need companionship, either with other birds or with people. They've been known to pull their feathers out when lonely or bored. Give them toys, bells, and mirrors so that they can keep themselves amused. Give them attention, too, just like you do with dogs and cats.

Keep them healthy. Birds don't need immunization shots like dogs or cats, but they should have regular checkups and diagnostic exams if they appear ill.

Empty their dishes. A bird will accept a wide variety of food for a balanced healthy diet if it is hungry at feeding time. But don't keep food dishes filled all day. Instead, set up feeding times and give the bird fewer seeds and more fruits and vegetables. Feeding time is also a special bonding time with your pet and a time for you to observe changes in its eating habits or health.

Recycle your seeds. Your pet birds don't always eat every seed. Save the leftovers and put them where outdoor birds can sift through and get the seeds missed by your pets.

Give pet birds exercise and attention. A lonely parakeet can actually get "lovesick" and act strangely. If your bird begins to preen before a mirror or a plastic cage toy (some birds may even regurgitate food onto the mirror or toy), it is practicing courting and nesting behavior, which is usually reserved for mates and offspring. The cure for "lovesickness" is to remove the "love object" from the cage for 2 to 3 weeks and give your bird more exercise and attention.

Note: Regurgitation by parakeets and other birds can also be a symptom of digestive ailments. If your bird regurgitates frequently but has no other "lovesick" symptoms, check with your vet.

Teach your bird how to talk. Just remember, repetition is the key. You can put the word (repeated many times) on a cassette tape and then play it for your bird when you don't have time to chat or when you go away on a trip and don't want your bird to forget.

Wild Birds

Keep squirrels away from bird feeders. Hang the bird feeder from a straightened wire coat hanger. It will hang far enough from the tree branch to keep squirrels and other unwanted guests from eating the bird food. Or hang the feeder with heavy filament fishing line; squirrels can't climb up or down on this. I keep a separate feeder for squirrels on the same tree with my bird feeder in an attempt to keep all of the critters happy.

Make a pinecone feeder. Spread a thin layer of peanut butter or honey onto a pinecone, roll it in birdseed, and tie it to a tree with a piece of string.

Scare birds away from fruit trees. Readers report that old compact mirrors, suspended in the trees with string or rope, work like a scarecrow. Also, hanging a few rubber snakes in a fruit tree scares birds—and sometimes the neighbors, too!

Save your seeds. If you dry watermelon and cantaloupe seeds during the summer, you can feed them to the birds in the winter.

Hint: If you begin to feed birds in the winter, they will depend upon you and may perish if you stop feeding them. So don't start if you don't intend to continue feeding until the weather allows "your" birds to find their own food as spring unfolds.

BLANKETS

Save the zippered bag. Blankets, mattress pads, and bedspreads often come in heavy-duty zippered bags that you can recycle for storing all sorts of linens, clothing, and just plain stuff. One reader keeps old picnic and football game blankets in the zippered bags and hangs them in the garage so that they are handy when the family goes on outings.

Wash your washable woolen blankets. If the care label says that the blanket is machine washable, here's how to get a comfy, clean, renewed blanket. Fill the washer with warm water, add detergent, and agitate to completely dissolve the detergent. Stop the washer and load the unfolded blanket evenly around the agitator. Soak for 10 to 15 minutes, then agitate on the gentle cycle for 1 minute. Stop the washer and advance the timer to the drain cycle and spin for about 1 minute.

Finish by filling the washer with cold water for a deep rinse. Add fabric softener and allow the washer to complete the rest of the cycle automatically. To dry in the dryer, set the temperature selector to the high setting. Place 3 or 4 bath towels in the dryer and turn the dryer on for a few minutes. Heated towels help absorb moisture so that the blanket dries more quickly. Place the blanket in the dryer and set the timer control at 20 minutes. Check after 10 minutes and remove the blanket while it's still damp. Overdrying and excessive tumbling may cause shrinkage. Place the blanket on a flat surface or stretch it over 2 clotheslines to complete the drying. Gently brush up the nap with a nylon brush. Press the binding with a cool iron, if needed.

Fix accidental shrinkage. If your blanket happens to shrink in the dryer and becomes too short, sew a strip of matching-color fabric to the bottom of the blanket. You can tuck this section under the mattress at the foot of the bed, and your bed will still look nice.

Find a new life for old electric blankets. If an electric blanket no longer works, unplug it and feel for the wires at the end of the blanket. Make tiny slits there, snip the wires, and pull them through the slits. (You may have to enlarge some slits to remove the thermostats.) After removing the wires, sew up the slits, reattach the loosened bindings, and you have a usable blanket.

If you don't feel like sewing up the slits, put the blanket in a comforter cover that coordinates with the colors in your bedroom. You can find them in some linen departments or in catalogs, and they serve well as cover-ups when blankets are moth-eaten, worn, or just don't match anything in your bedroom.

Keep the covers clear. Never layer bedding over an electric blanket while it's on. You can cause the wiring to overheat to the point of catching fire.

Tuck the cord out of the way. If you have a Hollywood-style bed (without a footboard), you'll know that the electric blanket cord tends to stick out from the foot of the bed and catch your ankle when you are making the bed. Try attaching a cup hook to the underside of the box spring, with the open part of the hook pointing toward the head of the bed. Thread the cord through the hook, and the cord will stay out of your sight and way.

Make your own dual-control blanket. If you need a king-size electric

Letter of Laughter

Blanket Wars

When a couple bought a dual-control electric blanket, they were disappointed. He complained that his side was too hot, and she said her side was too cold. For a week they adjusted control knobs, he turning his down and she turning hers up until they decided that the blanket was defective. Then, when changing the sheets—you guessed it—she realized that his control was on her side of the bed and hers was on his side. She had been "roasting" him, and he had been "cooling" her. I'll bet that's not the first time something like this has happened!

blanket and find twin-size ones on sale at a good price, tack the edges of two twin-size blankets together to make your own dual-controlled king-size blanket. The cost is much less.

Launder electric blankets safely. Take an electric blanket to a professional cleaner when it needs freshening, or, if so indicated on the care label, launder it yourself, as follows.

First, disconnect the electric control. Fill the washer with warm water and a mild detergent. When the machine is filled with water, let it agitate a bit so the detergent dissolves (if you use powdered detergent), then put the blanket into the water and let it wash for 3 or 4 minutes at the most. (Long wash or spin cycles may damage the blanket.)

After the water drains, follow with a short spin cycle. Rinse again, then spin briefly again so that only part of the water is removed. Press the remaining water out with your hands. Line dry the blanket over 2 parallel clotheslines. (Machine drying can damage the wiring.)

Caution: Never run an electric blanket through a coin-operated dry-cleaning machine. The solvent can damage the wiring and cause electric shock when you use the blanket.

 Recycle your blankets. Sew old baby blankets together for a memory blanket a young child can cover up with—especially at grandparents' house. It's extra nice to curl up under the blankets that comforted the child's parent, aunt, uncle, or other relative in the past. Another good use for an old blanket is to cut rounds or squares from it to place between nonstick frying pans, china, or other stackables that might scratch each other.

See also BEDROOMS.

BLENDERS

Discover the miracle of a self-cleaning blender. One tried-and-true method for cleaning a blender is to fill it about halfway with water, add a couple of drops of liquid dishwashing detergent, and put the lid on. Blend for a few minutes, rinse, and dry. If the blender is really soiled and has dried-on liquid, fill it with water and let it sit overnight.

See also APPLIANCES.

BLINDS

Prevent dust buildup. Prevent heavy dust buildup on blinds by frequent vacuuming; the upholstery attachment works best.

Use old socks. To dust miniblinds, put old socks on your hands (inside-out terry is good) and spray them with dust-attracting spray. Close the blinds, and then dust each slat separately starting at the top, going over them side to side, and then clean the back side. Similarly, to wash, put old socks on your hands and spray the socks with window cleaner. Then go over them as described above.

Try this for heavy-duty cleaning. For those instances when miniblinds are really dirty, take them down and put them flat on a surface that you can get wet and soapy, such as the sidewalk or driveway (or in the bathtub). Wash with a soft brush or nylon net (or old panty hose scrubber) dipped in a solution of mild dishwashing soap and water. Rinse well and dry immediately.

Caution: Be very careful when you clean blinds because they can scratch easily. Miniblinds can also break if handled roughly.

BLOODSTAINS

See STAINS for hints on removing bloodstains from fabric.

BOOKS

Mark the passages, quotes, and recipes you want to find again. If you can't bear to dog-ear or pencil-mark the pages of a book, attach a pocket to the inside flap. (Make this from an envelope by bending back the envelope flap and gluing it to the book cover). Write the page numbers you want to check later. Or just place a small sheet of paper in the front of the book listing page numbers, subjects, or the names of recipes.

Dress up a bookcase. The traditional brick (or concrete block) and boards student bookcase can be dressed up if you cover the bricks with cloth, felt or wallpaper scraps, or paint the whole thing. If you spray paint the parts, put them one-by-one inside a box when spraying so that you avoid a mess.

Hint: If the shelves are made from pressed wood, they will absorb lots of spray paint unless you apply primer with a brush before painting on the final color.

Decorate with bookends. Decorative tins (especially those from fancy gourmet teas) filled with sand will keep books standing in your bookcase.

Make wrapping paper bookmarks. That leftover strip of wrapping paper that is too narrow to wrap anything can be cut into shorter pieces for bookmarks. Take all of the strips and put them into the front of a cookbook so that as you use recipes you can mark the page with a gift-wrap bookmark to make it easier to find the recipe the next time. If you want to get even more organized, mark holiday recipes with appropriate holiday paper or colors. Note on the bookmark if you changed the recipe with different spices or other additions.

I have a friend who really needs this hint. She usually forgets which recipe she fixed and often adds other spices and ingredients to change recipes. When one of her innovations turns out to be good, her children say, "Gee, this is good. Too bad we'll never have it again!"

Remember sentimental moments with a bookmark. Press leaves or flowers between two sheets of clear laminated plastic to make a bookmark. Flowers from your wedding placed in your family Bible or in a photo album are a nice sentimental remembrance.

Keep your loaned books coming back to you. Stick your extra address labels inside each book or cover the book with brown paper (recycle grocery bags) and write your name and the date you lent the book on the cover. Or make note of who borrowed the book and the date. Record the information either in your calendar or in a card file. Ring-bound index card packs work well, too.

Move them easily. Books are heavy; packing them in cartons adds more weight. Try sorting books according to subject (or by price for a book sale) and then packing them in paper or plastic grocery sacks. Seal bags with masking tape; mark the contents for easy sorting at your destination. To move bagged books from one place to another without straining muscles or tempers, stack the bags on a hand truck (dolly) or a sturdy luggage carrier.

Remove price stickers easily. Heat the iron to "medium," put a pressing cloth over the book, and press the sticker for a couple of seconds. The warmth softens the stickers enough to let them be pulled off easily, and shiny covers won't be damaged.

BOOSTER CHAIRS

Give a young child a lift. Tape together several old telephone books or thick magazines. Or, if you don't want them so permanently joined, place them in a pillowcase, wrapping the "tail" around the stack to hold them together.

BOOTS

Dry them first for proper storage. Stuff boots with newspapers to keep their shape while drying and when storing. Newspapers also help absorb odors.

BOTTLE STOPPER

Unstick the stuck ones. For bottles that don't contain food, pour a bit of *thin* lubricating oil or mineral oil around the stopper and let it sit for a while (some take a day or two), then gently pull it out. Lubricating oil is thinner than cooking oil and will slide down more quickly and easily.

BOWL SCRAPERS

Make your own from plastic lids. Cut off the rim about halfway around lids from dips, sour cream, and cottage cheese, leaving the rim on the other half-side for a handle. These scrapers clean a bowl in seconds, and they're free!

BRAS

Measure the perfect fit. In order to find a bra that fits perfectly, there are two measurements you'll need: band size and cup size. To determine your band size, start by measuring your chest just under your bustline and then adding 5 inches to this figure (round up if the total is an odd number). For example, if your chest measures 32 inches, adding 5 will give you 37, so round up to 38 for the correct band size.

To determine your cup size, measure the fullest part of your bust while wearing a bra. This total, compared to the band size, will give you the cup size. For example, if the bust measurement is 1 inch more than the band size, your cup size will be an A; 2 inches over the band size is a cup size of B; 3 inches over the band size is a C; 4 inches over the band size is a D; and so on.

Try before you buy. Not all bras in the same size fit the same, so it's always a good rule to try on bras first to make sure they are a comfortable fit.

BRASS

 Clean brass hardware. Clean hardware on doors, drawers and other items with a good brass cleaner. Then, to prevent tarnish, rub on paste wax, let it dry, and polish to a shine or spray it with a clear lacquer finish. Sometimes it's easier to remove the hardware (street numbers and the like) to clean it. Or, knobs can be poked through a slit in cardboard or poster board so that the door or drawer finish is protected. (This is a good idea when you clean brass buttons, too.)

See also COPPER AND BRASS.

BREAD

Prevent plastic wrap from sticking to rising dough. Spray one side of the wrap with cooking spray and put that side against the dough. The wrap will peel off easily.

Recycle stale slices. Use a stale slice for a spoon rest while you cook and then toss it out for the birds to eat.

Getting Dough to Rise

If the hints readers send me are an indication, getting bread dough to rise is one problem that has as many solutions as there are bread bakers. Here are just a few.

1. Put the rack in your microwave, place a pan of very warm water on the bottom, and the dough bowl on the rack. (You don't turn on the microwave for this.) If your microwave has no rack, use a cake-cooling rack.

2. Turn the oven on "warm" for just 5 minutes, then turn it off, leaving the door closed. Cover the dough and pop it into the oven. The temperature should stay about right if you don't open the door too often.

3. Turn the oven light on, and it will usually maintain just enough low heat to work.

4. Place a pan of hot water in the oven on a lower shelf; change the water if it cools off.

5. Heat a slow cooker only to its lowest warm setting; then unplug it, put the dough in, and keep the cover on it during rising.

6. Turn the clothes dryer on for a few minutes, turn it off, set the bowl of dough in it, and close the door. Be sure to let people know that the dryer is being used for bread-rising!

   Note: One reader reported trying this method, but she forgot to turn the dryer off. When she closed the door, the drum revolved one full turn before she could stop it. The good news was that it all went so fast that disaster was averted. The bowl ended up in exactly the same place it had started. She suggests that an unbreakable stainless steel bowl would be best when using this hint, just in case!

Deep-freeze the leftovers. To prevent bread from getting stale or moldy, double bag the loaf with a bag from the previous loaf and store it in the freezer. Close the bags with twist-ties or a spring clothespin. When you remove a serving, always leave the "heel" plus 1 or 2 slices frozen together; they're a "lid" to protect the remaining slices from drying out. To thaw, either toast or zap in the microwave for 10 to 20 seconds for every 1 or 2 slices. Storing bread in the refrigerator may cause it to dry out.

 Use frozen bread instead of bread crumbs. Grate frozen bread if you don't have stale bread; it's easier to get "crummy" than fresh unfrozen bread. Another good substitute is crushing commercially packaged croutons with a potato masher in the bowl you'll use for mixing meatloaf. You can also substitute unprocessed bran, wheat germ, or dry corn cereal for a flavor change when you bread fish or meats.

BREAKFAST FRUIT

Heat up your fruit on cold mornings. If cold grapefruit is an unpleasant shock on cold mornings, heat it. Heat sectioned grapefruit halves in the oven at 350°F for about 10 minutes or in the microwave for 30 to 45 seconds.

See also PRODUCE.

BROCCOLI

Save money with stems. After removing the "flower" ends of broccoli, slice the stems thinly and toss into a green salad or add to stir-fry veggies for extra crunch and food value.

See also PRODUCE.

BROOMS

Store it with a magnet. Screw a magnet into your broom handle about halfway down and it will stick to the refrigerator between the fridge and the wall.

BROWNIES

Soften in the microwave. Place overbaked brownies in the microwave on "low" for a few seconds right before eating, and they'll get nice and soft.

BROWN SUGAR

Substitute another sweetener. This mixture will not have the same texture as store-bought brown sugar but can be substituted in a pinch. Mix together 1 cup of granulated sugar with 4 tablespoons of dark molasses. Mix with a fork to make sure the molasses is evenly distributed.

The reason this tip works is that molasses is one of the ingredients used in manufacturing brown sugar. The amount added determines light or dark brown sugar. You can substitute dark for light or light for dark in recipes. However, the dark has a stronger flavor because it contains more molasses.

BUGS

Make a critter cage for a budding collector. When children want to study fireflies, grasshoppers, crickets, little lizards, and other "nature pets," place a half-gallon milk carton on its side. Cut away two opposite sides, leaving two sides intact along with the bottom and top of the carton. Slip an old knee-high stocking over the container and tie a knot on the bottom, leaving about 6 inches on top.

The top can be opened and closed when the child puts grass, food, or another critter into the container. To close, pull the stocking tight and tie a loose knot. The critter gets plenty of air and can be seen by your budding biologist. Make sure your young scientist is instructed to be kind enough to set insect-eating critters free after observing them for a few hours and never to keep them overnight.

See also ANTS, FLEAS, and PEST CONTROL.

BUMPER STICKERS

Remove stickers safely. Heat the sticker well with a hair dryer, lift the corner with a sharp knife, and peel it off. Be careful not to scratch the bumper! If you don't get it all, repeat the process.

Hint: Next time you put a sticker on, remove only a 2-inch strip of the backing from around the edges and leave the center intact. Removing it will be easier; just split the center and pull it off.

Letter of Laughter

Bug Repelling

A cafeteria manager tried cucumber peelings as a repellent for ants; they worked very well when left on the kitchen counter overnight. Then a friend said that watermelon was even better, so they chopped some up and left it on the counter overnight. The next morning it was loaded with feasting ants. The manager decided to stick with the proven cucumber peelings!

BUNK BEDS

Reuse the ladder. When the ladder for bunk beds is no longer needed, paint it to match the room, hang it on the wall, and use the steps to hold knickknacks.

Make bunk-bed spreads in a snap. For two spreads that fit without hanging over the sides, cut a king-size bedspread in half lengthwise and hem the cut edges.

BUSINESS CARDS

Find uses for old cards. Punch a hole in the edge, write a description of clothing placed in a storage bag, and put the card over the top of the hanger outside of the bag. Or list the contents of a storage box on the back of the card and tape it to the box—no more guessing what's inside. Another good use is to write a brief description of a recipe on the back of a card's shorter edge and poke it into a cookbook so you don't have to look in the index.

BUTTER AND MARGARINE

Prepare some "pats." While the butter or margarine stick is still cold, slice it into individual "pats" with an egg slicer. "Pats" are less messy at the table, and if you are dieting, you'll know how many pats were in the stick and therefore how many you can take.

Measure on paper. Before you remove the paper from a stick of butter or margarine, score the stick on the measure lines provided. Then you can still get a measured "dose" when you need it without messing up a measuring utensil.

 Reuse the wrappers. When you unwrap a new stick of butter or margarine, fold it butter sides in and store in a zipper bag in the freezer. Then when you need to grease a pan, pull out a wrapper, grease the pan, and then toss the wrapper. Imagine if you could use every disposable thing that comes into your house at least twice instead of once. Imagine if everyone did likewise—our landfills would last longer!

See MARGARINE SQUEEZE-STYLE CONTAINERS for recycle uses for these handy containers.

See STAINS for hints on how to remove butter stains from fabrics.

BUTTONS

Prevent accidental pop-offs. The buttons on inexpensive blouses and shirts are sewn on by machine. A thread tail usually hangs loose, and if you pull it, the button comes off. Try putting a small dab of white glue on each button before wearing the garment. The buttons will stay on longer.

Make a match. Can't find the color button you need? Paint buttons with fabric-matching epoxy paint before sewing them on.

Sew on buttons with six-strand embroidery floss. It's stronger and matches any color. If you have to sew on a popped white button with colored thread because that's all you have at the office, cover the thread after sewing with typewriter correction fluid.

Tie them up. Extra twist-ties will hold similar buttons together in your button box, and you'll save time rummaging through loose ones.

Recycle stray buttons. When the container in which you keep stray buttons for emergencies is full, get creative.

- Decorate sweat shirts and T-shirts or sew different colors of buttons on a white blouse for a designer look.
- Glue buttons flat to thumbtacks to give them bigger heads and to make them "designer," too.
- String buttons to make jewelry for children or adults. Give them to children for rainy-day stringing of necklaces or bracelets. Glue two matching strays (or nonmatching if you like) to earring backs for boutique-look earrings to match a certain garment.
- Toss them into the bottom of glass flowerpots instead of rocks.
- Create a "garden" of button flowers on a sweatshirt or one flower on each mitten by sewing one larger button in the center surrounded by smaller ones for "petals." A bow can be the "leaves" beneath the "flower."
- Sew stray buttons in designs on sweat shirts and down the seams of sweat pant legs to make a boutique workout suit.

CABBAGE

Minimize the smells. To get rid of cooking odors when preparing cabbage dishes like corned beef and cabbage, add a bit of vinegar to the water while boiling it.

CACTUSES

Repot painlessly. Repotting cactus when it outgrows its original container can be a prickly situation unless you have some carpet scraps to handle the plants. Just wrap the carpet pieces around the ball of dirt at the base of the plant, and gently lower the plant into its new home. Shield your hands with the carpet scraps as you tamp down the soil.

CAKES

One reader wrote to tell me that when she was baking a cake with her 5-year-old granddaughter, she told the child that it was time to grease and flour the pan. Her granddaughter replied, "I'll get the scissors if you will tell me which flowers I need to cut." Now that she's older, they share a joke whenever they bake together about not forgetting to "flower the pan."

Baking

Pump up a German chocolate cake. Instead of water, substitute the same amount of club soda when making a German chocolate cake from a mix. You'll get a deliciously moist and tasty cake.

Make heart-shaped cakes. If you don't have heart-shaped cake pans, bake a 2-layer cake as directed on the package. But, instead of 2 round layers, bake one 8-inch square layer and one 8-inch round layer. To assemble the heart shape, cut the round layer exactly in half across the diameter. Place the square layer with one corner pointing down on a doily-covered tray. Add the straight cut sides of the round layer on either side of the top corner to form a heart. Frost to cover the "seams."

Bake a friendship cake. For a special event, like a Golden Anniversary, a friendship cake might be perfect. When you send out the invitations, ask each guest to bake and frost a small square cake using their favorite recipe. Then as the guests arrive, piece the cakes together to make a large patchwork cake.

Try football-shaped cakes. Grease and flour a roaster pan as you would a regular cake pan. After baking the cake, take the pan out of the oven and flip it onto a cooling rack. Flip the cake back over so the "dome" is on top. Color coconut with brown food coloring to frost the cake, and make "laces" with black licorice.

Make do with oddly shaped pans. If you need to measure the batter capacity of an oddly shaped pan (hearts, lambs, bells, and stars) to equalize the amounts used in different-shaped layers, fill the pan with water and measure the amount of water that the pan holds. Use *half* of this measurement to fill the pan halfway with batter.

Prevent dome-shaped layers. Try baking your cake at 250°F for 1 hour and 20 minutes; or, buy a special wrap from cake-decorating supply stores to cover the outside of the pan.

Try easy greasing. Keep a plastic sandwich bag in the shortening can so that you can insert your hand, grab some shortening, and grease your pans with the same bag over and over.

Make an in-a-pinch cake tester. When you're out of toothpicks, substitute a long thin piece of uncooked spaghetti to test angel food or other deep cakes for doneness.

Decorating

Decorate with dinosaurs. After frosting a regular cake for a child's birthday, decorate the top with graham cracker dinosaurs.

Quick-draw with spaghetti. Drain cooked very thin spaghetti and cut it to the desired length. Soak it in several drops of red or other food coloring while you decorate the rest of the cake. Then, after removing any drips of color, use the colored spaghetti to outline shapes. You can "draw" Easter bunny whiskers and mouths or anything else that compliments your theme.

Create the color black. Add some blue food coloring to chocolate frosting. Experiment until you get the desired results.

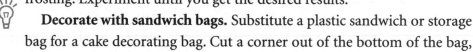

Decorate with sandwich bags. Substitute a plastic sandwich or storage bag for a cake decorating bag. Cut a corner out of the bottom of the bag, slip in the decorating tip, load it with icing, and close the bag.

Make easy chocolate drizzle icing. Instead of making drizzle icing, cut a chocolate bar into little pieces and put the pieces on top of the still-hot-from-the-oven cake.

Freezing

Don't frost before freezing. It's best not to frost and fill cakes before freezing; fillings can make the cake soggy. However, you can frost a cake with confectioners' sugar or fudge frosting (using frosting instead of cream fillings to join layers). Freeze the frosted cake, *then wrap,* place it in a heavy carton or other protective container, and refreeze.

Freeze layers without frosting. Wrap the cake as soon as it's thoroughly cool, then freeze. Store in a carton or other container to prevent crushing; cakes do not freeze solidly.

Thaw slowly. Wrapping will prevent moisture from forming on the cake's surface as it thaws. Large cakes take 2 to 3 hours at room temperature to thaw; a cake layer takes about 1 hour; cupcakes take about 30 minutes.

Heed these storage times. Unfrosted cakes may be kept frozen for up to 3 months, but frosted cakes are best stored only a month or two.

Troubleshooting

Cut unfrosted layers. It's easier to cut cake layers with a long, taut piece of heavy thread or dental floss than to mess around with a knife.

Pack cakes neatly for lunches. If you slice a piece of sheet cake in half lengthwise and then "fold" the two pieces so that the icing is in the center, the icing won't stick to the plastic wrap or to the lid of your container. No mess!

Prevent white "flour dust" on cake layer bottoms. After greasing the cake pan, sprinkle some of the mixed dry ingredients of the recipe or some dry cake mix on the pan to "flour" it. Return the excess to the mixing bowl and proceed with mixing the cake recipe as usual.

Remove a layer stuck in the pan. If you get distracted and the cake completely cools and sticks to the pan, put the stuck layer into a warm oven briefly. This will soften the shortening used to grease the pan. When the pan bottom is warmed, remove it from the oven and immediately turn the layer out onto a cooling rack.

See also POUND CAKE.

CALENDARS

Don't ditch your favorite. If you don't want to part with a special calendar (such as a school band picture or gorgeous scenery), leave it up. Then tear off pages from a freebie calendar and tape them over the corresponding months on the old one.

Record family activities. Have each family member post activities with a different colored ink so that you can tell at a glance who has to be where and when. You can also use colored dots to color code the labels on each member's possessions to quickly identify whose stuff is lying around the house and who owns which tube socks, T-shirts, or other articles.

Reuse desk calendars. Don't toss out the "days" of desk calendars. Write notes, grocery lists, phone messages, and other reminders on the backs, or send the cartoon "days" to people who might enjoy them.

Find new uses for old linen calendars. If you don't want to use old linen calendars for towels, sew them together to create children's quilts or tablecloths. If you crochet, you can connect them together for children's summer coverlets.

See also ADVENT CALENDARS.

CAMCORDERS

See VIDEO CAMERAS AND CAMCORDERS and VIDEOCASSETE RECORDERS.

CAMERAS

There are so many cameras with so many different operating procedures that I can't begin to give tips in this book, but here's one that will save you a trip to the repair shop. If your camera won't click and the shutter seems to jam, you may not have a broken camera. Get new batteries! Camera batteries power the whole camera, not just the flash mechanism. (Once, I thought I'd gotten sand in the camera at the beach and sand was jamming the shutter, but it actually just needed new batteries.)

Practice preservation. Take the batteries out when you aren't using your camera, and they will last longer. A small amount of "juice" is being drained from the batteries as long as they are in place.

Especially in damp climates, or if you've taken your camera to a damp place (like the beach), the battery connection point may corrode. You are less likely to have this problem if you make it a habit to remove batteries when you store your camera for a couple of weeks. If you've been at the beach or fishing, you might want to dab the battery section with a cotton-tipped swab to dry the area and to clean out dirt or sand specks.

Focus upside down. Since most pocket cameras are made to focus with your right eye, vision problems in that eye can also cause picture-taking problems for some people. But, if you turn the camera upside down, you can use your left eye for focusing. The camera and film don't care if the up side is down or vice versa.

Remember if it's loaded. Here's a tip if you've ever "taken pictures" when there wasn't any film in the camera. If you put a twist-tie on the camera strap when you put film into the camera and remove it when you take film out, you'll always know when your camera is "on empty," and you won't miss important photo shots.

Make memory gifts. If you are taking instant camera pictures at a special occasion, why not put the pictures into an album. Then, at the end of the party, present the album to the honoree as a remembrance. Honeymooners would enjoy taking the album along so that they can see their wedding pictures before the official ones arrive from the photographer.

Record the facts. When you move into a furnished apartment, take photos of the furniture and carpeting so that you can show how worn they were when you moved in. Or, on the other hand, if you are the landlord, photos will show how new the furnishings were when the tenant moved in. Include a sign or newspaper with the date to prove when the photos were taken. Likewise, if you own a furnished vacation cottage or home and rent it, take photos of each room, major appliance, or furniture piece, and the exterior of the house in case you have to make insurance claims because of damage or theft. It's also crucial that you should store your valuables.

Save the small stuff. Film containers are great to use as storage for all sorts of small things, such as paper clips in your purse or briefcase, coins for payphones and tolls, and many other tiny things.

See also FILM.

CANDIED FRUIT

Mince by machine. When a recipe calls for finely minced candied fruit, cut the fruit into small pieces and run it through the food processor to mince. No sticky fruit wads to deal with!

CANDLES AND CANDLEHOLDERS

Remove stuck-on wax. If wax has dripped onto metal holders, hold them under very hot water, and the wax will rub off. Or place them in the freezer for at least an hour; the wax will harden and you can easily pick it off. You can avoid the problem completely if you spray the inside of each holder lightly with cooking spray before inserting the candle. The wax will pop right out for easy cleaning. If you need to remove wax from your dishes, gently scrape off any large pieces, and then rinse or soak the dishes in very hot water. Finish by washing in hot sudsy water and, if necessary, scrubbing with a nylon scrubber. (Skin-buffing pads that have become too rough for your skin are good for removing wax or the sticky goo from labels.)

Deal with the drips on a wooden dining table. First scrape off as much of the wax as possible with an old plastic credit card or the dull side of a knife. Clean with a good quality wood cleaner. If the stain doesn't go away, it has probably penetrated the wood, and the entire table will need to be refinished.

Tighten candles that are loose in the holders. Put paper "cups" from boxed chocolates on the bottom of a candle to help it stay put in its holder. Or you can wrap the bottom of the candle several times with a thin piece of tape to make the bottom in a little fatter. If you wrap the tape sticky-side out, it really holds candles in place. You can also use thin foam sheets, the kind used for padding china and giftware. Cut the foam into small squares or circles and wrap them around the candle ends before poking them into candlesticks. (Cut the foam so that it extends up the sides of the candlestick hole but doesn't show.)

Give them a new life. Gather partly used candles and melt them in a coffee can placed in a pan of hot water. Use caution—do not overheat because the wax is flammable. Remove the wicks from the melted wax with a fork. Then dangle a long wick in the center of a mold as you pour in the melted wax. After the wax cools completely, remove from mold and trim the wick if it's too long.

Hints: Easy-to-use molds (because you can cut them away from the candle after the wax hardens) include clean milk cartons and long, narrow potato-chip cans. Just be sure the mold will hold hot melted wax. If you use metal cans, you'll need to place them in hot water for a few seconds to get the candles out. To get translucent effects as the candles burn down, put ice cubes or chunks of ice into large molds (like milk cartons or large shortening cans) and pour the wax over them.

Whiten yellowed candles. You might be able to get the yellow off older white candles if you rub the candle with a soft cloth and rubbing alcohol, or wash it in warm (not hot enough to melt), sudsy water, and rub gently. Polish with a pair of old panty hose. If you can't whiten it, try creative "play." Melt colored crayons or old colored candles and let the soft wax drop onto the candle so that each candle has its own unique design. Harden the wax by placing the candle in the refrigerator overnight.

Light your linguini. Light one end of a long piece of dry, raw pasta, and use it to light candles, especially on a birthday cake with many to light.

See STAINS for hints to remove candle wax from fabrics.

CANDY

Freeze leftover chocolate. Should a miracle occur and leave you with uneaten chocolate candy, freeze the extra pieces in plastic freezer bags. An unopened plastic-wrapped box can go into the freezer as is. Many people freeze chocolates to avoid the temptation to overeat, taking out only the allocated treat allowance for any time period.

Save it for a rainy day. Label a jar "Rainy Day Savings," and have children put all extra candy, such as from Halloween trick-or-treat or birthday party favors, in it. Then, when they're cooped up in the house during bad weather, they can take out the jar and have a snack—not all of it, but some! You'll be monitoring their candy consumption and teaching them about "delayed gratification" at the same time. They may also learn by this example the advantages of saving money for a rainy day.

See also CHOCOLATE.

CANNED FOOD

See FOOD STORAGE AND SAFETY.

CARE PACKAGES

Pack goodies with goodies. To send fragile items or food in a "care package" to a student or overseas service person, protect the goodies with foam packing popcorn and tuck in individual packages of marshmallows or peanuts, or candy—what fun!

CARPETS

Protect areas beneath children's chairs. Put a flannel-backed vinyl tablecloth under the chair. It's easy to wipe up, and liquids won't soak into the carpet.

Find new uses for old pieces. Lay carpet runners on garden paths between rows of vegetables to avoid walking in the mud; staple or nail pieces to garage walls and ceiling for free insulation; or wrap carpeting around a post to make a cat scratching post. Cut circles to fit drink coasters (using plastic lids from different containers), then the coaster won't stick to the bottom of a "sweaty" glass when you pick it up.

Remove crayon from carpet. After you've scraped off as much crayon as you can (a spoon works well), place paper towels over the stain and then gently press the towels with an iron on low-to-medium heat. Move the towels to a clean spot as they absorb the crayon and change them as needed. If color remains (red is very difficult to remove), try a good commercial spot remover specifically made for carpets.

Remove white school glue. Working from the outside in, use a damp sponge to wet the area, and then blot dry with a paper towel. Continue doing this until you've cleaned the entire stain. If some of the glue remains, wash the area by applying a solution of 1 teaspoon of mild dishwashing liquid dissolved in 1 cup of warm water, being careful not to make the rug too wet; then blot with a clean cloth. Remove the cleaning solution by rinsing well with a small amount of water, then blot until dry.

Repair the tear. Place a strip of carpet tape beneath the tear in the carpet and press down. To permanently repair, sew up the tear with a heavy upholstery needle and strong nylon thread and then reinforce the tear with tape. If the tear is in new carpet, it could be a defect. Check with the manufacturer or store about replacement or at least professional repair.

Repair a burn hole. Cut patches the same size (or a tiny bit larger) than the burn holes; clean all the burnt fibers from the carpeting by rubbing with a spoon or cutting with cuticle scissors. Put a bit of transparent or fabric glue on the patches and along the edges, then push each patch into a hole, cover with waxed paper and place a heavy book on top. After the patches are dry (about 24 hours), brush with an old toothbrush to lift up the fibers. If the burn is large and deep, you may have to call a professional to reweave the area.

Reverse indentations. When heavy furniture leaves indentations in the carpet, put an ice cube into each indentation and let it set overnight. The ice cube will melt slowly into the carpet. In the morning, blot up any moisture with paper towels and fluff up the carpet fibers carefully with the tines of a fork. You can also use a steam iron to remove indentations caused by furniture legs. Hold the iron above the indentation, but don't let it touch the carpeting. Let the steam penetrate the area. The fibers should spring back to normal. You may have to repeat the steaming for stubborn dents. Use a brush to fluff up the pile after steaming.

Consider carpet protectors. Before you decide to protect new carpeting from traffic-pattern wear with scraps of the carpeting, check the carpet's backing. If the underside is rough, it will wear down the carpet like sandpaper and you won't accomplish anything. Only rubber-backed rugs should be placed over carpeting to protect it from traffic pattern wear and soiling. Also, remove the rugs often, and vacuum beneath them so that dirt doesn't get ground into the carpet below.

Vacuum slowly. When you vacuum, take slow, overlapping strokes (at least seven) to really clean out embedded dirt particles. And remember that you can't vacuum well if the bag is full. Check the vacuum cleaner bag often and empty it as needed. To prevent dust clouds from polluting your home, empty the vacuum cleaner bag into a large plastic garbage bag— preferably outside.

Vacuum often to fight fleas. If you have a pet and the resulting problems with fleas in your carpets, your vacuum cleaner is your best ally in the battle against these pests. Always vacuum thoroughly after applying flea killers.

Don't be shocked by shedding. It's common in new carpeting, as loose fibers left over from the manufacturing process rise to the surface.

Control the static. Static electricity in some carpet fibers plagues us mostly in the winter months when humidity in the home is low. The commercial antistatic sprays made especially for fabrics and carpets (found in supermarkets) are effective. Running a humidifier can help. (It's also good for your skin and lungs if very dry air causes you to have dry skin or breathing problems.)

Close the drapes. It's a good idea to keep drapes closed on sunny days. Overexposure to the sun will fade some carpet fibers.

Eliminate musty smells. If your carpet smells musty, it's usually a sign that the carpet or padding is damp. If you cannot take the carpet or padding outside to dry in the sunlight, dry it with a fan. If you can tell that only a small area is wet, you can use a hair dryer on a low setting to dry it. If the odor remains after the carpet is completely dry, there may be mildew on the back. To get rid of the mildew, try sprinkling some baking soda underneath (if the carpet is not tacked down) and on top of the carpet as well. Wait a day, and then vacuum up the baking soda. Hopefully, your carpet will be fresh and clean.

See also RUGS.

Carpet Drying 101

It's important to clean all spills immediately because set stains will be more difficult to remove (especially those from beverages that contain sugar and from pet urine). And after using the appropriate solution for the spot or stain, rinse the area well. Of course, with clothing, you can just hold the garment under running water or immerse it. With carpets, after you rinse the area with clear water to remove all detergents or other stain removers, you have to blot as much of the moisture as you can to prevent rings from forming around the area you worked on. Here's how.

Place an old white towel or wads of white paper towels (use white to prevent any possible color bleeding) over the wet area. Then walk around on the towels, reversing them so the dry sides are touching the carpet. Keep doing this until the area feels mostly dry.

Then place another dry white towel on the area and weigh it down (with bricks, a heavy book wrapped in foil or plastic wrap to protect it from moisture, or a stack of magazines) to help draw out any remaining moisture.

Leave the weighted towel on the area overnight. In the morning or whenever the carpet is dry, fluff up the nap with your fingers, a brush, or the vacuum cleaner.

CARPOOLS

Create a code. Plan with your carpool that if you can't reach a driver by phone to say that you won't be riding that day, you will put a piece of colored paper or some other signal in a front window of the house. That way, the driver won't have to waste time stopping or annoy neighbors by honking a horn.

CARS

See AUTOMOBILES.

CASSEROLES

Prevent pre-potluck spills. To prevent spills in the car when transporting casseroles, put them inside a plastic grocery bag or a plastic bag–lined box. Use masking tape to tape lids tightly to dishes so nothing leaks out.

Get a basket. Why not purchase a pretty basket (square or rectangular ones work best) to transport your covered dishes? Look for baskets with wide, flat bottoms. Use dish towels to keep the dishes from sliding inside the basket.

Keep it hot. Put a folded towel in the bottom of a small foam ice chest; cover the casserole with another folded towel. With the lid on the chest, the casserole will stay hot until serving time, even up to an hour.

Caution: My sources say food shouldn't stand for more than 2 hours between preparation and eating. Keep food at 185°F, or reheat it to that temperature before serving.

See also COVERED DISHES.

CATS

Cats are affectionate pets. Who can resist their purrs? One reason for their increased popularity these days is that cats are such practical pets for apartment-dwellers. However, cat owners should know that even if Tabby never goes outdoors, she should be inoculated annually against disease. If your cat is of the outdoor variety, make sure the collar it wears is elastic and can slip off if your cat gets caught on something while climbing trees and

Cat Carriers

With newspapers on the bottom, try using the following to transport a cat.

- ♥ A bird cage will hold a small kitten en route to a new home.
- ♥ Two small laundry or storage baskets, one right side up and the other upside down, laced or tied together, will serve as an emergency cat carrier in the car.
- ♥ A sturdy case from bottled beer, tied shut with rope, will serve as a cat carrier. The handgrip spaces provide air and see-through windows.

rooftops. You can still attach a bell and rabies tag to an elastic collar.

Here are some other valuable tips for making sure your feline friend is safe, happy, and well-cared for.

Cat Adoption

Adopt with care. To save yourself heartache, before you get too attached to a sweet stray cat, take him to a vet for a checkup and testing for feline leukemia. Often the strays of an entire neighborhood have passed the infection around, and it's just a matter of time before the cat dies—sometimes only a couple of weeks. If the cat isn't infected, you need to see a vet anyway to have it spayed or neutered and to get all of its immunizations, including vaccination against feline leukemia. If you bring an infected cat into the house, you will have to wait 6 months before bringing another cat into that area to prevent infection of the new cat.

Care for abandoned newborn kittens. If a mama kitty abandons her litter, you need to keep the kittens warm. A box lined with shredded paper and a soft cloth will do. It helps to also have a thermostatically controlled overhead infrared lamp because kittens need to be kept at about 88° to 92°F when they are a week old; about 80° to 85°F when they get to 14 days old; about 80°F when they are about a month old. Also, keep a pan of water near the box to add humidity since dehydration can be a problem.

If you can't get to a vet to buy the proper formula, this emergency formula can substitute. Mix 2 cups of milk, 1 teaspoon of corn syrup, the yolk of 1 egg, and a pinch of salt. Keep the formula in the refrigerator and take out what's needed for each feeding. Formula should be room temperature. Feed only 8 to 10 drops per tiny kitten.

Prepare before adding a second cat to your family. A young kitten may be a better choice and less of a threat to an older cat. Try to match sizes so that the older, larger cat doesn't harm the smaller, younger one in play. Also, match personalities so that both are playful or both are tranquil loungers. Some vets suggest getting opposite sexes to lessen territorial battles and recommend neutering or spaying both pets to make them more compatible. When you bring the new cat home, put each cat in a separate room. Gradually let them get acquainted for short periods under supervision, extending the time as they get used to each other. Provide each cat with its own litter box, food dish, toys, and sleeping place. Be sure to show each cat equal affection and attention and allow time for them to adjust to each other.

Clever Cat Toys

Cats like to bat around just about anything. Try these with your kitty—under supervision.

- ♥ Put a few pebbles or a tiny bell into a small plastic pill bottle and close it tightly.

- ♥ Roll and tuck a sock into a ball.

- ♥ Toss your cat a tennis ball or even a wad of crumpled paper.

- ♥ Hang a fishing float on a string from a door knob and watch Kitty bat it around.

Caution: Don't give your cat a ball of yarn. He may become entangled and strangle himself while playing.

Cat Comfort

Install a cat cozy. When you have a cat that just won't stay inside, you can make a warm sleeping box from an old foam ice chest. Turn the chest upside down, place it on top of the lid, and cut a hole in one side just large enough for the cat to get in. Put some newspaper on the bottom and a fluffy towel over the paper. Kitty will be insulated and waterproofed by the foam.

Dish up cat food au gratin. If a finicky cat refuses the flavor of cat food you've bought, try sprinkling Parmesan cheese on it. While it's not usually good to give milk products to cats, a little cheese once in a while won't hurt, and you won't waste the cat food. Another treat is to give your cat the liquid that comes in canned salmon, tuna, and sardines. It's like kitty champagne to most of them!

Keep them safe. If the cats in your neighborhood lounge around on cars, you can bet that one will crawl under the hood looking for a warm engine "bed." I've received several letters from people whose cats were severely injured when motorists started their cars and instead of an engine's "purr" they heard the shriek of a cat caught in the machinery. Tap on the hood or toot your horn before you turn the key, wait a few seconds, and any kitty sneaking a cozy nap will be out of harm's way.

Create a snooze spread. If your cat likes to snooze on your bed and the result is cat hair on the spread, substitute a next-size top sheet for the bedspread, in a print that coordinates with your bedroom colors. You can more easily wash it than a heavy spread or quilt. Queen sheets cover double beds; kings cover a queen-size mattress.

Cat Health

Regular checkups are essential for good pet health. Still, it helps to know the early warning signs of those situations that require an immediate trip to the vet. Here are three to watch for.

- ⊛ **Loose stools, a lackluster coat, and bloated stomach.** Cats that look malnourished even though well fed could have worms.
- ⊛ **Changes to the eyes.** When a cat's membranous eyelids half-cover its eyes, it's generally a sign of intestinal illness. Constant discharge from a cat's eye can be a symptom of a local infection or systemic disease.

✿ **Trouble urinating.** If a cat stops urinating normally or seems to have trouble urinating, get it to a vet quickly. A cat with urinary problems may stop using the litter box because it associates the litter box with pain. Treating the problem will help get the cat to use its litter again. Cats really are clean animals and prefer to use their litter boxes.

Cat Scratchers

Lead them to the scratching post. Sprinkles of catnip can lure a cat to a scratching post, but don't be surprised if your cat ignores catnip; not all cats like it. If that's the case, you might try playing a game with your cat by getting it to chase a scratchable toy that you dangle from a fishing rod. Reel in the toy while kitty chases it. Then, use this game to lead kitty to use its scratching post by dangling the toy over and on the post. Soon kitty will play and scratch on the post whenever the mood strikes.

Make your own post. You don't need to buy a scratching post. Cover a length of log (cat-length high and about 6 inches in diameter) with carpet and nail its end to a flat board base. Some cats—those that are used to scratching the wooden fences they walk on—will be happy scratching on a 2- by 4-inch wooden wall stud that's about twice the cat's body length. Just saw off a piece and leave it on the floor. Kitty will stand on it and scratch at the same time.

Cat Scare

A reader whose cat, like many cats, liked to play with string wrote a chilling letter. Normally, when her cat finished playing with a string, the reader would pick up the string and put it away. The one time she forgot, she found her cat with a string in its mouth. Unable to remove the string, she took the cat to the vet, who also couldn't remove it. The string had worked its way through the cat's system and was wound throughout its intestines. Emergency surgery revealed 31 inches of string! The cat never gets string to play with anymore.

Cat Discipline

Spritz the cat with water. Direct a quick squirt from a spray bottle while you sternly say, "No!" each time the cat does something wrong or goes to a place that it doesn't belong. The cat will soon associate unpleasantness with what it was doing and will stop. You have to be consistent. Cats can learn the word "no" just as well as dogs can.

Let them taste some vinegar. Each time the cat goes to the forbidden place, dab a cotton ball moistened with vinegar on the cat's lips—just a dab. Don't rub in the vinegar or hurt the animal. If you are consistent, kitty will learn that going to the forbidden place means touching that nasty vinegar and will soon give up. You can leave the saturated cotton ball in the forbidden place as an added deterrent.

Protect the plants. Keep cats out of your plants by covering the soil with wads of nylon net, a layer of pinecones, or citrus rinds. Cats don't usually like the smell of citrus. You can water plants through the net or cones. Cats will steer clear of newly seeded plant beds if you lay rolled or crumpled lengths of chicken wire on the beds.

Cat Litter Boxes

Avoid changing or handling cat litter boxes if you're pregnant. Toxoplasmosis, a disease transmitted from cats to pregnant women, is responsible for about 3,000 birth defects annually, according to the March of Dimes Birth Defects Foundation. This disease, caused by passing parasites from cats to humans, also causes brain damage and death in people with poor immune systems.

Keep yourself clean. Wear rubber gloves and wash your hands carefully after you change that litter pan.

Minimize odors. Keeping an air freshener in the room with the litter box helps, but frequent changing of the litter works best to keep odors down.

Sprinkling baking soda on the bottom of a litter pan before adding the litter helps to deodorize it.

Caution: Don't do this if your cat is on a salt-restricted diet.

For a quick temporary deodorizer, sprinkle baking soda or litter freshener powder on top of the litter and stir it into the top layer with your "pooper scooper." It'll stay reasonably fresh for a few hours until you can change the litter.

Ease the cleanup. A newspaper section placed on the bottom of the litter pan makes it easier to dump out the litter. Newspapers strategically taped to the wall behind the litter pan will protect the wall from flying litter if you have an especially enthusiastic cat. You can also avoid a mess by putting the whole pan into a large plastic garbage bag before you tip it to empty it. Tap the back of the pan while it's still inside the bag to release any stuck litter, then hose off the litter tray. If you can, allow it to air in the sun for a while.

Make subtle changes. If you change litter brands, (to one with a different texture or odor), your cat might develop "litter phobia." The cat may refuse to use the new litter and actually suffer from urine retention and constipation. To avoid this, add new litter in increments of ¼ new litter to ¾ old brand of litter, increasing the addition of new litter gradually as you change the litter pans to allow your cat to get used to the new brand.

Consider newsprint. Some cat owners train their cats to use newspaper sections instead of litter in the litter pan. It's easier to lift out a newspaper section than to dump messy litter, and you won't have litter tracked around in the "litter room." But you have to believe that the cat won't use your newspapers *before* they get put into the litter pan!

See also PETS.

CATSUP

See STAINS for hints on how to remove ketchup stains.

CEDAR CHESTS

Refresh the scent. Lightly sand the inside of the chest with fine grade sandpaper. (Wrap sandpaper around a big rectangular sponge so the heat of sanding doesn't bother your hands.) Vacuum up any wood particles. You can also add cedar balls or blocks if this doesn't renew enough of the scent.

CEILINGS AND CEILING FANS

Speed-patch the hole. When you remove a swag lamp or planter hooks from the ceiling and you find that there's with a small hole to patch, try this. Plug the hole with a cork. Push it in until it's flush with the ceiling surface, then paint the cork to match the ceiling.

See WALLS for other ideas.

Distinguish the chains. If you have a hard time telling the fan chain from the light chain, put a large wooden or ceramic macramé bead on the light and a tassel on the fan or vice versa—anything that helps you tell one from the other. Cork or plastic fishing-line floats or plastic lime or lemon juice squirters are good quick-fix chain pulls for lights or fans. A plastic yellow lemon attached to a closet light pull makes it especially easy to find in semidarkness.

CELERY

Restore limp stalks. Put the stalks in cold water to recrisp them. They will keep in the fridge for a day or two.

Freeze extra celery. When there's too much celery to consume quickly, dice and cook it in a bit of water until just tender. Then cool it and divide it into small amounts for soup or casseroles and freeze.

Make a refrigerator bouquet. To make sure that you have celery to munch on even if you have no time to cut it up into sticks: Cut off the stalk end when you bring the celery home, rinse off the stalks, and place them bottom-side down in water in a large wide-mouth vase (like the freebies in which florists deliver cut flowers). Save the heart of the celery (either in the refrigerator or freezer) for cooking. To further avoid temptation if you are dieting, put your celery "bouquet" on the table for before-dinner munching. A vase will hold the celery vertically so it takes very little space in the fridge.

See also PRODUCE.

CEREAL

Keep it fresh. If the cereal isn't in a resealable bag, pour it into gallon-size zip-closing bags and return it to the box. It will stay fresh longer.

Reuse the inner bag. You can use cereal-box liners to cover foods cooking in the microwave, to hold scraps when you peel veggies, or to line drawers. Or use them to wrap potatoes for microwaving or as a base for rolling cookies and pie crusts. Crush crackers or cereal in one for breading. Open the bag to make a flat surface to hold crumbs and flour for breading and a place to lay coated meat pieces as they dry for 20 minutes before frying. (If you let breaded meats dry, flip the meat so each side is exposed to the air for 10 minutes or so, or place on a rack before deep- or pan-frying, and the coating will be crisper and cling better.)

Sip your cereal. There's no rule that says hot cereal must be served in a bowl. Put it in a cup, add a bit more milk so it's thinner, and then drink it. This idea is especially helpful when small children make a mess eating hot cereal with a spoon. Give them a straw and see them slurp up breakfast! If you get a late start, put the cereal in a lidded, insulated coffee cup, insert a straw in the lid hole and sip breakfast en route to work or to enjoy when you get there.

Keep the sugar from sinking to the bottom. I've received hints to avoid this problem, like dissolving sugar in the milk before pouring it on the cereal. But the easiest idea is to pour milk on the cereal first and then sprinkle on the sugar. The sugar granules will stick to the moist cereal.

Mix a batch of "cereal surprise." Mix the last few ounces of different cereals for a "custom blend" that uses up all the leftovers and tastes good, too.

Hint: When children prefer to eat cereals that have the nutritional value of a cookie, mix the sweetened favorites with "real food" cereals.

Avoid a sticky mess. To press rice cereal treat mixtures into the pan, place clear plastic wrap over the top and press or use a chilled mug as a "rolling pin" to press the mixture down.

CHAIRS

Take sags out of cane bottoms. Wipe the surface of the seat with a cloth that has been dipped in hot water and wrung out. Scrub thoroughly, then place the chair outdoors in the sun to dry.

Protect the walls when storing. Often, storing folding chairs and the extra table leaf can leave walls marred where these items lean. To prevent that from happening, put a pillowcase over each bridge chair or table leaf when storing it. You'll also keep the chairs or table leaf clean and nicely dust-free.

CHAMOIS CLOTHS

Make it last. Wash chamois cloths after each use in mild soapy water, leaving a little soap in the cloth to help keep it pliable between uses. After washing, wring it out gently and pull it to its original shape. Lay it out to dry, but not in direct sunlight or near a heat source. Also, never use a chamois with strong chemicals, oil, grease, or as a sponge when washing the car.

CHAMPAGNE

See WINE AND CHAMPAGNE.

CHANDELIERS

Try the twist-tie repair trick. If a crystal falls off because wires have broken, replace the wire with a twist-tie. Scrape the paper off the wire and put it through the opening of the crystal; rehang the crystal on the chandelier. Cut off the excess wire.

CHANGE

Use loose change. Someone I know calls coins found lying around the house or left in pockets "mad money" because it makes her mad to see her family treat money so carelessly. If that sounds like you, try putting these strategies to good use.

- Put a large decorative bowl in a catchall spot so that all family members can easily contribute. Then when there's enough money, treat yourself to a night out at a restaurant.
- Put parking-meter coins in your car ashtray so that people won't put ashes in it or will think twice before smoking in your car.
- Collect loose change from laundry pockets until there's enough "pocket money" to buy something for the chief laundry-doer, even if it's just an ice-cream treat.

CHARITY

Plan your giving. When you are asked to give to charities, you want to give to those groups that use your money wisely. One way to check on any charity—national or local—is to call your local Better Business Bureau. BBBs have information on charities and how they meet the BBB standards for money usage, public accountability, fund-raising practices, solicitation, and the accuracy of informational materials. They can also tell you how they are governed, and if they comply with laws and regulations.

CHECKBOOKS

 Keep track of the numbers. When you write a check while shopping, collect the receipt, note the check number quickly on the receipt, and place it in your checkbook. When you get home, record all of your purchases at one time and balance your checkbook. No more mystery checks that you forgot to record and therefore have no idea of the amount!

 Check your checks. Place a small bookmark or a piece of ribbon at the point in your checkbook where you have only 5 checks left. It's a reminder to put your next book of checks into your purse or checkbook case.

CHEESE

Don't mind the mold. Moisture can cause cheese to mold. If mold hasn't penetrated too deeply, scrape it off; you can still eat the cheese. (But yogurt, cream cheese, or cottage cheese that has mold should be discarded.)

Protect against moisture. If you want to prevent moisture from undermining your cheese, place a few sugar cubes in a self-sealing plastic bag with the cheese. When the cubes become soggy in a few days, replace them.

Use cheesecloth. To keep mold from forming on large hunks of cheese, the traditional way is to wrap the cheese in cheesecloth (what else?) that has been moistened—but is not dripping wet—with vinegar. Place the wrapped cheese in a plastic bag and into the refrigerator. The vinegar doesn't affect the taste of the cheese. You may have to sprinkle more vinegar on the cloth every now and then if you are storing the cheese for several weeks.

Employ the sniff test. When buying "surface-ripened" cheeses like Camembert or Brie, make sure to "sniff test" if you can. If they have even a hint of an ammonia scent, they are past their peak for eating. Don't buy them. It's a cheese seller's myth that the ammonia scent is okay.

Table of Common Cheeses

Generally, ripened cheeses keep longer than unripened cheeses, and you can buy enough to last for several weeks. Most soft, unripened cheeses are perishable, so it's best to buy only as much as you'll use in a short time.

Ripened Cheeses
Very hard: Asiago, Parmesan, Romano, Sapsago, Spalen
Hard: Cheddar, granular or stirred curd, Caciocavallo, Swiss, Emmentaler, Gruyère
Semisoft: Brick, Muenster, Limburger, Port du Salut, Trappist, Roquefort
Soft: Bel Paese, Brie, Camembert, Neufchâtel (as made in France), Gorgonzola, Blue, Stilton, Wensleydale

Unripened Cheeses
Soft: Cottage, cream, Neufchâtel (as made in the United States), fresh ricotta

Cut only what you'll use. If you have a large hunk of cheese, instead of serving the whole thing, cut off only the amount you expect to eat, and allow it to come to room temperature (best for eating). Going back and forth from fridge to table dries out the cheese and speeds up spoilage.

Slice with ease. Grasp each end of a piece of dental floss and slice away. Dental floss also neatly cuts cake layers horizontally.

Store cheeses in the refrigerator. Some American cheeses will crumble if frozen, which is fine if you plan to use them in a sauce or as a salad topping, but not so fine if you want slices. Refrigerate sliced cheeses in their original film wrappers. You can wrap cheese with waxed paper or plastic and then with foil before refrigerating it. Processed cheese, cheese food, and spreads sold in sealed jars or packages keep without refrigeration, but they must be refrigerated after you open the containers.

CHENILLE BEDSPREADS AND ROBES

Make dishcloths. Once no longer usable as a spread or a robe, cut 10-by 10-inch squares and hem them to make dishcloths. The chenille knots are terrific for removing stuck food from dishes and pans.

See also BEDDING and BLANKETS.

CHEWING GUM

See STAINS for hints to remove chewing gum from fabrics.

CHILD PROOFING

See BALCONIES, DOORS, and KITCHENS.

CHILI SAUCE

See STAINS for hints on how to remove chili sauce stains from fabric.

CHINA

See TABLEWARE.

CHINA CABINET LIGHTS

Enjoy the scenery. Instead of turning on the lights only when you have guests, plug the light cord of a lighted china cabinet into a socket timer and enjoy a few glowing hours each night without having to remember to switch them off.

CHOCOLATE

Melt chocolate like magic. If you are melting chocolate in a double boiler for fondue or other uses, don't let the water touch the bottom of the pan. It will scorch the chocolate and make it hard and gritty. Cooking chocolate too fast or in a lightweight saucepan can also make it gritty. The best way to cook chocolate is in a heavy saucepan over low heat, stirring it often. I stir with a pancake turner so that the whole pan is scraped fast.

Dip a chip. Place one or two pretzels, crackers, or cookies on a potato masher; dip in melted chocolate; and place the treats on a plate to cool.

Savor the syrup. When all that's left is a bit of chocolate syrup in the bottom of the container, make chocolate milk by adding milk and shaking until the syrup dissolves.

See also CANDY and COCOA.

See STAINS for hints to remove chocolate from fabric.

CHOPSTICKS

 Start a stake collection. Save the disposable chopsticks you get from Asian restaurants. They make sturdy plant stakes for indoor potted plants.

CHRISTMAS

 Keep track of after-Christmas purchases. Before you pack away those bargain Christmas cards, wrapping paper, and decorations that you bought during the after-Christmas sales, write down what you bought and make note of what you still need, and then attach the list to the November page of your next year's calendar. It's easy to forget what you have, and it's a chore to unpack early to find out what's needed.

Plan gifts for unexpected guests. Buy a variety of small gifts, like mugs, calendars, decorative candles, or candy, to keep under the tree to have a surprise for unexpected guests. You can code them by gender (red wrapping or with bows for females; green paper or with crinkle tie for males) if you want to be more specific, but I like to buy generic gifts.

Hang outdoor lights with ease. Attach cup hooks to the outside eaves of your house, about every 10 inches, and leave them in place as permanent anchors for holiday lights. Then, you can cut a notch in the end of a yardstick and poke the lights' wires into place each year without a ladder.

If you can't reach the eaves with a yardstick, screw a cup hook into the very end of a broom handle. The broom handle will be a useful "grabber" during the rest of the year, and you can hang it so that it doesn't stand on end squashing its bristles.

 Light with luminaria. Empty plastic jugs make beautiful "lanterns" for lining your driveway or walkway during the holidays. Cut an opening in the top, leaving the handle on. Spray them green or red, and then fill with an inch or two of sand to help anchor a small candle. Or decorate with

Christmas Ornament Recipe

Store these from year to year in a tightly sealed container. In some climates, they can attract insects. One reader stores hers wrapped in tissue and placed in a box with a few mothballs or cedar shavings to deter bugs.

Christmas ornament dough

2 cups baking soda
1 cup cornstarch
1¼ cups cold water

Mix the baking soda and the cornstarch in a saucepan. Add the water. Cook over medium heat, stirring constantly, until the mixture is the consistency of wet mashed potatoes. Turn it out onto a plate and cover it with a damp cloth. Let it cool. When cool, knead it until it's smooth. Seal it in a plastic bag, and store in the refrigerator until you're ready to use it.

Use either your hands or cookie cutters to shape the ornaments. Insert a wire hanger into the soft dough, or make a hole in each ornament with a plastic drinking straw so that you can hang the ornament with crinkle-tie or regular ribbon. Let the ornaments dry overnight, or heat them in a 250°F oven for 15 minutes. If they are not completely dry, put them back in the oven, and keep checking them every 5 minutes until they're done.

Paint dried pieces with watercolors, poster paints, acrylic paints, or felt-tip pens. Finish the ornaments with a coat or two of clear nail polish or varnish, and they'll last for years.

large 32-ounce juice cans. Use a nail to pound holes in the sides of the can, either in a random pattern or a particular design. (To keep the cans from bending when you pound nails into the sides, fill them with water, freeze until the water is a solid block, and then pound away.) Spray the cans with flat, black paint, pour in a couple of inches of sand and insert a candle.

Improvise your ornament hooks. Unbend the middle "bend" of a paperclip so that you still have a loop on each end, one for the ornament and one for the tree. Alternately, you can just put a twist-tie through the decoration loop and wrap the ends around the tree branch.

Note: My busy research editor has all of her ornaments permanently attached to her artificial tree. After Christmas, she covers the still-decorated tree with a plastic bag (sold for disposing of real Christmas trees) and stores it in a spare room. Then each year, she brings out the tree, already decorated.

Collect Christmas souvenirs. Instead of buying dust-catching knick-knacks as souvenirs, buy Christmas ornaments unique to the area you visit when on vacation. You'll have a very personalized Christmas tree with wonderful memories of vacations when you decorate it (and not lots of stuff to dust throughout the year).

Create a "stocking tree." When one reader's family's new home had no fireplace for hanging their traditional Christmas stockings, they substituted a pole planter that had a hook for each stocking.

Water with a funnel. Here's a no-mess idea for watering the Christmas tree. Insert a long funnel—the type designed for a car transmission and sold at auto parts stores—into the water pan. No more breaking ornaments and knocking things off when you're crawling under the tree to water it!

Decorate both sides of your door. If you have two holiday wreaths that are about the same weight, try tying a sturdy ribbon from one to the other and draping it over the door. The weights of the wreaths will balance like a teeter-totter. Apply a heavy-duty tape, like duct tape, across the ribbon on top of the door to keep the ribbon from sliding when the door is opened.

CLEANING

Work in one room at a time. When you get ready to do a serious cleaning of the entire house, you will sabotage your whole effort if you move the clutter from one room to another. What gets picked up should be stored where it belongs; and, if it doesn't belong anywhere, give it to a charity or throw it out. Along the same lines, don't switch to another room until the first room is finished, even if it takes several days. Seeing progress in one room will give you a greater sense of accomplishment than having several rooms half-finished.

Don't start a new room when you're already tired. If the first room's work has taken most of the day, wait until morning so that you're more inclined to clean thoroughly.

Do a little each day. Get rid of papers and junk as they accumulate, and vacuum and dust daily if you can. If you clean your living room every day,

The Cleaning Routine

Adopt a routine when cleaning so you are always closer to the goal of completing one room before moving to another. When you use the same routine over and over, it becomes so automatic that you can think about something else while you're doing it. Some people like to "plug in" to their radio or cassette earphones while they clean. Music with a beat helps beat the cleaning blues. Here's a top-to-bottom housecleaning routine to try.

1. Pick up all papers, magazines, or any other clutter.

2. Dust knickknacks, paintings, lamps, and other decorative items.

3. Dust or polish all wood furniture.

4. Vacuum floors, carpets, and upholstered furniture.

5. Dry mop, sweep, or scrub noncarpeted floors.

6. Do any heavy cleaning chores such as window washing, silver or brass polishing, and miscellaneous repairs.

7. Close the door and go on to another room. Closing the door keeps dirt and dust from getting back into clean rooms and gives you the satisfaction of having finished something.

8. If you pick up items that need to go to another part of the house, don't leave that room and let yourself get sidetracked. Put them outside the door and remove them all at once.

you'll always have one refuge from clutter. One clean room prevents your feeling overwhelmed by a whole house in need of attention. And, you'll have someplace to sit comfortably if a friend drops by unexpectedly for a coffee-chat break.

Create a storage tote. Leave the handle on, but cut out the top side of a large plastic milk jug to make a container to store bathroom cleaning supplies, sponge, and scrubber.

See also BATHROOMS, CLOSETS, and KITCHENS.

CLEANING FLUID RINGS

See STAINS for hints to remove cleaning fluid rings from fabrics.

CLOCKS

Stop annoying humming noises. Try turning the windup clock upside down and leaving it that way for a day or so; it "re-oils" the small parts.

CLOSETS

Closet cleaning may be a chore, but sometimes organizing one part of your life (in this case, it's your wardrobe) can lead to getting the other parts of your life organized.

If you don't believe me, think about the times when you are surrounded by the most household clutter. Is it when you feel as if the sun is shining just for you and the world is yours to dance on? Or is it when you feel as if the world is spinning so far out of orbit that you have lost your footing and are flying off into outer space?

The point is that when you feel in charge of your life and that everything is going your way, you can control clutter in your home and the rest of your life instead of having the clutter sneak up and control you.

Closet Cleaning

Start by taking all of your clothes out of the closet. As you put your clothes back into the closet, decide what you really want and will wear again. Be ruthless. It's okay to be sentimental and save the outfit you wore when you met that special person in your life—but don't get carried away.

Refresh the Scent

Step into a walk-in closet when applying spray cologne, and the extra fragrance will stay in the closet (to make it smell nice) instead of dissipating in the air.

Caution: Don't spray cologne on clothing because it can stain or damage certain fabrics.

(This is a good time to paint or clean the inside of the closet, as well as a good time to sew on loose buttons and repair other clothes that you want to keep.)

Take the 2-year test. Get rid of clothing that hasn't been worn in at least a year or two. I know we all say, "I'll wear that someday," and then we put it back into the closet to hang around for several more years.

 Try the "A, B, and C" method. Make 3 piles of clothing—A, B, C. You will definitely keep the A clothing. You might keep the B clothing. C clothing hasn't been worn for a year or so, for whatever reason, and won't go back into the closet. After returning the A pile to the closet, go through the B pile again. If necessary, redivide the B items into A's and C's. Put the second group of A's back into your closet and make a mental note that these were almost discards. (The next time you clean your closets, if these same items are B's, they should immediately go into the C pile for discarding.) Put all the C's together in large plastic bags and donate them to a nonprofit group.

Donating Discards

 Host a clothing swap. Hold a clothing swap party for your friends to clean out outgrown, no-longer-liked, or no-longer-worn garments. Donate garments that nobody claims to a women's shelter or other charity. I'm still wearing a "swap" garment from 10 years ago!

Recognize a good cause. Knowing that your discards have value to somebody makes it easier to be objective when you sort the "Keeps" from the "Keep-Nots." You will be helping yourself and somebody else at the same time. Battered-women's shelters across the country, for example, always need women's and children's clothing, bedding, and towels, because their clients often come in with only the clothes they are wearing and obviously can't go home to get their possessions. This is where everything I "go through" is taken.

Call the organization to find out what it will do with your donation. Preowned clothing is used by different organizations in different ways, depending upon its condition. Some organizations sell wearable clothing as a fund-raiser; others distribute it to needy people. Some organizations shred nonrepairable, nonwearable clothing, and then sell it by the pound to rag dealers.

Some national organizations, such as the Salvation Army and Goodwill Industries, will repair donated items before resale, thus providing jobs for various people, including the handicapped. Such organizations will accept just about any kind of discards. Often, if items are not sold during their allotted "rack life" of 6 weeks or so, they are passed on to individuals who use the clothing and household items to help the homeless and others in need.

Organizing Closets

Create more hanger space. Buy 18 inches of ¼-inch brass chain. Put a sturdy wood or metal hanger through the second or third link, and hang it from the closet rod. Let the remainder of the chain dangle and put other hangers through the links as desired. This is an excellent way to hang blouses, skirts, and children's clothes. You also can hang a chain in a soft garment bag to use the often-wasted space at the bottom. Or just suspend a chain from the ceiling of your closet.

Stack some crates. Plastic milk crates sold in most department and variety stores can be stacked on their sides to form shelves. Or use them to hold various items such as sweaters, shoes, and handbags, and then stack them on top of each other or on shelves in closets. When they're on shelves, you can just pull them out as you would drawers.

Create some boundaries. When children (or even adults) share a closet, you can set boundaries for each person's clothing with plastic coffee-can lids. Cut a hole in the middle of each lid large enough to accommodate the wooden clothes rod in your closet, and then make a slit from the center hole through the outer rim. Write each person's name on the lid with a permanent felt-tip marker and place the lid on the clothes rod between "territories" to divide (clothing) and conquer (closet complaints).

Color code your clothes. Hang blouses and shirts in the closet according to color. Then when you're in a hurry, you can find what you need to match whatever you're wearing. And you may find, as a dear friend of mine did, that she had over 30 navy blue blouses because that was her favorite color. So now when she shops, if she reaches for navy blue she closes her eyes, sees the vision of her closet, and chooses another color.

Hang a complete outfit. Put matching pants, shirts, socks, and even the underwear (for children) on one hanger. This hint helps young children who are learning to dress themselves and adults who are color-blind because getting dressed becomes a matter of grabbing a clothing "ensemble" from the closet and putting it on. No more kids in "clown" outfits; no more beige shirts with gray suits and brown socks.

Store your slips together. If you hang slips on a skirt or trouser hanger, they won't be wrinkled, and it's easier to tell the length when you have several of the same color.

Organize children's dresser drawers. Put matching clothing in large zipper-type plastic bags and put them in the drawers. Children feel grown up selecting their own clothing, and their outfits will match. You can help children and the babysitter by labeling each drawer's front. Identify the articles in each drawer on an index card or a stick-on note. It will save time and messes, since they won't have to dig through every drawer.

Make a place for hats, mittens, and gloves. Attach spring clothespins to the coat closet door with heavy-duty staples or nails so that hats, mittens, and gloves can be hung up and found the next day.

Cover the closet rod. Putting on a plastic closet rod cover is easier if you put a small bottle inside the plastic roll and then push it along in front as you fit the cover onto the rod. No more cut fingers, broken plastic, or broken fingernails! Another idea: If you want your hangers to slide more smoothly, apply paste floor wax to the closet pole.

Storing Clothes

Store wedding gowns with care. After cleaning, wrap the gown in unbleached muslin or acid-free white tissue paper, and then wrap it in blue tissue paper and store it in a sealed box in a cool, dry place. It can last for generations.

Use under-the-bed boxes. Often on sale at variety stores, these under-the-bed boxes are really convenient for storing your out-of-season clothing. They're out of the way, but still easy enough to get to when needed.

Don't store furs, leather, or leather-type garments in plastic bags. These types of clothes need to breathe. If you must prevent them from gathering dust, cover them with old cotton pillowcases or sheets. You can also buy special "breathing" bags in the notions departments of fur and leather shops. Considering the price of these garments, a few dollars more for the proper storage bag doesn't seem like an extravagance.

Let them breathe. Closets need fresh air, too. To prevent musty odors in them, be sure they are well-ventilated. Open the windows in the bedroom and open the closet doors for a few hours each day.

Never put dirty clothes back into the closet. Not only will dirty clothes cause odors and attract fabric-damaging insects, they won't be fresh and clean when you want them to be. If you must hang a jacket in the closet after wearing it—and it's not as fresh as you would like but it's still clean—turn the jacket inside out and hang it on a hanger outside the closet, allowing it to breathe before putting it back into the closet.

Minimize fading. Always store your clothing out of direct sunlight and

Jog Your Memory in the Closet

Mark a 1-year calendar with birthdays, anniversaries, and special events, and then hang it up in your closet so that you will get a reminder each day when you get dressed. The reader who sent in this hint said his wife gave him a calendar like this one and noted their anniversary date in big red letters. Very, very smart!

Plastic Garbage Cans

Use plastic garbage cans to keep clothes clean, off the menu of munching moths, and out of your way in your crowded closet. It may sound unbelievable, but I got 17 skirts, 7 blazers, 4 vests, and 11 sweaters in one 30-gallon can. Here's how.

1. Lay the garbage can on its side and start with your skirts. Roll them vertically, hem-to-the-waistband, until you have a long, thin roll. Place the hem against the bottom of the can. If the waistband extends outside of the can, that's all right.

2. Next fold blazers, lining side out, and roll them. Place hem side down on top of the skirts.

3. Continue with vests, slacks, dresses (fold from the waist and roll). By putting all hem ends down, the wider top portion of the can allows more room for bulk, such as the shoulder padding in blazers.

4. When the can is filled, stand it up and fold over skirt tops.

5. Place an inventory list on top of the clothes, put the lid on, then close the lid tightly or seal it with tape.

6. Store the can at the back of your closet until you need the contents again. If you store this can in an attic or dry basement, be sure to label it so that it doesn't accidentally get pitched out. You want to see your clothes again. Or place a round piece of plywood over the top of the trash can, throw a pretty tablecloth over it, and you have a corner table.

strong artificial light. Some brighter-colored fabrics and many silks can oxidize and fade.

Create a clothing code. Before hanging a garment that needs some sort of attention—take to the dry cleaners (at the end of the week or after wearing one more time), replace a button, fix the hem, or other repairs—back in the closet, place a large bangle bracelet on top of the hanger.

CLOTHES

Well-made clothing that is properly cared for will fit, look, and wear better than poorly constructed clothing. Expect to pay for quality construction, but don't assume that all expensive clothing is carefully constructed. Here's what to look for and how to care for it when emergency clothing situations crop up.

Shopping

Examine the sewing. Seams should be flat and smooth. If the seams show signs of puckering when a garment is bought, they will only get worse after wear and laundering. Patterns should be matched well at the seams, collar, and armholes. Buttonholes should be properly reinforced, and buttons should be in proportion to the buttonholes and the design of the garment. Top-stitching should be even, and threads should not pull or pucker.

Check the interfacing. Shirt and blouse collars or cuffs with stiff fusible interfacings should have these interfacings smoothly fused to the fabric. If they appear to be improperly fused in a new garment, they may pucker when the garment is washed. No matter how you struggle to iron the collar or cuffs, they'll still look rumpled.

Examine the trim. It should be sewn on properly and constructed of materials that are compatible with the garment. For example, nylon lace on a cotton blouse will surely melt at the heat you'll use to iron the cotton part of the blouse, but it may be compatible with polyester blouse fabrics. Beading or other trim should be sewn on instead of glued; glued trims don't stand up well to repeated washing or dry cleaning.

Check the care label. Make sure that the garment can be cleaned by a process that you can afford. With a few exceptions, clothing is required by the Federal Trade Commission to contain a permanent label with the care instructions. Manufacturers must specify only one care procedure—even when several are safe—and are required to warn consumers when garments will be damaged by certain cleaning methods. Take special note of instructions for lined garments. Lining and garment fabrics may be incompatible. For example, while the outside of the garment may be washable, the nondetachable lining may need to be be dry cleaned.

Recognize that sizes vary. Different manufacturers and designers use different size standards. It's possible to wear a size 8 or 10 in one label and still need a size 12 in another. On one particular shopping day, I went from one store wearing a size 4 and 6 to three stores down where I couldn't squeeze into a size 12. You can imagine what that did for my psyche.

Sometimes this inconsistency in size standards makes you feel as if you have to go home and weigh yourself to make sure you haven't gained a size. Wouldn't it be wonderful if all the manufacturers would get together and decide upon standard size charts for men's, women's, and children's clothing? I would think that the time saved by not having so many gifts returned to stores would make it worthwhile.

Check for motion. When trying on the garment, walk around and sit down in the clothing to be sure you can move and sit comfortably in it.

Consider when and how often you'll wear the garment. Fabrics should be compatible with your use of the garment. Obviously, fragile fabrics are better suited to special-occasion wear than they are for everyday wear and the resulting frequent laundering or cleaning. Remember, very soft or loosely woven fabrics have a tendency to pill or ball up easily if subjected to a lot of friction, like fidgeting on that office chair. Certain fabrics, such as rayon, lose their pleats quickly. Pleated fabrics can be expensive to dry clean, since most cleaners have cost-per-pleat rates. Lightweight wools and jerseys keep their shape and need little ironing. They make good traveling clothes.

Make a perfect match. When shopping for a particular garment to match something already in your closet, don't take a chance on guessing what color is right. Snip a very tiny piece of fabric from an inside seam, and carry this with you to find a perfect match.

Evaluate the price. When you are looking at a very expensive garment or even an inexpensive one, figure it on a cost-per-wearing basis. If you are going to buy the perfect smashing black dress, blue blazer, or winter coat, plan to wear the garment for 4 to 5 years, 10 to 20 times in a season. Even if it's a very expensive garment, the cost per wearing breaks down to less than $5 or $10 per wearing. But, if you're buying a nice little shell or T-shirt to wear with shorts in the summertime and expect to wear it only 3 times or so, it isn't worth spending more than $50.

Know the right lengths for men's clothing. Shirtsleeves should reach to the end of the wrist bone. Jacket and coat sleeves should cover the tops of the wrist bone.

Save receipts and tags. When you shop for clothing, make a shopping list of planned purchases on the front of an envelope. Circle items you buy and insert the receipts. Write down any purchases that were not on the original list. When you return home, put the envelope into a manila folder labeled "receipts" or other file drawer for that purpose, and you'll never have to search for receipts again.

Alternately, note a description of the garment on the label and then save the tags in a file, envelope, or shoebox so that you can refer to them when you need to launder or dry-clean the garments.

Avoid emergency shopping whenever you can. It's a lot easier to select a special party dress or good suit that makes you look terrific if you aren't shopping for a party or job interview that's (Gasp!) tonight or tomorrow. And that's the time to find the best bargains.

Take advantage of back-to-school clothing sales. If you have teens and preteens, it may be better to save some of the budget money for those things that parents never heard of but that "everybody is wearing"—especially if your child is attending a new school. Children need not be slaves to fads, but it helps them fit in if they have some "everybody" clothes, backpacks, notebooks, or lunch boxes. It may also help to shop in stores located near the school your child will attend. They'll be catering to the local tastes and the school's requirements.

 Make over a full-length slip. When you need a full-length slip to match a formal gown, buy a full-length nightie in the matching color, cut it off at the right length and hem. Nylon nighties are less expensive.

Repairing

Use the tried-and-true stapler. If your skirt hem becomes unstitched at an inconvenient time, staple from the inside out to avoid snagging your stockings.

Try tape. Transparent or masking tape will hold on some fabrics—at least until you can get home to change.

Face the interfacing. The best way to mend holes in knit shirts is to iron lightweight fusible interfacing onto the wrong side of the shirt.

Battle the buttons. Buttons with shanks can be pinned on with safety pins until you have time to reattach them. When you need a heavy-duty repair for buttons that keep coming off certain garments, sew them on with thin nylon fishing line or dental floss. You have to cut it with scissors to remove the buttons. Hunting, work, and children's clothes and coats seem to be the chief offenders in the button-popping world.

Extend the waistband. To extend a skirt waistband in an emergency, loop two rubber bands through the buttonhole. (The official encyclopedia name for the loop knot that works here is "cow hitch," but somehow that sounds depressing when you find yourself in this situation!) Next, loop the rubber bands over the button.

If you sew, and want to make a more permanent waistband extender, take a piece of 1-inch-wide elastic the length you need to extend the waistband. Sew a button on one end and put a buttonhole on the other. Put the button into the waistband buttonhole and put the elastic buttonhole over the skirt button. Of course, if you use either of these extenders, you'll have to wear an overblouse so the "quick fix" doesn't show. Also, you'll have to decide if you want to buy all new clothes or whether you need to get rid of those extra waistline inches!

Apply an appliqué. Personalize bargain garments by replacing buttons or by adding trims and appliqués. Appliqués and trims can also hide small permanent stains or burn holes.

Hide a burn hole. If a burn hole is very small and the fabric texture allows, you can hide the burn hole by cutting a tiny piece of fabric from the seam allowance and gluing it in place using fabric glue, fusible tape, or iron-on mending tape placed under the hole with stick-on side up. (Place a small piece of lighter-weight fabric underneath as backing.) These mends won't hold well or have a satisfactory appearance with all fabrics, but are worth a try if you don't want to have the hole professionally mended. (With some fabric textures, you can glue frayed threads from the seam allowance instead of a small piece of fabric.)

See also BELTS, CLOSETS, and SOCKS.

CLOTHESPINS

Keep them handy. When hanging a large bedspread or blanket on the line outdoors, clip clothespins to your shirt bottom. They'll always be within arm's reach.

Keep them clean. Remove mildew from wooden clothespins by soaking them for about an hour in a bucket with water, a bit of laundry detergent, and about a cup of bleach. Then rinse and let dry before using.

 Find unconventional uses. Use clothespins to clamp the end of a plastic bread or snack bag; hold sheet music in place on a stand, even in the wind; or clamp scarves, skirts, and other clothing onto hangers.

 Stash one in your car. Clamp a clothespin on your keys so when you switch your car lights on during the day you don't forget to turn them off. Of course, you'll have to remember to clamp on the clothespin when you put the lights on!

Create a coupon holder. Clip coupons together when shopping. Clip a second pin to the cart to hold coupons that you'll be using.

COCOA

Store it separately. Some cocoa cans have openings too small for measuring utensils. The solution is to sift the whole 8-ounce can of cocoa into a 2-pound plastic margarine tub with an airtight lid. You can scoop with any measuring utensils, and the cocoa won't get lumpy either.

See also CHOCOLATE.

COFFEE

Such a simple, unassuming, pick-me-up, coffee is truly one of life's pleasures. Here are some hints on making and storing the stuff.

Making Coffee

Use distilled water. Brewing coffee with distilled water is the best way to avoid the need for excessive equipment cleaning. It makes better coffee, too.

Brew a homemade blend. If you'd like to try a homemade version of those more expensive gourmet-flavored coffees, blend the following ingredients in a blender or food processor until powdered (substitute appropriate amounts of powdered creamer for powdered milk, if you wish). To serve, put 2 rounded teaspoons of coffee into a cup filled with hot water.

- ⊗ Orange Coffee: Blend ½ cup of instant coffee, ¾ cup of sugar, 1 cup of powdered milk, and ½ teaspoon of dried orange peel.
- ⊗ Mocha Coffee: Just mix ½ cup of instant coffee, ½ cup of sugar, 1 cup of powdered, and 2 tablespoons of cocoa.
- ⊗ Cinnamon Coffee: Blend ½ cup of instant coffee, ⅔ cup of sugar, ⅔ cup of powdered milk, and ½ teaspoon of cinnamon.

 Add a dash of flavor. Add a sprinkle of cinnamon to the ground coffee before brewing. Or, add a drop or two of almond, vanilla, or other extract to the ground coffee. For mocha, add chocolate syrup or cocoa mix to brewed coffee.

Have some coffee olé. This is an often-requested recipe. To a cup of regular coffee, add a little extra skim milk and a tablespoon of powdered skim milk. Add sugar or artificial sweetener to taste. Blend the mixture in the blender until it is foamy. Pour the mixture into a microwaveable coffee mug and heat it on warm for a couple of seconds. Enjoy.

Ice your leftovers. If you don't feel like reheating leftover coffee in the microwave, make yourself a glass of iced coffee from your morning pot's leftovers for a tasty coffee break during the day. I like iced coffee with a dash of cinnamon or nutmeg as a treat.

 Add a splash to sauce. Try adding about ¼ to ½ teaspoon of instant coffee to spaghetti sauce. It gives the sauce a nice, less acid flavor and adds a bit of brown color to the bright red tomato sauce that makes it look more homemade "cooked-for-hours."

Make a low-fat coffee creamer. Combine nonfat dry milk with low-fat liquid milk; store in fridge and shake before pouring. If low-fat isn't your goal, a spoonful of sweetened condensed milk puts both cream and sugar in your coffee.

 Stretch a cup on a tight budget. Try making the first pot in a drip coffee maker with the regular amount of ground coffee. Then, for the second pot, leave the grounds in the basket and add half the normal amount of ground coffee on top of them. Brew as usual. For the third pot, throw it all out and start again. It's okay to pinch pennies but don't pinch so hard that Mr. Lincoln says "Ouch" or everyone who tastes the coffee says "Yuck."

Warm your mug. Place your coffee mug on top of the drip coffeemaker when it starts brewing. By the time the coffee is ready, your mug will be warm enough to keep your coffee hot longer as you sip those first eye-openers to get your day off right.

Caring for Supplies

Fake an easy substitute for 1-cup cones. Ordinary filters cost less than special cone ones. To make filters for 1-cup cones, fold a regular filter in half, then in half again. Open one side and you have a cone.

Keep a Thermos on hand. If you put your just-brewed coffee in a Thermos instead of on the coffee machine heater, it will stay hot for a late morning cup without getting stronger. A Thermos also comes in handy when you have houseguests and need two pots quickly. Just pour the first pot into a Thermos as soon as it's brewed so that you can start the second pot immediately.

Hint: Don't forget to rinse out the Thermos with hot water to heat it before you pour in hot coffee. The coffee will stay hot longer, and you aren't likely to crack the glass insert.

Evaluate the need for a vinegar bath. Bad-tasting coffee in a drip coffeemaker can mean there is too much hard water mineral deposit accumulating in the brew chamber. To clean a drip coffeemaker, run the fullest measure the pot allows of white vinegar through the cycle, followed by a cycle or two of the fullest measure of fresh water. (Some coffeemaker brands suggest that you run the vinegar through twice or have you unplug the coffeemaker to make the vinegar work longer. Check your manual for instructions.)

Avoid wasting vinegar that has been used to clean a coffeemaker. Collect the filtered vinegar in a coffee pot after it has run through and store it in an empty jar. The vinegar can be used again in cleaning the coffeemaker a couple of times. (You can also use the stored vinegar to clean and "sweeten" drains.)

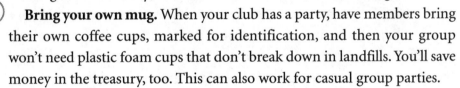

Scrub burnt bottoms with salt. When you discover that an electric pot has been left on or the glass pot is burnt, pour table salt into the pot and let it stand for a few minutes. The burnt crust will loosen, and you can wash the pot clean. (This hint came from an office worker who used salt because nothing else was handy; that's how most hints come into being!)

Bring your own mug. When your club has a party, have members bring their own coffee cups, marked for identification, and then your group won't need plastic foam cups that don't break down in landfills. You'll save money in the treasury, too. This can also work for casual group parties.

Storing Coffee

Make your own coffee filter packs. Place a coffee filter in a large margarine tub, measure the coffee, add another filter on top of the coffee. Continue until the tub is full. Seal with the lid to keep the coffee fresh.

Don't make a mess. To pour coffee into a canister from a can, cut a "spout" hole in the plastic lid. You'll save time by not having to wipe up spilled grounds.

Switch it off. Is there anyone who hasn't left the coffeepot on for hours and hours? Make it a habit to plug a night-light into the same socket with the coffeepot when you start the coffee, and unplug the night-light when you switch off the pot. The extra light can be a reminder, especially if the "on" light of your pot is not very large or bright.

Keep the beans cold. Freezing coffee (whole beans or ground) in a well-sealed container or zipper bag is a great way to preserve flavor. Also, you can keep various kinds of coffee in the freezer and have different "house blends." I like to mix decaf and regular for a milder brew.

COMBS AND HAIRBRUSHES

Clean with ease. Fill the bathroom sink with hot water and add a couple of squirts of dishwashing liquid or shampoo. Swish everything around in the soapy water and soak for 30 minutes or so. Then run the wide end of a comb through the brush bristles to remove hair, hairspray residue, or other dirt. Drain the water from the sink and rinse each item thoroughly under hot running water. Place the brushes on a towel with the brushes' bristles-sides down; let drip dry.

COMPACT DISCS

Keep the sound clean. Although CDs are considered to be virtually indestructible, they should always be stored away from heat and dust and handled carefully to prevent scratches and fingerprints. Fortunately, your player will ignore some dust. Beware of grease or skin oils from handling that fill the tiny pits in compact discs. This can "confuse" the laser and cause it to reflect the wrong way, resulting in garbled sound.

Clean a CD safely. To clean a CD, just wipe it with a dry, soft, lint-free cloth. You can rinse it under running cool water and blot it dry with a lint-free towel. Always wipe your CD in a straight line from the center to the edge. Never clean CDs with solvent or abrasive cleansers. Some sources say that you can use ethyl alcohol as a solvent if necessary, but most say commercial cleaning kits are the safest way to clean CDs.

COMPLAINTS

Make a case with clout. If you find yourself in a situation where you have to register a complaint about faulty merchandise or service, be businesslike rather than emotional, and type the letter, if possible. (If not, be sure to write legibly). Include all pertinent information, as follows.

⊛ Your name, address, and work and home phone numbers

⊛ Date and place of purchase

⊛ Serial and model number of merchandise

⊛ Name of the person who did the work if it's a service complaint

Keep copies of all complaint letters and allow a reasonable amount of time for a response. Send complaints by registered mail for proof that the company received your complaint.

COMPUTERS

Avoid back and neck tension on the job. Place your terminal so that the top of the screen is at your eye level or just below; keep your feet flat on the floor and your elbows at 90 degrees so your fingers just reach the keyboard comfortably. Position your work station so that the screen receives the least amount of glare from windows or indoor lighting, and make sure your chair provides good back support. Finally, remember to take short breaks from your computer or desk—at the least, stretch your arms for a few minutes each hour.

Clean the screen properly. Don't clean your computer screen with wet cloths. Instead, wipe it with a slightly damp cloth. Commercial antistatic cleaning pads are the best choice. Buy them in office supply or computer stores.

Put your shredder to good use. Shredded office paper can be used for packing materials. One reader uses shredded computer paper instead of hay on the farm to line chickens' nests and says she thinks the hens like it better!

CONFECTIONERS' SUGAR

Try a savvy substitute. Mix 1 cup of granulated sugar and 1 tablespoon of cornstarch in a blender a half cup at a time at high speed for a few minutes until it reaches a fine, powdery consistency. As with most substitutes, the consistency and texture of the dish may be altered slightly.

See also BROWN SUGAR and SUGAR.

CONSUMER INFORMATION

Find it fast. If you can't find a number to call in the manual that comes with your appliance or on a product label, dial (800) 555-1212 to get the toll-free consumer information number of a company. If the company has no toll-free number, the main library branches in large cities usually have information services you can call to get the addresses and phone numbers of national firms.

CONTACT LENSES

Make a travel kit. Use a plastic soap case to hold all the accessories for cleaning your contact lenses when you travel.

Clean with care. Don't clean contact lenses with regular hydrogen peroxide, even though this peroxide is safe for other uses. It may contain additives or impurities that can cause soft-lens discoloration or irritate your eyes. Instead, always clean and disinfect contact lenses with the cleaning solutions made especially for them.

COOKIES

Scoop the dough. One reader wrote that she makes 25 dozen chocolate chip cookies at one baking session. To save time she scoops the cookie dough onto cookie sheets with a large melon ball maker or small ice cream scoop. All the cookies are the same size and are just right for grandchildren and parties.

Note: Save a teaspoon of chocolate chips when you are mixing the dough. Then when you get down to the last spoonful of batter and all of the chips have been used with the first scoops of dough, you can add the reserved chips to make all of the cookies equally chocolatey.

Use a muffin mix. For one dozen delicious fresh cookies, add 2 eggs and ½ cup of oil to a box of store-bought muffin mix. Drop by teaspoonfuls onto an ungreased cookie sheet and bake until firm enough to remove from the cookie sheet. For extra flavor, add optional ingredients like a spoonful of peanut butter, chopped nuts, or raisins.

Letter of Laughter

Christmas Cookies

This Christmas cookie recipe letter appeared about 20 years ago in my mother's column. It was sent to me by one reader when it was requested by another reader and I couldn't find it in my files. It proves that some recipes are timeless!

Christmas Cookies

1. Light oven; get bowl, spoons, and ingredients; grease pan; crack nuts; and remove 10 blocks, 7 toy autos, and 1 wad of chewing gum from kitchen table.

2. Measure 2 cups of flour, remove Johnny's hands from flour, wash flour off him, measure 1 more cup of flour to replace flour on floor.

3. Put flour, baking powder, and salt in sifter. Answer doorbell. Return to kitchen. Remove Johnny's hands from bowl. Wash Johnny. Answer phone. Return. Remove ¼-inch salt from greased pans, grease more pans. Look for Johnny. Answer phone.

4. Return to kitchen and find Johnny. Remove his hands from bowl. Wash shortening and everything else off him. Take up greased pan and take out shells from it. Head for Johnny, who flees, knocking bowl off table.

5. Wash kitchen door. Wash table. Wash kitchen walls. Wash dishes. Wash Johnny. Call baker. Lie down!

Smash 'em as you go. When making peanut butter cookies, flatten the dough balls with a potato masher or a plastic fork.

Make the most of cookie crumbs and pieces. Wondering what to do with the leftover bits at the bottom of an almost-empty cookie jar? Add them to bread pudding for extra "Yum!" (It's not true that the calories don't count when you eat broken cookie pieces instead of whole cookies!)

Make cookie cutters do double duty. Plastic cookie cutters come in many shapes and colors for Christmas, Thanksgiving, Valentine's day, Easter, and other holidays. In addition to making great cookie shapes, they can serve as festive but inexpensive napkin rings.

Minimize the sprinkles mess. After preparing the dough and cutting out the cookies, place the cookie cutter around the cut-out cookies before sprinkling on colored sugars or sparkles. The cutter will corral the sprinkles and keep them from being scattered about. This tip is especially valuable when your "assistant cook" is a small child.

Watch your waistline. Fill the cookie jar with low-sugar dry cereal. It's a great snack and helps develop better eating habits!

Shave off some calories. To cut a few calories from chocolate cookies (or at least to feel like you're trying!), substitute ½ cup of mini-chocolate chips for 1 cup of regular-size chips. Few cookie munchers will notice the difference.

COOKING SPRAY

Avoid sticky messes. To keep sticky ingredients like honey, corn syrup, or molasses from making a mess in a measuring utensil, spray it with cooking spray before measuring to make cleanup easy.

COOLERS

Chill with concentrates. Instead of buying bagged ice, which will just melt and be tossed away, buy frozen orange juice concentrate. Four cans of frozen concentrate will keep 2 cold beverage six-packs cool in a small cooler. When you're done using the cooler, you can mix up the juice for breakfast during the week after your picnic.

Use your washer. Ice down canned and bottled beverages for a party by lining the bottom of your clothes washer with a heavy towel and then filling the machine with ice and cans. When the party is over, remove any remaining cans and use the water for a cold water wash that includes the towel.

Ban the mildew. To prevent mildew from forming in a tightly sealed cooler that's been in storage, place a spacer—like a piece of wood or folded cardboard—between the lid and rim. This prevents the cover from sealing tightly and lets air circulate inside it. Don't forget to sprinkle in some baking soda to prevent odors.

COPPER AND BRASS

Tame the tarnish. Commercial cleaners and homemade cleaners, such as those described below, work great to remove tarnish. Those made with lemon juice or vinegar give copper and brass a bright finish; the oil and rottenstone cleaner add a soft luster to these metals.

- Sprinkle table salt on a wet sponge, rub off tarnish, rinse, and dry. Or, rub darkened places using half a lemon (with or without table salt), rinse, and buff dry.
- Rub metal with a paste made by adding flour to the salt and vinegar or lemon juice, rinse, and dry.
- Make a thin paste from rottenstone (an abrasive powder available at hardware stores) and oil such as cooking or salad oil. Wipe off the excess oil after rubbing; polish with a clean cloth.

See also BRASS.

CORKS

Make it vanish. If you want to remove a cork that has been pushed into a wine bottle that you want to save, pour ammonia into the bottle and leave it somewhere where air circulates. The cork will disintegrate in about a week. Wash the inside well with soap and water, and the bottle will be ready for display or to root a sprig of ivy in water.

Put them to good use. No need to toss old corks when there are so many interesting ways to use them. Consider the following.

- Protect the points of knives, barbecue forks, ice picks, and knitting needles.
- Save your fingers from pokes from safety pins, map pins, thumbtacks, and other small, sharp items.

☸ Color them with fabric or craft dyes for craft projects.

☸ Glue corks into frames of various sizes to make trivets and coasters.

☸ Cut them lengthwise so that there is one flat side and glue to plywood, fiberboard, or cardboard. (This project's gluing phase could keep a vacation-weary child busy for a long time!) Or, glue to the side of a kitchen cabinet to make a message center.

☸ Glue on backings for picture frames, Christmas wreaths, or refrigerator magnets.

☸ Make tiny sailboats with toothpick-held sails to occupy a child.

☸ Place them in the bottoms of potted plants to help drainage or around the roots of orchids to stabilize them.

CORN

Avoid sharing with the birds. Cut off the bottoms of used beverage cans and place the cans on sweet-corn ears a week or so before the corn is ready to pick. The cans keep the birds from eating the corn before you do and don't harm the birds.

Grill some corn on the cob. After pulling off the corn husks, boil the ears of corn for about 5 minutes and then toast the corn for several minutes over hot coals in the barbecue pit.

CORN SYRUP

Substitute for corn syrup. You can substitute honey for corn syrup in a recipe, but the flavor and texture may be altered because honey tastes sweeter and is often thicker. You cannot substitute corn syrup for granulated sugar and vice versa because one is a liquid and the other is a dry ingredient. It's difficult to adjust the recipe ingredients to get the same result.

COSMETICS

See STAINS for hints to remove cosmetics from fabrics.

COUNTERTOPS

Make more space. A great temporary solution to lack of counter space is to turn a dish drainer upside down inside a sink and put your chopping board on top of it. Then you can chop vegetables and fruit with the easiest-ever cleanup. Just turn on the faucet and send the peelings down the disposal, or collect them in the sink by hand and rinse the rest of the mess off.

Use a cookie sheet. Alternately, you can open a drawer all the way and put a cookie sheet on it, then close the drawer until the cookie sheet fits tightly. A lower drawer can be an extra "table" for a child if you don't have enough space at the main table. Put a place mat over the cookie sheet after following the extra-space directions.

See also KITCHENS.

COUPONS

I recently found a coupon taped to a product on the shelf by some generous donor. I don't know if the store manager would like to see flaps of coupons taped to items on all of the shelves, but I appreciated the 50 cents I ended up saving!

Donate unused coupons. When you know you're not going to use coupons, there are other opportunities to consider. You might want to give them to charities when you donate clothing and other items; senior citizen or other community centers; food banks for distribution to needy families; and in some communities to coupon exchanges run by churches, libraries, and other social service organizations.

One reader shared with me how she figured out a way to give several items weekly to her church "care bank" without breaking her budget or raiding her pantry for donations. Instead of wasting good money-off coupons for foods that she doesn't usually eat, but which are good staples, she allocates $1 per week to spend on coupon items to give to the church.

Whether you use coupons for yourself or as a way to extend your charitable giving, here are the some great ways to maximize the way you use these budget savers.

Using Coupons Wisely

Coordinate coupons with your shopping list. To make couponing easier, when making a shopping list, place a "C" next to items that have a coupon to be redeemed. If you are shopping with a roommate, spouse, or child, make two lists—one for coupon items and one for regular shopping. Have one person go off with the coupons and a separate cart, and then both of you can meet at the checkout counter in half the usual shopping time. Reading the coupon requirements is not only fun for kids, but it teaches them how to be aware of details. If you ask a child to hunt for coupons, always offer an incentive by making sure that some of the coupons are for favorite cereals and other goodies.

Double up. When grocery stores accept double coupons, check the newspaper section to see how many coupons will be useful to you. If there are a lot, you can save money by buying another copy of the paper.

Keep them close by. I always keep a few coupons in my purse for items that I frequently use and need. The money they save really adds up.

Let the kids do the cutting. Keep a box handy when you read newspapers or magazines. When you see coupons, tear out the entire page and put it in the box. When your children are bored or watching television, they can cut them out.

Note expiration dates. Go through your coupons every other month and pull out those due to expire in the next 2 months. Clip these together and put them in front of the others. If there's no expiration date, write the word "none" across the coupon. Also, when you clip a coupon out of a newspaper, underline the expiration date or mark it with a highlighter. This helps to organize coupons and helps the cashier to find the expiration date, saving the cashier's time and yours.

Organizing Coupons

Organize by aisle or by date. One way that works well is to arrange your coupon file in the order of the supermarket's aisles. Or file them according to the expiration date instead of storing by category (dairy, meats, or baking goods), leaving an extra envelope for those coupons that have no expiration dates.

Have a handy holder. I use an accordion-style canceled check file to avoid the bulk of a recipe file box, but a spare napkin holder, an old checkbook cover, or even those little wallets that you get with traveler's checks will do the job. You can even use a clothespin to hold coupons you plan to redeem, leaving your hands free for shopping.

Contain them with a list. Attach a legal-size envelope to the refrigerator with a magnet, then write your grocery list on the envelope, and tuck the coupons to be redeemed inside it.

Consider size. If you have hundreds of coupons to handle, a plastic recipe box is just the ticket. Use the index card dividers to separate food groups. You can also keep coupons in a large metal or plastic lunch box, using file box dividers to separate the coupons into groups. The lunch box fits into the seat portion of the shopping cart and makes handling coupons easy as pie.

COVERED DISHES

Make sure they come back. Getting plates and casseroles returned is often difficult and certainly a chore for the event organizer. Readers have sent in many solutions, including the following:

- ✿ Write your name on masking tape and stick it to the bottom of the dish, or stick an address label to the bottom.
- ✿ Cover several thicknesses of paper plates with foil; or cover sturdy cardboard with foil, cover with a paper doily, and send a cake on this disposable "plate."
- ✿ Buy 12-inch square floor tiles, cover with foil and place cakes on them.
- ✿ Buy casseroles, plates, salad bowls, and other serving dishes and utensils at flea markets (sometimes for only 25 cents), and run them through the dishwasher a couple of times to make sure they are sanitized. You won't care if they don't get returned.
- ✿ If the covered dish event is at a friend's house, buy a dish that might match something in her house (or a clear glass one) and make it a hostess gift.

See also CASSEROLES.

CRACKER CRUMBS

Try this crushing advice. I've received letters describing all sorts of shortcuts for crushing graham or soda crackers to crumbs, including these. Put crackers in the blender, put them in a sealable bag and use a glass to crush them when you don't have a rolling pin, or step on a bag full of crackers until they are reduced to crumbs. But one reader topped them all—she puts the crackers in a sealable bag and drives over them with her car. I don't think I would do this myself, but it makes a good story!

CRADLES

 Give them new life. Doll or antique baby cradles can have a variety of new uses. Use them to store magazines, display older children's stuffed animals, or to hold throw pillows or a folded bedspread from the bed overnight.

CRAFTS

Crafts are cottage industries for many women who want to remain at home but still supplement the family income. Selling in consignment shops, in addition to the usual summer craft shows, can generate year-round income if you make the right connections.

Look for a consignment shop with variety. Avoid shops that buy most of their products wholesale from other craftspersons or those that also sell lots of imported or commercial gift lines. Remember that seasonal orders are placed months in advance, and it's probably too late to sell Christmas items in November.

Call attention to your work. If you exhibit at craft fairs, offer to distribute flyers to promote the shop or gallery that handles your work. Make sure that your retail prices are in line with those of the shop.

Keep careful records and get all agreements in writing. If the shop doesn't have a printed consignment form, print your own. The agreement should note if the shop is insured against theft or other loss, such as damage by fire or flood; who pays postage and insurance if you send your crafts by mail; the exact percentage of commission the shop gets (store markups are typically 100 to 150 percent), and whether payment is monthly or upon sale; where your crafts will be displayed (Will they be left in a storeroom or worse, in a window where they will fade?); how long will the item be displayed, and how it will be returned to you if it's not sold.

CREAM CHEESE

Perk up your breakfast. Sprinkle flavored fruit gelatin on cream cheese after you've spread it on your English muffin or toast.

CREDIT CARDS

Keep purchases at your limits. Get an extra checkbook register and list your credit cards, noting the monthly charge limit for each card. When you use a card, immediately write the purchase amount in the appropriate column in the checkbook and subtract it from the total charge amount allowed. You will always know your exact balance and when "the well is dry." If you can't get a checkbook register, a small, lined notebook will do. Check out the spelling-test notebooks sold in school supplies departments; they're good for lists.

Keep them away from magnets. Don't allow the magnetic strips of credit cards to rub against each other in a billfold—the cards can become demagnetized and useless. Other troublemakers include money clips with magnets and magnetized card keys used to enter buildings. And leave your credit cards behind if you will be in a magnet field like an industrial area. The good news is that airport x-ray devices do not harm credit cards.

Keep a record. Make photocopies of all your credit and bank cards so that you have records of all the numbers and expiration dates on one sheet of paper in case you have to report a loss.

Caution: Don't forget to take all of the credit cards out of the copy machine and to store the information in a safe place.

CROCHETING

See KNITTING AND CROCHETING.

Overcome Application Rejection

If you apply for a credit card and are rejected, use the following steps to try to reverse the problem.

1. Write to the bureau that gave information to your prospective lender (their name should be included in the denial letter you receive), and ask for a free copy of your credit report and the information that caused your application's denial.

2. Look for incorrect or out-of-date information in your file. If you find any, write to the credit bureau and ask them to verify it for you. Also notify the creditor of the problem and try to resolve it yourself. You will need copies of bills, canceled checks, and other papers to back your claim. Send copies, not originals, to the creditor.

3. File a report of the problem, and ask to have it placed in your credit file if you can't clear up the matter with the creditor.

4. Before applying for credit, check with your local credit bureau to see if any negative information is in your report. In fact, an annual check is recommended by some of my sources. Making sure your credit file is up-to-date and accurate avoids problems when you need to borrow money. Credit-reporting firms charge a small fee to review your files; you get a free report only when a credit application is denied.

CRYSTAL

See GLASSES and TABLEWARE.

CUPBOARDS AND DRAWERS

Loop a helping hand. People with arthritis often have trouble pulling drawers and doors open with their hands. One reader put fabric loops through her mother's kitchen cabinet handles so that she could open them by slipping her arm through the loops.

Create your own canisters. Cut off the top half of plastic 1-gallon milk jugs, leaving the top of the handle on. Then you can place bags of flour or sugar into the remaining part of the jug. They won't spill and are easy to pull in and out of cabinets.

Keep them closed. Reinforce the cabinet closures with self-gripping fabric tape. You can get stick-on dots and strips in neutral colors.

CURLING IRONS

Remove hairspray buildup. Cool and unplug your curling iron before cleaning. Then dampen a clean cloth with rubbing alcohol and wipe the wand several times until it's clean. Avoid buildup by cleaning with alcohol about once a month.

Iron other items. Run ribbons, dress sashes, and some scarfs (depending on fabric) through the curling iron to press them.

CURTAINS

Make them crisp and fresh without ironing. Just wash and rinse as usual. Add 1 cup of Epsom salts to a sink filled with water, and rinse the laundered curtains in the solution; hang to dry. No need for ironing!

Reuse your rods. When you switch from window shades to curtains, make the curtain casing large enough to accommodate the shade rollers and save yourself the trouble and expense of buying curtain rods. The bonus is that you don't make more holes in the walls!

Remove wrinkles without ironing. When you wash sheers or similar fabrics, rehang them while still damp, and put heavy dinner knives in the hem openings. The added weight helps to pull out wrinkles as the curtains dry.

Color code the rods. If the rods show through colored sheers, spray paint the rods with the appropriate color.

DECANTERS

Remove stains. Fill the decanter with white vinegar, and let it stand overnight. Then add uncooked rice and shake the decanter to remove the stains on the inside that a sponge or brush won't reach. Rinse and dry.

Try this dealer's trick. Sometimes stains in antique decanters cannot be removed. For particularly stubborn stains, some dealers mix about ¼ cup of dishwasher detergent with hot water. When the water cools, fill the decanter to the top, and let it soak for a few hours or overnight. A bottle brush may remove stubborn stains, too, but some may remain.

DECORATING

I like to visit people whose knickknacks are personal treasures (which has nothing to do with price) instead of just decorator dust catchers. I have many things in my home that are heirlooms, gifts, or just things that entertain me every time that I look at them. For example, I have a butler at my door—a mannequin dressed in full tuxedo. Everyone who visits me has fun talking to my butler.

Not everyone will have a butler, but we all accumulate treasures that we are fond of and that give our homes a personal look rather than a magazine photo layout look.

Maximize your memories. To give a room a focal point, group photographs or any other souvenirs and personal collections in one place rather than scattering them about the house. This way, you'll create one large, memorable, attractive display.

Make every item work. If you tend to collect things made from a specific material—such as shell, brass, wood, copper, or porcelain—you'll find that when you group your collection, everything will match no matter what color, size, or shape it is.

Picture anything. Frame anything that appeals to you, such as an old map, family documents like Grandpa's citizenship papers, children's artwork, a nice piece of print paper, or needlework art.

All around the House

Have some pillow talk. Throw pillows always add new color and brighten a room. If you sew, you can make them from fabric remnants and stuff them with recycled panty hose, foam dryer sheets, foam packing materials, or bits of other soft material.

Fix up a fireplace. A nonworking fireplace, primed and freshened with paint, makes a cozy niche for an aquarium or for pretty flower or plant arrangements.

Discover towel power. Colorful, fringed fingertip towels bought at white sales can be no-iron inexpensive place mats, especially at the children's table for family dinners where they'll also absorb spills.

Conceal blemishes. Dresser scarves can cover a multitude of sins, such as stains, nicks, and scratches on a tabletop, buffet, or dresser. Or substitute place mats or napkins (like the one remaining unstained member of a set), colorful serapes, or fringed stoles for traditional dresser scarves.

Cover stains. Discover a stain on the tablecloth with no time to change it? Make it look as if the cover-up is really your purposely placed decoration. Hide the stain with a centerpiece, trivet, a wide runner down the center, complementary colored napkins (placed diagonally), place mats (one in the center or one on either side of the centerpiece), or doilies located so they will be beneath serving dishes or the centerpiece. Scatter holiday flowers or greenery so that spots are covered as part of your decorating scheme. (Cut stems off flowers so that they'll lie flat, and hold things in place with tape loops.)

Make an instant centerpiece. A branch cut from any blossoming tree or bush makes an unusual centerpiece on a dining or coffee table. Use greenery of any kind. Just add something appropriate for the season, such as artificial red holly berries, decorative peppers, or Easter eggs.

Improvise. Just about anything that holds water can be a vase. Display flowers in a crystal ice bucket, fluted champagne glasses, mugs, or cocktail pitchers.

Don't discard. You don't have to throw away a favorite crystal water glass or pitcher when it gets a chipped lip. Use it to hold fresh or artificial flowers. Silk flowers can be arranged even in favorite containers that don't hold water.

Let gourds evolve. Buy gourds in the fall at the supermarket. Use them for a month or so in an arrangement, then put them someplace warm and dry for a while. The gourds become very light as they dry, and the colors mute beautifully with age.

Spice up your kitchen. Garlic braids or dry, hot peppers threaded on a long string make a kitchen decor cook! (And the garlic, according to legend, keeps away vampires. I've never seen a vampire in a kitchen that has garlic hanging in it. Of course, I've never seen a vampire in a kitchen without garlic either!)

Frame a window with fabric. Use this framing technique instead of curtains or accent curtains. Start by making a frame with wood molding that is 4 or 5 inches wide and ½-inch thick and cut it to fit the length and width of your window. Cover the frame with foam padding, tack fabric to the back of it, and attach to the wall.

Wallpaper

Consider your colors. When you are selecting wallpaper, remember that if the wallpaper has one or more of the dominant colors already in the room it will tie everything together.

Work with room size. If you have a large room and want it to appear smaller and cozier, choose wallpaper with a large, bold pattern. Don't, however, use bold patterns in a small room, because they will close in on you and make the room look small and crowded. Instead, consider mural-pattern wallpaper, which makes a small room appear larger.

You can also make a ceiling appear higher or lower with wallpaper. A high ceiling seems lower if the walls are papered with a bold pattern. A low ceiling seems higher if the walls are papered with a small print or a texture.

Carry color chips. Gather paint sampler color chips that match sofas, comforters, curtains, rugs, and other unmovables so that you can take the chips shopping for wallpaper, paint, or whatever else you need to buy for redecorating.

See also WALLPAPER.

Painting

Know the effects of color. When selecting paint colors, remember that blue, green, and violet have a tranquilizing effect. Use these cool colors in rooms where you want to relax. Warm colors like yellow, orange, and red will energize.

Try sponge painting. Sponging one paint color over a neutral color is a popular decorating technique. Choose the type of paint strategically. Water-based paints dry faster, so you won't have to wait as long to dab on the second layer of paint. Oil-based paints dry more slowly. If you use them, you won't have to work as fast, and you'll have time to correct mistakes.

Windows

Rely on "living curtains." Hanging plants can substitute for curtains on windows. (And talk about no-iron, drip-dry!)

Hang a bedspread. An Indian print bedspread can become an instant drapery. Hang it full width across a window on a round rod, pick up a bottom corner to open the "drapery" diagonally across half the window, and then secure with a tieback.

Go with gauze. For an airy, summery window, try stretching gauze or chiffon between two dowels, and hang them inside the window frame.

Customize window shades. Glue fabric to cheap window shades, finish the edges with braid or fringe, and you won't need curtains. In bedrooms, an inexpensive way to achieve a coordinated look is to buy extra matching sheets to use as window dressings, table covers, and even as throws over chairs.

If your fabric is rather heavy, the roller springs won't work well and you may have to keep the shade at half mast all the time, so plan the pattern accordingly.

Work with sheets. Turn colorful, printed bed sheets into curtains for any room in the house. They can also be stapled to walls for a fabric "wallpaper" look.

Trim with shelves. Frame a window with bookshelves, either built-in or freestanding. You can top store-bought shelves with a board if they are as tall as the window to add an extra shelf across the top of the window and tie the two bookshelves together. You'll be adding storage space and avoiding curtain maintenance at the same time.

Wall Hangings

Make use of mementos. Group pictures and other hanging mementos such as plaques or plates to dramatize a wall or room area.

Display properly. Not everything should be matted and framed. Oil paintings, for instance, usually are not matted or covered with glass. Etchings and delicate flower prints are usually covered with glass and put into lightweight frames.

Save your hooks. When preparing to move, as you take down wall hangings and pictures, remove the nails or hooks from the walls at the same time and tape them to the back of each object. Then, when you're ready to rehang them at the new place, you won't need to look for hooks or nails.

Affix with can tabs. Tabs from aluminum cans make great hangers for lightweight pictures. Drive a nail or tack through the rivet into the picture frame, then bend the tab to the desired shape. This won't hold heavy pictures, but it works well on lightweight pictures and wall plaques.

Go fishing. If you're hanging a picture from a molding, but you don't like to see the exposed picture wire, substitute nylon fishing line. The transparent nylon is almost invisible, and your picture can star on its own.

Faux-finish your pictures. Giving an inexpensive, glossy picture the texture of an oil painting is easier than most of us would think. Purchase some nylon net, and cut it to overlap the picture. Tape the corners to keep the net flat and taut. Brush shellac on lightly, let it set for a couple of seconds, carefully remove the net, and let the picture dry. After the picture dries, it will have the texture of canvas and look like an oil painting.

Place pictures precisely. Picture hanging can be frustrating if you simply try to "eyeball" the right spot to put the hook. Some people measure with tape and yardstick and still don't get the picture where they want it. You can place a picture exactly where you want it the first time by following this method.

Cut a sheet of paper to the exact size of the frame. Position the pattern on the picture's back side and pull the picture's hanging wire up taut so that you will see an inverted V. Mark the "V" point on the pattern, and poke a hole through that marked point.

After you determine where you'll hang the picture, place the pattern on the wall, and use the V point hole to make a pencil mark showing exactly where the nail should go. The picture will hang precisely where you want it.

Leave fingerprints. If the picture isn't too heavy, another time-saving method is to hold the picture itself by its wire and decide where you want it positioned. Wet a fingertip and press it on the wall to mark the wire's inverted V point. The fingerprint mark will stay wet long enough for you to drive a nail and hook on target.

Get it on paper. Take the guesswork out of arranging several pictures on the wall; do it like a pro. Spread out a large sheet of wrapping paper or several taped-together newspapers on the floor and experiment with frame positions.

When you decide on a pleasing grouping, outline the frames on the paper, tape the paper to the wall, and drive hooks through the paper into the wall. Then remove the paper and hang the pictures.

Create an artful arrangement. Group pictures of similar subjects, colors, frames, or sizes. When putting a grouping over a large piece of furniture such as a sofa, it's usually better to keep the bottom line even. But no rules are set in stone. Use an arrangement that pleases you.

Keep things straight. Sometimes a picture that was positioned correctly has a mind of its own and won't hang straight. Give it some gentle guidance by wrapping masking tape around the wire on both sides of the hook so the wire can't slip. Or install parallel nails and hooks a short distance apart. Two hooks are better than one for keeping pictures in their places.

Try a double-faced fix. Squares of double-faced tape affixed to the frame's two lower back corners also will keep pictures from roving.

Be on the level. If you are hanging a shelf and have no level, try filling a tall straight-sided plastic bottle three-quarters full of water. Tightly close the lid so that you can lay the bottle on the shelf on its side. Adjust the shelf until the water is level. Then screw the shelf to the wall.

Try toothpick placeholders. Don't lose a perfect picture grouping when you repaint a room. If you insert toothpicks in the hook holes and paint right over them, when the paint dries you can remove the toothpicks and rehang your pictures in the same holes. Another quick, easy way to remember the grouping is to take a photo of your picture arrangement before you take the pictures off the wall.

Protect plaster. To prevent a plaster wall from crumbling when driving a nail or hook into it, first form an X over the nail spot with two strips of masking tape or transparent tape.

Make the most of mirror magic. Make small rooms look larger and brighter by installing mirrors on one wall to create double width with reflections of opposite walls. This works whether you are installing mirror tiles or hanging a mirror collection. Just make sure that your mirrors are not in direct sunlight, which can adversely affect some mirror backings.

When hanging a mirror with screws that go through mounting holes in the glass, don't tighten the screws all the way. Leave enough play so the mirror won't crack if the wall shifts.

See also QUILTS and SEASHELLS.

DEHUMIDIFIERS

Know when you need one. In some climates and some tightly constructed homes, high humidity is a problem, especially when showers, wet towels, drying clothing, cooking, floor washing, and ground moisture add to the situation. Common symptoms of too much moisture include mildewed shoes in closets, musty smells throughout the house, and general physical discomfort for the people in the house.

Conquer the steam. Attic fans can replace warm, moist air with cool, dry outside air, and dehumidifiers recirculate room air and reduce the relative humidity. Dehumidifiers work by drawing moist air over refrigerated coils. When the air hits the cold surface, moisture condenses and drips off into the collection bucket or to a drain hose connected to a drip tray.

If you're in the market for a dehumidifier, look for one that has the following features: an adjustable thermostat that regulates the on and off cycles; exposed air-drying coils that let you clean the unit easily and keep it at peak performance, with resulting lower operating costs; catch buckets that hold at least 10 quarts of water and are easy to remove and empty without spilling; an automatic water overflow control that prevents spills by shutting the unit off when the water bucket is full; and recessed wheels to increase stability and mobility (two are usually enough).

DENTURES

Keep them clean. Combine 1 teaspoon of water softener, 1 teaspoon of liquid bleach, and 8 ounces of water. Soak dentures in the solution for 10

Six Ways to Use Dental Floss

There are many creative uses for dental floss around the house. Here are some to try.

- ♥ String beads for necklaces.
- ♥ Sew on buttons with white or new colored flosses; they'll stay on!
- ♥ Faucets with clear plastic covers on the "Hot" and "Cold" knobs can be hard to clean. When you are in the mood to strive for perfection, dental floss cleans not only the nooks and crannies between your teeth but also those of covered faucet knobs!
- ♥ Cut cake layers. (Thread also works better and neater than a knife.)
- ♥ Lace up a chicken or turkey for cooking.
- ♥ Make quick household repairs, such as reattaching umbrella material to a spoke.

to 15 minutes daily. Scrub with a denture brush and rinse well before replacing them in your mouth.

Caution: Don't use this or any solution containing bleach if you wear a partial denture with metal, wire clasps, cast chrome, or gold frame.

Leave the cleaning cup at home. A resealable plastic bag fits easily in a shaving or cosmetic bag and dentures can soak overnight as easily in the bag as in a hard-sided container.

DEODORANT

Discover a gentle solution. For a nonchemical deodorant, apply dry baking soda to the underarm area, and then brush off the excess. It's not likely to irritate skin like some commercial preparations can.

DESSERTS

Cut them up. When only one or two people live in a home, desserts can get stale before they are eaten. The solution is to cut all freezable desserts into single-serving sizes and freeze them in plastic freezer-safe bags. A few seconds in the microwave brings them back to freshness.

See also COOKIES.

DETERGENT

 Get extra mileage. When you empty a plastic squirt bottle of dish-washing detergent, don't throw it away. Instead, fill it with water and shake to dissolve the detergent that remains inside. The resulting diluted detergent is powerful enough to squirt on eyeglasses, your hands, or on a sponge to quick-wipe dishes. Plus, it will rinse off more easily than when you squirt full-strength detergent on washables.

Hint: When washing eyeglasses with plastic lenses, remember that paper towels, napkins, and tissues can scratch. Instead, dry with a soft cloth.

Make sand scoops. Caps from liquid laundry detergent can be stacked like building blocks or used as sand scoops at the beach (please don't leave them there!) or in a child's sandbox.

DIAMONDS

Remove your rocks. Don't wear diamond jewelry while doing housework or gardening. Cleaning products can harm diamonds and gold. Contrary to popular belief, one good knock can chip a diamond.

Avoid scratches. Because diamonds can scratch other gem stones, store each piece of diamond jewelry in a separate case or jewelry box section.

Beware of the sink. When you wash your hands, don't take your ring off and leave it near the sink. It can fall down the drain or be forgotten when you leave. I've seen people hold their rings between their lips while washing their hands.

 Clean them easily. Powders, skin oils, soaps, and lotions dull diamonds. To clean them, soak the diamond jewelry for a few minutes in a small bowl of warm water to which you've added a squirt of mild liquid detergent. Then brush the diamonds with an old soft toothbrush or eyebrow brush, rinse well, pat, and buff dry.

Use alcohol. Try dipping each piece of diamond jewelry in a bit of rubbing alcohol and buff dry. It really makes diamonds sparkle.

DINNER

See ENTERTAINING.

DIP DISH

Use a pepper. Carefully cut off the top of a bell pepper and stand it on end in the middle of a veggie platter to hold dip. The pepper can be red, green, or yellow depending upon the color you need to perk up the platter.

Try a cabbage. Put cocktail sauce in a hollowed-out cabbage. Skewer a few shrimp on colored toothpicks and stick the opposite ends into the cabbage like antennae on a satellite. Place the rest of the shrimp artfully around the cabbage.

DISHES, HAND WASHING

Some things just don't go into the dishwasher. Also, not everyone has a dishwasher that operates on electricity. Some "dishwashers" are run by human energy.

Use some vinegar. Dip washed dishes in a vinegar water bath to rinse them clean.

Protect your crystal. To help protect your fine crystal, line the sink with a thick dish towel or washcloth. Be sure to wear rubber gloves, because you can rinse glasses with hotter water that way, which means they dry faster.

Clean your baking dishes. If your glass baking dishes have burned-on grease, fill the dish with hot, soapy water and add a bit of vinegar. Scrub lightly with a plastic scrubby pad. This is especially important if the glass dishes are used with silver holders, where burned-on gunk looks especially bad.

Eliminate dried food. Soak dishes and pans with dried egg or milk in cold water. Hot water actually cooks these foods onto their containers and makes cleaning more work.

Presoak to save time. If you soak gunky dishes in hot, soapy water as you are preparing a meal for family or guests, you won't have to do as much scraping during the final cleanup. Just fill the sink with water, and then add utensils, pots, and dishes as you finish with them.

Be careful with knives. Never drop knives into a sink full of dishwater, because you might cut your hand while you're groping around for dishes.

Use a makeshift periscope. If you have lost something in the dishwater, use a drinking glass to peer past the suds and get a clear view of the bottom of the sink.

Safely retrieve broken glass. If you break a glass, let the water drain out, and use a paper towel to retrieve it so that you don't cut your hand.

Add a strainer. Have an extra sink strainer handy to accommodate the extra dishes you use when you have company. If you have people drying dishes as you wash, you can put one strainer on each side of the sink and ease the traffic congestion in the kitchen. (With two strainers, you can also give the more fragile pieces to the more careful dish dryers, especially if you have children helping you!)

Create a disposable strainer. Here's how to make a spare strainer and avoid clutter in your cupboards. Simply layer several clean towels on your counter. The towels will absorb the dripping water and keep it from flowing across your countertops. Once the dishes are dry, just wash the towels.

 Clean your dish drainer and tray. Fill the kitchen sink with about 2 inches of hot water and add a couple of "glugs" of chlorine bleach. Place the drainer and tray in the sink and let them soak for about 15 minutes. If you can't put your hands in bleach and have no rubber gloves, after soaking is over, unplug the sink with barbecue tongs, and let the bleach water drain away. Rinse items. Best quality dish drainers can be placed upside down in the dishwasher on normal or light setting for easy cleaning. Just be sure that the moving arms are not blocked by the rack.

Stack wisely. If you are hand washing stacks of dishes, put the whole stack into the dishwater at one time so that the bottom ones soak while you swish off the top ones. This is much easier than stacking dishes beside the sink and putting one at a time into the dishwater for washing.

DISHWASHERS

If you follow the directions in the booklet that came with your dishwasher, and you still get enough film and water spots to feel like you're in a TV detergent commercial, it's probably because the water isn't hot enough. Some machines have built-in boosters that heat the water when it's in the machine. Whether yours has a booster or not, here are some hints for keeping your dishwasher in tip-top shape.

Regular Use

Test the water. To test if your hot water is hot enough to dissolve powdered dishwasher detergent and help your dishwasher do its job, run hot water in your sink until it's the hottest it can get. Then, fill a tall glass with hot water and put a tablespoon of dishwasher detergent in. If the detergent dissolves before it gets to the bottom, the water is hot enough.

Let it run. Let the water run from the faucet until it's hot before you start the dishwasher. Keep the water heater setting at 120°F.

Caution: If the heater is set for 140° to 160°F, the water is too hot. Children and even adults have been scalded by hot bath water, often with serious consequences.

Play it safe. Don't run the dishwasher while the washing machine is running or during or after showers unless you have more than one water heater. (Running the dishwasher or clothes washer during showers in homes with limited water pressure can be harmful to the health of relationships. Nobody wants cold water to suddenly spew out on a shampoo-lathered head! Also, fluctuating hot water flows can burn if the hapless bather adjusts the shower to the hot water flow during the washer's fill cycle.)

Load properly. Glasses will become etched from improper loading or overloading of the dishwasher, a blocked filter, a spray arm that doesn't move as it should, or any other situation that prevents water from adequate washing and rinsing. If the proper water action is blocked, detergent will remain on the glassware too long and will not rinse off completely, thereby etching your glassware. I wash and dry my best crystal by hand. It takes only a few seconds to do this.

Try some vinegar. If your glasses are cloudy because of hard water buildup, soak them in warm vinegar for several hours, and then try to wash off the cloudy part.

Rinse first. If you have an older-model dishwasher, you may need to rinse the dishes well before loading them.

Beware of starch. Starchy foods such as rice seem to cause the most trouble if you don't rinse dishes before loading the dishwasher. Also, dishwasher efficiency depends upon how long you've let food dry on the dishes.

Watch the filter. Check your dishwasher filter regularly (if your model has one) and keep it clean. The cleaner the filter, the cleaner the dishes. If the filter is dirty, food particles will recirculate over your clean dishes.

Clean the door. Check the bottom of the dishwasher door if you have a front-loading dishwasher. Use a wadded paper towel or thick sponge to

Dishwashing Facts

An efficient automatic dishwasher, properly used, conserves water and energy, according to the Texas Energy Extension Service at Texas A&M University. For best results, heed these tips.

♥ Most dishwashers have "air dry" or "energy miser" buttons. These features save you money because they turn off the heat during drying.

♥ Dishwashers with booster heaters allow you to get hotter water for dishes than elsewhere in the house. You won't have to keep your water heater set as high.

♥ Look for dishwashers that can dispose of food residue so that you don't have to rinse dishes before putting them into the dishwasher. Just take a used paper napkin or a rubber spatula and wipe off solids—then let the machine do its work. If your dishwasher consistently leaves residue on your dishes, check for blocked drainage along the line, including your main kitchen drain pipe or sewer line.

♥ No dishwasher? You use a lot of water and energy if you wash dishes and rinse them in running hot water. You use less if you wash in one pan and rinse in another.

protect your hands when you wipe this area because some dishwasher doors have sharp bottom edges.

You will be surprised at the gunk (mostly hardened fats and oils) that accumulates here. It is more likely to accumulate when the dishwater isn't hot enough and can ultimately damage the seal in some washers. I've found broken glass and even a missing spoon!

Check the cup. If you rinse all of your dishes before loading, you'll surely have family members confused about whether dishes in the dishwasher are clean or dirty. One good signal is to put one cup right side up when you load the dishwasher. This cup will get filled with water during the cycle. and you'll know that the dishwasher has been run.

Send strong signals. Some people like to put magnets on the front with little notes that say, "Wash me" or "I'm washed." Some new models have green lights that glow if the dishwasher has gone through its cycle.

Selecting Detergent

Choose detergent carefully. To get maximum dishwasher efficiency, start by choosing the right detergent. Shake the box of powdered detergent; if you can't hear the granules rattling inside, don't buy it. Lumpy dishwasher detergent won't dissolve well enough to do its job.

Store detergent properly. Find a better place to store detergent than under the kitchen sink, where it's moist and warm. Place it in a cool, dry place instead.

Buy detergent accordingly. If you find that the larger box of the powdered dishwasher detergent gets lumpy, you might want to consider buying smaller boxes. You'll use them up more quickly, and they won't go bad in the interim.

Shop around. Try different detergents. Some people may get better results with thick liquid dishwasher detergents. Also, different brands of detergent seem to work better in one part of the country than another because of variances in water hardness. The one your mom used when you were living at home may not work in the city you live in now. Use coupons to try the smallest sizes of different brands to see which works best in your area.

Use less. If you have softened water, don't forget to use less than the full recommended amount of detergent. Using too much detergent can etch your glasses, causing them to look cloudy and "dirty," and nothing will make them clear again.

Cleaning

Wait! Don't skip this section because you think this is a useless chore or one to totally avoid. Often the reason your dishwasher won't clean properly is that it needs a cleaning beyond its own self-washing. Also, a real ogre of a landlord who's determined to keep your apartment damage deposit will have one less point to pick on if you put a sparkle on the appliances. Sparkling appliances help sell your house, too.

Do the powdered-drink trick. Remove dishwasher stains by wetting the stains and sprinkling instant powdered orange breakfast drink or powdered lemon drink on them. Let it stand for at least 1 hour. Then, wipe a bit off to see if the stain has disappeared. If it has, load the dishwasher, add the dishwasher detergent, and let it run through the cycle. The citric acid removes the stains.

Take two steps to success. Here's a two-step method to get the dishwasher and its contents clean and sparkling. First, pour one cup of bleach into a bowl and set the bowl on the bottom rack of the dishwasher. Run it through the "wash" cycle only. Do not dry. If your dishwasher can't be stopped after a cycle, then punch the "cancel drain" button.

Next, fill the bowl again, this time with one cup of vinegar. Let the dishwasher run through the entire cycle this time. Your dishes will be sparkling clean, and the discolorations, film, and mineral buildup on the interior of your dishwasher should have disappeared; if not, repeat the entire process.

Caution: Never combine the bleach and vinegar for a one-step process. It's dangerous! Also, do not put gold-trimmed dishes, glassware, or silverware in the dishwasher when you use this process, because it damages such trim and objects.

Troubleshooting

Fix silverware basket "leaks." Put a piece of nylon net in to the bottom of the dishwasher silverware basket if you have small-handled pieces that seem to poke through and possibly interfere with the rotating sprayer in the bottom of the dishwasher.

Stop cup flipping. To stop cups from flipping over and getting filled with water and sediment during the wash cycle, line up the cup handles and run a ¼-inch dowel pin through them. Dowel pins are sold in most hardware stores.

Repair the rack. A commercial liquid plastic product made just for repairing missing plastic and nicks on dishwasher racks is available from appliance or dishwasher service stores. It comes in several colors to match different brands.

Keep dishwashing sponge fresh. Clip it to the top shelf of the dishwasher at the end of the day so that it won't fall to the bottom and damage the machine while the dishwasher's hot water and detergent deodorizes and cleans it.

Recycle parts. When a dishwasher can't be repaired, salvage the racks for use as organizers of wrapping paper and ribbons. Rolls and ribbon spools fit on the upright prongs and flat packages of tissue or gift-wrap fit in slots. Also, some old dishwashers have silverware baskets with handles that can carry flatware to the picnic table and be used for informal outdoor buffet serving.

DOGS

Watch their weight. At ideal weight, you should be able to feel a pet's ribs with your fingers without pressing. Generally, if you can see the pet's ribs, it is underweight. In either case, don't put your dog on a weight-loss or weight-gain diet without your vet's advice.

Play music. If you have to leave your dog alone at home for several hours, leave your radio on. The sound will reassure your pet and make him feel less abandoned. Dogs are pack animals, and since their humans become their pack when they are brought into a family, many dogs panic when left alone.

(A radio that's on also deters would-be housebreakers. They're likely to assume that someone's home.)

Leave your scent. Leave a rag or towel and old bathrobe or shirt that you have used with your dog when you go away, or, in the case of a new puppy, when you go to bed. Your scent will comfort him. Send along something with your scent on it or a rawhide bone that your dog's been chewing on when you board your dog, too, to make him feel at home.

Wipe his eyes. Each day, wipe away the daily rheum that gathers at the corners of your dog's eyes with a dab of cotton dipped in warm water.

Praise while training. Praise is the key. Pat, hug, and tell your dog "What a good dog!" when he responds properly to training, and reward him immediately with a treat. Hitting only teaches fear to an animal and is not training. It's abuse.

Always have water on hand. When you take your dog in the car, also take a small plastic water bowl or a bowl made by cutting off the bottom of a gallon milk jug and a jug of water.

Store food wisely. If you store pet food in a garage, protect it from insects and rodents by storing it in a clean plastic garbage can with a lid.

Make no-tip food dishes. Buy a tube baking pan and put it over a stake you've driven into the ground. You can put food or water into the pan and the dog can't tip it. Or put dog food or water into heavy-based, wide-mouthed crocks.

Keep his ears clean. A reader wrote that she puts a stretchable headband over her cocker spaniel's head, tucking his ears under it, and he's so interested in eating that he doesn't notice.

Unleash her in the car. It's best not to keep your dog on a leash in the car. A leash can get caught on door handles and other projections, and your dog could be injured.

Avoid the heat. Exercise your dog early in the morning or late at night

Heartworm Medication

Heartworm can be avoided if you take your dog to the veterinarian for annual blood tests and give him the preventive pills. Heartworms are transmitted by mosquitoes and affect only dogs.

Bear in mind that heartworm pills are now given all year long instead of just during the summer as was the custom in the past. (Infected mosquitoes, carriers of the disease, have been found indoors when it was 7 degrees below zero outside!)

If your dog hates the pill, wrap it in half of a cheese slice. (Wrap the cheese around the pill, and then hold the wad in your palm for a minute. You'll have a pill-stuffed cheese ball that fools the dog into eagerly eating it.) Or coat the pill with peanut butter or liverwurst if that's what your dog likes. Pills are available in monthly doses; ask your vet for advice.

during the summer. Midday heat can cause heat exhaustion. Dogs are so eager to please they will run well beyond their capacity to tolerate heat and get into trouble.

Consider skin protection. Don't walk a newly clipped dog in the peak sunshine because her skin could get burned.

Clean his feet. Salt and chemical deicers can irritate and cause cracks in the skin on a dog's feet in wintry climates. Wash the dog's feet off when you bring him in from a walk.

Pause for a little lotion on the paws. If the pads of your dog's feet become dry or cracked, rub a little petroleum jelly into them. Wipe off the excess to protect your carpet. You can also put creamy lotion on them to help healing. This is a special treat for both Cabernet and me in the wintertime.

Winterize the doghouse. A reader wrote that the first night's freeze made the leftover carpet placed on the floor of her dog's house wet and frosty—unsuitable for the dog to sleep on. So her husband built a platform about 10 inches high to elevate the house from the cold ground and removed the carpet. Instead, they put tar paper on the floor, covered it with layers of newspaper, then topped it all with a layer of hay. This insulation kept the dog warm and dry.

Make a sweater. For a small dog, recycle an old ski mask so that the dog's front paws go through the eyeholes and its head goes through a hole you open in the seam at the mask's top. The dog's tail wags from the neckhole, of course, to thank you for the warmth and kindness!

Cover yourself. Stay dry while washing your dog by making a cover-all apron by cutting holes for your head and arms in a plastic trash bag.

Use a plastic pool for bathing. Some dogs won't stay put when being washed out in the yard with a garden hose but will at least stand in one spot if you have them stand in a child's plastic wading pool or other large low-sided water holder. The advantage is that the dog's feet will be soaked clean while you lather and hose the rest of him.

Deodorize your dog. In between baths, try dusting your dog with baking soda. If you leave it on for 10 minutes or so, you can brush it out and enjoy a sweet-smelling dog again.

Stop the shakes. Try firmly grasping the dog around his nose. For some dogs, "the shake" starts there, so if they can't shake their noses, they can't shake anything else either. You'll stay drier and have less mess.

Puppies

Provide a birthing bed. A child's small plastic swimming pool makes a good puppy-birthing bed. It's easy to clean and has no sharp edges. Plus, the dog can step over the side, but tiny puppies will stay in.

Make the transition comfortable. On puppy's first night home, if you place a ticking clock wrapped in a soft towel near him in his bed at night, it will help him think he still hears his mother's heartbeat. Sleeping on a hot water bottle wrapped in a towel will comfort him, too.

Block rooms with pegboard. You can use 2-foot by 4-foot pegboards as temporary doorway barriers for puppies. Prop the pegboards in place with a chair or other furniture. There's no need to make holes in walls or woodwork. With only a "half door" in place, your puppy won't feel as isolated as he would with the door closed, and if he scratches up the pegboards it won't matter as much as if he scratches up a door.

Some dogs get the idea that the pegboard means "no admittance," and then you can use the pegboards to bar your dog from any off-limits room (bookcase, chair, or other furniture, too) at any time by just using a pegboard piece as a "stop" sign. The pegboards can be used to hang things in your garage after the puppy gets free rein in the house.

Cure car sickness. Common with puppies, car sickness can be outgrown more easily if you take your dog on 15-minute trips every other day or so, then increase the time gradually.

Housebreaking

Place him strategically. When you take a puppy outside to "outside-break" him, don't just plop the puppy on your porch, patio, or doorstep. He will use those places to relieve himself. Instead, place him where you prefer to have him perform his duties.

Mark the spot. Take a rag that you've used to clean up a mess and place it where the puppy should relieve itself, and then always take him there. His acute sense of smell will tell him that is where he is to go.

Time it right. Be sure to praise the pup when he performs as you want him to. If your puppy relieves himself in the house, discipline the pup only if you catch him in the act. A puppy has a short memory and will not understand why you are scolding him half an hour later.

Use a playpen. Until a puppy is well housebroken, keep it in an old baby playpen with newspapers layered over an old shower curtain or other waterproof mat. Then puppy can stay in the room with you without causing "accidents" on the carpet.

Confine him. It helps if you confine your new puppy to one certain room, especially a room with a wipeable floor, until he is housebroken.

Consider the crate advantage. Crate-training a dog will also help to housebreak her. Animals don't soil their own environments, and if a crate

Letter of Laughter

Springing Spaniel

One reader tried the playpen hint above and wrote that it was not for springer spaniels. As soon as her springer pup learned to "spring," he would spring up and down like a yo-yo, landing with a reverberating crash on the playpen floor. It was hilarious to watch but definitely wearing on the nerves after a while!

(or cage) becomes a dog's inside bed, she won't urinate or defecate in it unless it's too long between potty runs.

While some people don't like the idea of a dog in a cage, a crate-trained dog is a happier dog at the vet's when she's ill or in a boarding kennel if you're on a trip. If you don't treat the crate as a "punishing place," the animal will soon look upon it as her secure home and will be content to sleep in it and be put in it when "nondog" people are visiting your home.

Don't forget water. While it seems counterproductive to give your dog water while you are crate-training him and housebreaking him at the same time, the dog needs water at all times.

Spill-proof the water bowl. Some crated dogs will step in and tip over their water bowls. The solution is to buy a "rabbit cage" bottle at the pet store. A rabbit-size bottle holds about a quart and comes with a wire holder that you can attach to the crate.

See also PETS.

DOLLS

Make a stand. Dolls with small bodies and full skirts can stand up in a wide-mouthed mayonnaise jar. The jar makes a good skirt hoop.

Clean carefully. While some people wash cloth dolls in a washing machine, I must stress that you do it at your own risk. Resort to this method only when the doll is heavily soiled and all other cleaning attempts have failed.

To ensure the best possible results, remove all clothing, ribbons, and accessories. Pretreat heavily soiled areas with prewash spray. Put the doll in a pillowcase and close it by tying a knot in the open end. Place the pillowcase in the washing machine, set on a gentle cycle, and add warm water and regular laundry detergent. Add a few sheets or towels in with the doll to cushion the bumping.

After the washing cycle is complete, remove the pillowcased doll and place it directly into the clothes dryer on low heat for about 10 minutes. After 10 minutes in the dryer, remove the doll from the pillowcase and place it in a well-ventilated area to finish drying overnight so it doesn't smell musty.

Customize gifts. Buy a doll from a craft store and make doll clothes that resemble clothing worn for special occasions in the doll collector's life, such as First Communion and first day of school.

DOMINO CONTAINERS

 Play a game. Wash and dry a white or colored (just not a see-through plastic) gallon-size plastic jug and cut an opening in the top half opposite the handle large enough to admit an adult's hand. Then you can keep dominoes in the jug and pass it from player to player to draw from. Passing the jug also speeds up alphabet word games, and the jug can also be safe storage so that you don't lose pieces.

DOORS

Find the hinges. Ever feel silly pushing on a door you're supposed to pull open? When you approach an unfamiliar door, scan the frame to see if the hinges are on the inside (PUSH) or outside (PULL).

 Make furniture. Add legs to a door and paint it to make a desk or table. The height is up to you.

QUICK REFERENCE

Dead-Bolt-Lock Checklist

Here are some handy hints about dead bolts.

- ♥ The bolt should extend at least 1 inch from the edge of the door. (This is called a "1-inch throw.")
- ♥ The connecting screws holding the lock together should be on the inside of the door.
- ♥ The strike plate should be attached to the door frame with screws that are at least 3 inches long.
- ♥ The cylinder has a steel guard—a ring around the key section. The cylinder guard needs to be tapered or needs to rotate around the key section when twisted to prevent wrenching.

Protect small fingers. Prevent small children from slamming or closing doors on their little fingers. Throw a thick folded towel over the tops of doors so that they won't close completely.

De-squeak hinges. Take the squeak out of door hinges by lubricating the pin with petroleum jelly. Unlike oil, petroleum jelly won't drip on the floor.

Protect the finish. When you need to polish door hardware (on furniture as well as entryway doors), cut a cardboard shield so that it fits around the metal parts, and then hold the shield in place with masking tape while you work on the hardware.

Practice sliding door safety. Many people already do this, but it bears repeating. Apply a decal on sliding glass doors at eye level so that nobody will mistake a closed door for an open one. I even have one down at eye level on the special door for my schnauzer.

Mark door screens. People have been known to walk into lightweight screens, too, so you might want to put a decal or sew a zigzag of colored yarn on the screen.

 Clean a louvered door. If the louvered panel on a door to a hot-water heater, furnace, or air-conditioning unit is screwed in place, carefully unscrew the screws, remove the panel, and wash it in a sink or tub of warm, sudsy water with a soft scrub brush. Rinse, wipe dry, and replace. Trust me, removing the panel for cleaning is much easier than leaving it in place and making a mess on the floor while you spray on cleaning solution and try to clean the louvers.

Consider security versus safety. Dead bolt locks that need latchkeys inside and out to operate them are the most secure, but those that can be opened from the inside without a latchkey are considered safer in case of fire. Some communities have safety codes restricting inside/outside latchkey-only dead bolt locks. Check with local building inspectors or other suitable authorities.

Use a lubricant. A lock that doesn't open may not be broken, just stuck. To unstick locks and keep them working well, squirt the lock mechanism at the door's edge with lubricant regularly.

Don't forget to use them. Locks provide security only if you use them. Always lock doors even if you leave the house for only a few minutes.

Types and Uses of Door Locks

Are you curious about types of locks? Read on.

♥ Double-cylinder dead-bolt lock: Placed on doors with glass panels or on all doors, they can be opened only with a key from either side. You can keep the key near the door, but make sure it can't be reached from the glass panel. Intruders won't be able to break the glass and get the key, but your family can get out in case of fire. Before installing these, check with local law enforcement agencies, because some communities restrict use of these locks.

♥ Police lock: For rear and basement entrances, this is a metal bar bracketed against the inside of the door at an angle. It slides into a small hole on the floor and prevents burglars from jimmying the lock or kicking in the door.

♥ Padlock: It's usually used for garages, sheds, and workshops. Buy sturdy padlocks that don't release the key until the lock is locked. A padlock should have a rugged laminated case with ⅜-inch shackle so it can resist smashing. A padlock is only as good as its mounting hasp, which should be secured with bolts and mounted on a metal plate. Bolts must be concealed when the padlock is locked.

 Unstick with graphite. Try some graphite in the lock before calling the lock repair service. Often that will clear up the problem immediately.

DOUBLE BOILER

Know when the water is low. If you place a small, metal jar lid in the bottom of a double boiler, the rattling sounds will warn you when the water is getting too low. Marbles work, too, but be prepared for quizzical looks if, when someone asks, "What's that noise," and you reply, "I'm boiling my marbles." They may think you've lost your marbles!

STEP ♥ BY ♥ STEP

Quick Fix with Hardware

New hardware gives your kitchen or bathroom a new look. Before you buy, do the following.

1. Be sure to measure drawer handle spreads so that you can use the existing holes when attaching the new handles.

2. If you want to switch from handles to knobs, buy backplates to cover the old handle holes, and then drill a new hole in the center for the knob.

Note: Someone once told me that your mind is like a cartridge and ideas are like marbles. When your cartridge (mind) gets too full with too many marbles (ideas), some of them start to spill out, and that's where we get the expression "losing your marbles." However, I haven't been able to verify this with my usual sources.

DOWN-FILLED GARMENTS

Know whether to wash or not to wash. The International Fabricare Institute and most garment manufacturers recommend that down-filled garments be dry-cleaned. As always, consult the care label for exact instructions for your particular garment.

DRAFT GUARDS

Make your own. Make draft guards for doorjambs and windowsills by filling double or triple thicknesses of newspaper bags with sand. Tie the open end securely with a twist-tie, and then put the "snake" into a long tube sock.

DRAPERIES AND BLINDS

Clean metal blinds. An aerosol spray made for cleaning crystal chandeliers will clean painted metal blinds. With the blinds in a semiclosed position, spray and then wipe off the dirt droplets with paper towels or terry-towel rags. Liquid window cleaner and our homemade cleaner will also work, but you'll have to totally wipe each slat instead of just wiping droplets.

Remove dust and freshen. When drapes need a good dusting but not actual cleaning, you can toss most washable fabric drapes into the dryer with a fabric-softener sheet. Set the dryer on "Air Fluff."

Identify drapery cords. Either put pieces of colored tape or a dab of colored nail polish on the cord that opens the drapes, or take the letters left over from videotapes to stick "open" on one cord or "o" and "c" for open and close.

DRAWERS

Substitute wooden beads for knobs and pulls. Small wooden blocks and large beads used for macramé craft already have holes for screws and make novel pulls.

Prevent plastic organizers from sliding. When plastic silverware organizers slide around in a kitchen drawer, keep them in place with double-sided adhesive tape. You can still remove them for cleaning.

See also CUPBOARDS AND DRAWERS.

DRESSES

Hang spaghetti straps. Don't hang garments by spaghetti straps; they aren't strong enough to support the garment's weight, especially if the fabric is extra heavy like velvet or satin. If the manufacturer has not attached long loops of seam binding to the upper side seams for hanging, make some with seam binding or woven hem facing. Be sure to tack the loops to the side seam allowance.

Alternately, you could hang the dress over a pants hanger at the waist or clip the bodice to a skirt hanger. (Be sure to put foam padding under the clips to prevent crushing or marring velvet, satin, or silk.)

DRIVEWAY OIL STAINS

Use engine degreaser. Try spraying engine degreaser on driveway stains. Apply, let set about 10 minutes, and then wash away with a garden hose.

DRY-CLEANER'S BAGS

 Make a trash can liner. Tie a knot in the end, turn the bag inside out, and it will line a tall trash basket. You can insert a paper grocery bag to prevent things from poking through. Or you can double bag for heavier paper trash.

 Save for travel. Put bags on clothing to be packed in hanging-type bags when you travel. It helps prevent crushing and helps prevent clothing from getting wet if rain should fall on the zipper area. You can also stuff bags into sleeve arms to prevent crushing.

DRY CLEANING

Act fast. Don't store clothing that needs dry cleaning. Any soil or stain left on a garment too long can become impossible to remove without damaging the fabric. This is why it is very important to point out any stains to your dry cleaner when taking the garment in. This includes any that are light in color or invisible, such as soft drinks or white wine. The heat from the drying process of dry cleaning can turn such stains brown or yellow.

Extend the life of clothing. Frequent dry cleaning prolongs the life of a garment. Not only do stains set with age, making the garment unwearable, but ground-in dirt and soil act as an abrasive (like sandpaper), causing rapid wear of the fibers, and they can attract moths to wool garments.

Protect from personal products. Protect your garments from perfumes and colognes, as well as deodorants and antiperspirants, by applying these items before dressing and allowing them to dry. Garments made of delicate fabrics, such as silk, can be seriously damaged by perfumes and hair sprays.

Be kind to your dry cleaner. Remember, a good professional dry cleaner is the next most important thing to a good hairdresser. Be honest with them when you take in your garments and point out any stains; tell them anything that you have tried to use to remove the stain before bringing it in. They can work their miracle only if you help them. Many stains are impossible to remove regardless of what is attempted. So please remember that your dry cleaner is only human, too.

DRYERS

Clean the lint trap. A baby-bottle brush sweeps the filter clean with one whisk.

Fix a door seal. Self-adhesive weather stripping will replace a broken dryer door seal if you can't get an "official" one from an appliance parts store.

Clean the filter. Try using an old fabric softener sheet, a comb, hair pick, pen, or pencil to remove the lint from the filter.

Loathe the lint. Lint buildup will cause your dryer to take much longer to dry the clothing. Not only can this buildup damage the machine, but it will cost more money in electricity or gas to dry your clothes, and there is also the possibility of fire if the dryer overheats.

Appliance service agents say that even though you "clean" the lint filter often to remove all the fuzz, a fine film forms on the filter that keeps air from circulating properly. You need to wash the filter with liquid dish-washing soap, a stiff brush, and warm water every so often. Let the water run through to remove every particle of lint.

DUST AND COBWEBS

Clean the corners and crevices. Secure an old sock on a yardstick with rubber bands and poke it into hard-to-reach places like under or behind

Dryer Troubleshooting

If your dryer suddenly stops working, do the following:

- ♥ Check the outside vent to make sure nothing is clogging it.
- ♥ If it's a gas dryer, check that the striker is working properly and that the pilot light is on.
- ♥ Check that the door is closing tightly.
- ♥ Check if a fuse has blown.

the fridge or the stove. You can also reach cobwebs in corners with this handy "extension wand."

Clean silk flowers and plants. "Dust" with cold air blown from a hair dryer or clean by shaking them in a bag with table salt.

Brush it off. An animal hair pastry brush or natural bristle paintbrush removes dust from the inside corners of picture frames, light bulbs and globes, chandelier chains, bric-a-brac, cloth lamp shades, pleated tops of draperies, and other nooks and crannies.

Vacuum it. Gently vacuum moldings, air-conditioning and heating vents, and corners of walls to get rid of fuzzy dust and any cobwebs that may be on the ceiling.

If your vacuum extensions aren't long enough, you may be able to reach corners with a broom, mop, or fishing pole covered by an old pillowcase, T-shirt, or nylon net.

Play ball. Unreachable cobwebs can sometimes be "caught" if you wrap a racquetball or tennis ball in a dust rag and then toss it up into the cobweb corner.

Caution: Don't get too enthusiastic when tossing the ball, or you'll "score" costly knickknack-breaking rebounds.

Keep crystal free of dust. Cover party crystal with plastic wrap when you put it away, and it will stay clean between parties.

DUST RUFFLES

Keep them in place. Dust ruffles can be kept in their place if you sew them on to an old fitted sheet or quilted mattress pad either by machine or hand-tacking. The fitted sheet will hold tight to the box spring.

EARRINGS

Curb the crunch of clip backs. Place spongy nose pads sold in optical shops on the clip part and a piece of moleskin on the back of the earring, or cut small moleskin adhesive pads (those made for protecting corns and blisters) to fit and stick them on the offending earring back and the front of the clip so that the pads sandwich your poor, suffering earlobe.

Hold them straight. Cut small circles from plastic lids, such as those from coffee cans, and place them behind your ear on the pierced-earring post before you put the back on. You can also buy clear plastic disks for this purpose at costume jewelry stores.

Prevent earring-related skin irritation. Putting a bit of antibiotic ointment on the posts helps earrings go in easier and helps to prevent skin irritation.

Keep them from getting lost. If you take off your hook-style pierced earrings at the gym or doctor's office, poke them into a plastic foam packing peanut so the wires don't get bent or lost. When traveling, poke them through half of a washcloth and then fold the other half over them for protection.

> ### When You Lose One of a Pair
>
> There are many ways to recycle a surviving earring. Consider the following ideas.
>
> ♥ Poke posts through scarves or knit ties to hold them in place.
>
> ♥ A button-style pierced earring can be a stud for a missing button or a small lapel pin.
>
> ♥ Turn an earring "dangle" into a small pendant and hang it like a charm on a bracelet or necklace.
>
> ♥ If you have several leftover dangle earrings, put them all together on a charm holder (sold at jewelry counters in silver or gold) and then put the holder on a chain or velvet ribbon for a multipiece "pendant."
>
> ♥ Poke large earrings through the screen door to prevent people from bumping into it when it's closed.
>
> ♥ Break or cut off posts from the earring back; glue the earring "button" with a hot glue gun to a plain gold or silver ring and you have a new piece of jewelry.

Keep them handy. Inexpensive, lightweight, clear plastic fishing tackle boxes will store many pairs of pierced earrings for easy selection. Some have 20 or more compartments, each with enough space for several pairs of similar earrings.

 Store pierced earrings with ease. For pierced earrings, another storage technique is to poke them through a piece of recycled cloth, such as an old necktie, place mat, fabric belt, strips of ribbon from gifts, a not-so-perky scarf, sock, or sentimental baby T-shirt.

EASTER

 Innovate with Easter baskets. Instead of buying baskets that will just get broken and thrown away, buy useful items to hold Easter goodies such as bicycle baskets, a football helmet or baseball cap, special milk mugs or cereal bowls, or anything else your imagination conjures up.

 Try a skein of rug yarn instead of plastic or paper grass. The problem with disposable grass, besides the fact that it's disposable, is that it seems to get everywhere before it's finally discarded. If you want to try yarn instead, undo the wrapper, fluff it up, and add eggs, bunnies, and other clean items. In other words, skip the unwrapped chocolate and sticky candy. The bonus is that you can save the yarn for next Easter or crochet or knit with it later in the year. Or, buy only green yarn instead of purple and yellow so that you can tie up Christmas packages with it later on.

Consider Easter-basket substitutes for adults and older children. Fill a straw or other hat, a small trashcan, a mug, collector glass, flying disk, or nut bowl. For nonsweets eaters, substitute cheese and crackers, fruit and nuts, travel-size cosmetics, lunch snacks, cassette tapes, or a plant.

Use your baskets all year long. Fill a basket with fruit and make a centerpiece; have it hold powder, lotion, and pins in the nursery; store clippers, pins, and scissors in the bathroom; use it to hold spices and other small things on the kitchen counter; fill it with the remote control, TV-listing guide, and your eyeglasses atop the TV. Serve hard-boiled eggs in Easter baskets any time of the year.

 Boil a batch of all-natural Easter eggs. Boil eggs with onion peels to make them yellow, with spinach or turnip tops to make them green, or with a fresh beet to make them red.

EGGS

Realize that you can't judge an egg by its color. The American Egg Board has the final word to dispel an old wives' tale that's been around as long as the "Which came first, the chicken or the egg" riddle.

Eggshell and yolk color may vary, but color has nothing to do with the quality or nutritive value of an egg. The breed of hen determines the shell color. White breeds lay white eggs, but brown or reddish-brown breeds (such as Rhode Island Red, New Hampshire and Plymouth Rock) lay brown eggs. Most Americans want white eggs, but in some parts of the country, especially in New England, brown shells are preferred.

Cascarones: "Confetti Eggs"

Popular in my hometown, San Antonio, at Fiesta time, these party eggs are easily made.

1. Whenever you use a fresh egg, don't crack the shell in half. Instead, carefully poke a pin or thumbtack hole in the small end, and tap out a dime-size hole in the opposite larger end with a spoon.

2. Hold the egg over a bowl, and use a straw or baby bulb syringe to blow into the pin hole, forcing the egg out the dime-size hole. Gently run water into the empty eggshell to rinse it out, and place it on paper towels to dry.

3. Decorate the eggshells with dye or paint them as you please. Then fill the inside with confetti. After inserting confetti, paste a small piece of tissue paper over the larger opening to hold it in.

4. Have a Fiesta party, and pop cascarones atop the head of someone for a lot of laughs and a lot of flying confetti. At Fiesta, you know someone really cares when he or she cracks a cascarone over your head! Olé!

Generally, brown eggs cost more because the breeds that lay them are larger and require more feed, therefore the market price is higher in some sections of the country. But why pay more for brown shells when you eat the inside of the egg, not the outside?

Remove a piece of broken shell. Scoop out the piece of shell with a spoon or the tip of a knife.

Easily clean the one that dropped. If you don't have an eager dog or cat to lick it up, pour salt over the broken egg and let it set for about 15 minutes. Cleanup is a cinch!

Know the storage limits. The American Egg Board tells us that fresh eggs can be stored in their cartons in the refrigerator as long as 5 weeks and that the store carton is the best container for storage. The reason for this is that if you take the eggs out of the carton and put them in the egg holder in the door, every time you open and close the door the eggs are subject to temperature variation and to movement, which causes them to spoil more quickly. Also, contrary to what we would think, the shell is porous; it does allow odors to penetrate.

Eggs can be stored 8 to 10 days if hard-cooked in shells. You can store egg whites in a covered container or egg yolks covered with water for 2 to 4 days.

Freeze eggs for future use. Eggs cannot be frozen in their shells, but raw whole eggs, whites, and yolks and hard-cooked yolks can be frozen.

To freeze egg whites, seal them tightly in a freezer container that is labeled with the number of whites and the date.

To freeze whole eggs or yolks, add either ½ teaspoon of salt or 1½ teaspoon of sugar or corn syrup for each four yolks or two whole eggs. In addition to the date and number of yolks or whole eggs, note whether you've added salt or sugar to the eggs so that you'll know if they can be used for main dishes.

Thaw frozen eggs overnight in the refrigerator or under cool running water. Yolks and whole eggs should be used as soon as they're thawed; thawed whites will have better volume when beaten if they are kept at room temperature for about 30 minutes.

Recycle the cartons. Place a cardboard or plastic foam egg carton, spread open, into the bottom of a trash bag when you put it into the can. It will prevent the bottom of the bag from getting soggy and tearing.

 Substitute egg whites for whole eggs in baking. When 2 egg whites are substituted for 1 whole egg, you need to add 1 tablespoon of oil and 4 teaspoons of liquid to your recipe to make up for the fat in the egg yolk. One reader saves all the yolks she removes from whole eggs in a plastic bag. When the bag is full, she cooks the egg yolks in a greased microwave dish and sets the "egg casserole" out for wild animals to eat. Raccoons, opossums, and even foxes feast at her country home.

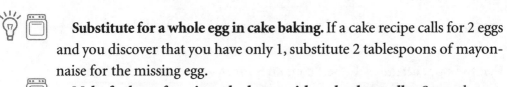

Substitute for a whole egg in cake baking. If a cake recipe calls for 2 eggs and you discover that you have only 1, substitute 2 tablespoons of mayonnaise for the missing egg.

Make foolproof semipoached eggs with no broken yolks. Spray the pan lightly with cooking spray, fry eggs until the whites are barely set, and then add about 1 tablespoon of water. Cover tightly and turn the heat down very low. It won't take long at all!

Spot a cooked egg without breaking the shell. There's no rule that says you can color eggs only at Easter. Add a few drops of food coloring or onion skins to the water when you cook them and the colored eggs will be the cooked eggs. The onion skins make a nice mottled marbled look!

Hint: If you didn't happen to color your eggs before they became confused, just remember that hard-boiled ones spin and raw ones will wobble.

Keep old and fresh eggs straight. Mark the old eggs with a pencil when you add new ones to the fridge.

Stop run-away eggs when you are cooking. To keep eggs from rolling down the counter, sprinkle a few grains of salt or sugar on the counter. Place the egg on the grains and it will stay put.

Separate the yolks from the whites. If you hold a funnel over a container and break the egg into it, the white will slide into the container and the yolk stays in the funnel. Another method involves breaking the egg into a small bowl and then lifting the yolk out with a large slotted spoon. Try both methods to see which one works better for you.

Expand the deviled filling. To make the halves of deviled eggs appear fuller, add about ⅓ cup of low-fat cottage cheese to 6 eggs' worth of yolk filling. Mash all together and add the usual seasonings.

Don't despair the double-yolk. The American Egg Board says double-yolk egg yolks are usually smaller than regular yolks and so can be substituted one for the other.

ELDERLY PEOPLE

Know the signals. In apartment complexes where many elderly people live and watch out for each other, many have the custom of putting a red

Letter of Laughter

Elbow Grease

After I'd used the term "elbow grease" in a column, a reader shopping in the supermarket overheard a young woman asking the store manager where she could find the "elbow grease" she'd read about in Heloise's column. He thought she was kidding until a second shopper came up and said, "That's what I'm looking for, too!" Neither shopper had ever heard the term before and thought it was a new product. When the manager explained to them that it was a term meaning a good old-fashioned rubbing and scrubbing, they all had a good laugh, and so did I when I heard about this generation gap gaff. But wouldn't it be wonderful if somebody would package "elbow grease" so you wouldn't have to use all of your own?

bandana or other marker on the doorknob at night and then removing it in the morning as a signal that all is well in that apartment. If the bandana is still on the doorknob by midday or afternoon, someone checks on the person who lives in that apartment to see if all is okay.

Help an elder with poor vision. Write friendship letters in large, bold print with a felt-tip pen. Some eye conditions make red felt-tip pens easier to see than a black one. Then be sure to include a self-addressed, stamped envelope with the letter so that the elder can write back without having to address an envelope.

Bypass the buttons. When fingers won't button shirts, turn a button-down shirt into a pullover. Simply sew a seam from the second button from the top down to the next-to-last button so that the shirt can be pulled on overhead.

ELECTRICAL WORK

Repair safely. If you have turned off a circuit breaker to do electrical work at home, tape a sign on the circuit breaker that says: DO NOT TURN ON, to prevent people with good intentions from flipping the switch and causing you harm.

EMBROIDERY FLOSS

Store in nine-pocket plastic sheets. You can wrap floss on cardboard spools when it's long enough, but to store shorter strands, buy nine-pocket plastic sheets used to display baseball card collections and you can insert the label with color number along with the leftover pieces of floss. Keep pages in a three-ring binder and just remove the page when you need to take samples to the store for matching or coordinating colors.

Keep them in place. Wrap the thread around the post of a permanent wave roller, using a separate roller for each color, and clip it in place. It's easy to remove the clip when you need more thread.

EMERGENCIES

Know your numbers. If your area does not have a 911 emergency system, have the emergency number taped to your phone so it can't be lost. If you have a programmable phone, program emergency numbers into it and clearly mark the emergency button.

Try to remain calm. When you call, simply say "I want to report a (robbery, suspicious person, or fire)." Prepare to be asked questions, such as: Where? When? Can you describe the person or situation? Weapons present? Injuries? Which way did the criminal run?

Get the number or name of the operator. If you know who took the information, you'll save time if you need to call again with more information. You can give it to the same person and avoid repeating what was originally reported.

Call back with updates. Do call back if the situation changes or if you get more information. Remember, because of computerized communications systems, a police car can be on the way before you finish your

Getting Proper Medical Care

When should we go to an emergency room or urgent care center, call the doctor for an appointment, or just wait and see? With the different deductibles on medical insurances, cost of different facilities is as much a worry as the illness itself. *The Mayo Clinic Health Letter* advises the following:

Seek emergency care when you are ill or in pain if there is:

♥ Chest pain or upper abdominal pain or pressure

♥ Sudden, severe pain anywhere in your body or sudden severe headache with no prior history

♥ Dizziness, sudden weakness, or sudden change in vision

♥ Severe or persistent vomiting

♥ Difficult breathing or shortness of breath

♥ Fainting or feeling faint

♥ Suicidal or homicidal feelings

Call your doctor for an appointment if there is:

♥ Unexplained weight loss

♥ Lump in your breast

♥ Blood in your urine

♥ Abdominal cramps lasting 2 weeks

Wait and see if you have:

♥ Vomited once in 6 hours; no fever, pain, or other symptoms. *Note:* Age, past medical history, and other conditions change what is "wait and see" for one person as compared with others. Chances are that if you think your symptoms are an emergency, they are, and you shouldn't delay getting medical attention. The sooner a doctor treats your illness, the better the chance for a good outcome.

first call. Any additional information will be forwarded to the officers and can help with your emergency.

Remember the details. Try to remember the description if a car is involved, such as the color, make, and any damaged parts. If you can only get part of a license plate number, the first three numbers are more important than the last three.

Make it easy to find you. Place your house numbers on the rear of your home if you have a back alley to help police and firefighters.

Contribute to neighborhood safety. Cooperate with local Neighborhood Watch organizations or help start one if your city promotes them. Install lighting between houses if you live in a city neighborhood.

Within your own home, take time to rehearse emergency procedures with your family and emphasize the seriousness of false alarms to children.

Make a personal affairs checklist. In case of an emergency, keep an up-to-date list for your family. Include a copy of will and trust agreements; doctor and hospital information; family records (births, marriage, divorce, social security, military service, and citizenship); insurance policy information (numbers, agent, beneficiaries); funeral information (preferences, location of cemetery plots, and deeds); safe-deposit box (key, key location, and person authorized to open it); bank account (number and locations); debts (your own and owed to you); pension plans, IRAs, Keoghs, financial/legal advisors' names and phone numbers, brokerage accounts (with brokers' name and phone number); all business records; and all of your charge accounts.

Note: Keep irreplaceable documents in a safe-deposit box, but keep copies for your home records. Remember that a safe-deposit box can be sealed when a person dies so that important information may not be available when it's most needed, such as for funeral preferences and wills.

ENGAGEMENT CALENDARS

 Make special recipe collections. Convert your pretty (but outdated) engagement calendars into specialized recipe collections. Copy recipes in bold print on appropriately sized blank cards and then paste the cards over used pages of past engagements. You can arrange recipes alphabetically or by general subject and put a tab on the first page of each category.

ENTERTAINING

Color the mood and hide the dust. Colored bulbs in lamps when you have holiday parties look festive and make dust invisible. They let you spend more time on the food and less on cleaning before the party. You'll have to clean after anyway!

Don't look a gift horse in the mouth. My best hint on the topic of cleaning up after entertaining is to say, "Yes, thank you" when guests offer to help bring food or clean up after. If you have a close friend who entertains as much as you do, you might consider trading "maid-services." You "do" her party and she "does" yours.

Ask older children to be in charge of entertaining younger ones. Provide board games and other playthings, such as "dress-up" clothing for "pretend" games and plays, in a room out of the food preparation traffic. Offer a reward to older children of a movie or other entertainment for childcare and cleanup after family dinner. Adults who remember their teens also recall that they were bored with adult-style visiting after the main feast is over.

See STAINS.

 Substitute the large containers. For family reunions and other large parties, buy new brightly colored plastic dishpans in which to mix and serve potato and pasta salads.

See also HOLIDAYS, PARTIES, TABLECLOTHS, and TABLES.

ENVELOPES

Leave a spot for notes to yourself. If an envelope is addressed and ready to go, but not yet, you can write notes to yourself on the upper right-hand corner about when to mail a birthday card, if photos or other items are to be included, or when the bill is to be paid, and then cover the note with the stamp at mailing time.

Don't recycle "junk mail" envelopes. While it's tempting to reuse the unused envelopes you receive in the mail, do not mail out your bill payments or letters in them. First, it is illegal to use postage-paid envelopes for anything other than the original intended use. Also, many reply envelopes are printed with bar codes that direct them to the intended address no matter what you write on them. Sticking on a label is no assurance of covering up addresses either; a reader wrote me that her label came off so her car payment went to a book club instead and, as a result, she got a late-payment charge on her car loan that would have bought a lot of new envelopes.

Seal the unsealable. Dab the inside flap with a bit of clear fingernail polish and close it up. I use up the decorative stickers and return address labels that I get from various charitable organizations to reinforce the seals, especially on envelopes containing checks.

Steam them open. Set your iron on a hot setting, then place a slightly dampened cloth over the envelope seal and press with the hot iron for a second or two. This should open the envelope. To reseal, briefly touch the closed flap with the hot iron. If it doesn't stick, try a drop of household glue, tape, or nail polish.

Avoid stuck-together envelopes. To avoid stuck-together envelopes, place something between the flap and the envelope such as waxed paper or regular paper or just raise the flap of one envelope and place the next envelope under it. Or in really damp climates, don't buy the kind that need licking to seal; instead, buy self-sealers. Sometimes, spending a few pennies more saves a lot of aggravation!

EYES AND EYEGLASSES

Soothe tired, puffy eyes. Working on computers or doing demanding needlework can be a strain. To soothe eyes quickly, put wet, used tea bags into the freezer for a few minutes. While they chill, dab olive oil on your eyelids. Place a tea bag on each eye and lie down for 15 minutes or so. Then carefully remove the oil by dabbing lightly with a clean tissue or cotton ball.

Alternately, soak a couple of cotton balls in cold milk, apply to closed eyes, and lie down for 10 minutes. Or try the time-honored cucumber trick. Just place a slice of cold cucumber on each eye and lie down for 10 to 15 minutes.

Pull off an emergency eyeglasses repair. If you lose the tiny screw from your eyeglasses, use a twist-tie with the paper removed. When the point comes out the other side, cut off the ends you can see. If the screw is just loose and you don't have a tiny screwdriver, try a pencil eraser. It works great, especially on metal-framed eyeglasses that seem to always have a screw loose!

Remove paint splatters from your eyeglasses. Rub lenses gently with a soft cloth dipped in soapy water. If you have glass lenses (not plastic, plastic coated, or other special coating), carefully apply acetone or mineral spirits with a soft cloth to remove paint. Then wash with soapy water, rinse, and dry.

FACIALS

Treat oily skin to a home facial. First, make a paste of dry oatmeal and water. Next, spread it on your face, being careful not to put it on the delicate eye area skin. Let the mask dry and then splash your face with warm water to remove it or remove it with a washcloth. After all of the paste is removed, splash a little cool water on your face for a delicious, refreshed feeling. Your face will feel clean and smooth.

FAMILY IDEAS

Make a newsletter for grandparents. Have children assemble family news in newspaper style—sports, editorial, world and local issues, and an advice column—and send a monthly family newspaper to their grandparents.

Keep the peace with a kitchen timer. For a very young child who dislikes naps, set the timer and leave it in the child's room to show when nap time is over. (Side benefit—the ticking lulls some children to sleep!) Kitchen timers are also useful as a way to limit teen phone conversations, especially if you set the timer to limit your own conversations to make the process seem fairer to the teen.

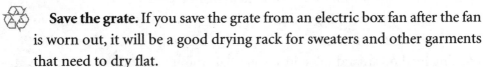

Letter of Laughter

Family Wake-Up Call

Tired of repeating children's wake-up calls on school days? One reader gives her children 5 minutes to get up after being called or she spray-mists them with a spritz water bottle. It took only a few spritzes, and now she has no problems.

FANS

Save the grate. If you save the grate from an electric box fan after the fan is worn out, it will be a good drying rack for sweaters and other garments that need to dry flat.

Use a ceiling fan. There's absolutely no question that ceiling fans make air-conditioning and heating units work more efficiently and economically. If you are installing a ceiling fan in a high hallway or in a room with a cathedral ceiling, a fan with a remote control can be more convenient, since you won't have to reach for different chains and pulls.

FAST FOOD

Keep the condiments. Buying fast food usually means extra plastic ware, ketchup, mustard, and salt and pepper packets. Instead of throwing the extras away, save them for picnics and camping. They take less space in your food basket than whole jars of condiments, and there's no mess either.

FAT

Minimize frying spatters. Place an inverted metal colander over a skillet. It lets steam escape and the meat brown without splattering fat all over the stove area for you to clean up.

Fry foods safely. If you need to turn the foods you're frying, minimize your risk of injury. Place one pancake turner on top and another on the bottom when you flip over fried patties, and you won't spatter grease by plopping the patty into the pan.

Reduce the cholesterol. If you substitute vegetable oil for butter or lard in recipes other than bread or baked desserts, you will need one-third less vegetable oil—for example, 2 teaspoons of vegetable oil sub for 1 tablespoon of solid shortening (1 tablespoon = 3 teaspoons). Corn oil stick margarine works also. And when you substitute 2 egg whites per egg in a recipe, you may also add 1 teaspoon of vegetable oil for each yolk omitted so that the recipe has a better texture.

Substitute the dairy. If you want to use low-fat or nonfat yogurt for sour cream in a recipe, your sauce may separate and get watery. To keep this from happening, stir some flour into the yogurt before cooking or, if possible, add it to dishes after removing them from the heat.

Consider other cooking methods. Simply put, frying meat adds fat to your diet. When you want to reduce the fat in your diet, try these other cooking methods that don't add substantial amounts of fat.

⊛ Roasting: Roast leaner beef and lamb on a rack in a roasting pan. When you cook in the oven by dry heat, the temperature of the meat should be between 135° to 140°F. Cook pork to 160°F, veal to 170°F, and whole chickens to 180°F.

⊛ Broiling/Barbecuing: Cook quickly and by direct heat in your range broiler or on a barbecue grill. Marinades add flavor and soaking meat in an acid solution tenderizes it. Make a marinade with a base of vinegar, wine, or lime juice, and your favorite herbs and spices.

- Poaching/Braising: In a nonstick pan, add a little oil and brown the meat. A regular pan, sprayed very lightly with cooking spray can also be used. Cover the meat and let it finish cooking in the simmering liquid until tender. This can be done on top of the range or in a medium oven.
- Stir-frying: Fry meat, which has been sliced thinly across the grain, uncovered in very little oil (or in a very small amount of bouillon if you want to avoid fat altogether).

FAUCETS

Raise the garden faucet. If leaning down to turn on the water is difficult for someone with a back problem or an elderly person, try raising the faucet to a more reachable height. Remove the faucet and put on an elbow fitting. Connect a 2-foot length of pipe to the fitting and then attach the faucet to the pipe. Be sure the pipe is attached to the house so that it doesn't break or pop loose if jarred. If you aren't handy, have a plumber do the job.

FAXES

 Create reusable cover sheets. In my office, we made one standard cover sheet for all fax transmissions. We put it into a clear plastic sleeve (the kind that lets you fax a cover sheet within it) and then write in all pertinent information with a dry erasable marker. When we finish transmitting, we erase the marker with a blackboard eraser and the cover sheet is ready for the next transmission. If several companies are using one fax machine, each can have its own logo on a master cover sheet and then just change cover sheets in the plastic sleeve for transmission. If you frequently fax information to one certain person or business, reuse the same cover sheet—just have several lines on which to write the date and subject of each fax.

FEATHERS

 Blow-dry the dust away. When ostrich or peacock feathers get too dusty for just a blowing with cool air from a hair dryer, gently swish them in cold water, then gently blow-dry them with a hair dryer set on low cool setting. Hold the dryer at a safe distance from each feather so it dries gently. Don't try to reshape the feathers with your hands. A gentle swishing when dry would be enough to bring back the natural shape.

FEET

Restore your aching feet. Pour baking soda into a pan, add warm water, and soak your feet. The bonus is that the soak softens rough skin. It also softens cuticles so that you can give yourself a pedicure.

Give yourself a foot massage. Put dry beans in your tennis shoes, and walk around to get a foot massage.

FELT

See STAINS for hints on how to remove finger marks from felt.

FIBERGLASS

 Clean tubs and showers surfaces gently. Fiberglass is easily scratched with harsh abrasives. If you don't have cleaners specially formulated for fiberglass (sold in places that sell tubs and shower stalls), or a cleaner recommended for fiberglass from the supermarket, you can clean this surface with baking soda. Apply with a damp cloth, rub and rinse off residue well. I've also found that cheap shampoo "degunks" soap film on fiberglass.

Readers say they get good results if they wax fiberglass tubs and showers with car or boat wax. Clean with a nonabrasive cleaner, and apply wax to the walls and sides. Buff the fiberglass with an electric buffer for a super shine.

Caution: Never wax the shower floor or tub bottom. It makes them too slippery for safety.

FILES

Make your own filing cabinets. Buy plastic milk-type crates in colors you like, then insert hanging files. The crates can be stacked easily and are lightweight if you need to carry them around.

Identify important papers. To avoid having to unfold each document to see what it is, fold papers so that the letterheads face out. You can just thumb through the files in a hurry.

FILM

Make identification in a snap. To prevent loss when having film developed, print your name and address on letter-size paper and take a picture of it when you start a new roll. If you are traveling, take a picture of a sign printed with the city's (or other location's) name so that you can identify your photos when you get home if your memory is fuzzy.

 Reuse the 35 mm film canisters. Don't pitch 'em. They can hold jewelry when you're at the gym, address labels and stamps, children's jacks, marbles, lunch money, coins for the laundromat, sewing supplies at work or travel, styling gel in travel kit, and so on.

For more uses for film canisters, see LUNCH.

FINGERNAILS AND FINGERNAIL POLISH

Mend broken or split nails easily. A drop of instant glue will repair a split. For a bad tear or split, strengthen it by gluing on small torn bits of white tissue paper. Simply glue a small piece of torn tissue (facial or toilet tissue or newspaper border, if you have no wrapping tissue) over the tear, then cover it with a larger piece. After the glue dries, gently file the paper with the smoothest side of an emery board. Add several coats of clear nail polish to smooth and, if you wish, colored polish to cover. This mend will last long enough for a bad tear to grow out and save you a lot of finger pain!

Use an "emergency" fingernail file. When a fingernail breaks and you don't have an emery board or file to smooth the rough edge, try the striking edge of a matchbook. One reader discovered this hint when she assumed that if the striking edge was rough enough to ignite a match it could file a fingernail—creative thinking!

Keep the polish from spilling. Put a droplet of polish on a scrap of heavy paper or piece of cardboard, then place the bottom of the bottle over it. The bottle will adhere to the paper and tipping is almost impossible. When you are finished with your nails, either remove the bottle from the paper with a drop or so of polish remover or leave it stuck for the next time.

Make the bottle easier to open. Wind a rubber band around the bottle top to get a better grip on it.

Other Uses for Fingernail Polish

Mark the following items with red or any other vivid color.

- ♥ Levels for measuring amounts in cups or buckets
- ♥ The start of the washer's rinse cycle on the dial
- ♥ The VCR stop (or other) button that's hard to find
- ♥ A light switch that's supposed to be left on
- ♥ The line-up arrows on child-proof medicine bottles
- ♥ Dab different colors (like white pearl and red) on the "On" and "Off" switches of the remote TV control to ID them without glasses

Use clear nail polish to make the following quick repairs.

- ♥ Stop runs in stockings—an all-time favorite repair (I carry clear polish in my travel kit for this purpose.)
- ♥ Glue the thread tail on a machine-sewn button so it won't pop off
- ♥ Spread some polish around the caps of cologne when you travel, replace the caps, and they'll stay firmly in place—no leaks
- ♥ Mend small holes in a window or door screen
- ♥ Mend a little hole in a window by building up a few layers of polish
- ♥ Paint on jewelry to keep it from tarnishing where it touches your skin

Thin your polish. Add a few drops of enamel solvent (found in drugstores) to dilute thickened nail polish. Nail-polish remover will thin polish but it contains oil and fragrance and so is not recommended. Avoid the problem of buildup, which prevents a tight seal and allows air to dry out the polish, by wiping the neck of the bottle with nail-polish remover on a tissue or cotton ball.

Reuse the bottle. After cleaning thoroughly with polish remover, fill an empty nail polish bottle with white latex paint to make a little touch-up bottle handy when you need to cover nicks in the wall or correct mistakes in your checkbook register. (Latex paint can be homemade correction fluid.)

Make a travel-size polish remover kit. Insert a small piece of sponge into a small, plastic trial-size bottle and add just enough fingernail-polish remover to be absorbed by the sponge. Then when you need to remove polish, dip a finger into the container. There's no damage from leaky containers and the smaller one takes up less space.

Keep your fingernails clean. If you dig your fingernails into a bar of soap before starting messy chores like potting plants, the dirt will wash right off when you wash your hands.

Don't let them yellow. Nail polish can stain fingernails yellow. The trick is to apply a base coat of clear polish before adding color. To remove yellow, put your fingernails in a cut lemon half for a few minutes. Cleaning things with baking soda also bleaches fingernails white, but it may dry some people's skin and nails, so apply hand lotion after cleaning sessions.

Strengthen your nails. To make fingernails strong, apply white iodine (from drugstores) every day for 7 days and then once weekly. Don't overdo it, or your nails will become brittle. You can polish nails over the iodine. The following hints help you save wear and tear on your fingernails.

- Pry up the tabs of soft drink cans with the plastic fasteners from bread bags instead of fingernails.
- Clip a steel wool pad with a spring clothespin when scrubbing.
- Wear rubber gloves to protect hands from cleaning solutions. Reinforce new gloves at the fingertips by inserting tips cut from old gloves.

FINGER PAINTS

Make your own nontoxic formula. Mix ½ cup of cornstarch with 2 cups of cold water in a saucepan. Bring the mixture to boil and continue to boil until it thickens. Let cool slightly. Pour equal amounts into clean baby-food jars and color each with food coloring.

FIRE DRILLS

See EMERGENCIES.

FIREPLACES

Winterize wisely. Have your fireplace inspected by a professional chimney sweep and arrange for cleaning if needed. If you seldom use your fireplace, it may not need annual cleaning, but frequent use may cause more creosote buildup inside, which can ignite and cause fires. If you have a fireplace insert, which is basically a wood stove fitted into a fireplace opening, the fans and blowers should also be serviced by a professional chimney sweep. Older models need to be checked to make sure they meet current safety standards.

Make energy-wise modifications. Despite expensive modifications (fireplace inserts can cost hundreds of dollars, depending upon accessories), fireplaces are not considered to be efficient heaters by any of the experts on this subject. About 90 percent of the heat generated by a fireplace goes up the chimney.

Glass doors and inserts may not prevent this heat loss, but they do prevent embers from popping out and starting fires. If you have glass doors, keeping them closed during burning allows for more air control for combustion, but cuts your fire's radiant heat output in half.

You might consider having a fan-driven heat exchanger system. This can be built in or added to your fireplace to enable the fire to warm the room's air instead of merely radiating heat on objects in the room. Or, perhaps an insert would be more right for you. Basically they are wood stoves designed to fit into fireplace openings, and they can significantly improve heating efficiency and still retain some of the ambiance. These either fit into the fireplace or protrude onto the hearth. Protruding inserts are more efficient. A well-fitted fireplace insert also limits the amount of warm room air that goes up the chimney and the amount of air in the combustion chamber.

Don't forget to decorate in the summer. Place several large candles in your fireplace and light them for a cheery glow instead of a dark, yawning hole.

 Remove fireplace ashes efficiently. Take a tip from barbecuing. Line the bottom of the fireplace with heavy-duty aluminum foil so that the foil covers the bottom and extends a couple of inches up the sides. Then you can just roll the ashes up in the foil and pitch the whole mess.

Remove smoke and soot from regular bricks. An art "kneaded" eraser, sold at art supply stores, lifts smoke and soot stains from some porous surfaces such as brick and stone. Knead the eraser until it's pliable, then press it against the smoke-covered bricks. When the eraser becomes soiled, knead it again, and continue until the bricks are clean. Repeat the procedure until the eraser has removed the stains.

When a fireplace is surrounded by smoother brick or stone surfaces, a kneaded eraser may not work well to remove all of the stain. After cleaning with the eraser, you may need to wash the brick with a solution of ½ cup of trisodium phosphate (sold in hardware stores) to 1 gallon of water.

Caution: Always wear heavy-duty rubber gloves to protect your skin when cleaning with strong solutions such as trisodium phosphate, and follow the box directions exactly.

 Clean soot and smoke from white bricks. Before you begin, cover the floor and hearth to protect them from bleach, wear gloves, and make sure the room is well-ventilated. Next, mix equal parts of bleach and water, and put into a spray bottle. Spray bricks with the mixture, and scrub gently with a soft-bristled brush to remove soot and smoke stains. Rinse with plain water.

Burn the right woods. Don't burn heavily oiled papers or chemically treated wood products such as railroad ties or outdoor lumber. Dangerous toxins can be released into the air when these materials are burned.

Make your own starter logs. Roll newspapers tightly, and fit them into empty cardboard paper towel tubes.

FIRST AID

Keep a well-stocked kit. For camper or boat, put the following in a fishing tackle or old lunch box: different sizes of adhesive bandages, gauze, medical tape, elastic bandage, antiseptic, rubbing alcohol, cotton, swabs, tweezers, ointments, sunburn pain reliever, sun block, small scissors, eye drops, special items needed by family members, a current first-aid book, a snake bite kit (from camping supply stores) if you are going to the wilderness, and an emergency ice pack (the kind that activate by tapping them on a hard surface). Then tape some quarters to the lid so that you have change for emergency phone calls.

Store supplies in the same box. Keep the tube of antibiotic ointment in the box with the adhesive bandages.

FISH

Although fish don't require walking, litter changing, or regular trips to the vet for inoculations, they do require care and attention. Saltwater aquariums require even more attention than freshwater ones.

Whether or not hand-feeding many saltwater tank inhabitants, such as invertebrates (sea urchins and anemones), is fun or a chore for you is one factor to consider when you are choosing between saltwater and freshwater aquariums. The other is that saltwater aquariums require frequent testing to maintain the proper pH and salt concentration in the water, and the inhabitants are more sensitive to temperature changes. If you just want to watch fish swim, you may prefer a freshwater tank. But the biggest thing to keep in mind is that an aquarium is a community of fish that functions best if the community is planned.

Setting Up a New Aquarium Community

Season the water. If you are starting up a new saltwater tank, be aware that the water has to be seasoned for several days before you put any living creatures into it. Use your test kit to see if the pH and the salt content are suitable for fish. You will put invertebrates such as sea urchins, anemones, crabs, and starfish into the tank first, wait several days or weeks for the water to be seasoned again, and then add vertebrates—the actual finny fish.

Remember, you're planning a "jungle." First off, plan on buying fish of similar size and maturity to keep them from becoming each other's dinner. You should also select fish according to their natural characteristics. For example, although they eat their own young, peaceful platy will be compatible with other live-bearers and Mexican tetras. Tetras and barbels like to live in schools, so buy three to five of them at one time. The common angelfish we see in fish stores will live in pairs and with other peaceful species but need to have the cover of seaweed to swim in. However, regal angelfish are very aggressive and territorial; you can have only one in a large tank with other similarly sized fish. A lionfish can be kept in a tank only with fish its own size or larger; it will corner smaller fish and eat them. Tiger fish are so aggressive that they can be kept only with their own species. And so on. . . .

Consider fish at every level. Choose the fish according to the aquarium level at which they prefer to live. Observe the fish in the store tanks and get advice from someone knowledgeable. For example, catfish breeds tend to live and feed at the bottom, tetras swim around in schools near the top, and angelfish and gouramies tend to stay around the middle of the aquarium. When fish have their own territories, they are more likely to leave each other alone.

Give them temporary amnesia. When you add new fish to an established aquarium community, disorient the "home" fish so that they "forget" which part of the tank they've claimed as their territories. Do this by rearranging the foliage, shells, ceramics, or other tank decorations at the same time that you add the new fish. All the fish will then have a chance to stake out their squatter's rights as if it were a new tank, and you'll have fewer fish fights.

Use a holding tank. Prevent introducing fish diseases into your aquarium by having a holding tank for new fish. Quarantine new fish for about a month before putting them in with the rest unless you deal with an aquarium store that quarantines fish before selling them. Sometimes, they'll have holding tanks in a back room if they quarantine new fish.

Let them adjust. If your aquarium store has already quarantined the fish, you can add them to the tank from their plastic bags, but don't just dump the fish in, whether it's into the main or holding tank. Allow the bagged fish to float in the tank for about 15 to 20 minutes so that the new fish can become acclimated to your tank's temperature. After the waiting time, open the bag while it's still in the tank and allow the fish to swim into its new home.

See also AQUARIUMS.

Keeping Fish Nourished

Know the symptoms of poorly fed fish. Fish suffering from dietary deficiencies can lose weight, have cloudy eyes, pale color, scoliosis (twisted spine), or a bloated appearance known as ascites. Although dried commercial fish foods are made to be nutritionally balanced, they can lose their nutrients during processing or while sitting on the shelf.

Boost your fish feedings. Make this homemade supplement and give it to your fish once or twice a week. Mix 9 parts of minced, partially cooked beef liver with 1 part of commercial food, plus 400 mg vitamin C, in a blender, and process until combined. This mixture can be frozen for future use.

Inspire a feeding frenzy. When you buy fresh shrimp, save a few raw pieces for your fish. Cut finely and drop the pieces into the tank, but feed only the amount that can be totally consumed in 5 minutes. You can buy a fish feeder that holds individual pieces of shrimp or other fish food and lets you hand-feed invertebrates like anemones or sea urchins. Freeze the leftover shrimp for future fish treats.

Uneaten food can spoil and pollute the tank; that's why you should feed only the amount your fish will consume in a single feeding frenzy, which usually lasts 5 to 10 minutes. Also, feed enough food so that the top and bottom feeders get their share.

Rely on a no-mess food sprinkler. Transfer small amounts of fish food (small flakes or grains) into a shaker-topped spice jar so that food can be sprinkled in. It helps avoid spilled containers of fish food when children are in charge of their own aquarium.

FLASH CARDS

Make math flash cards in a flash. Remove the face cards from a deck of new playing cards or one that has some cards missing or marked. To "play" math, shuffle the cards. Then, deal two cards face up and ask your child to add or subtract the numbers. These homemade flash cards also work for multiplication and division of small numbers. The math game can be played in an airplane, too. Ask the flight attendant if cards are available, or bring your own.

FLASHLIGHT

Find it in the dark. Stick on a strip of glow-in-the-dark tape (or paint a stripe with glow paint from a craft store) around the flashlight head, then you'll be able to find it when the electricity is off.

Note: This is so very practical that it's amazing nobody thought of it sooner—obviously you are most likely to need a flashlight when it's too dark to find one!

FLEAS

In some parts of the country, flea season is torture for animals and humans. Animals can develop hot spots (irritated skin patches that are actually hot to the touch and that are rendered hairless by the animals' efforts to bite the fleas), and humans, too, suffer from itchy bites.

To give you an idea about the magnitude of the flea problem, consider this. One female flea can create 800 virtually indestructible eggs in her lifetime, and under good conditions 10 fleas can produce a quarter of a million new fleas within 30 days! To keep these numbers down, read on.

Extermination Strategies

Be persistent. You need to interrupt the flea cycle because fleas multiply so rapidly. Flea bombs and sprays work, but you need to use these chemicals every couple of weeks in the beginning to kill the flea eggs as well as the fleas. Otherwise the eggs hatch and you're back to square one! And please consider whether you want to spray these chemicals at all.

Don't forget the great outdoors. Treat your lawn at the same time as you treat your pet and your house; otherwise the fleas just come back into the house. Follow insecticide directions exactly and do not allow children or pets to walk on the lawn while the insecticide is wet or fresh. Pets, especially, will lick the insecticide from their paws and it could be toxic.

Consult the experts. Your best resources for ways to rid your home of fleas is your vet or your county extension agent.

Stick it to 'em. Fleas can jump as far as 12 inches or more in one leap and can accelerate 50 times faster than the space shuttle. You know that if you've ever tried to catch one! Wrap adhesive tape around your fingertips, sticky side out, to form a tape band for dabbing up the fleas when you see them. Fleas stick to the tape and won't be able to escape like they do when you try to capture them with your fingers only.

Make your own flea trap. Since fleas are attracted to heat, you can make a flea trap with a light-colored, shallow pan, and a 25-watt lamp, without shade. Every night for several weeks, fill the pan with soapy water and set it on the floor; position the lamp next to the pan so that the bulb is a foot or so above the water. (This should be the only source of light in the area.)

When the light is turned on, fleas will jump toward the heat and fall into the water. Rinse out the pan in the morning.

Prevention Strategies

Vacuum floors, rugs, and furniture at least weekly. Vacuuming is a great way to collect fleas and their eggs, being especially careful to vacuum in dark corners and crevices. Then throw out the bag!

Avoid skin irritations from too-potent flea collars. Let the collar air out for several days before putting it on your dog or cat. But air the collar where it's away from people and pets!

Try a flea dip. If you have a water-hating cat or a dog too large to dip for fleas and ticks, thoroughly wet the animal's coat, and then spray the dip (mixed in proportions according to directions) onto the pet with a spray bottle. It's better to let your pet dry naturally after being dipped since towel drying will remove some of the dip.

Avoid dry skin. Shampooing your dog more than every 10 to 14 days can dry out its skin. If your flea shampoo and dip aren't effective for the entire interval between bath and dip, you'll need to use sprays or powder in between shampoos.

Brush off the extra flea powder. If you have a cat or small dog that really resists being powdered or sprayed for fleas, powder or spray a bath towel and then wrap the animal in the towel, holding it wrapped for about 15 minutes so the chemicals can work their magic. It's also important to know that excessive amounts of flea powder in a pet's coat can be licked off and may make your pet ill. So brush off all excess flea powder within 30 minutes after it's applied to prevent your dog or cat from ingesting or inhaling the residue.

Don't use flea preparations formulated for dogs on cats. Cats groom themselves more than dogs do, and cat formulas take that into account when the chemical strengths are determined. Some preparations available from your veterinarian are safe for both dogs and cats. Be sure to get advice from your vet!

Don't combine prevention remedies. Flea and tick powders and sprays should never be combined with each other or with a flea collar because you may overdose your pet with these chemicals. This is especially true of small breed dogs. Please don't take a chance.

🌐 **Try a natural repellent.** Cedar shavings or pine needles will repel fleas from animal bedding and doghouses. Salt also repels fleas, so washing your dog's doghouse periodically with salt water is a good prevention.

Go green. Wash your pet and yourself with green soap. Fleas supposedly don't like the dye that turns soap green.

FLOORS

Nowadays, there are more types of flooring available that ever before. Vinyl flooring is usually referred to as "resilient flooring," in contrast to "hard-surface" flooring such as wood, stone, concrete, marble, terrazzo, and ceramic tile. Linoleum, asphalt, rubber, and cork floorings are no longer manufactured, but some people still have these materials in their homes. Most of these materials, except wood and cork, can be cleaned with water, mild detergent, or household cleaners. For more specific cleaning and care tips, read on.

Wood Floor Care

Keep them clean. The best thing you can do for wood floors is to sweep or dry mop as often as possible. The culprit is ground-in dirt so the more you sweep the floor, the better it will look. Generally speaking, water is wood's enemy and should not be used to clean wood floors unless the manufacturer's instructions say it's okay.

Try a spritz of spray wax. Zap your mop with a little spray wax before dusting wood floors and you'll keep them shiny-clean with only a few minutes of effort each day.

Caution: Don't let wax puddles accumulate on the floor. You'll have the equivalent of slippery and dangerous ice patches, which people won't see but that they will find the hard way—by falling on them.

Prevent scratches. When moving heavy furniture across uncarpeted areas, slip scraps of old carpeting, facedown, under all furniture legs.

Give them a fresh start. Very old and dull wood floors may need to be sanded and refinished. You can refinish them yourself. Many new, easy-to-use products are available at hardware stores.

Save your skin. Sanding floors by hand causes so much friction that you can get friction burns on your fingertips even through work gloves. Some people have even sanded the skin right off their hands. If you are determined to sand by hand, apply masking tape to your fingertips and wear gloves.

Remove slivers easily. If you get small slivers from steel wool or some types of soft wood in your fingers, instead of poking around in your skin with tweezers, try spreading a film of white school glue over the sliver areas. Let the glue dry, then peel it off. This method works eight out of ten times.

Don't wait to stain. Sanded wood should never set longer than 12 hours before you apply the stain or finish. Raw sanded wood absorbs moisture, which could affect the way it absorbs stain colors or the way the finish adheres to the wood.

Make a homemade buffer. You can hand buff a floor to a beautiful shine with a pad made by inserting a folded old bath towel into an old panty hose. The wax buffs to a shine faster than you'd think could be done by hand. The stocking will get snagged and you'll have to change it frequently, so gather up a bunch of old ones.

Prevent the need for floor fixes from furniture. Dancing chair legs (or actually chair feet) often mar hardwood floors. Try applying self-adhesive-backed moleskin to the bottoms of chair legs to help them glide smoothly across the floor without making marks.

If furniture feet have dented your floors, you may be able to fill the dents with clear nail polish or shellac. Since they are clear, the floor color will show through and the dents will be less noticeable. (Now remember, this is a Heloise homestyle hint, but it sure does work in a pinch and will alleviate some of the aggravation from staring at that dent day after day after day.)

Squeaky Floors

Consider the benefits. Whether or not you want to silence a squeaky hardwood floor probably is determined by the ages of your children. While the pitter-patter of little feet added to squeaky boards can drive a parent a

Four Quick Fixes for Floor Care Emergencies

Floors sure do put up with a lot. The hints that follow can help if yours has a major problem.

♥ Shoe heel scuff marks on resilient flooring can be removed by rubbing them with a pencil eraser.

♥ Crayon marks come off when rubbed with a damp rag containing toothpaste or silver polish.

♥ If you drop a raw egg on the floor and don't have an eager dog to clean it up for you, sprinkle the egg glob with salt, let it sit for 10 to 20 minutes, and then sweep it up with a broom.

♥ You can patch a gouge in resilient flooring if you grate a flooring scrap with a food grater, mix the grated flooring with clear nail polish, and then plug the gouge. This tip is not for dents, just gouges or holes.

bit balmy, such squeaks can be a parenting aid when you have older children. Many teens have inadvertently announced their late-night arrivals with squeaky floorboards.

Silence the squeaks. Try sprinkling talcum powder over the musical areas for a dry lubricant. Sweep the talc back and forth until it filters down between the cracks, and you'll probably get blessedly quiet floorboards.

Tack it down. If the squeaky wood floor is under tile or carpet, you might be able to eliminate the squeak without removing the floor covering. It's sometimes possible to reset loose boards by pounding the loose nails back into place. Place a block of scrap wood over the squeaky area to protect the flooring and then pound with a hammer.

Care of Vinyl Floors

Clean according to level of dirtiness. When floors are only slightly soiled, just sweep or vacuum, then damp-mop with a clean sponge mop and warm water, pressing hard enough to loosen surface dirt. When you wet-mop, attack small areas at a time, and be sure to rinse the mop frequently in the bucket of clean water; otherwise you are just smearing dirt around the floor instead of cleaning it up. Change the water when it's dirty, which may be several times for a large room.

Know when to use the tough stuff. Really dirty floors need to be washed with a no-rinse cleaner or a general-purpose liquid detergent. Flooring manufacturers warn against washing with soap, dishwashing liquid, or gritty powders or cleansers. Always follow the directions on the no-rinse cleaners. For most of them, you apply them with a sponge mop and just wipe them up.

Always rinse floors with clean water. Always make sure you follow this advice, even when the directions for the floor cleaner say you don't have to. Flooring manufacturers tell me that the reason no-wax floors get dull is that they are not rinsed properly after detergents and floor cleaners are used on them, or the incorrect floor cleaner is used on a no-wax floor. It's very important to check with the manufacturer of the no-wax floor that is in your home to be sure you're using the proper cleaning agent, if any agent is to be used at all on it.

Try a vinegar rinse. When your floor dries after rinsing and still has a dull film, try mopping again with a solution of one cup or so of white vinegar to a bucket of water. (Yes, I know, where there's Heloise and a bucket of water, there's a cup or so of vinegar. But, believe me, when it comes to shine, vinegar does it.)

Avoid yellowing. Buildup of soil between polish layers can cause white or light-colored vinyl floors to yellow. Removing all of the polish and starting over can help. Exposure to strong sunlight or being covered with a rug with a rubber backing or furniture also can yellow such floors. Sometimes, such yellowing is permanent.

Make do with a disposable dustpan. In a fix and don't have a dustpan when you're sweeping the floor? Just take a paper plate, cut it in half (and a really easy hint is to moisten the edge), set it on the floor, and there you go—a disposable dustpan.

STEP ▾ BY ▾ STEP
Floor Mopping Basics

When using the detergents recommended for your type of floor, prepare the bucket of detergent and water according to label instructions. Use two buckets, one for detergent solution and one for your rinse water. Scrub the floor as follows.

1. Dip the sponge mop into the detergent bucket.

2. Don't squeeze or wring the mop out before you spread the cleaning solution over a small area.

3. Wait for a minute for the detergent action to loosen the dirt. The detergent is supposed to work for you, not you for your detergent.

4. Scrub the area with the mop, and then wipe up the liquid.

5. Rinse well, being sure not to leave any detergent on the floor. Be sure to change the rinse water often.

Waxing 101

Know your products. Always read the directions on the wax container. Some products will specify that you have to remove all other finishes first, and you may not be up to that chore. Other products, such as paste waxes, may require machine buffing, and if you don't have a buffer, you'll have to rent one for waxing day. Above all, make sure you never use liquid wax made for vinyl flooring on wood floors. It tends to darken wood. Use paste wax or liquid waxes specifically for wood instead.

Remember: Out with the old before in with the new (wax). Before you put a new coat of wax on your linoleum or tile floors, you'll need to remove the old wax to get good results for your efforts.

Make your own floor wax. If you're all fired up to wax your floors and find out that you have no commercial wax, don't quit when you're on a roll.

You can "wax" some floors with a solution of 2 tablespoons of furniture polish and ½ cup of vinegar added to a bucket of warm water.

Get rid of sticky, tacky buildup. If a newly cleaned floor continues to be sticky or tacky after more than 20 or 30 minutes of drying, or if the polish layer powders, flakes, or scratches easily, it may be due to old polish that was not removed, cleaner residue not well rinsed off, too much polish, or not allowing enough time between polish applications. The solution is to clean the floor thoroughly, removing all polish, and then to reapply polish according to directions on the container.

Use your own tools. A long-handled paint roller can be used to apply wax to floors when you don't have an official waxer. Rollers work fast and reach under furniture for you.

FLOUR DUSTER

Place a brand-new powder puff in your flour canister. This is a handy way to dust baking pans. Or, keep flour in a large-holed sugar or salt shaker for dusting pans with flour.

FLOWERS AND FLOWER POTS

Cover dry arrangements. Here's an easy way to help keep dry arrangements from gathering dust when they're not being displayed. Take a piece of fabric (a remnant or one that matches the decor) and cut it a few inches longer and wider than the pot. Sew a casing along the top and bottom sides of the fabric. Insert string or elastic to ensure a snug fit. This won't work for a clay pot with real plants because water seeping through the clay can cause mold on the fabric.

Dry the filler. If you've received a fresh flower arrangement, after the fresh flowers wilt, remove the dried baby's breath and straw flowers used as "filler" and make them into your own arrangements of dried or silk flowers. (Look for seasonal sales on silk flowers at craft stores.)

Clean silk flowers and foliage. Silk-type flowers are usually made from nylon or polyester with plastic steams and can be washed in a basin with cool water and a few drops of mild detergent. Immerse flowers, gently swish around for a minute or so, rinse, and air dry. Most fabric flowers can be dusted with a blow-dryer on cold-air setting. Or, put ¼ cup of table salt in a brown paper bag and place the silk flowers stem up in the bag. Gather the top shut and shake well; they'll come out cleaner.

Dye carnations two colors. Popular when dyed in school colors, they're easy to do at home; it takes about 2 days. First, slit the stem in half lengthwise, about halfway. Then, using two containers, put a cup of warm water in each and add different food coloring to each one. Set the containers next to each other and put each half of the stem into each one. Leave them in water for 2 days. To dye a flower just one color, make a fresh cut at the bottom of the stem and place in a container of water to which food coloring has been added.

Make graveside flower arrangements. Fill a coffee can with sand for weight; cut several small slits in the plastic lid put it back on the can. Then, arrange silk or plastic flowers and artificial evergreens by putting the stems through the small slits in the lid. To finish, cover the can with foil and add a ribbon for color.

Keep cut flowers fresh. When you buy a bouquet, remove all leaves below the water level and cut off ¼ to ½ inch of the stem. Change the water every other day and recut the stems each time. Many of my readers say adding an aspirin or a teaspoon of sugar to the water prolongs the life of cut flowers.

And some say cut flowers stay fresh long if you put the arrangement in the refrigerator overnight when nobody is looking at them anyway.

Preserve flowers and leaves in wax. The quick-fix way to press leaves and flowers is between two sheets of waxed paper and seal with a hot iron. (Don't forget to put an old towel or cloth on the ironing board to keep the wax from getting melted into it.) Another method involves carefully melting paraffin wax, letting it cool slightly, and dipping each leaf or flower in it. (Hold it with tweezers or tongs to prevent burning your fingers). After dipping, lay the leaf or flower in the proper place directly on construction paper of a suitable color. No need to glue them, the wax sticks them to the paper.

Gather free seeds. If you have cut flowers that you like, dry the flowers and collect the seeds for spring planting. To get the seeds out easily, put the flowers in a large paper sack when they are partially dry. When they finish drying, shake the bag to get the seeds to fall to the bottom, pour the seeds into a clean dry jar, and save for planting. Remember to label the jar so you'll know which seeds are which.

Mix and match fresh and dried. Use dried flowers in flower arrangements to replace dead blooms or to replace dead flowers in planters. Attach dried flowers to a comb and wear in your hair or pin to your lapel or blouse. Scatter dried blossoms when setting your table to cover spots on your table linens or attach them to a fan for a wall decoration.

FOOD PROCESSORS

 Do all of your grinding and chopping in a single once-a-week session. If you do, you can cook creatively when you're short on time. Making your own bread crumbs and buying chunks of cheese rather than grated cheese saves money, too. To avoid lots of processor bowl washing, first chop bread crumbs, next grate hard cheeses such as Parmesan, then grate soft cheeses like Cheddar, and chop parsley and onions last. You can freeze the chopped ingredients, and they will still taste fresher than store-bought processed foods.

FOOD STORAGE AND SAFETY

Food costs too much to waste it by improper storage, but waste isn't the only reason you should store food properly. The Centers for Disease Control and Prevention (CDC) estimates that millions of people get bacterial infections each year that cause diarrhea, fever, and vomiting, and thousands die annually from common food poisoning. Most salmonella poisoning is traced to contaminated meat, poultry, eggs, or milk, but the bacteria can also be harbored in other foods that come in contact with contaminated water or foodstuff. For information on salmonella and other food poisoning, you can call the U.S. Department of Agriculture's hot line, at (800) 535-4555. Put your tax dollars to good use.

Generally, you should keep foods in cool, dry places, and avoid overloading your refrigerator, which prevents it from cooling food properly.

The temperature in the refrigerator should be 42° to 44°F in its warmest part and 40°F or less in its coldest part (other than the freezer).

Canned Foods

Store fruits and vegetables in cans for the short term. The U.S. Department of Agriculture says it's okay to leave leftover food in the can and store it in the refrigerator for a couple of days. However, don't store acidic foods (such as tomatoes) in cans because they may get a tinny taste. Don't buy dented, damaged, or bulging cans; you can get food poisoning.

Avoid the raw edges. Drop the lid removed from canned food into the can before disposing, and you won't cut yourself if you have to rummage through the trash to find a lost item.

Know the score. If you want to reduce sugar and salt in your diet, it's not a good idea to reduce the amounts in canning recipes because ingredients such as sugar, salt, lemon juice, and vinegar control spoilage. Instead look for newer recipes that allow less sugar and salt while still keeping home canning safe. To get the new recipes and methods, contact your county

---

QUICK REFERENCE

Canned Food: Old Recipes Updated

Older recipes may call for a specific size can, rather than an ounce or cup amount. Use this handy reference chart to measure accurately every time.

- ♥ No. 1 can = 10 to 12 ounces
- ♥ No. 300 can = 14 to 16 ounces
- ♥ No. 1½ or No. 303 can = 16 to 17 ounces
- ♥ No. 2 can = 1 pound, 4 ounces or 1 pint, 2 fluid ounces
- ♥ No. 2½ can = 1 pound, 12 ounces to 1 pound, 14 ounces
- ♥ No. 3 can = 3 pounds, 3 ounces or 1 quart, 14 fluid ounces
- ♥ No. 10 can = 6 pounds, 8 ounces to 7 pounds, 5 ounces

---

home economist. Look in the U.S. Government section of the phone book, under Agriculture Department.

Reduce the fat. If you are on a low-fat diet, keep unopened cans of soup or chili in the refrigerator. After the food is sufficiently chilled, you can easily skim off the congealed fat, then heat as usual. You'll never miss the fat, and the flavor will be as good as before.

Store in a cool, dry place. Canned goods should be kept in a dry, cool room with a temperature of about 70°F. Never store canned goods near steam pipes, furnaces, kitchen ranges, or in the garage because both freezing and too much heat will affect the quality of canned goods.

Know the limits. Nonacid canned foods are safe in the above conditions for 2 to 3 years, with some vegetables such as potatoes keeping as long as 5 years. Acid foods, such as tomatoes and fruits, are safe for about 18 months.

Examine the can. If you see rust or discoloration on a can at the seam or anywhere else or if a can bulges at either end, throw out the can without opening it and certainly without tasting it. Consider any discolored or off odor food to be spoiled and poisonous. Discard it and make sure children and pets can't get at it. Whenever you are in doubt about the age of canned foods, or if they even hint at being spoiled, it always makes sense to be cautious and throw them out. No amount of money saved is worth taking a chance of making yourself sick.

In fact, never taste-test any type of questionable food, whether it's canned, home-cooked, or even fresh from the market. Always throw out foods that you suspect may be spoiled. When in doubt, throw it out!

Dispose of spoiled or questionable foods carefully. Seal them in containers. If possible, flush spoiled foods down the disposal or toilet to keep them away from animals that might raid your garbage. To prevent garbage jamming in the pipe of your garbage disposal, be sure to always run lots of water when you turn it on. Let the water run a few seconds after turning it off to thoroughly flush out the pipes.

Cereals, Flour, and Grains

Use containers. When I buy raw cereals, flour, rice, and certain packaged foods, I put them into glass jars to prevent bug traffic from one food to the

(continued on page 192)

Storage Limits for Keeping Food

Wrap food airtight and always identify and date purchases. If foods are properly handled before purchase and stored in a cool, dark cabinet or the average, properly working refrigerator, the following times are the storage limits suggested by the U.S. Food and Drug Administration's *FDA Consumer,* various U.S. Department of Agriculture publications, and *Good Housekeeping* magazine.

Apples, cherries, and other fruits: Store without washing in a crisper or moisture-resistant wrap. Apples keep about 1 month; citrus fruits, 2 weeks; most other fruit, 5 days—except berries and cherries, which keep 3 days in crisper or moisture-proof wrapping, and pineapple, which keeps about 2 days. Canned and cooked fruits (in covered container) keep 1 week; unopened canned fruit keeps 1 year; dried fruit, 6 months.

Baby foods: Keep 2 to 3 days if covered in their original jar.

Bananas: Should not be refrigerated.

Beef, fresh: Variety meats such as heart and liver, 1 to 2 days in the refrigerator; ground beef, 1 to 2 days; chops and steaks, 3 to 5 days; sausages, 1 to 2 days; roasts, 3 to 5 days.

Bread: Commercially frozen, baked bread can be frozen for 3 months; for unbaked bread, check label.

Butter: In the refrigerator, 1 to 2 weeks; freeze 9 months.

Casseroles, stews: 3 to 4 days in the refrigerator; frozen cooked meat dishes, 2 to 3 months; and cooked pastry dishes, 4 to 6 months.

Cheeses: Opened cream cheese, 2 weeks; cottage cheese, 10 to 30 days; opened Swiss, brick, processed, 3 to 4 weeks.

Fish: Fresh fish and shellfish (all wrapped loosely) are best if kept only 24 hours in the refrigerator. Cooked fish and shellfish (covered or wrapped), canned fish and shellfish (opened, covered), 1 day.

Fruit juices: 3 to 4 days in covered container.

Gravy: Can be kept 1 to 2 days in the refrigerator and can be kept frozen up to 1 month.

Ice cream and sherbet: 1 month in the freezer.

Lettuce: Unwashed, head lettuce keeps 5 to 7 days in the refrigerator crisper; washed and drained, 3 to 5 days.

Mayonnaise and salad dressing: Unopened on the shelf, 2 to 3 months; in the refrigerator after opening, 6 to 8 weeks.

Meats: Generally, processed or cured meats (such as sliced ham) keep 1 week in the refrigerator, 1 to 2 months in freezer. Bacon and franks will keep 3 to 5 days in fridge; bacon keeps 1 month in the freezer; franks, 1 to 2 months. Ground meat (loosely wrapped) is best kept only 24 hours in the refrigerator. Lunch meats can be refrigerated 3 to 5 days. (Always look at the date on the package.)

Milk: Keeps about 5 days in the refrigerator. Cream that's in carton will keep 1 week; 1 week for evaporated milk (in opened can). (Always check the date on the carton when buying milk or cream.)

Pasta: Dried pasta has a shelf life of 2 years.

Peanut butter: Best kept refrigerated. Keeps 6 months unopened; 2 months after opening.

Pork: Fresh, 3 to 5 days for chops, 1 to 2 days for ground; 3 to 5 days for roasts. Frozen, 3 to 4 months for ground; 3 to 4 months for chops; 4 to 8 months for roasts.

Potatoes: Store in cool, dry place but not in the refrigerator.

Poultry: Refrigerate 2 to 3 days. A whole turkey will keep for 12 months, a whole chicken for 9 months, and chicken or turkey pieces for 6 months in the freezer.

Rice: White, up to 2 years if kept in a tightly closed container, in a cool, dry place; brown, 1 year.

Soup: Refrigerate for 1 to 2 days; freeze for 1 to 4 months.

Sugar: Granulated sugar keeps 2 years in a tightly closed container. Brown sugar keeps 4 months.

Vegetables: Store-bought frozen vegetables can be kept up to 8 months in the freezer; fresh vegetables, from 1 to 7 days in the refrigerator. Root vegetables (carrots, rutabagas, etc.) keep up to 2 weeks in the refrigerator.

other. I save the cooking instructions and put them into the jar or tape them on the outside. Gallon pickle jars are my favorites.

Freeze them first. If you put foods made from grain, especially flour and cornmeal, into the freezer for at least 7 days after bringing them home, any visible or invisible infestations will be destroyed and you won't have to share your groceries with uninvited crawling creature "guests."

Note: The FDA recommends storing cornmeal in the refrigerator, especially in the summer.

Frozen Foods

Select only the best. You need to have quality foods for freezing because what comes out will be no better than what you put into the freezer! It's like your computer instructor said, "Garbage in; garbage out!"

Work quickly. Control growth of bacteria, yeasts, and molds and stop the chemical action of enzymes; to do this, you need to handle, chill, and freeze foods as quickly and exactly as directed for each food.

Remove the moisture. To keep food from drying out and to preserve its nutritional value, packaging should be moisture and vapor proof. Rigid containers and plastic bags need airtight seals, and wrapped foods should be stored in extra-heavy aluminum foil. Use freezer tape around the edges of rigid container lids to ensure a seal. Squeeze air from bags before sealing. Always label containers with the name of the contents, the date of freezing, and, if you rent food lockers, include the locker number on the package.

Freeze fruits and vegetables quickly after packaging. Either put them in the freezer a few packs at a time as they are ready or keep packs in the fridge until all are ready. If you use a locker plant, transfer packs from your home freezer to the locker in an insulated box or bag.

Don't freeze too many items at one time. The heat given off by non-frozen foods can raise the freezer temperature. Try to place lukewarm products away from those already frozen to avoid heating up frozen products. (Many upright freezers have a special shelf designated for quick freezing nonfrozen foods; see the book that came with the appliance.)

Reevaluate refreezing. Fruits, vegetables, and meats that have not completely thawed, or those that have been thawed for a short time and have been refrigerated, can be refrozen, but they will have lost quality and flavor. Refrozen vegetables toughen. Refrozen fruits become soft and mushy, which makes them suitable for cooking but not for eating uncooked.

Low-acid foods like vegetables and meats spoil rapidly after thawing and reaching 45°F; it's not advisable to refreeze them. Acid foods, like most fruit and fruit products, are likely to ferment after thawing and reaching 45°F. Slight fermentation of acid foods may change and spoil flavor, but the food is not unsafe to eat.

Use thawed food immediately after thawing. Not all bacteria are killed by freezing; bacteria become active as food thaws so food not used after thawing will begin to lose its nutritional value and spoil. Foods that have reached temperatures of 40° or 45°F may be unsafe to eat as well as deteriorated in quality.

Safeguard against power failure. A filled freezer will stay frozen for about 2 days; a half-filled freezer may not stay frozen more than 1 day. Prevent spoilage by packing the freezer with dry ice. About 50 pounds of dry ice will hold the temperature below freezing in a 20-cubic-foot home freezer for 2 to 3 days if you act quickly after the power is lost.

Caution: Don't handle dry ice with bare hands; it burns.

Recommended Temperatures for Food Storage

The recommended temperatures for preserving raw foods are between 30° and 50°F, depending upon the product. (Most fruit should be stored at 32° to 35°F; fish should be iced and kept at the same temperature.)

After processing or cooking, foods should be cooled quickly to below 60°F. If you can't cool the food immediately, it must be kept at a temperature warmer than 140°F until it can be cooled.

Know your freezer temperatures. Make sure your freezer stays at 0°F. Fluctuating temperatures cause frozen foods to lose moisture at a faster rate than normal and result in their becoming rough and dry.

Note: You can always fill up the freezer with ice if you don't have it full of food. Use bagged ice from the supermarket or recycle clean plastic milk jugs; fill with water and keep frozen. The bonus with milk jugs (or 2-liter soda bottles): You can take them camping or on picnics to ice foods in your cooler; as the ice thaws, you have drinking water.

See also FREEZERS.

Spices

Store in a cool, dry place. Spices and most canned and packaged foods should never be stored above the stove. Because heat rises, the shelves above the stove are pretty warm when the stove is in use. If you have a gas stove with a pilot light, the heat will be constant. Spices especially will lose their flavor if stored near heat. Like other foods, color and odor changes indicate loss of quality. For best use, buy the smallest quantity.

The FDA and cooking experts say that keeping spices and herbs refrigerated or frozen is the best way to preserve flavor. The next-best way is in a cool, dry, dark cupboard, where most of us keep them.

Keep track of the age of spices. Mark the date of purchase on a strip of masking tape and stick it to the bottom of the container.

Store them yourself. If you grow your own herbs for drying or if you like to make your own spice mixtures, you can store them in clean, dry baby food jars. If you're short on cupboard space, nail or glue the jar lids to the underside of a shelf so that you can just unscrew the jars from their lids when you use spices.

Special-Care Foods

Take care with eggs. All uncooked or cooked foods containing eggs should be refrigerated at all times.

Chill creams, custards, and meringue pies. All cream-based foods and foods with custard fillings—including cakes, cream puffs, and éclairs—should not be kept at room temperature. Cool slightly and then refrigerate. If such foods are taken on picnics, keep them in a cooler.

Store salad dressings in the fridge. Salads and sandwiches made with salad dressings containing eggs or milk products and little vinegar or other acids also need refrigeration.

Give caviar special care. This extra-elegant treat needs special care because it is highly perishable. It should be removed from the refrigerator 15 minutes before eating, and the lid should be removed only at the last moment. Unopened, a container of fresh caviar may be stored in the refrigerator for up to 4 weeks. Serve caviar in its original container placed in a bed of ice. If the caviar is oversalted, serve it with chopped hard-cooked egg; if it is fishy, serve it with chopped onion; if it is somewhat sour, serve it with lemon juice.

See also OLIVE OIL.

FOOTBALL BIRTHDAY CAKE

See CAKES.

FORMAL DRESS

Go to the right lengths. Just like you read labels at the supermarket to avoid raising your cholesterol level, you read party invitations to avoid raising eyebrows. Invitations usually explain the dress expected for men—the dress expected for women is implied in the men's dress code. Different communities have different interpretations of "formal." If you're new in town, ask someone who knows. The following are general rules.

⊛ When men wear white tie and tails, women wear long or at least ankle-length dresses.

⊛ When men wear black-tie tuxes, the event is called "semiformal" and women can wear short, very dressy dresses. If the invitation specifies black-tie/cocktail, women can wear strapless dresses with or without beading and other glitter.

⊛ When men wear dark suits, women wear cocktail or dressy, dinner dresses. A dressy dinner dress is less revealing than a cocktail dress and looks right at a restaurant after the cocktail party.

✻ For dinner, theater, or the symphony in most communities, women wear less revealing dresses made from rich fabrics such as silk. Revealing strapless dresses are appropriate at black-tie events but not at restaurants or dinner parties in someone's home.

FRAGRANCES

Work around your allergies. One reader solved her problem of sneezing when wearing perfume or cologne by adding a drop or two of her favorite perfume to her bath along with a few drops of mineral oil. She's not bothered by the fragrance when it's diluted by bathwater and still enjoys a bit of the scent when it's left on her skin in the mineral oil, which also softens her skin.

Caution: Take care when adding any oil to the bath; it can make the tub bottom slippery.

FREEZERS

Defrost chest freezers quickly. Turn an all-day job into a 1-hour one. First, unplug the freezer and empty the food into newspaper-lined laundry baskets, cartons, or picnic coolers. Next, place several large buckets of very hot water inside the freezer and shut the lid. Change the water every 15 minutes. After a couple of changes, most of the ice and water will have dropped to the bottom. Use a wet/dry vacuum or bath towels to remove it. When clean, wipe up the residue, plug in the freezer, and load it up.

Caution: Always be careful using electrical appliances near water; never stand in a puddle. Make sure the vacuum is rated "wet." A regular vacuum won't work and is dangerous if used for this purpose.

Form your food into frozen squares. Save cake-mix boxes so that when you put food in a freezer bag, you can put the bag into the cake-mix box. It will freeze in a block that will take less space in the freezer than various lumpy-shaped frozen foods. Either label and date the bags before filling them or remove them from the box when frozen hard and then label and date them. You can reuse the boxes throughout your food-processing season.

Rely on freezer labels. Cut labels from foods and tape them to containers or packages when you freeze leftovers to make identification easier. For example, if you freeze spaghetti sauce, cut those words from the sauce jar label and tape to the container before freezing.

Monitor your freezer while on vacation. Place a small, clear bag of ice cubes in the top basket or shelf of your deep freeze when you go away. After you return, if you find the ice cubes melted and refrozen into one chunk, you'll know that your freezer has been off for a considerable amount of time and that it may not be safe to eat perishable foods. Also, fill up all empty spaces with bags of ice or frozen water in plastic jugs to help keep your freezer cold in case of power outages. This is a good idea anyway, because a full freezer uses less energy going on and off to maintain the right temperature.

Conserve space. Freeze soups and casseroles in freezer bags set inside of bread tins or square pans. They will be easier to stack and fit.

See also FOOD STORAGE AND SAFETY.

FRENCH BREAD

Transform your loaf. If not eaten the day it is baked, real French bread is nearly a brick the next day but wonderfully edible if you turn it into something else. Do what they do in New Orleans—make bread pudding. Or slice the bread, and then bake it until it's brown and hard. If you sprinkle the slices with your favorite grated cheese and then let the cheese melt for a few minutes in the oven, it becomes the perfect crispy bread slice to float in a bowl of any kind of soup.

Create some croutons. Bake cubes of French bread in a 275°F oven for

French Toast for Chocoholics

One reader mixes a bit of chocolate syrup with the egg coating for French toast and then drizzles a syrup of mixed maple and chocolate syrups on the cooked French toast before savoring it.

30 to 45 minutes or until golden brown and crunchy. For flavorful croutons, before baking drizzle them with the following spiced butter mixture. For ½ loaf of French bread, simmer together 1 stick of butter or margarine, 1 teaspoon of minced basil (fresh is best), and 2 cloves of minced garlic, while you cube the bread. Place the cubes in a roasting pan, drizzle the spiced butter mixture over the cubes, and bake as directed above. Store in a tightly sealed plastic container or jar.

Do as the French would do. Make French toast! Add a dash of vanilla to the batter to perk up the flavor and sprinkle with powdered sugar before serving. Or, for a quick breakfast or light supper, cut stale bread into cubes, mix with beaten eggs, and fry in a small amount of butter or margarine as you would French toast. Serve with or without syrup.

FRUIT

See PRODUCE.

FRUIT JUICES

See STAINS for hints on how to remove fruit juice stains from fabrics.

STEP ♥ BY ♥ STEP

Candied Fruit

No need to buy candied fruit. Here's how to make your own.

1. Wash and dice fruit peels to appropriate size. You can collect peels as you eat the fruit. Store them in the freezer until you have about four each of oranges, lemons, and grapefruit.

2. Slowly boil 2 cups of sugar, 1 cup of water, and ¼ cup of corn syrup over low heat for 30 minutes. Add peels and cook for 45 minutes to an hour. It's done when all the syrup is absorbed.

3. Sprinkle sugar on waxed paper, lay peels on it, and toss to distribute. Allow to dry for a couple of days. Keeps indefinitely in the refrigerator.

FRYING OIL

Improvise a temperature gauge. Drop a kernel of popcorn in the frying oil. If the popcorn pops, the oil is hot enough to begin frying the food.

FUNNEL

Fill your own spice jars. Cut one corner of an envelope to make a funnel for filling spice jars or creating designs with colored sugar on cakes.

FURNACES

See HEATING AND COOLING.

FURNITURE

To see a Cinderella develop from an Ugly Duckling is a very rewarding experience. You can find many new products on the market for deep cleaning and refinishing old, pre-owned (sounds better than "used") furniture nowadays, all of which save time and energy. You can also find excellent-quality unfinished furniture to stain in colors of your choice and blend in with furniture you already own.

Some people like to totally refinish antique or old pieces, but others feel that the antique value is destroyed when anything beyond cleaning and functional repairs are done. Whatever your preference, here are the tips to keep your furniture just the way you like it.

Dusting and Polishing Wood Furniture

Use a double-barreled approach. Dampen two old cotton gloves or socks with furniture polish, slip them on, and then dust with both hands.

Stock up on steel wool. Buy fine (0000) steel wool. Do not use any that is coarser; make sure the package has at least four zeroes. This will remove any residue that your cleaner leaves behind. Be careful to rub the wood very gently, with the grain, and only until the buildup is removed. Don't rub excessively or you will scratch the finish.

Forego the fingerprints. To avoid leaving fingerprints while polishing furniture, wear cotton gloves. They'll protect your hands from the polish, too. If you sprinkle a little cornstarch on furniture after you've polished it, and then rub it to a high gloss, you'll find that the cornstarch absorbs excess oil and leaves a glistening, fingerprint-free surface.

Wax and polish sparingly. The good news and excuse for not waxing and polishing too often is that using too much oil on furniture eventually darkens it because dirt and oil form a film on the surface. I once used a commercial furniture cleaner on a very old piece of furniture bought at an auction and was amazed to find very elaborate light fruitwood-colored veneer designs underneath what I thought was a plain, dark walnut finish.

Match the right product to the right finish. In all cases, when you are planning to wax or oil furniture, remember that the finish on the furniture determines which method you will use. Generally, high luster furniture needs a liquid polish or paste wax, which dries to high shine. Low luster or satin finish furniture needs a greaseless cream polish or wax that protects without shine. Natural oil-finished furniture needs to be reoiled with the type of oil originally used by the manufacturer (or boiled linseed oil). Most manufacturers say it's not good to switch back and forth with different products, using wax one time, oil the next, and some other polish later.

Furniture Polish

Aerosol sprays and chemicals in personal and home products cause air pollution inside our homes. The following polishes are inexpensive and safer. However, you should always test new polishes on an inconspicuous place.

Polish #1: Add 1 teaspoon of lemon oil to 2 cups of mineral oil for a lemon-scented oil polish.

Polish #2: Mix 1 teaspoon of olive oil with the juice of one lemon, 1 teaspoon of brandy or whiskey, and 1 teaspoon of water. This must be made fresh each time.

Polish #3: Mix 3 parts of olive oil with 1 part of white vinegar.

Make your own Heloise furniture polish. Here is the often-requested recipe. Mix together ⅓ cup of vinegar, ⅓ cup of turpentine, and ⅓ cup of boiled linseed oil. Moisten a soft cloth with polish and rub over furniture. Polish with a clean cloth.

Caution: Never attempt to boil linseed oil; it's highly flammable. Buy it at the hardware store. Also, always clearly label homemade cleaning compounds and keep them away from children and pets.

Refinishing Furniture

Renovate resourcefully. You may not need to refinish marred and scarred furniture. Instead, cover scratches with colored markers, shoe polish, the meat of a pecan or walnut, or commercially prepared lemon or boiled linseed oil. Or you can often renew a piece of furniture by cleaning it with mineral spirits (read container for directions and for surfaces it will not damage) or use my Heloise furniture polish above.

Evaluate the finish. To determine what type of finish your furniture has, dampen a cotton ball with nail-polish remover and rub it across a small, inconspicuous area, like the underside of a chair. If the finish gets gummy or sticky, it's either clear oil-base varnish, shellac, or lacquer. You can use liquid furniture refinisher to remove it.

If the finish remains intact with no damage, it's probably a plastic-resin base. It can be removed with paint remover.

Keep dust circulation to a minimum. Switch off the central heating system in your house before you begin refinishing and varnishing furniture indoors. However, you must always keep your workspace well-ventilated and with a constant temperature over 70°F. Cooler temperatures prevent finishes and glues from working properly.

Use thick gloves. Many furniture strippers and stains will dissolve ordinary rubber gloves; buy heavy-duty gloves to protect your skin and fingernails. Wear cloth work or garden gloves when sanding or steel-wooling raw wood to prevent putting your fingerprints on the wood. Oils in your skin can make marks that show up when you wipe on the stain.

Stain with secondhand socks. Old socks and cotton knit underwear make great wiping cloths for stain. Inside-out terry sports socks absorb well

Letter of Laughter

Furniture Polish

On some finishes, you can apply mayonnaise for a healthy-planet alternative to furniture touch-ups. Just rub it in, wipe it off, and buff with a clean cloth to touch up scratches or remove white areas caused by heat. But this may have unintended consequences. When one reader tried mayonnaise to polish a low wooden chest, she applied too much, so she left the room to get a cloth to wipe off the excess. When she returned, she found her big old tomcat purring happily as he licked it off. She says she sat on the floor and laughed while he finished his snack. So, evidently furniture polishing can be fun sometimes!

for wiping off stain, and fuzzy nylon men's crew socks make good applicators for some stains and sealers.

Repairing Furniture

Most of us can do simple repairs on most furniture ourselves. Really valuable antiques are best repaired by professionals. Check with a few of the best antiques stores in your town to find out where they send their work. Ask to see samples of repaired furniture before you release your valuable pieces to a repair shop. Agree beforehand what will be done—repairs, replacement of parts or hardware, reupholstery, refinishing wood, or just cleaning and polishing.

Iron out the dents. Small dents in wood furniture can be ironed out. Really, they can. If you have a dent (where wood fibers are not actually cut, just bent), set your electric iron on medium heat and get a damp cloth. Place the cloth on the dent, and then hold the iron on it until the cloth begins to dry. Repeat the process, redampening the cloth each time, until the dent is raised.

Eliminate the wobble. When your chair wobbles because one leg is shorter than the others, you can lengthen the short leg by molding a piece of wood putty in the shape of the chair leg tip. After the putty dries, sand and stain it to match the leg and glue it in place. No more wobble-rocking!

Stop drawers from sticking. When wooden drawers stick, you can make them glide better if you rub the contact surfaces with a bar of soap or an old candle stub. (Just remember that you've unstuck the drawer the next time you open it; otherwise, you'll pull with your usual "darn this stuck drawer" force and end up with everything dumped on the floor for an unplanned drawer-cleaning session.)

Tighten loose furniture leg casters. Wrap the caster stems with rubber bands before reinserting them.

Improve with a groove. When you are repairing furniture or putting together unassembled new items fitted with dowels, most of the glue gets pushed into the bottom of the hole and the rest of it squishes out of the rim when you insert the dowel into its hole.

This happens because the dowel is exactly the size of the hole, and the result is that the joint may not hold as well as it should. If you cut a few grooves into the dowel, the glue will distribute itself along the dowel surface into the grooves, and you'll get a better bond.

Prevent wicker furniture from getting wobbly. Lightly mist old wicker pieces with water, using a plant mister every now and then. You can tighten wobbly wicker furniture by washing it outdoors (or in the shower if it will fit) with hot, soapy water; then, rinse with a hose and let it air dry. The water treatment will shrink and tighten the wood and cane.

Keep track of the parts. If you need to dismantle a piece of furniture to repair it, number or label the parts with strips of masking tape so that you can put them all together again. Use this tip for furniture that disassembles for moving. It's hard enough to get your life back in order when you move without adding extra confusion to the chaos.

Turn to tiles. You can cover the damaged top of a dresser, buffet, or coffee table with tiles. Look for tile kits in craft or hardware stores.

Make furniture booties. Basement furniture and storage cabinet "feet" can get damp and even wet if storms cause water on the floor. Putting on plastic cap "booties" keeps them dry and prevents rust stains on the floor from metal furniture or feet with metal "buttons" on them.

Cleaning Upholstered Furniture

Uphold the code. Upholstered furniture sold after 1970 usually has a letter code on its tag that tells which cleaning or spot-removal methods are safe for the fabric. The code is as follows.

- ❀ W: Use water and cleaning agents or foam mixed with water.
- ❀ S: Use no water. Use dry-cleaning solvents.
- ❀ W-S: Use either water-based or dry-cleaning solvents.
- ❀ X: Don't use liquid or foam cleaning agents. Soil can be removed by brushing or vacuuming only.

Lather the leather. Upholstered leather furniture should never be cleaned with oils or furniture polishes; these may make the leather sticky. Clean leather chairs or tabletops by rubbing with a lather of warm water and castile or saddle soap. Wipe with a clean cloth and buff dry with a soft cloth.

Wipe down vinyl furniture. Clean vinyl furniture with a solution of warm water and mild detergent. Rub to loosen soil, rinse, and then dry with a towel. Commercial vinyl cleaners are available and best used for greasy or stubborn stains. Vinyl fabrics can be waxed with milk paste wax such as automobile wax.

Remove the ink. The most-often-asked-about stain to remove from vinyl or leather furniture is ballpoint pen ink. Simply dip a cotton swab in a little rubbing alcohol, then gently dab at the stain. Some people use hair spray on the cotton swab, but you must be careful because that does leave lacquer. After removing the ballpoint ink, wipe with a damp sponge, and recondition the leather or vinyl.

Troubleshooting

Remove the rings. Most water rings on wood tables can be removed easily if you get to them right away. Immediately moisten a cloth, dip it into cigar ashes (some people claim cigarette ashes work well, too), and rub the milky spot gently. You can also mix mayonnaise or vegetable oil in with the ashes. If no one in your house is a smoker (and we sincerely hope they aren't), using mayonnaise or vegetable oil and a dry cloth first just might do the trick.

Alternately, you can try this homestyle treatment: Rub the spot with equal parts of nongel toothpaste and baking soda, applied with a soft, damp cloth. Rinse out the cloth and wipe off any residue. When the finish is smooth, buff with a clean soft cloth. Restore color and shine by rubbing the spot with the meat of half a pecan, then buff.

Use some shoe polish. Paste shoe polish covers small scratches, marks, or discolorations on furniture, cabinets, or wood paneling. Use dark brown on dark wood or tan on lighter wood. It works like magic and leaves a nice glow.

Remove paper that's stuck to a polished table. Saturate the paper with cooking oil, let it sit awhile, and peel it right off.

Touch up black-painted metal. Buying office furniture at an office supply store "scratch-and-dent" sale is a real bargain. Cover scratches on black-painted metal file cabinets, bookcases, or desks with permanent wide felt-tip marker. Apply wax over the marker to finish.

See also WICKER.

FURS

Never store furs in plastic bags. Believe it or not, furs need to "breathe." Instead, make a protective cover from an old sheet or place a king-size pillowcase over the garment. You'll need about a 3-inch deep or wide shoulder cover to keep dust off without crushing the fur.

GARAGES

Garages tend to get dumped in, and stuff just accumulates in them. In climates where people don't have basements, garages serve as combination basement/garage/storage areas, and you really can get an accumulation of jumbled-up "junque." ("Junque" is plain old junk that you don't admit to being junk.) If this image describes your garage, read on to find the solution that's right for your situation.

Doors and Windows

Seal the surfaces. An unpainted garage door can swell and warp and then be hard to open. Let the door dry out when you have dry weather for a few days, and then paint all surfaces, including the edges, to seal the wood so that it won't absorb moisture.

Know when to unplug an automatic door. If you have an automatic garage door opener, you may find that your garage door mysteriously opens and closes when you haven't meant it to. It's possible that someone else has an opener set on the same frequency as yours. If you can't reset the frequency or have it done by the company that installed the door, unplug the opener mechanism when you are at home (especially at night) or when you are on vacation to keep your garage door closed.

Perform regular maintenance. Have all garage doors checked, adjusted, and reset each year. The clutch can stick if not reversed often or not used for long periods of time. Doors can shift during the years and get out of line. To check to make sure that your garage door reverses immediately, put something solid (such as a two-by-four) under the door that will stop it. When the door touches the item, it should lift up immediately. If you have any doubt about your unit, get a garage door company to inspect and adjust the lift mechanism.

Secure the windows. If you don't want to put old curtains or draperies on your garage door windows, you can buy window-frosting paint or apply frosted adhesive-backed plastic for privacy.

Hint: To apply plastic, hold a piece of the adhesive-backed plastic up to one of the panes and cut it with a razor for a perfect fit. Remove the backing and apply carefully, smoothing out wrinkles. If you get a small bubble, let the air out with a tiny pinprick and press down.

Greasy Garage Floors

Collect the leaks. Grease and oil spots are unsightly in a garage, but the real problem is that people step in them and bring the gunk into the house. An old cookie sheet or cake pan filled with cat litter or sand placed at the drip site will collect leaking grease or oil. If you don't have cat litter or sand handy, use a piece of corrugated cardboard cut to fit inside the cookie sheet and change it as necessary.

For a disposable drip pad, staple heavy-duty aluminum foil to a piece of corrugated cardboard. And then there's the obvious solution. Get the car fixed so you won't have to deal with leaks.

Clean up oil and grease spots. Apply paint thinner to the spots, then cover them with cat litter, dry cement, sand, baking soda, or cornmeal, and let the absorbent remain on the spot overnight. Sweep up the absorbent material and repeat the process if you have to until you've got a clean-enough garage floor.

Use a stain-removing solution. If the absorbents don't work, try dousing the spot with full-strength bleach and wiping up the excess with rags or paper towels.

Caution: Wear protective gloves when you're using bleach or other strong chemicals.

Camouflage. If you still can't get rid of the stain and it bothers you, paint a wide black stripe the width of the space between your car tires and use the stripe as a centering aid.

Safe Parking

Make a focal point. Paint bright or luminous stripes or stick reflector tape on the rear garage wall to help you aim the car down the center.

Identify the object in your way. Stick reflector tape on anything that seems to be in your way at night if you don't have good lighting in the garage.

Know when you should stop. Hang a ball on a string from the garage ceiling so that it touches the windshield at about eye level when you have the car in the right place. If you hang the ball in the center of your parking space, you can use it for a centering guide as well as a stop sign. Bright colors and a piece of reflector tape will help you see your guide.

Protect with padding. Old inner tubes cut in pieces can be used to pad anything that you tend to brush against with your car or touch when you open the car door, such as support studs, framing, or even the nearest walls. Other padding materials include carpet scraps, old rubber mats, and foam rubber. If you like to back into the garage, an old tire hung at bumper height can be a wall-protecting, dent-preventing stopper.

Storage

Build storage shelves on side and back walls. If you're handy, you can use up all that air space in the top half of your garage by building storage shelves on side and back walls. If you're not handy, peg boards and ready-made shelving are for you. If you're not afraid that your family will over-load them, you can install deep shelves in the back end of the garage so that your car hood will be under them.

Save floor space. Hang garden tools, sports gear, bikes (on special heavy-duty hooks for that purpose), or anything else that will hang up.

Garage Sales

First, consider asking neighbors and friends if they want to join you; sales advertised as "several families" or "neighborhood" attract more buyers. Then follow these steps to a successful sale.

1. Check with your city to learn if there are any garage sale restrictions in your area and if you need to get a permit.

2. Advertise in local newspapers, noting several of the best or most unusual items for sale in the ad.

3. Separate clothing by size and hang it up for easy pickings.

4. Mark prices on each item so that people don't have to ask.

5. Price items objectively and reasonably. If several families are participating in the sale, use colored stick-on tags with a different color for each family. Then as you sell an item, remove the tag and stick it in a notebook; each family will know exactly how much it has earned.

6. Place large eye-catching items on the lawn or in the driveway to attract customers.

7. Have boxes, newspaper, and bags to package sold items.

8. Be ready for the "early birds" who show up an hour or two early to get the best bargains.

9. Keep someone at the money box at all times, and arrange the tables so that buyers have to pass the "checkout" to get out. Of course, never leave the cash unattended.

10. Don't accept personal checks unless you know the buyer. Also, have plenty of change ready at the beginning of the sale. You can separate coins in muffin tins.

11. Since the object of the sale is to get rid of the stuff, be ready to bargain with buyers. There's no money at all if you give or throw away the items, so why not give discounts?

12. Donate leftover items to a charity.

Lay a platform or shelving across ceiling joists. This is a quick way to store seldom-used or seasonal items, such as storm windows and screens.

Take a tip from your city's parking lots. Paint parking area lines on the garage floor to designate spaces for bikes, the lawn mower, or other large objects, so that these targets have their own spaces. If they're within their parking spaces, you'll be less likely to hit them with the car when you're pulling into the garage. (Isn't it annoying to have to get out of the car to move a bike or lawn mower a couple of inches so that you can drive in?)

GARBAGE DISPOSALS

Rely on water. Always run lots of water while using a garbage disposal and for a few seconds after use. This is the most important instruction for using a disposal. My husband, who is a plumbing contractor, has told me that if the garbage disposal ever backs up, it's my fault because I always forget to run a lot of extra water. If you don't run enough water when using your disposal, food waste will back up into the disposal and damage the unit, not to mention clog the plumbing. One other tip to live by: Never use drain cleaners in the disposal because they may damage it.

Distinguish it from the light switch. Is there anyone who has not switched on the disposal and got startling noise instead of the light you expected? Mark the disposal switch with red nail polish, a stick-on frown face, a red stick-on dot, or colored tape—anything to avoid the grating shock!

Unjam a jammed garbage disposal. Look carefully at the disposal. There's usually a red restart button. Press it and then turn the garbage disposal on. Many times this will do the trick. You may have to try this once or twice. If this does not work, place a broom handle or a very sturdy stick into the disposal and turn it counterclockwise to try to unjam the motor. Pull the stick out, run water, flip the switch, and see if that does it.

Feed it vinegar ice. Fill an ice tray with water mixed with ½ cup of white vinegar; then freeze. (Don't use that tray for your drinks; mark it.) Put the vinegared ice cubes down the garbage disposal about once a week; they will freshen it and clean the disposal and blades as well.

Caution: Be sure your disposal is of a good, sturdy quality if you do this. The less expensive brands may not be capable of chopping up the ice cubes.

Grind orange and lemon rinds to get rid of odors. This strategy is a real time-saver because you were probably going to grind them up to get rid of them anyway!

Check the garbage disposal gasket. This is the rubber piece that fits in the drain hole. If you can remove it, take it out and clean it thoroughly. If you can't remove it, put on rubber gloves, be sure the disposal has no chance of being turned on (unplug it to be sure!), stick your hand down the disposal, and scrub underneath. That will help eliminate a lot of the bad odor.

Chuck the stringy stuff. If you add other foods when you are grinding up tough, stringy stuff, you won't be as likely to get a garbage jam in the disposal. However, under no circumstances should you put artichoke leaves, asparagus, or very stringy vegetables or food down the garbage disposal. You're only asking for trouble.

Perform a fill and flush. Occasionally, flush the disposal drain by filling up your sink with water and then draining the sink with the disposal running. The volume of water should help whirl away grime.

Clean the cleaning machine. If your dishwasher drains through your garbage disposal, flip the unit on when hot soapy water is running through it so it gets a good cleaning.

Steer clear for safety's sake. Never position your head directly over the disposal when you turn it on. If a knife or spoon or any utensil has fallen into the disposal without your knowledge, turning the disposal on could turn the utensil into a dangerous projectile when the disposal force shoots it out of the opening. Also, never put your hand or any nongrindable object down the disposal while it is running. Keep the cover on it at all times until ready to use.

GARDENS

Make a plan. Start small by first planning the area in which you spend the most time, then gather information about your yard before you go to your local nursery to get advice and buy bedding plants or shrubs. Make sure you ask about plants native to your area; they will thrive with less effort than "imports."

(continued on page 214)

Winterize Wisely

Here are the basics for preparing your lawn and garden for a care-free winter. Because growing conditions vary so much across the nation, you should also find out about winterizing trees and shrubs in your climate from your Cooperative Extension Agent (county agent), local gardening columns, and local garden centers.

Manage with mulches. In cold climates, mulches of straw, salt hay, evergreen boughs, pine needles, and nonpacking leaves prevent the alternating freezing and thawing of the soil. In warm climates, mulches prevent soil from drying and crusting and keep it cool during hot weather. Before layering mulch on your garden beds, remove dead or diseased plants to ensure a healthy start in the spring.

Plan for low-maintenance evergreens. These hardy trees and shrubs grow in almost every state, but evergreens aren't just another pretty plant. Placed strategically, they can be windbreaks, privacy screens, hedges, background plants, and foundation plantings. Plant evergreens adapted to your local climate so that you don't need to wrap them for protection against winter winds and freezing temperatures. You'll continue to enjoy seeing them year-round.

When heavy snow and sleet blankets shrubs in the winter, sweep or shake branches to relieve them of the weight as soon as you can, because ice buildup can break branches and cause deformed shapes. Winter winds can dry evergreens and cause browning of needles in certain species; water evergreens right up to the freeze-up if your weather has been dry. Because they don't lose leaves in the fall like deciduous trees, evergreens continue to lose moisture by transpiration through the green needles all winter long.

Protect your roses. If your area temperatures regularly drop below zero, you need to protect your roses. If you have climbing roses, remove canes from the supports and tie them together in several places. Place a round object, such as a plastic bucket, on its side at the base of the plant and then bend the tied canes over it. Keep them pinned to the ground by tying them to a notched stake. Then cover the whole plant with at least 10 inches of soil or soil-mulch mixture.

Prune rose bush tops back to 6 inches, using slanted cuts at about ¼ inch above the strong outside buds. You should have three healthy canes remaining after pruning. Apply wound compound to the cuts as directed on product. Make a collar around the base of the plant with builder's felt and then mound soil over the stubs for winter protection. The mound should be 8 to 12 inches deep. In the spring, when new shoots are about ½ inch long, remove the mounds by spraying them with the hose.

Apply fertilizer in the fall. This is the best way to encourage root growth and help your lawn build up nutrient reserves for the winter. Good organic fertilizers include cottonseed meal, blood meal, composted cow manure, and straight compost sifted fine enough for a top dressing. Before you feed the soil, it's best to have it tested by your county agent or local garden center to determine what it needs and what pH your soil is.

Aerate in the fall, too. To aerate the soil, you punch out small cores of soil 2 to 4 inches deep with an aeration machine, which you can rent.

Thatch before the deep freeze. Early fall is the best time to have your lawn thatched so that the lawn has a chance to recover before growth slows down for the winter. Thatching means removing the thickly matted organic material such as old, dead roots and runners. If your lawn has a very thick layer of thatch, a rake won't do. It's best to rent a dethatching machine from your local gardening-supply store. You can toss the material that you remove into your compost pile for next spring's fertilizing session.

GARDENS (*cont.*)

Also, before you go, measure the space, draw a picture (graph paper helps you keep to scale) or take a photo that shows the plants that are already there; note if a fence is near (for climbing or tall plants); determine if the area gets morning or afternoon sun and how much sun (shade, partial shade, or full sun); and check drainage and type of soil (sandy, rich black earth, or clay). Garden centers and your county agent can test soil for you if you bring them a coffee can full.

Start an indoor winter garden. If you have a sunny corner, make a pattern or take measurements to a sheet metal shop and have them make a planter deep enough to hold a ficus or other indoor-growing tree and other plants at the base. Fill the planter with a couple of large rocks for bottom-weight, and then add soil and your favorite plants. If you need more light, install a grow light in the ceiling above.

Discover the delicacies of an herb garden. Herbs can grow in the ground, hanging baskets, window boxes, pots indoors in a sunny kitchen window, outdoors on a porch or apartment balcony, or even in a terrarium made from an old fish tank, large jar, or bowl. Remember, the farther away from the kitchen that herbs are planted, the less likely they are to be used!

See also HERBS.

Grow tomatoes in containers. Read the tags on plants to find out the plant's mature size. Larger plants (30 inches high) will grow in 2 gallons of soil, and smaller ones (12 inches high) will flourish in hanging baskets. You may have to stake or tie up plants in containers

Find the end of the garden hose. Use yellow paint to mark about 12 inches from the end of the hose. Then you can always find the end when the hose is tangled up.

Repair a leaky garden hose. Lightly sand the area around the holes with sandpaper. Cut patches from an old rubber tube and sand the patch lightly, too. Apply contact cement to both surfaces, let it dry to the touch, and press firmly over the hole. Keep the patch in place by wrapping it with black electrical tape or duct tape.

 Make a healthy-planet drip irrigation system. With a large nail or ice pick, poke more holes into an already leaky hose at strategic intervals on

one side. Then lay the hose between garden rows or in flower beds so that water dribbles through the holes into the ground without evaporating as it would with an ordinary sprinkler.

Another strategy is to pierce a tiny hole in the bottom of a gallon plastic milk jug and put it next to a young tree or shrub and fill it with water. The water will drip out slowly and seep down to the roots. Fill the jugs early in the morning and at night, during dry spells, and you won't waste water through evaporation.

Use a smaller plastic bottle the same way to drip-irrigate houseplants. Or you can mix plant food and water in a plastic jug; freeze it; then poke three or four holes in the bottom of the bottle and set it on the pot's soil.

Make the most of mulch. Mulching the soil surface maintains moisture and prevents evaporation of water. It also regulates soil temperatures so that you get better root growth.

Garden with black plastic. You can keep soil temperature and moisture constant by "mulching" plants with black plastic. Plants are inserted in holes made in plastic sheeting or plastic sheeting is used to cover the soil around them. Or, use organic mulch to reduce soil temperature and moisture fluctuations. (In some areas, heavy rainfall can cause rot when plastic mulch is used; check with your county agent, local botanical center, or gardening experts.)

Spruce up your landscape by pruning trees and shrubs. If you have a tree or shrub that has outgrown its location, you can prune as much as ⅓ of the total plant. However, it's best to prune and shape plants each year on a schedule to avoid such major cutting.

STORAGE SOLUTIONS

Garden Tools

Put rakes, hoes, shovels, and other large tools into a large garbage can and hang smaller tools on S-hooks around the rim. Then you can drag all of your tools along with you as you work.

You'll want to cut crossed branches that rub each other; remove one to prevent damage to the other. Remove dead or diseased wood. If a plant has been damaged by winter, wait until new growth occurs so that you know what parts are really dead.

Plan to prune spring flowering plants after they bloom. Many roses are pruned after their blooming period, in fall in most parts of the country, to a height of 18 to 24 inches, leaving 4 to 6 strong canes for the next year's growth.

Exercise caution with the garden edgers. Protect your eyes from flying debris by wearing a mask or goggles. Protect your shins as well with soccer pads or pads made for that purpose.

Be careful with the trimmer, too. The monofilament lines used to cut grass and weeds can damage shrubs, vines, and young trees by removing part of the bark. If you trim so closely that you remove parts of the bark, you can damage the cambium tissue just beneath it, thus preventing the flow of nutrients to the root system.

Make your own borders. Instead of buying garden timbers to border flower or vegetable beds, tie rolls of old newspapers with wire, old panty hose, or twine, and place them end to end.

Start seedlings in egg cartons. When planting seedlings in egg carton cups, place an eggshell half in the bottom before adding soil. Then it's easy to lift the whole seedling at planting time.

Buy some beautiful bulbs. Select bigger bulbs for bigger blossoms. Don't buy soft, mushy, moldy, or heavily bruised bulbs. But, you can buy bulbs that have loose or torn "tunics" (the outer papery skin like on onions). Loss of the tunic does not damage the bulbs and may actually promote faster rooting after planting. Remember to get planting instructions from the garden center if you are buying bulk bulbs. Packaged bulbs usually have printed instructions.

Sow small seeds in a spice shaker. Pour seeds into an old spice shaker, put the lid on, and sprinkle over each garden row to evenly disperse small seeds. Cover seeds lightly with soil, water according to package directions, and wait for results.

Consider rainfall when making a watering schedule. Newly planted trees and shrubs need watering every 5 to 7 days. Even well-established trees and shrubs need water when less than 1 inch of rain falls during a 1-week period. If your area hasn't had rain in 7 to 10 days, you'll need to water to maintain healthy plants.

When you water, apply a thorough soaking so that enough moisture gets to the roots and helps them become well established. Don't water more often than every 5 days. Roots will suffocate because too much water removes oxygen from the root zone.

Maintain a gardening calendar. On a gardening calendar, note what was planted when; when plants sprouted; and when they were watered, fertilized, and harvested. You can plan the next year by seeing what grew, produced well, and in how much time.

Manage your time with a timer. Take a kitchen timer outdoors with you so that you won't get so absorbed with gardening that you're late for other activities.

Take a gardening tray with you. A rubber garbage can cover will hold small plants, gardening tools, and other necessities so that you can carry them around the garden and avoid back and forth trips.

Keep a handle on garden tools. Paint handles of your rake, shovel, and other garden tools bright orange so that you can see them at a glance if they are left somewhere in the yard. Also, if you lend the tools to anyone, they'll be identified easily as yours (unless the borrower also has orange-painted garden tools). If you frequently lend tools, it's best to put your name on them! I even put my mailing labels on my books so that they get back to me instead of spending eternity on someone else's shelf.

See also PLANTS.

GELATIN

Don't add fresh pineapple to the mix. Fresh or frozen pineapple has not been processed and contains the enzyme bromelain, which breaks down gelatin and won't let it set. Canned pineapple has been processed so it can be added to gelatin.

GERBILS, HAMSTERS, AND GUINEA PIGS

These little animals can be wonderful pets, especially for apartment dwellers. They live in self-contained environments; are clean and odor-free if their cages are kept clean; and don't bark, claw the carpet, or otherwise annoy landlords. Also, they make entertaining pets for children who are bedridden or confined to wheelchairs because they are always busy exploring, chewing, and climbing.

Create a perfect habitat. A 10-gallon aquarium with a wire screen or mesh cover over it is a perfect home for gerbils and hamsters. (Guinea pigs need a bit more space.) There is no mess from litter falling out of the bottom, as with a regular cage.

Many plastic aquarium or tunnel homes can be bought for gerbils and hamsters. If you are handy, you can make a habitat from Plexiglas panels bolted together (much larger and wider than, but similar to, an "ant farm" container); then, fill it with cedar shavings and other critter bedding so the gerbils or hamsters can make their own tunnels and hideaways. If you make your own, don't forget the air holes and a secure place to hold a water bottle.

If you're in a pinch, a small birdcage will usually hold a gerbil or hamster well, but be sure to tie the lift-up door shut, because they are smart enough to get out through such an escape hatch.

Let them adjust to handling. Small rodents should be handled for increasing periods of time to tame them. They like to burrow in pockets and sleeves, and if they are gently and frequently handled, they become pleasant, cuddly pets.

Know the gender differences. Males are generally more docile than females. The females will become very restless when they are in heat and if they can, they may find a way to escape from their homes. Always be certain that lids and tunnels are properly fastened, especially during the females' restless periods.

Open up a gerbil gym. An exercise wheel or ball will help your guinea pig, gerbil, or hamster get rid of excess energy and will entertain you, too. Just don't forget that your pet is in the ball and leave it without food and water for too long. As an added bonus, an exercise ball is a good carrier for a gerbil or hamster if you have to return it to the pet store or take it to a new home.

Diversify their diets. Small rodents will eat carrots, lettuce, and many other foods in addition to store-bought pet food. They like to take their food from the food dish and hide it as if they were in the wild and have to stock up for the winter. They also eat live insects that might get into their cages. And although they don't drink much water (they get some of their water needs met by eating lettuce and other vegetables), these animals need to have a supply of fresh water in a stopper bottle at all times.

 Use metal jar lids to hold seeds and other food. These small rodent pets will often eat plastic items, so it's best to use judgment about what you put into their cages. Small, ceramic food bowls can be bought at pet stores.

Give them something to chomp. Rodents, and that includes gerbils and hamsters, need to chew, so provide them with chew sticks and carrots to satisfy their needs; otherwise they will chew on their cages. Cardboard tubes from paper towels and tissue also make nice treats to chew on. The bonus here is threefold: the shredded scraps are perfect for the nest, you recycle, and the gerbil gets something to do.

Don't consider cardboard. You simply can't try to keep a gerbil, hamster, or guinea pig in a cardboard box "home." Cardboard is just another munchie, and they will chew their way our in no time at all. You'll find many chew holes in the boxes they are put in for transport to their new homes before they get carried through the doorway!

Prevent the great escape. These animals also are very supple; a grown hamster can squeeze out through a hole the size of a quarter. So inspect their homes often for holes.

Capture escapees safely. If your hamster or gerbil escapes, find a box with a lid on and line the bottom with a small towel or crumpled newspaper. Make a hole in the lid large enough for the "escapee" to drop through, then lay a paper towel or hanky over the hole and put some food on it to entice the hungry pet to the trap.

Educate yourself. Most pet stores have inexpensive booklets on raising gerbils, hamsters, and guinea pigs, and you can get information from the library to help you, too.

GIFTS AND GIFT WRAP

Make a thought-provoking gift. A reader whose younger brother was in the hospital recovering from a serious back operation wanted to give him something to show that she was thinking about him even if she couldn't visit him often. Recalling that he said he remembered little of his childhood, she bought a school composition book and wrote stories about things he did, their family's history, and important people in their lives. After receiving the book in the mail, her brother called to say that if she'd sent him a million dollars, he would not have been happier. She had included things he'd always wanted to ask his parents but didn't. I think this gift shows that not all treasures cost money!

Keep the guessing fun. Place some loose, raw macaroni in the box with a gift so that those who like to shake before opening will have a harder time guessing what's inside.

Wrap a gift quilt in a bed box. Since it's so large and hard to wrap anyway, put a quilt in an under-bed storage container so the recipient can store the quilt in its own box.

Consider the gift wrap wisely. Wrap a going-away present in a road map to the recipient's destination. Wrap a baby present in a baby blanket or diaper to which you've pinned a rattle or other toys with diaper pins.

Recycle balloons for gift wrap. Foil party balloons, after they deflate, make great gift bags. Cut the little neck off the bottom, and staple or tape it closed. Then cut across the top, either in the shape it is or straight. Then insert tissue paper with the gift and tie it shut with a ribbon.

Decorate your gift wrap. You'll have wrap handy for all occasions if you keep plain white, not glossy, paper, on hand. Then decorate and personalize it with stencils and colored markers or crayons. Top your artwork with a matching ribbon or bow.

Keep rolls of wrapping paper from getting mashed or mangled. Slide the roll into the good leg of old panty hose and hang the "leg" on a small nail inside your closet. I think that if you had several rolls to store, you could leave the panty hose whole, put one roll in each leg, let the legs straddle a hanger, and then put the hanger with three to five panty hose paper rolls in your guest closet. Then wait for comments from surprised guests!

Use a handy kitchen substitute. No gift wrap in the house? Wrap the gift in aluminum foil, shiny side out, covered by a sheet of colored plastic wrap, then add a ribbon, yarn bow, or a flower. The foil holds its shape so you don't even need a box. If you cut the plastic wrap larger than the foil and press both sheets together, you don't even need tape.

Work around large or awkwardly shaped items. Place the item in a colored plastic trash or department store bag and tie it shut. If the item is so large that it requires two bags, join the seam where the open ends of the bags come together and cover the joint with a wide ribbon.

Wrap your gift in a bottle. When a 2-liter soda bottle (with opaque bottom "bowl") is empty, run hot tap water over the outside to remove the colored bottom from the clear part. Then cut a hole in the bottom of the clear part and put a gift inside the bottle. Stick the colored part of the bottle back on and tie a ribbon around the neck. Then, have fun as people try to figure out how you got the gift into the bottle!

Hint: A 2-liter soda bottle also can be a terrarium for small plants, which can also be a gift!

Refresh gift-wrap bows. A curling iron will press crumpled bow loops and make them look new in a few seconds.

Protect bows in the mail. Place a clean margarine tub upside down over them before packing. Secure with a bit of tape.

Substitute with ribbon. Forget the ribbon? Cut strips of the remaining wrapping paper, curl them with scissors, and glue them to the package. These curls match better than ribbon!

GLASS

Clean up shards of shattered glass. After carefully picking up large pieces, wet a piece of newspaper, and then put the paper on the tiny bits and pieces. Lift it up and the glass will cling to the paper. Be sure to blot the entire floor. When glass shatters, it's amazing how far the pieces will fly!

GLASS CLEANER

See BATHROOMS.

GLASSES

Unstack the stuck ones. Put cold water in the top glass and dip the bottom one in warm to hot water. Gently pull the glasses apart. Or pour some baby oil or mineral oil between the glasses, allow them to set for a while, and then gently pull them apart. Wash in hot soapy water and rinse.

Avoid water spots when you wash them by hand. Wash with the proper amount of liquid dishwashing detergent, rinse in the hottest water safe for the glasses and your hands, and then dry with a soft, lint-free cloth.

Hint: Wear rubber gloves to get a good grip and protect your hands from hot water. If your area has hard water, rinse the glasses in water to which a splash (less than a glug but more than a spritz!) of vinegar has been added.

See also EYES AND EYEGLASSES.

GLUE

Avoid glue if you can. To avoid harmful chemicals, use staples or reusable metal paper clips. If glue is a must, use a glue stick (made from petroleum derivatives), white glue (made from polyvinyl acetate plastic) or yellow glue (made from aliphatic plastic resin).

Make your own glue. Here are three recipes for paper glues that you can make with ingredients from your kitchen and hardware or drug stores.

1. Blend 4 tablespoons of wheat flour into enough cold water to make a smooth paste (about 6 tablespoons). Boil 1½ cups of water and stir into mixture, stirring until mixture is translucent. Use when cold.
2. Blend 3 tablespoons of cornstarch and 4 tablespoons of cold water to make a smooth paste. Stir paste into 2 cups of boiling water, and continue to stir until mixture becomes translucent. Use when cold.
3. Blend ¼ cup of cornstarch, ¾ cup of water, 2 tablespoons of light corn syrup, and 1 teaspoon of white vinegar in a medium saucepan. Cook over medium heat, stirring constantly, until mixture thickens. Remove from heat. In separate bowl, mix ¼ cup of cornstarch and ¾ cup of water until smooth. Add this to the first heated mixture, stirring constantly. This glue will keep for 2 months in a covered container.

Don't get burnt by a glue gun. When you use a hot glue gun to glue trim on fabric, press the trim in place with the end of a chopstick (the cheap wooden ones that come in packages), and you won't burn the tip of your finger.

See STAINS for hints on how to remove glue from fabrics.

GOLF BALLS

Make your own storage containers. Rather than letting your golf balls roll loose, slip three balls into a tube from a roll of toilet tissue. Mark the outside with the brand of balls inside and then just peel off a portion of the tube to extract a ball. Egg cartons will hold a collection of golf balls in neat stacks.

GRABBER

Make a "grabber." These do-it-yourself gadgets are great for picking up small items, pulling the oven rack in and out, and to hook on other unreachables. Here's how to make one. Attach a cup hook to one end and a coat hook to the other end of a ½-inch wooden dowel cut to a 3-foot length. (It also reaches that place in the middle of your back that itches!)

GRAHAM CRACKER CRUMBS

Sneak in a cone substitute. When she had no graham crackers to "crumb" for a dessert bar recipe, one reader substituted 1½ cups of crushed ice-cream cone crumbs for 1 cup of graham cracker crumbs and loved it!

GRANDPARENTS

Give gifts that make the distance seem smaller. So that very young children who live far away can understand who sent the gift, take a photo of Grandma or Grandpa holding it and enclose it with the gift.

Keep grandkids entertained so adults can visit, too. To keep children occupied while adults talk and visit after dinner at the table, keep a bookcase in a nearby room filled with coloring books, picture books, storybooks, crayons, markers, games, bubble pipes, and plastic building blocks. Adults can excuse the children with some hugs and kisses and continue to talk while the children play.

Hint: Cut puzzles and games from newspapers and save them for older children to work on. You could even paste them in a scrapbook or spiral notebook to make a puzzle book if you feel ambitious.

Keep a grandparent's scrapbook. Write down young children's cute sayings and add their "quotables" as they get older, and you'll end up with a wonderful and funny record of the joys and sorrows of childhood and teens. Keep the original and make a copy for your grandchildren when they leave home.

GRAPES

Freeze them for a frozen treat. Buy too many grapes? Freeze grapes in a plastic zipper bag or a well-sealed container for healthy, sweet treats. Also, holding a frozen grape in your mouth for a while is a good dieter's trick for fighting an attack of the munchies.

GRASS STAINS

See STAINS for hints on how to remove grass stains from fabrics.

GRAVY

Liven up pale gravy. Add a tablespoon of low-salt soy sauce or Worcestershire, depending upon your taste. Also, sprinkle paprika into the gravy as it boils to thicken and watch how it gets a nice warm brown color. Paprika doesn't affect the taste unless you add massive quantities of it.

Hint: Sprinkle in paprika until the color improves, but don't sprinkle directly from the can or jar. Steam rising from gravy or sauces causes powdered spices to cake and lose their zip! Instead, sprinkle some in your hand, and then sprinkle from hand to pan.

Lump-proof your gravy. Always add powder to liquid not vice versa. Pour liquid (water, milk, or bouillon) into a clean, empty jar with a tight-fitting lid. Add flour or cornstarch, screw on the lid, and shake until completely blended. Add this mixture to casseroles, soups, gravies, and more.

Serve gravy without the mess. Try a large teapot for no-mess gravy pouring at family dinner. It'll stay warmer, too, with a lid and tea cozy on it.

GREASE

See STAINS for hints on how to remove grease stains from fabrics.

GREETING CARDS

Decorate and display. Toss Christmas and other greeting cards into a pretty basket and keep it where it can cheer you up anytime.

Recycle old greeting cards. Recycle them by cutting off the fronts and using them for gift tags or postcards (draw a dividing line for message and addresses). Sometimes preschool or day care centers and elementary schools can use the cards (and suitable magazines) for arts and crafts projects.

Hint: If you include a handwritten note in your Christmas card, write the current Christmas message on last year's card fronts and each card you received will be used twice!

Organize the spares. When you buy extra cards, file them in an accordion record file or pattern file box according to "birthday," "thank you," or "get well," and you won't have to dig through them all when you want one.

GRILLED CHEESE

Savor a super-speedy sandwich. Toast two slices of bread in the toaster, put cheese in between, and zap in the microwave for 20 to 30 seconds (depends on type of cheese and your microwave wattage). No frying, less mess, and fewer calories!

Hint: If you like the toast to stay crisp, put the sandwich on a paper plate, which absorbs the moisture, before zapping.

GROCERY BAGS

Use paper bags as kindling containers. Put kindling wood in paper grocery sacks, and then put sack and all into the fire as a firestarter.

Or when you buy charcoal for the grill, divide it into paper grocery sacks so that you have a "dose" ready for the fire without having to handle the charcoal again.

Carry them "cowboy style." If the handles of heavily loaded plastic grocery sacks cut into your hands when you carry them into the house, try hooking three to five bags on a boot hook (the kind used to remove cowboy boots). No more pain!

GROUT

Keep on top of regular cleaning. If bleach won't work, you may have to replace the grout. Oil that gets into grout of ceramic-tiled kitchen floors cannot usually be removed. You have to remove the stained area and regrout. An alternative can be to stain all of the grout, but that's a major project.

Protect grout, too. To avoid the problem of cleaning grout, protect grout from stain, mildew, and washing out by spraying a water-seal product on the area. Spray, then wipe excess from tiles while the product is still wet. The seal will remain in the grout and make it look good longer.

See also BATHROOMS.

HAIR

Check out your grocery store's hair care section. Sometimes it seems like they have more lotions and potions for your hair than for every other part of your body combined. Read on for some easy, inexpensive hair care ideas and tips.

Color

Many hair dye products contain potentially carcinogenic chemicals. They also contain chemicals that are absorbed through the scalp and can cause problems for people who are allergic to them or have sensitive skin. These chemicals include coal-tar dyes, ammonia, detergents, hydrogen peroxide, and lead. Here are some planet-friendly alternatives.

Darken or highlight your hair with henna. The safest commercial hair color product, henna can darken or highlight hair, and it washes out gradually over a 6-month period. Henna is often sold at health food stores. Generally speaking, with plant materials like henna, you process the product as directed and then strain and cool before using. Pour the liquid through your hair 15 times, catching it in a basin so that you can rerinse with the same liquid. Then wring out the excess, allowing the

Choosing Shampoos

Each shampoo seems to have some magical ingredient—wheat germ oil, aloe, collagen, jojoba, sheep's placenta, ammonium lauryl sulfate—that also makes the price "magic." Research reported by the *University of California, Berkeley Newsletter* confirms that many claims are meaningless, and costly ingredients just go down the drain. Here are some hints to help when you read those labels.

Wash oil out. You can wash your hair with bar soap, but it leaves a film. Shampoos have detergent to remove oil and dirt. Most shampoos have foam boosters because suds make people feel clean.

Put oil in. After detergents take the oil out, people want conditioners to put it back in. Using a separate conditioner makes hair feel better to the touch. Conditioners include lanolin, balsam, glycerol, propylene glycol, and other oils.

Know which additives don't add up. Proteins such as keratin and collagen are supposed to make hair look fuller, and botanicals like mint, chamomile, or other herbals are supposed to add luster. These usually just add price and go down the drain when you rinse. Other additives are scents, colors, and preservatives. Citric acid is added to counteract the alkalinity of shampoos—the "pH"—but it makes little or no difference to your hair's look.

Don't be a flake. Dandruff shampoos contain active ingredients like pyrithione zinc, selenium sulfide (a sulfursalicylic compound), or coal tar. They remove dandruff if used frequently, but so do ordinary shampoos. Everyone has some dandruff; it's natural for the skin to shed its outer layers. If you have severe dandruff that causes crusting, itching, or redness, see a dermatologist.

Scissor split ends. Don't believe the hype! Hair shafts are dead tissue; the cure for roughened hairs is to cut off damaged parts.

Reduce your use. Price does not determine shampoo quality, and most people can't tell one shampoo from another in blind studies. Try using less. I often dilute my shampoos; they last longer and are easier to rinse off. Also, ignore the manufacturer's instructions to lather up twice, especially if you shampoo frequently.

rest to remain in your hair for 15 minutes, and then rinse with clear water.

Try the coffee shop solution. You can also darken hair by rinsing it with strong black tea or black coffee.

Use lemon to lighten. Rinse with mixture of 1 tablespoon of lemon juice to 1 gallon of warm water.

Add some red. Try rinsing with strong tea, rosehips, cloves, or strong black coffee.

Cover the gray. Simmer ½ cup of dried sage in 2 cups of water for 30 minutes, then steep for several hours. Apply tea to hair after it cools, allow to dry, then rinse and dry hair again. Apply weekly until you have the shade you want and then monthly to maintain the color.

Remove green from chlorine. Try dissolving 6 to 8 aspirin tablets in a glass of warm water, saturate hair strands, leave on for 10 to 15 minutes, rinse thoroughly, and shampoo. Also look for special shampoos formulated to remove discoloration caused by chlorine and minerals. They are usually referred to as swimmer's shampoo and can be found in beauty supply stores and some hair-care product sections in supermarkets.

Shampoos

Let it shine. Castile soap is tried and true for shiny hair! Grate castile bar soap and mix it with pure water in a blender or food processor, then blend 1 cup of this liquid with ¼ cup of olive, avocado, or almond oil and another ½ cup of distilled water. Store in a marked squirt bottle. Use this solution sparingly.

Don't be a flake. Here's my baking soda again! This time it's a dandruff remedy. Wet your hair, rub in a handful of dry baking soda, and then rinse. This may make your hair seem drier than usual for the first weeks of use, but soon your hair's natural oils will make your hair very soft.

Get a grip. Wrap a couple of fat rubber bands around your shampoo and creme-rinse bottles, and they won't slip out of your hands in the shower.

Styling Products and Hair Accessories

Soften your hair, not just your sheets. Laundry fabric softener diluted 1 teaspoon to 1 cup of water can be used after you shampoo.

My Favorite Homestyle Conditioner

Massage a dollop or two of real mayonnaise (not salad dressing) into your hair before shampooing, wrap your hair with plastic wrap, and cover all with a bath towel. Leave on for at least 30 minutes, and then wash hair as usual with warm or cool water, not hot. Rinse very well and enjoy great-feeling hair.

Make your skin silky, too. Smooth on hair conditioner as a body lotion after a bath or shower. Or substitute conditioner for lather when shaving your legs; it won't leave your skin as dry as soap or shaving cream. For an inexpensive manicure or pedicure, put conditioner in warm water for a soothing soak.

Camouflage thinning hair. Try blow-drying in the opposite direction from the way you normally style or brush it, starting at the roots. Or, blow-dry your hair while bending forward from the waist. Don't brush too much after you've poufed it with the dryer, or you'll flatten it.

Reuse your hair accessories. If you cut long hair short, your favorite barrettes, ponytail rings and other hair accessories can be recycled as scarf rings and clips.

For storage ideas, see also BARRETTES.

Store headbands neatly. Empty 3-liter soft drink bottles, washed and dried, will hold headbands neatly, and you won't have to worry about the ones with bows or ruffles getting crushed.

Perms

Catch the drips. Put on a terry-cloth exercise headband and tuck the cotton roll inside. It will catch drips better than cotton stuck to your skin with petroleum jelly, the usual drip solution.

Use twist-ties. If you don't have hairpins or clips to hold sections in place, try twist-ties. Just make sure no metal wire touches the permanent solution because it might discolor.

Try coffee filters. Run out of permanent papers? Coffee filters cut to the proper size work just fine.

Save extra perm papers. When you have leftovers, carry them in your purse to absorb oil on your face without disturbing your makeup and to blot lipstick. They work so well you may want to buy the papers for that purpose from a beauty supply house.

Loosen tight curls. Speak to the salon about the problem or if you've overdone it at home, try styling with a hair dryer to straighten it. Other ways to help the curl relax include applying a conditioner after each shampoo and controlling your hair with mousse or gel.

HAIR SPRAY

Take cover when you aim. To keep hairspray out of your ears and off your earrings, cover your ear on the side you are spraying with the spray-can cap.

HALLOWEEN

Give candy substitutes. Instead of candy, buy small party-favor toys, balls, baseball cards, and other inexpensive items and let children pick some from a bowl.

Create a scented jack-o'-lantern. After carving, sprinkle the inside of the lid and inside bottom of the pumpkin with a bit of nutmeg and cinnamon. Then when you light a candle, the jack-o'-lantern will look bright and smell nice, too.

HALL TREES

Plant them anywhere. Keep a hall tree handy in the bedroom or walk-in closet for airing clothing that doesn't get washed after each wearing. A hall tree is a good "guest closet," too.

HAM BONE BROTH

Store this simple seasoning. Place the bone with leftover ham still on it into a large pot and cover with water. Bring to a boil, and boil until all meat falls off. Cool and skim off the fat. Place the ham and broth into small individual containers and freeze. You can use the broth to season beans, vegetables, and more.

HAMMERING SAFELY

See TOOLS.

HAMSTERS, GERBILS, AND MICE AS PETS

See GERBILS, HAMSTERS, AND GUINEA PIGS.

HANDBAGS

Stash more than cash. Recycle broken or worn-out handbags as storage containers. They hold craft items to work on when traveling or visiting, store small items in the closet, hold tools for odd jobs around the house, corral tools and other emergency items in a car trunk, organize temporary files, and more.

Keep the shoulder straps from slipping. If one strap keeps slipping off your shoulder, join the straps by machine-stitching a 2-inch strip of self-adhesive tape to them. They will automatically stick together, and you can still pull them apart if you want to. If the straps are too thick to stitch yourself, you can have a shoe repair shop do it.

HANGERS

Color code your closet. Durable plastic hangers in assorted colors can help you find your clothing quickly, and they're also great for heavy jackets and sweaters. One reader codes blue for blouses, red for slacks, yellow for skirts, white for dresses, and so on. She can always find blouses if they've been "misfiled" among the skirts or slacks.

 Don't give them the slip. When garments slip off their hangers, make a nonslip hanger sleeve by punching a hole in the center of a piece of fabric and slipping the fabric over the hanger hook so that it hangs over and covers the "shoulders" of the hanger. Use old sheets cut to size, leftover yardage from sewing projects, old diapers, terry-cloth towels, or just an old T-shirt hung normally. Once fabric is against fabric, it's less likely to slip.

Prevent snags. Sand wooden hangers smooth with sandpaper and then brush on clear shellac.

See also CLOSETS.

Hardy Hangers

Once you've organized your closet and made sure every item will stay put, you can recycle any spare wire hangers. If your dry cleaner doesn't take them back, call local thrift stores, preschools, or Scouting organizations; they may be happy to have them for hanging clothes or for crafts. Or try these ideas out yourself.

- ♥ Remove the paper tube from pants hangers and bend the wire ends inward to make a paper towel holder outdoors or when camping.

- ♥ Unhook one end of a pants hanger, put rolls of gift ribbon on it, and replace the end. You have a multiroll dispenser.

- ♥ Bend both "arms" of a wire hanger upward to hold spaghetti-strap garments in the closet or to hang bra straps on for drying indoors.

- ♥ Straighten a hanger and hang a bird feeder from it so squirrels can't get to the food.

- ♥ Bend the wire into a circle and cover with old panty hose to make a small leaf skimmer or paint strainer.

HEATING AND COOLING

You can save energy and dollars—in summer or winter—by making just a few simple changes to your daily routine.

Keep Cool in Summer

Turn the lights off. Lights, especially incandescent bulbs, which furnish more heat than light, make your air conditioner run harder. Please remember to switch them off.

Change the air conditioner filter at least monthly. You may need to change it even more frequently if you have shedding pets to reduce the load on the air conditioner unit and therefore cut costs.

Lower the thermostat. Set your air conditioner thermostat no lower than 78°F. In some climates, shut off the air conditioning and open windows to take advantage of cool evening breezes.

Trap moisture. Close off humidity-producing kitchen, bathroom, and laundry areas to keep moisture from the rest of the house. You'll feel cooler in dryer air. When you shower, open the bathroom window or turn on the exhaust vent if you have one to let moisture out.

Cook conscientiously. Cover pots on the stove to confine heat and humidity. Covering the pot makes the contents heat up faster, too, so the stove

Hints for Using Window Units Wisely

For some, window units are energy and utility bill demons. If you use a room air conditioner unit, check the filter now and clean or replace it. Clogged filters make the unit run longer than needed and operate inefficiently. If you can do it safely, clean the condenser coils and fins (those grills on the outdoor side of the unit).

Set the temperature control no lower than 78°F and don't set the control to a cooler temperature at start-up. It won't cool the room faster, and you may forget to set the control lower once the room is comfortable, thus wasting energy. Most window units don't have specific degree settings, so place a thermometer somewhere in the room away from the air conditioner air flow to get an accurate temperature reading.

Remember that lamps, TV sets, or other heat sources placed near a window unit can cause the AC to run longer than necessary. A window fan uses as little as $\frac{1}{10}$ the energy of an air conditioner, so buying one to bring cool air into your home is good energy economy.

If your air-conditioning unit has an outside air control to bring in fresh air, you can use it without using the cooling mechanism. The unit's compressor motor guzzles the energy, not the fan. But remember to close the outside air control when you start cooling again.

won't be heating the room as long. (But then your mother told you that!) To save even more energy, if you turn off the electric stove 3 minutes before you're done cooking, it will stay hot for at least that long.

Show heat the way out. Warm air rises so open second floor and attic windows to let heat escape. In the evening when it's cool, you can let the cooler air into the house and close the windows early in the morning to keep the cool air inside.

Use fans wisely. A large window fan uses ¼ the energy and costs ⅕ as much as an air conditioner to operate. Placing one in an attic window can push hot air out and draw cooler air in through downstairs windows.

Shop smartly. When buying an air-conditioning unit, bigger is not always better. Look for the Seasonal Energy Efficiency Rating (SEER). The higher the number, the more cooling efficiency you'll get for electricity costs.

Take advantage of shade. AC units work more efficiently when installed on the shady side of your house. Some people shade their units with awnings or trees. Awnings, of course, also help to keep hot sun from shining into windows.

Stay Warm in Winter

Lower the heat. Turn down the heat to 60°F in unoccupied rooms. Do this by closing duct covers, turning down radiators, or lowering individual room thermostats.

Take advantage of secondhand warmth. If you have the oven on in the kitchen for a long period of time, such as while cooking a turkey or baking Christmas cookies, close off your kitchen hot air duct. You'll get enough heat from the oven.

Keep it cool when away. If everyone will be away from home for 8 or more hours, turn down the heat at least 8°F. The first one home can turn it back up.

Snuggle at night. When you are snug under a comforter at night, you can have the temperature reduced to 61° to 64°F.

Get with the program. If you have a programmable thermostat, you can set it so the heat will go off and on when it's needed, resulting in lower heating costs and less fuel waste. Heating costs increase by 5 percent for each degree you set your thermostat above 68°F.

Make it a game. Cover all cracks in doors and windows to prevent heat from escaping. Get the children in on this project; they can be "air-leak police." Have them take a 6-inch piece of ribbon or strip of paper and hold it near places at windows where air may be escaping, then make a map showing where these drafts are so that the family can stop them.

Keep it down. In newer homes, power ventilators cool the attic in the summer. Turn them off in the winter to prevent their drawing warm air up from the house. Such warm moist air can also cause frost buildup and damage in the attic.

Preheat your bed. If you don't like to sleep under an electric blanket or with a heating pad, use them to preheat your bed and turn them off when you get in—wearing warm PJs and socks, of course!

 Save money with maintenance. Keeping your home furnace in good condition can decrease your energy consumption by as much as 10 percent, which can save about 50 gallons of oil (multiply by oil costs in your area to get saving) and keeps 1,089 pounds of carbon dioxide emission a year from our air. In addition to keeping your filters changed winter and

---

Energy Rate Your Home

In some cities, public utility companies offer free energy-efficiency checks; others charge a minimal fee. If a utility company does an energy check for you, the results will be mailed along with recommendations for improvements, estimates of your initial investment costs, and predictions of your long-term savings.

To be an energy miser, check if your home has adequate insulation in the attic and walls, weather stripping and caulking in good condition, and the proper insulation and temperature setting for your hot-water heater. Check if appliances, heaters, and air conditioners are operating efficiently. When you replace these items, look at the energy ratings on their tags before you buy.

summer, have regular maintenance inspections and cleanings of your furnace by an authorized company. Often, by contracting for regular service (spring and fall each year) you can save on the overall service fee.

Consider zone heating. Room heaters help if you are trying to save energy costs by practicing "zone heating." In zone heating, you close off unused rooms' registers or heating vents or shut off the furnace and heat only used rooms with room heaters. Although room heaters are not as efficient as furnace heat, in some houses room heaters can heat one or two rooms at less expense than a big heater.

When selecting a portable heater, you need to check the wattage. The rule of thumb is that you need one watt per cubic foot of air volume in the room. Portable heaters use 110 volts.

HEIRLOOMS

Pass them on. Many people like to pass on family heirlooms before they pass on themselves because they enjoy seeing the heirs using them. For example, a silver service that is seldom used by parents who don't entertain much anymore is a treasure to a daughter who is just beginning to entertain more formally. The trick is to give possessions when the time is right, to the child or children who will really love, use, and appreciate them. A good time is on happy occasions when all the people involved are present so they all share lifetime memories. My father and I share certain special family treasures that we trade back and forth.

HELPING PEOPLE

It's always a good idea to help people, but sometimes the way in which you offer help makes it easier to accept. Here are tips to smooth the way.

Be specific. Say, "I'm going to the dry cleaners on Wednesday. I can stop by and get your cleaning, too." Or, "I'm grocery shopping on Friday. If you make me a list, I'll shop for you."

Make it disposable. If you take over a casserole—and this is a wonderful help, especially when there's a new baby in the house or the family cook is sick—take it in a disposable container, and maybe include paper plates, napkins, and cups so there's no cleanup or returns.

Run errands. Offer to mail items or buy stamps for shut-ins or to take a shut-in's pet to the vet or groomer.

Be their arms and legs. If you have a friend who is disabled or who has a periodically disabling disease like arthritis, offer to change beds, dust, wash windows, clean blinds, rake leaves, sweep sidewalks, do minor repairs, or take care of other everyday chores that are difficult for someone who isn't agile.

Offer to host. Throw a birthday party for a disabled friend's child or offer to take the child somewhere where the friend can't go, such as trail hiking or roller-skating. If your friend is having a party, offer to come over an hour early to help with preparations.

Ask, then move on. People who have disabling or chronic illness say they would rather answer questions about their problems than have people wonder about or assume certain things about the illness. Then, after the questions are answered, they would like to move on to lighter conversation and not dwell on illness.

Give hugs. A hug is always welcome even if it's awkward to hug someone who's bed bound or in a wheelchair. If your friend has arthritis, a hug is better than a handshake, which can be painful to arthritic fingers.

HERBS

Brew an herbal concentrate. For herbs that don't dry well, brew a concentrate and freeze it in cubes so that you can thaw one cube for a cup of hot tea or add melted cubes to lemonade. To prepare, mash leaves, cover with hot water, steep for a day or so, strain liquid, and then freeze in cubes.

Using Herbs Wisely

Do not experiment with unfamiliar herbs when making homemade tea blends. Some herbs are actually poisonous (like some ferns) and others (like some mints) have medicinal properties that could be harmful to people with certain health conditions. Get information from your county extension agent or local botanical center.

Make Some Mint Tea

To make tea from fresh mint, choose larger leaves or pinch off leaf clusters at the stem end (instant pruning). Drop a handful or so into a quart of boiling water, steep 10 minutes, strain, and serve. To dry mint leaves for tea, cut branches before blooming, hang in a shady place until dry, then gather dried leaves and store in an airtight jar. To make frozen concentrate, add about 2 cups of coarsely chopped mint leaves and stems to a pint of boiling water, and allow water to boil. Remove from heat, cover, let cool about 1 hour. Strain, then freeze in ice-cube trays. For tea, heat a cube with enough water to make 1 cup or add cubes to other teas, punches, or soups. For a special treat, freeze a block of mint concentrate (with a nice sprig or two in the middle for decoration) and let it float in the punch bowl.

Make a tea infusion. Strip leaves from stems and chop. Measure twice as much water as you have chopped leaves. Add leaves to water when it boils. Boil for 5 minutes. Let cool; strain into a jar for storage in the fridge. For a cup of tea, add twice as much boiling water as infusion, then sweeten to taste with honey. Add lemon if you wish.

Dry herb leaves for tea. Cut branches just as they mature or flower, hang for about a week in an airy, shady place, and then crumble dried leaves into airtight jars. To make 1 cup of tea, place a few leaves in a cup, pour boiling water over them, and then add honey and lemon juice to taste.

Make herbal vinegars. Heat your favorite vinegar in an enamel pan, but don't let it boil. Pour it into a vinegar bottle. Add one or several culinary herbs to taste. Let the mixture steep for 2 weeks before using.

Whip up herbal butters. To 1 stick of unsalted butter, add 1 to 3 tablespoons of dried herbs or 2 to 6 tablespoons of fresh herbs, ½ teaspoon of lemon juice, and white pepper to taste. Combine ingredients and mix until fluffy. Pack in covered container and let set at least 1 hour. (See "10 Common Herb Combinations for Cooking" on page 240.)

See also GARDENS and TEA.

10 Common Herb Combinations for Cooking

Here are some Heloise-tested herb combos. When you cook herbs—especially bay leaves and whole peppercorns, cloves, or all-spice—in soup or stews, put them in a mesh or perforated metal tea ball so that they are easily removed and nobody bites into a peppercorn or risks choking on a piece of bay leaf.

1. **Fine herbs:** Parsley, chervil, chives, and French tarragon (If you'd like, add a small amount of basil, fennel, oregano, sage, or saffron.)

2. **Bouquet garni mixtures:** Bay leaf, parsley (two parts), and thyme (The herbs may be wrapped in cheesecloth or the parsley can be wrapped around the thyme and bay leaf.)

3. **Barbecue blend:** Cumin, garlic, hot pepper, and oregano

4. **Italian blend:** Basil, marjoram, oregano, rosemary, sage, savory, and thyme

5. **Vegetable herbs:** Basil, parsley, and savory

6. **Tomato sauce herbs:** Basil (two parts), bay leaf, marjoram, oregano, and parsley (If you'd like, add celery leaves or cloves.)

7. **Salad herbs:** Basil, lovage, parsley, and French tarragon

8. **Poultry herbs:** Lovage, marjoram (two parts), and sage (three parts)

9. **Fish herbs:** Basil, bay leaf (crumbled), French tarragon, lemon thyme, and parsley (If you'd like, add fennel, sage, or savory.)

10. **Egg herbs:** Basil, dill weed (leaves), garlic, and parsley

HINTS

Put hints where you'll use 'em. When you cut out diet or food hints, put them on the fridge door. If you cut out makeup or bathing hints, tape them inside the medicine cabinet. When you store hints where they'll be used, you're more likely to remember to try them.

HOLIDAYS

Store decorations safely. When holiday decorations replace knickknacks in certain places, solve the problem of where to safely put the knickknacks by storing them in the containers that normally hold the holiday decorations.

Scout the linen sales. Wait for after-holiday sales to buy Christmas Santa, Easter bunny, Valentine heart, and other fabrics. Then make special holiday pillowcases for cheery decorations in children's or adults' rooms.

Create festive dessert topping. Add a few drops of food coloring to dessert topping to make it festive. Try orange-colored topping on a Thanksgiving pumpkin pie, red and green for Christmas, red for Valentine's day, green for St. Patrick's day, or a favorite color of the birthday person.

See also ENTERTAINING.

HOME FIRE SAFETY

Get out quickly. This is the number one, most important, tip. Never spend more than 30 seconds fighting a fire. If the fire can't be extinguished, warn others and get out of the house. Go to a neighbor's house to phone the fire department.

Practice for the real thing. Hold family fire drills on a regular basis and make sure that everyone knows what to do in case of a fire. Make doubly sure that everyone can actually get out of the house according to the plans you have made.

Meet and count heads. Have a designated meeting place well away from the house where all family members will congregate for a head count to make sure that everyone got out safely.

Stow combustibles and gas engines safely. Keep combustible materials away from the furnace, which can give off flames or sparks at times, and keep them away from all pilot lights, such as on the hot water heater.

Don't keep lawn mowers that contain gasoline in unventilated rooms with hot water heaters. Here in Texas where I live, we have one or two explosions each year because of the intense heat that builds up under such dangerous conditions.

Be careful with cords. Don't run extension cords under rugs. They can wear, fray, bend to expose wire, or be bitten by pets, and then short out to cause a fire. The U.S. Consumer Product Safety Commission has been conducting a study of the causes of appliance cord failures because such failures result annually in thousands of home fires, hundreds of injuries, and many deaths. Check your appliance cords and extension cords for the beginning signs of wear, and then get them repaired or replace them before they are totally worn. Your life is worth more than any repair bill or extension cord cost.

Be prepared. Buy a fire extinguisher and check its effectiveness date regularly. Also, keep baking soda on hand for extinguishing small, emergency kitchen fires.

Install smoke detectors on each floor of your home, usually in the hallway near each separate sleeping area. They're easy to install with just a screwdriver and the set of instructions that comes in the box.

Don't mount a smoke detector too close to areas such as the kitchen, where smoke and steam from cooking will activate the alarm, in a bathroom, where shower steam may activate it, or in the garage, where combustion products from the car's engine can set it off.

When you buy your smoke detectors, you will get instructions for proper placement and for checking the batteries to make sure they are still working. If the batteries are dead, you are not protected, so test the batteries regularly.

Keep curtains away from gas flames. Don't install a gas cooktop near windows where curtains can blow into the flames or where wind could extinguish the cooking flames. If you already have such an installation, keep that window closed, don't have curtains over the stove, or vent the drafts by installing draft guards, which you can buy in hardware stores or through some catalogs.

Get out safely. More people are overcome by smoke and inhalation of chemicals produced by burning textiles and other parts of the building than are burned by fire. If you have to go down a smoke-filled hall, crawl on the floor and put a wet cloth over your nose and mouth to serve as a filter.

If you are in a room and suspect there is fire outside of it because of smoke or an actual alarm, touch the door before opening it. If it is hot, do not open it. The fire is likely to rush—more likely, explode—into the room before you can get the door closed again.

Heat rises, so the top of the door will warm up first. If the door feels cool but you see smoke curling in at the bottom, the area on the other side is filled to the floor with smoke, and you must find another way out. Smoke rises and fills a room or a hallway from the top down. If you are on the first floor, get out through the window and don't worry about breaking it or pushing out the screen. If you have to break a window, put a blanket over yourself or find a way to protect yourself from cuts.

Caution: Before you open any windows, if you are in a bedroom, take wet sheets, blankets, or towels, and stuff them around the door. Opening the windows can cause the heat and smoke from the hall to explode into the room.

Signal where you are. The universal way to signal firefighters when you are in a multistory building is to hang a sheet out of a window to say, "Somebody's in here; come get me."

See also EMERGENCIES.

HOMES

Take photos. If you are building a home, make sure to photograph everything that goes underground, like pipes, wires, septic tank, and gas lines, and then it will be easy to find them when you need repairs. Hopefully, with a new home, you won't need repairs too soon!

Determine how much you can afford. The general cost formula is that the home price should not exceed two to two and a half times your annual family income or the monthly mortgage, electric, water, and maintenance bills should not exceed 25 percent of your total monthly income.

Look for problems. Get a house inspector or construction expert to look for flaws, damage, and possible repair problems in the future before you buy, unless the price is such a bargain that repair costs are not a factor.

Consider location, location, location. To make sure you've chosen the right house, consider distance to schools, availability of bus service, and how long it would take family members to get to work or school. Are there shopping malls, grocery stores, a post office, and a hospital nearby? How high are area taxes? Are ambulance and fire services available?

Check the rules. Are any unusual restrictions enforced? Ask area neighbors if they have encountered any unique problems.

HOME SECURITY

Borrow boots. One reader puts a large (size 14), dirty pair of men's work boots outside her front door to dissuade would-be intruders. She occasionally runs a little water over them to make them appear as if they had recently been worn. This may be false security, but if I were an intruder, I'd think twice before risking confrontation with a guy who wears size 14 boots! The do's and don'ts below will also help you to feel safe and secure, with or without the boots.

Plant a key. Don't leave spare keys in the traditional places, such as in mailboxes, under doormats, under potted plants, and so forth. Find a secret way of concealing the extra key, such as putting it in a film canister or a small can or wrapping it in a wad of foil and then burying it in a special place in the garden where it can easily be dug up when you've forgotten your keys.

Don't advertise your absence. Don't leave notes for repair people or family members on the door where anyone can read that you will be away for a specific time.

Turn down the ringer. Unless you have an answering machine, adjust your telephone ring to its lowest volume if you plan to be away from home for a day or longer. Prowlers know a home is empty if the phone rings unanswered.

It's all in the timing. Use timers to switch lights, radios, and TV sets on and off when you're not at home so that your house appears to be occupied at all times.

Keep the mail coming. When you go on a trip, don't cancel your mail and newspapers; you'll just be letting a lot of strangers know you'll be gone and for how long. It's better to have a neighbor take in your mail, newspapers, and any flyers left on your door so that your house looks occupied.

Hire a house sitter. If for some reason your plans to be away from home have been publicized, as through announcements of a funeral or wedding, hire a house sitter or have a friend stay in your house while the event is going on. Burglars often use newspaper announcements that tell who will be where and how long to schedule their "working hours."

Get a dog. A barking dog is the best prowler alarm and burglar deterrent. Even a small yappy dog is an effective announcer of people presence.

Get new keys for your kingdom. Have a locksmith reset all of the lock tumblers when you move into a new house, or buy new locks. Nobody knows how many sets of keys are with how many people!

Make double trouble for intruders. If you don't already have them, install double cylinder locks that need to be opened with a key from the inside and outside. Then, if a thief breaks a pane of glass in your door to get in, he'll still have to fiddle around with a lock instead of just a knob.

See "Types and Uses of Door Locks" on page 145 for more information.

Don't become unhinged. If you have door hinges set on the outside of your house, a burglar only has to knock out the pins from the hinges and the door will come off for easy entry. It's best to reset hinges inside.

Beware of breaking glass. Burglars can easily break glass panels set beside doors and then reach around to open the door from the inside. If you have such doors, put a grille over the panel to fortify it.

Protect patio doors. Burglar-proof your glass patio doors by buying adjustable safety bars at hardware stores or by cutting a pipe, metal bar, or broom handle exactly to the measurement of the inside bottom track of the door so that you can wedge it in on the track when you want to bar the door.

If your sliding door is installed so that you can't drop a broom handle in, simply drill a hole through both sliding doors and insert a bolt or a nail to keep the doors from sliding.

Be discrete with a "C" clamp. If you think that someone can enter your house through your attached garage, a C clamp can provide extra security. Tighten the C clamp on the track next to the roller on the door track so the door cannot be opened.

Make windows frosty. Prowlers can't tell that you are gone because your car is not in your garage if you cover your garage windows with a frosted, adhesive-backed plastic or spray with a can of window frosting paint.

HONEY

Soften sugared honey. If honey gets sugared in storage, microwave the honey in the jar for a couple of minutes and it will return to a pourable state.

Caution: Microwave time will vary according to amount; better to zap it for less time than too much. Also, do not place metal containers in the microwave, and for extra caution place the honey jar in a dish you know is microwave safe.

See MICROWAVES.

Use corn syrup in a pinch. Generally, corn syrup can substitute for honey in most recipes, but since it's not as sweet as honey, the dessert won't be as sweet. As with all substitutions, the texture and flavor can be slightly altered.

HOSE

See PANTY HOSE.

HOT TUBS

Don't get overheated. My sources say that the maximum temperature of the water in the hot tub should be 100°F; heat stroke can occur in some people at temperatures above 104°F. Many people find that 95°F is perfectly comfortable.

Caution: People with certain health problems, such as high blood pressure, diabetes, or epilepsy, shouldn't soak when home alone.

HOUSEHOLD INFORMATION

 Keep a notebook. Record all floor and window dimensions to make buying new curtains and flooring a snap. Record the different paint colors and brands and glue the paint-store samples of paint colors of the different rooms on the page with the description of that room; do the same for swatches of wallpaper.

See also BILLS.

HOUSEPLANTS

Tag it. Keep the name tags on your plants and record their botanical names so that if a curious child or pet tastes any part of it, you can give an accurate description and proper name to your Poison Control Center. Call information to get the number, and then keep it by the phone or program it into a programmable phone before you have an emergency.

Take it. If you have to rush a child or pet to an emergency facility, take the plant along with you to confirm its identity. If the plant's too large, cut off a twig. If it has flowers, seeds, fruits, or exposed bulbs, take them, too.

Water neatly. Place a few ice cubes here and there on the dirt of your plants. They'll melt slowly, and you'll have no spillovers.

Water while you're away. Water plants thoroughly, then set them on a

Poisonous Plants

If ingested, some common plants can be harmful to children and pets. *Philodendron*, *dieffenbachia*, *rhododendron*, and various *anemone* species can all cause illness. Even the medicinal aloe vera plant, popularly used for skin irritations, can be harmful if eaten.

small rock- or pebble-filled tray. Fill the tray with water, but don't overfill it so that plants are soaked. Place the tray with plants in indirect sunlight (direct may be too hot), and they will wait happily for you to return from a short vacation.

See also PLANTS.

HUMIDIFIERS

The relative humidity ratio is always given as a percentage at a given temperature. The ideal indoor comfort range, according to my sources, is 40 percent relative humidity, plus or minus 5 percent, at a temperature of 68° to 70°F. But comfort aside, people with respiratory difficulties can benefit from humidifiers (either freestanding units or those that can be attached to a furnace), adding moisture to the air. Even people who are normally healthy can get sore throats from environments that are too dry.

And it's not just people who benefit. Humidifiers prevent electric static in cold climates, help keep your furniture's joints from drying out and getting loose, and ensure that home fabrics don't become brittle and wear out sooner than they should. They also make your houseplants happy and help you save about 15 percent of fuel costs in the winter since you tend to feel colder in a dry room. Here's how to maintain your humidifier.

Choose the right spot. When you are deciding where to put a humidifier, consider that bathrooms and kitchens produce a certain amount of moisture. Therefore, it's best to locate a humidifier in an area that's not too close to these rooms. In a two-story house, you can put the humidifier at the bottom of a stairwell, but it's really better to have one unit for each floor. If you place your humidifier in front of or near a wall heater or radiator, their heat and air movement will increase evaporation.

Keep it clean. Always check the manufacturer's instructions for details on cleaning your room humidifier. Keeping the humidifier clean and free of deposits helps it work better and last longer. If you don't have instructions, the following method works for most humidifiers.

Remove deposits with vinegar. Fill the humidifier bowl with white vinegar and soak it for a couple of hours or overnight for heavy buildup. Pour out the vinegar and rinse the bowl with fresh water. If deposits remain, repeat the procedure.

To soak an impeller (the little rod that actually sticks down into the water), fill a tall glass or jar with vinegar and immerse the impeller in it. Be careful not to bend the impeller or to get vinegar or water into the motor. Regular soaking will cut down on the amount of buildup and soaking time. Using distilled or mineral-free water will also help prevent buildup.

Avoid algae. When small humidifiers get algae buildup in the water, frequent, thorough cleaning is needed to remove the yucky slime. Add about 1 tablespoon of bleach each time you fill the reservoir, and the water will stay nice and clean. This small amount of bleach won't give off an unpleasant odor. Keeping your humidifier clean not only prevents musty odors, it helps avoid the possibility of spreading the mold and algae, which can really play havoc with allergies.

Replace worn parts. Maintenance includes replacement of worn pads, belts, plates, and orifices for solenoid valves, plus cleaners recommended by the manufacturer's manual that dissolve mineral deposits and lime, mold, and algae.

See also VAPORIZERS.

ICE CREAM

 Freeze individual portions. Save on the cost of individual ice-cream portions (vs. quart or gallon sizes) and recycle clean 1-cup lidded yogurt containers at the same time. Buy large containers of ice cream and put individual portions in the yogurt cups. There's no mess when children serve themselves, and dieters aren't tempted to take larger portions than allowed.

Make quick containers of ice for homemade ice cream. Freeze water in empty quart-size milk cartons overnight. Then, take a hammer and strike all four sides of the frozen carton a couple of times. Open the top and the crushed ice will drop neatly into the ice-cream maker. Five quarts of ice with a layer of rock salt after each one is enough for the average ice-cream machine processing.

Soften it to scoop. Zap a half-gallon of ice cream in the microwave on low for about 30 to 45 seconds, depending on the wattage of your microwave. Experiment to find the right amount of time. It will be easier to scoop.

Prevent drippy ice-cream cone messes. Place a small marshmallow in the bottom of the cone before you put the ice cream in. Then, if the ice cream melts, the marshmallow keeps it from dripping out of the bottom.

Keep crystals at bay. Crystals form when temperatures fluctuate and can indicate that the freezer is opened and closed too often or that there is a problem with the freezer itself. Keep track of your family's freezer use. If fewer openings and closings don't help, the freezer may need servicing.

Save ice pop sticks. Wash and save them for stirring coffee, scraping mud or other goo from shoe bottoms, leveling off measuring cups, marking depth measurements to help you plant seeds and bulbs, and using as plant markers.

Also, these sticks can spread condiments at picnics and glue, paste, and grout. Or use them for anything else that requires a disposable spreader. They can also stir paint in small containers. Check out craft books and shops for children's "keep-busy" ice-cream stick projects.

ICE CUBES

Go for the grande. When the weather is hot and you need serious-size ice cubes to keep drinks cool, freeze them in muffin tins.

Plant an ice cube surprise. Freeze a maraschino cherry or a couple of mint leaves in each cube for pretty drink decorations.

Use a slick strategy for stuck cubes. Most ice-cube trays are coated. Putting hot water into them and washing in hot, soapy dishwater or in the dishwasher melts off that coating. If cubes stick in your ice-cube trays, try spraying the trays with cooking spray every now and then.

Freeze more than water. Freeze leftover tea and coffee in ice cube trays to avoid dilution by regular cubes in your iced tea or coffee.

ICE PACKS

Treat lip injuries fast. A frozen juice treat stops the tears and swelling when a child falls, hurt a lip, and needs a distraction as well as an ice pack.

Make a homemade ice pack. Mix 1 part rubbing alcohol with 2 parts water and freeze in a zipper plastic bag. It will be pliable enough to conform to a knee or elbow and can be refrozen after each use.

Caution: Be sure to place a damp cloth between the skin and the ice pack to prevent frostbite.

INGREDIENTS

Keep special ingredients safe from family foragers. If you don't want a family member with a case of the munchies to eat certain ingredients bought especially for a recipe or meal, have a code worked out with your family such as placing a red dot sticker on the container or just stick a warning note on the item. You'll save emergency trips to the store and avoid those moments when you've got ingredients all prepared, and you reach for the last one, and . . . need I say more?

INSURANCE

Take inventory. Whether or not you are moving, having photos of your possessions is proof of ownership, their description, and condition. If you have a lot of jewelry or other valuables, you may want to use an instant camera; then you can immediately write on the back (or on a label to put on the back) the original cost and any other information that will help you make a claim if the item is lost through theft or fire. The photos should be stored in a fireproof safe or safe-deposit box so that they don't get damaged with your possessions in fire or flood.

INVITATIONS

Include extra phone numbers. When sending invitations to weddings or other similar events, include an emergency phone number for out-of-town guests. For example, wedding invitations tell the location of the church and reception, but parents of small children hiring a sitter for the event would want to also be provided with the phone numbers, just in case of an emergency.

IRONING

Ironing is one of those household chores that can be delegated to teens and other members of the family, who can, at the very least, iron their own clothing and, at best, be kind to their parents and iron a few extras. Here's how to get the most return on your ironing time and make sure clothes look great.

Ironing Basics

Start with the details. Iron detailed parts first then press the rest of the garment. You'll find you have fewer wrinkles to deal with.

Consider a spray. I like to use sprays. I'm not sure if anyone mixes starch anymore, because it's so time consuming. You can choose a fabric finish spray to renew the hand or body of a garment or a spray starch to give a garment more body and stiffness. Some people sprinkle garments with water to dampen them before ironing, but if you use fabric finish, it dampens the garment and adds body at the same time.

Refrigerate the "leftovers." If you've sprinkled garments with water or starch and then don't finish ironing them all in one spree, you can freeze or refrigerate the clothing in a plastic bag until you can iron again. If you just let damp clothing lie around, it will mildew or smell musty.

Ironing a Shirt or Blouse

Yes, it's a seven-step process, but this is the best way to iron a blouse.

1. First iron the back of the collar, then iron the front of the collar. Some collars are cut so that they will curve around the neck smoothly. Iron these from their point toward the center, stopping short when the fabric shows a fold. While the collar is still warm, you can fold it along the seamed fold line where the collar and neck facing meet, and wrap it around your waist to curve it.

2. Some people like to iron the underside of the button and the button-hole facing next; some omit this step entirely.

3. Iron the back and front of cuffs (also, pocket tabs if there are any; these should be unbuttoned).

4. Iron the backs and fronts of sleeves. Some garments shouldn't have the crease that forms when you flatten the sleeve from underarm seam to shoulder line to iron it. You can buy a sleeve board to insert into the sleeve when you iron it.

5. Iron the shoulder parts—the yolk across the back, and the front yolk, if there is one. With some garments and some ironing boards, you can do the whole shoulder area without moving the shirt, which is good.

6. Iron the two front sides or the front if it's one piece. If the front parts are ironed before the back, the spray is less likely to dry out on one side while you do the back and cause one side of the front to look better than the other.

7. Iron the back. If the back has a pleat and it's important to you to have this pleat ironed, you can line up the pleat folds with the shirttail, and give them a good hard press, dampening them well and pressing dry the first time you wash the shirt. Often the pressed lines will stay in the fabric through many launderings and will be a guide for future ironings.

Don't overload the dryer. Most of the time, blends of polyester and cotton will come out of the dryer either ready to wear or needing only a touch-up ironing. To prevent wrinkling, don't overload the dryer, and try to dry clothing of similar weight in each load. For example, if you wash a bunch of heavy towels in with cotton-polyester blouses or dress shirts and then dump the whole load into the dryer, the towels will smash up the shirts and require a longer drying time for the whole load. Ultimately, you'll have more creases to iron than if you put just the shirts and blouses into one dryer load and the towels in another.

Consider clothing on a case-by-case basis. Some of the crushed-look cottons really shouldn't be ironed or, at the most, should just be touched up with a steam iron. And whether or not you iron such things as jeans is a matter of taste and energy.

Iron dark-colored fabrics and damp silks inside out. You can also use a pressing cloth to prevent shine. Commercial press cloths are very good, but you can also use a cotton handkerchief or a linen dish towel if you don't have a commercial cloth.

Iron embroidered areas from the inside. For extra depth, place them embroidered side down on a terry towel or soft, folded dish towel for ironing.

Drop a drop cloth. When ironing long dresses, large tablecloths, curtains, and so on, it's best to put a sheet on the floor under the ironing board so you don't dust the floor and iron at the same time. (I know it saves time to do two things at once, but this isn't one of those times when it's a good idea.) And don't forget to use the large, squared end of the ironing board for ironing these things.

Test the temperature. Use the temperature guide on your iron to determine which temperature goes with which fabrics. Since iron temperatures vary, test the iron on an inconspicuous spot when you are touching up delicate fabric that might melt from too much heat. Follow the temperature guide on the label or hang tag, too; that's what it's for!

Make a sleeve roll. Dresses and blouses with puffy sleeves can be ironing headaches. Make a simple homemade sleeve roll from a roll of toilet tissue covered with foil, then with terry cloth or any fabric that will withstand the

Ironing a Skirt

Here's my favorite way to iron skirts.

1. Iron pocket flaps or facings, the undersides of button and button-hole facings (if the skirt opens down one side), and with certain machine-stitched hems, especially on heavy cotton or denim, iron the hem from the inside after spraying it with fabric finish to flatten it. This keeps the hem from rolling up.

2. Iron the body of the skirt.

3. Iron the waistband and, if needed, press the tops of pleats on a pleated skirt. If you are so unfortunate as to own a totally pleated skirt, you can line up the pleats and stick a nonrust straight pin at the hemline and into the ironing board to hold the pleats in place. (Bet you're sorry you bought it! And to make matters worse, dry cleaners charge by the pleat to press such garments!) And now you know why.

Note: If you have a gathered dirndl skirt and a bit of a "pooched out" tummy, lightly flatten the gathered areas when you iron the waistband so that they won't add more mid-section bulk.

heat of an iron. A half-used roll of paper towels can also be used as a sleeve roll for wide or capped sleeves.

Remove creases carefully. To remove creases from let-out garment seams or hems, wash the garment first. There may be dirt on the crease that will leave a line if ironed. Apply white vinegar directly to the seam or hem line until it is thoroughly damp. Place a dry, clean cloth over the line and press with a medium-hot iron. Hang the garment up to air. Vinegar odors dissipate quickly.

Caution: Always test on an inconspicuous place before putting vinegar on fabric.

To remove creases or wrinkles from wool garments, like those you get in

Ironing Pants

Pants can be trickier than you might think to iron. Here's how I do it.

1. Iron pocket facings.

2. Insert the ironing board into the pants, one leg at a time, ironing the entire pant top and as far down on the leg as the ironing board will go.

3. To iron the pant-leg bottoms and put in the crease at the same time, match each pant leg seam to seam, and lay the pants across the ironing board. Tuck the pant leg closest to you under your chin so that you can work on the other leg without having the pants fall to the floor.

4. Starting at the hem, match the seams and iron sections until you have ironed the inside of the pant leg as far as the crotch. Turn the pants over, tuck the ironed leg under your chin, and repeat. After both inside legs are ironed, lay the pants flat across the ironing board and iron the outsides of the legs.

5. When pants have pleats at the top, the front crease needs to go from hem to the major pleat. If you use the system above, this usually happens automatically. Then all you have to do is insert the ironing board into each pant leg to touch up about an iron's width of the pleat.

Note: Some people like to do all this by laying the pants along the length of the ironing board. It works if you have short-legged people in the house or a very long ironing board.

the back of a pants leg, lay the pants (or other garment) out on the ironing board. Dampen a cloth with white vinegar; place it on the wrinkles to be removed. Iron over the cloth and the wrinkles should come out. Repeat this step if needed, but when repeating, leave more vinegar in the cloth the second time. Continue until wrinkles and creases are out. Let the garment air out thoroughly.

Improvise in a pinch. Nowadays, many hotels provide an iron and ironing board for their guests. If you find yourself in a hotel room without such amenities, use this traveler's secret—hang your garments in the bathroom while you shower to let the steam "iron" it. If the fabric is not very fragile, you can also "iron" some creases out over hot light bulbs. (Just remember to put the shade back on the lamp.)

Ironing Boards

Replace the pad. If you find that you have to press hard or go over sections of clothing many times to get them ironed properly, you may need a new ironing board pad. Most of the time, we replace the cover only. We forget that we eventually iron the padding too flat to be a cushion when we iron.

Reflect the heat. You can put a piece of heavy-duty foil under the ironing board cover and over the pad so that heat is reflected to the undersides of garments to make ironing faster. Many of the silicone-type ironing board covers accomplish the same heat reflection.

Discover other uses for an ironing board. You can cover the cloth top with a plastic sheet or an old flannel-backed plastic tablecloth to make an adjustable worktable for crafts or wrapping gifts that's kind to your back because you can adjust the height.

Iron Care and Maintenance

Run your iron over a washcloth saturated with white vinegar. Place the cloth on a flat surface and run the warm iron over it several times, pressing gently. You'll see all the brown goop come off. Now run the iron over a clean, damp cloth, to wipe off any remaining residue so that it will not mark the next garment you iron. The secret is to clean the bottom of the iron frequently so that it doesn't get a major gunk buildup.

Clean the inside with vinegar, too. If the manufacturer's care instructions don't advise against it, you can use white vinegar to clean the inside of your iron. Fill the iron with vinegar. Let it steam for about 5 minutes, and then let it rest a while. Empty the vinegar and rinse the iron well with water. Then heat it and run the bottom back and forth across a damp washcloth before using it to prevent mineral stains on your clothing.

Clean with steel wool. One way to clean a steel iron sole plate is to rub a small piece of very fine (0000) steel wool gently over the bottom of the iron.

Caution: Never use steel wool on a nonstick iron.

Keep your iron from clogging. Use distilled water and drain it after each use. Distilled water prevents mineral buildup, the major cause of clogged irons.

Consider a commercial cleaner. You'll find many excellent iron cleaners on the market that will remove any buildup on the bottom of an iron.

IRON RUST

See STAINS for hints on how to remove iron rust stains from fabrics.

IRON SKILLETS

See POTS AND PANS.

JACK-O'-LANTERNS

See HALLOWEEN.

JAMS AND JELLIES

Make multiuse gifts. Homemade jelly makes a lovely gift. Next time, instead of putting the jelly in plain old jars, divide it into coffee mugs, seal with paraffin, and top it off with a bow and ribbon.

Keep cool when making jelly. Put on a clean pair of oven mitts to protect your hands while stirring and to tighten lids after processing. No more juggling hot, wet jars with pot holders or dish towels.

Savor the last drop. When there's just a bit of jelly or jam left in the jar, add some milk and shake vigorously to make a delicious, fruity shake. Delicious!

JAR LABELS

Remove them easily. When you need to send a label for a special offer, moisten paper towels or a cloth with hot water and wrap it around the jar.

Keep Necklaces Straight

Tired of spending hours trying to untangle a jumbled mess of inter-twined necklaces? Here are some tips for avoiding twists and tangles and preventing damage to your jewelry.

Hang 'em up. Hang necklaces on a mirror with clear suction-cup hooks or on an expanding peg coat rack on a wall or in the closet.

Lay 'em down. Line shoe box lids with a piece of soft fabric (to keep necklaces from slipping), and then layer the necklace-filled lids in a drawer. Or place your necklaces lengthwise on pieces of felt, roll necklace "sausages," and store them in a drawer.

Leave it on for a few minutes. When you remove the wet cloth, the label should slip off. If not, remoisten the cloth and try again. Or, soak the whole jar in warm water until the label comes off.

Note: Labels tear easily when damp; handle gently.

JEWELRY

Extend a short necklace. Create your own extension by fastening the clasp of a thin metal bracelet to the necklace. The collar will cover the bracelet so your extension won't show.

Create a simple cleaner. Mix sudsy ammonia with an equal amount of water. Soak jewelry (except for gold electroplated items, opals, jade, pearls, and soft stones) for a few minutes, and then carefully clean around stones and designs with a soft toothbrush. Rinse well, dry, and then buff with a soft cloth.

For a quick fix, rub a bit of toothpaste on gold or silver jewelry with your finger, rinse well, and polish with a soft cloth. Don't do this too frequently because it may be abrasive. And avoid this method for soft gems such as pearls, opals, and jade. They could be damaged.

Don't dump it down the drain. Place jewelry in a tea strainer to rinse

Jump Starts

Put a copy of these directions to jump-start a car in your student driver's glove compartment and maybe in your own, too.

1. Position both cars so they face each other. If your car is against the curb, park the other car next to yours on the battery side. Put both vehicles in park. Apply the emergency brakes, and turn the ignitions off.

2. Remove the cap from the top of each battery. This is an important safety measure.

3. Locate the jumper cables' positive cable (red clips) and the negative cable (black clips), as well as the positive and negative terminals on the batteries. (You may need to clean the battery surface around the terminals to find the markings—there should be a "+" or "pos" to denote positive and a "−" or "neg" to denote negative.)

4. Attach one of the red clips to the positive terminal of the dead battery. Attach the other red clip to the positive terminal of the good battery.

5. Then, connect the negative cable to the negative terminal of the good battery and to the engine block of the stalled car, away

after cleaning. It's a good way to prevent it from accidentally going down the drain.

Keep it safe and sparkling. Remove rings and other jewelry before doing housework. Various precious and semiprecious stones can get scratched by housework or have their surfaces dulled by household compounds. Pearls, opals, and jade are especially at risk.

As far as metals are concerned, silver jewelry tarnishes when exposed to rubber gloves and ordinary household compounds such as mayonnaise, salt, vinegar, eggs, and some cleaners. Gold is damaged by exposure to mer-

from the battery, carburetor, fuel line, and any tubing or moving parts. (NOT to the negative terminal of the dead battery.)

6. When the jumper cables are properly hooked up, start the car with the good battery. Then try to start the car with the dead battery; when it begins to run, let it idle with the motor on for a minute or two.

7. Disconnect the cables in the reverse order. Remove the black (negative) clip from the engine block first, then the red (positive) clips. To avoid electrical sparks, don't let the positive and negative cables touch each other.

Note: Most newer batteries have vented caps. With these, you must check to make sure they are tight and level before hooking up the battery to be jump-started. If a damp cloth is available, place it over the vent caps to decrease the chance of a spark igniting any fumes that might be released from the battery.

Caution: Serious eye injuries can result from batteries exploding. Exercise caution and wear safety eyewear to protect yourself, and never stand face-down over a battery when jump-starting a car.

For more about cars, see AUTOMOBILES.

cury and some chemicals. Alloys in gold and soldered areas are weakened by chlorine and so it's best to remove jewelry when swimming in a pool or cleaning with bleach solutions.

Avoid turning green. If you have any jewelry that turns your skin green, paint the part that touches your skin (like the inside of a bracelet) with clear fingernail polish or have it coated by a jeweler.

Share it with a princess (or a pirate). Instead of just tossing your old costume jewelry, give it to children to use as prizes when they play games.

Pin it to everything but your skin. To prevent losing a brooch because it has ended up in the washer, which is usually what happens when it's left attached to clothing, try pinning the brooch through your blouse and onto a slip or bra strap. Then, you can't undress until you take it all off.

JUICE

Avoid frozen juice frustration. Does mixing frozen orange or other juices in the morning rank equally in your life with untangling wire coat hangers? Instead, try breaking up the frozen juice chunks with a potato masher. Or, at bedtime, dump the frozen juice out of the can into a container, add the required amount of water, and place the container in the fridge. When you take it out in the morning, the juice will be thawed and you need only shake or stir.

KETCHUP

See STAINS for hints on how to remove ketchup stains from fabrics.

KEYS

Pin them on. It may be a sign of the times, but readers have begun sending me safety hints in case of mugging or theft. Some readers suggest attaching your house key to the band of your skirt or pants with a large safety pin; then if you are mugged, you can still get into your house. This also prevents giving a thief your key along with the address found in your wallet. My mother used to pin my key inside my coat pocket when I was a child.

Use them as reminders. Put your car keys on anything that you need to remember to take with you or to check before you leave. For example, hang them near the kitchen stove or coffee pot, and you'll remember to check that the kitchen appliances are off before leaving the house. If you tend to forget if you've unplugged your curling iron or hot rollers, hang your car keys there so that you have to check these gadgets before you leave. Put them on your "doggy bag" in the refrigerator and when you leave "Mom's"

(or some other generous nice person's home), you won't forget the goodies.

Make a paper pattern. When you get new keys, trace a copy of them on a sheet of paper that you keep in your household files. If you keep and label tracings of every key, then you have a pattern to match when you are trying to identify "mystery" keys.

Chime in. Attach keys with fishing line to a clothes hanger, tree branch, wooden embroidery hoop, or other hanging device to create a novel wind chime. Old keys can also substitute for missing parts of an existing wind chime.

Let Fido carry the spare. One reader attaches the spare house keys to her dogs' collars along with the rest of their ID tags. She says neither dog "takes kindly" to having a stranger mess with its collar, but relatives and friends who need the key can easily get it from one of the dogs.

Reuse your key tabs. Plastic fluorescent key tabs, often given away as promotional items, make great glow-in-the-dark light pulls in a closet or basement. Others may be attractive enough for ceiling fan pulls.

KITCHENS

In many ways, cleaning a kitchen is just like cleaning any other room in the house. But because kitchen surfaces are usually subject to heavy use and inevitably come in contact with your food, extra-special care is warranted.

Countertops

Don't be harsh. Never use abrasive cleansers on plastic laminated tops; they scratch and eventually remove the finish. If stains occur, squeeze fresh lemon juice over them; allow the juice to soak about 45 minutes. Then sprinkle baking soda over the lemon juice and rub with a soft cloth.

Wipe and rinse daily. A solution of mild dishwashing liquid and water does the daily cleanup job. Just wash, rinse with clear water, and your countertop should look good for a long, long time.

Pour a bit of bubbly. You can also clean countertops by pouring club soda on the counter and wiping up the soda with a soft cloth. Then rinse with warm water and wipe dry. You can finish the job on dull-finished countertops by polishing the countertops with a plastic laminate cleaner, which gives them a low luster.

Maintain the shine. Shiny-finish countertops will stay shiny if you apply lemon oil about once a week and wipe dry. It not only cleans but also preserves the finish.

Chopping Blocks

Treat the cuts. Tiny knife cuts are natural wear for these tops because they serve as cutting surfaces. Scrub them with soap and water. Small crevices can harbor bacteria, so occasionally you may want to disinfect the chopping block with a mild bleach solution (2 to 3 tablespoons of bleach to a quart of water). Rinse well, and then rejuvenate the surface with a thin coat of mineral oil; let it soak for a half an hour and buff.

Scrub the stains. A baking soda scrub will also clean chopping blocks and remove stains and some light burn marks. Rinse, then rub with oil as described above.

Tile

Get rid of grungy grout. Grout is no problem at all if you seal it with a grout sealer, found in tile or hardware stores. Follow the directions on the box. You may have to repeat the process once a year.

Nonetheless, the grout between kitchen tiles can become dirty. To bleach it out, make a mild solution (2 tablespoons of bleach to 1 quart of water), and dab at just the grouting with a cotton swab.

Make tile sparkle. Wash tiles with dishwashing liquid and water or vinegar and water when they look grimy. You'll get the best results if you scrub them with a nylon brush or nylon net. Just wash, rinse, and then step back to admire your handiwork.

Get artsy economically. If you've always wanted hand-painted wall tiles like those in decorator shops but can't afford to rip out your old tiles and replace them, try decals. You can either make a border of decal tiles or make your own design by alternating decal tiles with plain ones. If you want to make any changes later, you can buy a decal remover kit wherever decals are sold.

Sinks

Clean stainless steel. Never clean a stainless steel sink with abrasive cleaners. You'll scratch the surface and never be able to get the sink to look good again. If you feel you must use a powdered cleanser, be sure to rub with the grain of the stainless steel rather than in circles or in the opposite direction.

To clean stainless steel sinks, use baking soda; even some liquid cleansers may scratch surfaces. Always read those labels! Just sprinkle some baking soda in the sink and scrub with a damp cloth. Vinegar is great for removing water spots and attacking gunk buildup.

Wipe the sink dry after each use. To keep the sink shiny or for a hurry-up sparkle, wipe it with a little oil or vinegar on a soft, clean cloth.

Clean your porcelain with bleach. White and light-colored porcelain sinks sometimes need a good whitening treatment to get rid of accumulated stains. Fill the sink with cold water (enough to cover the bottom) and add ¼ cup of household bleach. Let it soak for at least ½ hour. Tell your family what's going on, and watch out for children or pets, especially sneaky cats who drink from sinks, so that they won't be accidentally harmed by the bleach.

Caution: Never use any kind of bleach on colored porcelain sinks because it fades the colors. Instead, clean colored porcelain sinks with mild liquid detergents, baking soda, or vinegar. Similarly, powdered abrasive cleansers and mild liquid cleansers can still be abrasive enough to wear off the glaze of your kitchen or bathroom sink. Once the glaze is gone, your sink will never be shiny again, and it will be harder and harder to keep clean.

KITES

Fly them safely. Fly your kite in an open field, away from electric power lines and public roadways. Never take a chance!

Don't rediscover electricity. Never use any metal in making a kite, including wire or string containing metal fibers. Also, never fly your kite on rainy or stormy days, and always make sure your kite string is perfectly dry. Wet strings conduct electricity.

Walk away from danger. If a kite becomes tangled in an electric power line or catches on a utility pole, leave it. It is simply too dangerous to try to retrieve it.

Along the same lines, never climb on utility poles, towers, or other utility equipment. Aside from the obvious risk of being electrocuted, you could fall and injure yourself.

KNICKKNACKS

Keep track of their locations. When you are dusting shelves that hold figurines, framed photos, or other collection arrangements, snap a picture of the display with an instant camera so that you can put them back as they were when you are finished. This is especially helpful if you're dusting at a relative's or friend's house. It's also a good idea to keep the photos for insurance records.

Clean them carefully. You can wash most knickknacks in less time than it takes to dust them if you swish them in water containing a touch of liquid detergent. Then rinse and drain on a towel. If you want to make sure every crevice is dry, use a hand-held hair dryer to blow away moisture. For fragile objects, put them on a towel-covered tray in the sink and spray them first with window cleaner and then with water. Let them air dry on a towel.

KNITTING AND CROCHETING

Color it smart. Knit with two different-colored, same-size needles, and you will always know which row you are on—even or odd.

Hold your place. Keep a pad of self-sticking notes near your chair. When the phone rings as you are deciphering pattern instructions, you can stick a note on the line you were on when interrupted.

Label your hand-knit gifts. Enclose a label from a skein of the yarn that you've used so that the person receiving the gift will know how to care for their new garment or blanket.

LABELS

Remove gummy glue. To soften gummy glue on a glass jar, put it in the microwave with a damp towel over it. Microwave it on low and check it every 30 seconds or so. The heat softens the glue, and you can usually pull the label off easily.

LADDERS

Tack up a tool holder. Instead of climbing up and down the ladder to get this tool or that, hammer some nails along the edge of a wooden ladder so that before you start a job, you can assemble all the tools you need and hang them at the height at which you will work. If you hang your tools at your usual workbench with self-gripping fabric tape, you can stick self-gripping tape to a metal ladder. Either way, your work will be easier if you don't have to climb a ladder as often.

LAMPS AND LAMPSHADES

Let the light shine through. Clean lampshades and see how much more light your lamps will give off. Don't forget to clean the bulbs, too! You can dust them with a new, soft paintbrush or your vacuum cleaner dusting brush. If you need to go beyond dusting, you can wash some lampshades. For example, when lampshades aren't glued to their frames, you can gently wash them in the bathtub with warm water and a spray hose. Dry them quickly after washing so that the frames won't rust. An electric fan or hair dryer can speed the drying process.

Of course, your best bet is always to check the instructions that came on their labels. (You did save the labels in your household file, didn't you?)

LANDSCAPING

Hang your plants. Turn a plain fence or apartment balcony railing into a garden focal point by hanging potted plants from it with S-hooks. Or, if you are handy and have a wood fence, attach some shelves for plants.

Create a fish pond. If you are installing a fountain outdoors and plan to have fish in it, make sure it is at least 10 inches deep. If you install the pond at ground level, you can insert a fiberglass pool like those used for children's swimming pools or a heavy-duty rubber or plastic liner into the hole you've dug. Fiberglass or copper pools made specifically for fountains can be above ground, but they're more expensive than make-it-yourself models.

Find a fountain. A water fountain in a garden room or outdoors in the yard makes a soothing, therapeutic sound and adds a luxurious touch to the decor. Many need no plumbing at all because they operate with water-recirculating pumps. If you buy the complete fountain "works" from a specialty shop, all you do is fill it with water and plug in the pump; no skills required!

Caution: Make sure all electrical outlets are grounded.

See also GARDENS and PLANTS.

LAUNDRY

Following these simple guidelines will help you manage your laundry easily and efficiently, whether you do your laundry at home or at the laundromat. Plus, these hints will give you much brighter washes, even the first time.

It's not necessarily your fault if you don't always get bright-as-new clothing. Manufacturers of white goods sometimes add brighteners to white fabrics that wash out, starting with the first wash. This is especially true of cotton-synthetic blends. When the brighteners wash out, a slight graying sometimes results.

Keep Laundry Tangle-Free

You can avoid the frustration of sorting through a load of tangled, wet clothes if you make sure all hooks are fastened (especially bras and other undergarments) and zippers are closed before starting a wash. If shirt or blouse sleeves seem to be the cause of tangled laundry, button each sleeve to a buttonhole on the front.

As you place clothing into the machine piece by piece, lay each garment in a circle around the agitator. Make sure you set the appropriate water level and washing time. For example, if you have a load of mostly delicate clothing, such as bras, long-sleeved, soft or silky fabric blouses or shirts, or nylon slips, use a delicate or knit setting and make sure the water level is higher than when you had the tangles. More water and less agitation time in the washer-machine may prevent agitation of the washer-person.

Laundry Tips 101

Sort the clothing. Group your clothes into the following separate loads: whites that can be bleached, whites that can't be bleached, light colors, dark colors, heavily soiled items, and lint-giving articles.

Soak bleachable stained items. Mix ¼ cup of chlorine bleach with 1 gallon of water in a sink or pail and soak bleachables for 5 minutes.

Note: Chlorine bleach doesn't remove protein-type stains such as egg, grass, or blood. These are best removed with a presoak product. Please see STAINS.

Test fabrics for colorfastness. Here's an easy way to test if an item is colorfast. Make a solution of 1 tablespoon of bleach and ¼ cup of water. Put a drop or two of this solution on an inconspicuous spot such as an inside seam, and check for color loss.

Let hot water help. To get white clothing whitest, always use the hottest water that is safe for the fabric. If you have hard water, add water softener or baking soda along with the detergent to increase the detergent's efficiency.

Add bleach after a few minutes. If bleach is necessary, add it after the load has washed for about 5 minutes for maximum effectiveness. Never wash colored clothes with white ones because color can easily transfer to the whites, and bleach can take the color out of colored fabrics.

Don't skimp on spot treating. Scrubbing the bottoms of socks and collars before washing is always a good idea. An inexpensive way to scrub out stains is to wrap a bar of soap in nylon net, bunch it around the bar so that it's rough, and then tie a knot in the net or secure it with rubber bands.

Make your own prewash spray. Mix equal parts of water, ammonia, and dishwashing (not dishwasher) liquid. (Read the label to be sure that it doesn't contain bleach.) Put it into a clean spray bottle, and label it as prewash spray.

Caution: When you apply this solution, wash the clothing immediately. Allowing it to set for any period of time may create a difficult stain to remove.

Note the cycle. Here's an easy way to remember when to add the fabric softener. Watch the dial closely to see where the last rinse cycle starts. Mark that spot with an arrow-shaped triangle of masking tape or red nail polish. This is the place you'll add your fabric softener. (Naturally, this is for machines without automatic softener dispensers.) Thereafter, only a quick look at the dial will tell you if it is time to add softener. Mark each cycle (normal, permanent press, and gentle) the same way.

Don't overuse fabric softener. This is particularly important on towels. Overusing fabric softener will decrease the absorbency of the towels.

Don't overload the dryer. If your clothes usually come out of the dryer wrinkled, you might be overloading the dryer, which keeps the clothes from tumbling freely. To remove the wrinkles, wet a washcloth or hand towel, wring it out well, and put it in the dryer with the clothes. Let the clothes spin a while longer, and they will be just as wrinkle-free as can be.

Dust your drapes. To remove dust and freshen drapes, valances, and quilts, put them into the dryer set on "air fluff," and add a fabric softener sheet. They will come out wrinkle-free and fresh-smelling.

Save the lint. Dust and lint buildup in dryer filters and exhaust ducts is a major cause of tens of thousands of home fires. Clean the filter after each load and check the exhaust duct regularly. Also check the outside vent tube to make sure that excess lint isn't plugging the air exit; this also can be a fire hazard.

In the spring, save the lint you removed from the filter. Put it outside and watch the birds pick it up to use as nesting material. They'll have the softest nests in town!

Check the dryer. If you own a cat, be careful to check inside your dryer before you turn it on. Many a tabby, seeking a nice warm place to nap, has taken a spin in the dryer, with disastrous results. Always check before you toss in a load and start the machine. It's a good idea to close the dryer door in between taking clothes out and putting clothes into it. You won't have to change the light bulb so often either, and you will save money on electricity!

Improvise the littlest lint brush. A clean mascara brush will get lint out of hard-to-reach places on clothing like shirt-front plackets, shirt pockets, and hems.

Wash sweaters wisely. To hand wash, use cool or lukewarm water. With the sweater inside out, immerse it for 5 to 10 minutes, turning it over once or twice and gently squeezing suds through the fabric. Rinse the same way

Six Hints to Limit the Lint

Today's dryers catch most lint in their filters, but some people still have problems with it. Most of the time, poor sorting before washing, overdrying, and static electricity are what cause lint to cling to clothing. Here are some hints to limit lint.

- ♥ Sort properly. Don't wash and dry lint-makers like bath towels with lint-collectors like synthetics or permanent press.

- ♥ Remove all papers and tissues from pockets before washing and drying clothes. Tissues seem to expand when laundered.

- ♥ Use fabric softeners to reduce static electricity.

- ♥ Don't overload washers and dryers; they won't work as well as they can.

- ♥ Try to remove clothing when it's still slightly damp. Static electricity builds up in overdried clothing so that lint clings more easily.

- ♥ Clean the dryer lint screen after each load so that it can catch more lint; you'll be saving energy, too, because the machine is working more efficiently.

in basins of water until the water is clear. Block the sweater back into shape, and let it air dry flat.

To machine wash (if care label says so), turn the sweater inside out (place delicate sweaters in a mesh bag or pillowcase), use cool or lukewarm water, and remove before the spin cycle. Some machine-washable sweaters can be put into the dryer for a short time and then removed while damp so that they can be dried flat and blocked. But some synthetics require tumble drying for the full cycle to be blocked into shape; check care labels.

Make a laundry bag for traveling. Sew a drawstring into the open end of an old pillowcase. It will fit to any shape in your suitcase if traveling by plane; it protects souvenirs on the way home, too. When traveling by car, you can toss the laundry bag into the trunk fender well so it's out of the way.

Carry laundry baskets safely. If you have to carry your laundry down steep steps to a cellar, it may be unsafe to carry a basket that limits your vision and puts you off balance. Instead, put your laundry in a plastic bag or in pillowcases and just toss it down the steps ahead of you! If it won't hit anything, you could also just let a plastic basket of laundry slide down the steps. P.S.: However you do it, considering how most of us feel about doing laundry, tossing it down the steps any way at all could be a happy, frustration-releasing experience!

Prevent laundry powder lumps in damp climates. Store powdered laundry detergent in a clean, plastic gallon milk jug with a tight-fitting lid. It will be easier to handle, too.

Getting Help from the Family

Enlist everyone's help. Tape-record detailed sorting instructions as well as instructions on using the washer and dryer. Your family members won't be able to use the time-worn excuse that they didn't know what to do. Or write down clear instructions of how to do these steps, from sorting, to washing, to drying, to folding and hanging, and tack or tape this up in the laundry room.

Give each child a personal laundry basket. Explain that the basket of dirty clothing is to be brought to the laundry room each morning before

Healthy-Planet Energy-Saving Checklist

Here are a few easy ways to save power while doing laundry.

♥ **Match water level to the load size.** Set lower water levels for smaller loads or delay washing until you have a full (but not overloaded) large load.

♥ **Pretreat spots and stains.** Then set the cycle and wash time to the type of load to avoid rewashing.

♥ **Go from lightest soiled to dirtiest.** Does your washer have a water return system? When you reuse water, you need to start with lightly soiled items first. You may need to add more detergent for additional loads.

♥ **Use hot water only when necessary.** Hot water is best for heavy or greasy soils and whites. Wash with cold for light soils. Rinse all loads in cold water.

♥ **Reduce dryer time.** Use a high spin speed in the washer for highly absorbent fabrics.

♥ **Dry full (but not overloaded) loads.** And separate lightweight and heavyweight items for faster, uniform drying.

♥ **Don't overdry.** In addition to wasting energy, it can give a harsh feeling to some fabrics and shrink others. Allowing garments to stay in the dryer after it's shut off causes wrinkles, which cause the need to iron.

♥ **Use residual heat.** Reload the dryer while it's still warm from a previous load.

♥ **Keep lint screens clean.** Buildup increases drying time and can be a fire hazard.

♥ **Do laundry during off-peak hours.** This is usually early morning and late evening. Check with your local utility company to find out about off-peak hours.

breakfast. Children can then take their clean laundry back to their rooms in the same basket at the end of the day.

Teach children to sort laundry when they bring it down. Have a framed cloth hamper for each load, each of a different fabric according to how you sort your laundry. For example, a denim hamper is for jeans, pants, and heavy clothes; a sheet fabric hamper holds sheets, towels, and whites; a print fabric hamper is for lightweight colored clothing. Or buy several plastic laundry baskets in different colors. For example, you could sort whites in a white basket, jeans and dark colors in a blue basket, and delicate clothes in a pink basket. Even the youngest child or adult with "selective incompetency" can sort laundry when it's coded this way, and it trains children to do their own laundry for when they leave home.

Laundering at the Laundromat

Wear an apron or smock with pockets. Use the pockets for quarters, etc. You can also buy a carpenter's apron at a hardware store and keep it stocked with things you need at the laundromat, such as change, sealable bags of detergent, tissues, and a small box of raisins and a toy if you have to take children with you. Or use a heavy plastic self-sealing bag to carry laundry change in.

Ease your load. Liquid detergent in the large containers is cheaper but harder to carry than small ones. Save syrup or dish detergent bottles with the pull-push tops and fill them with smaller amounts of detergent. Use one for laundry detergent and another for fabric softener.

Along the same lines, powdered detergent can be pre-measured into reusable margarine tubs or sealable plastic bags so that you don't have to tote a heavy, giant-economy box of detergent with your laundry. Plastic rinsed-out yogurt cups work perfectly, too.

Mark your spot. An easy way to identify the washer and dryer you're using is to put a brightly colored magnet on it. It not only helps you, but others will know it's being used.

Use the three-bag method. This laundry-sorting strategy lets you sort your clothes before washing. Or sort as you finish wearing them if you have the space. Put permanent press in one basket, white clothing in a second, and colored clothing in the third.

When your family takes something off, they can learn to drop things directly into the proper basket. It's a great time saver

This tip, of course, helps whether you use the laundromat or wash at home.

Have hangers on hand. It's a good idea to take some hangers with you to the laundromat so that you can hang up clothes from the dryer and avoid ironing them.

Putting Away the Laundry

Sort as you go. Save sorting and folding time by folding socks together as you take them out of the dryer or off the line. The rest of the laundry seems to get folded faster when there's no pile of socks to deal with.

Send it to the bottom of the stack. When folding clothes after washing and drying them, put fresh laundry under the existing stack (sheets, towels, handkerchiefs, underwear, etc.), so they will be rotated and the same ones won't be used all the time. Or place the fresh sheets on top and always grab off the bottom of the stack.

Fold, and then roll. Save space in a small linen closet by folding the towels, then rolling them.

Use a soap sachet on your sheets. For a fresh scent, put bars of soap between the sheets and towels in your linen closet and in your dresser drawers. As an added bonus, the soap will last longer when you do use it in the bath because it will have hardened.

Keep fabric softener sheets. Used fabric softener sheets will also prevent musty smells wherever you store linen. Do not allow them to come in contact with clothing, especially natural fibers, though.

Develop a code. When children or adults in a household wear nearly the same size or have matching outfits, it's hard to tell which clothes belong to whom. You can use a laundry pen to initial clothing in an inconspicuous place. Or, if there are several children whose clothing is unsortable, clothing can be color coded. Assign a different color to each child and mark each one's clothing accordingly. A stitch of thread or dot of permanent ink marker in the child's assigned color on the neck or waist seam of undergarments and on the toe seam of socks ensures matching instead of mixing.

For more laundry tips, see DRYERS, IRONING, LINENS, and WASHING MACHINES.

LAWN MOWING

Remember safety first. Wear proper protective clothing, including long pants, sturdy shoes, and protective eyewear. And always walk the area to be mowed beforehand to find and pick up objects that could be thrown by the mower or could damage the mower.

Take care of the equipment. Never disconnect safety controls; they are there to protect you. And never refuel the machine while it is running or the engine is still hot. Gas fumes are flammable.

Don't mow wet grass. Wet grass can clog the mower and may damage it.

Store the mower in a well-ventilated area. This is especially important in hot weather to prevent combustion of the gas remaining in it after you finish.

For more lawn care tips, see GARDENS.

LEFTOVERS

Leftovers are great time and money savers. I like to think of them as pre-cooked convenience foods. They can be popped into the microwave or conventional oven whenever you need a quick meal and cooking is the farthest thing from your mind.

Don't hesitate to serve the same foods 2 days in a row. If it's a nutritious meal on Monday, it will be a nutritious meal on Tuesday, and it may even taste better. If your family rebels, there are ways to disguise almost any food. When you look into your refrigerator, don't think of the food as leftovers; think of it as the beginning of your next meal. Build around it and consider it a bonus.

Being Creative with Leftovers

Add some fresh ingredients or spices. The leftover stew that's enough for only two might became a hearty soup, enough for four, if fresh or canned stewed tomatoes, some frozen or canned mixed vegetables, and noodles or rice are added. Some casseroles, stews, and pot roasts actually taste better the next day, after their flavors have blended. Texas chili, for example, is always better the second and third day.

Experiment with bouillon. I once read in a French cookbook that just about anything you add water to will taste better if you add bouillon instead. Many types and flavors of bouillon are available. Some liquid bouillons also add color to stews and soups.

Use every last drop. Add water to an almost-empty ketchup bottle and flavor noodle, rice, or meat dishes with the "puree."

Make a hot dish using accumulated leftover vegetables. A combination of vegetables, macaroni, and that last hot dog or slice of meat, can be put into a pan with a can of beef vegetable soup. If you are using a lot of left-

Leftover Magic: Bread

It's easy for time to get away from us and to have bread go stale before it's eaten. Here are some great uses for leftover bread.

♥ Stale bread makes good bread pudding.

♥ Dried bread can be cubed and oven-toasted for croutons or made into bread crumbs if it's dry enough. (Take dried bread, put it into a sturdy plastic bag, place it on the floor, and step on it until you have bread crumbs. You can also place it on the counter and use a rolling pin, but it won't be as much fun.)

♥ Sliced bread that's stale but still soft can be pushed into greased muffin cups, baked until toasty, then used as an egg cup.

♥ Use old bread for French toast or cut bread into cubes and mix with egg or egg substitute for "egg cubes."

♥ Make quickie cookies by dipping day-old bread slices in sweetened condensed milk, then in flaked coconut. Finish by placing on a baking sheet and toasting it in the oven until the bread is hot and coconut is brown.

overs, you may want to add a bouillon cube to flavor the soup and possibly cornstarch to thicken the sauce.

Prepare your own TV dinners. Cook extra portions and then freeze them. When you find three-sectioned heavy paper plates or heavy plastic plates on sale, stock up and keep extras on hand to freeze leftover portions that you can later reheat in the microwave. Fill each plate with one serving, place it in a freezer-safe plastic bag, and freeze. Use aluminum plates for leftovers that will be reheated in conventional ovens.

Have a homestyle buffet. When you have accumulated several meals of leftovers, have a family "Buffet Day" to eat them up. One reader makes a joke of her leftover day by posting a menu on the fridge that has the name of a leading restaurant of her city printed on top and a list of the "Choices du Jour."

Try freezing larger amounts of leftovers in a plastic-lined bowl. Fill a freezer-safe bag and set it inside a bowl. When the food is frozen, lift the bag out of the bowl. You can put the bag in the freezer, sans bowl. This way you haven't lost a bowl to the freezer, and this also helps save valuable freezer space.

Using the plastic bag or foil and this idea, you can also freeze casseroles in the same casserole dish in which they will be heated so that the block of food will fit into its proper cooking container. Always date everything you put into your freezer; it's so easy to lose track of time.

Freeze your fruits. Too many grapes? Freeze them for snacking later. Too many bananas? Freeze them and use them (sliced in hunks) instead of ice cubes and malt to froth up blender milk shakes.

Keep the best parts. Slightly bruised fruits? Cut off bad parts and make a fruit salad or pie or add fruit to tuna salad. Apples and grapes are especially delicious!

Make a sandwich. Any leftover meat can be used as slices in a sandwich or ground up to make sandwich spread. (Add commercial sandwich spread or mayo and chopped carrots, celery, and mushrooms for filler.) Heat meat slices in leftover sauce for hot open-faced sandwiches or to serve over leftover rice or noodles.

Leftover Magic: Cake

Leftover cake isn't too common in most households. But just in case you find yourself with some, here are two creative uses.

1. Break the cake into pieces and layer with slightly softened ice cream, freeze, and slice for a new dessert. (You can drizzle an appropriate topping over each serving, such as coffee-flavored liqueur over chocolate ice cream and angel food cake.)

2. Prepare one package of cooked chocolate pudding mix as directed, cool. Whip 1 cup of whipping cream with ⅓ cup of confectioners' sugar and fold into cooled pudding. Cut up one layer of cake (white, yellow, or chocolate) and place it in the bottom of an 8-inch square baking dish. Pour pudding over cake and sprinkle with ½ cup of chopped nuts (optional). Chill several hours in fridge before serving. Serves 4 to 6.

Transform hot dog and hamburger buns into garlic bread. Butter, add garlic and other spices, and broil for a few minutes to make garlic bread to serve with spaghetti or other meals.

Cook up a cheese sauce. Bits of leftover cheese can be melted with canned skim milk and turned into cheese sauce for veggies or noodles or for cheese dip. The more kinds of cheese, the better the flavor.

Stock up on soup fixings. Keep a tightly covered container in your freezer and add all bits of leftover veggies and their cooking water. When you have enough, make vegetable soup by adding browned onions, bouillon, or stock, and your favorite herbs and spices to the mix. Simmer at least 20 to 30 minutes to blend flavors.

Savor with a salad. Add leftover cooked veggies to any salad, such as mixed combination salads, sandwich spread, or just on top of your lettuce.

Whip up potatoes and eggs. Cut up leftover potatoes and add them to scrambled eggs or scrambled egg substitute. Brown the potatoes and add some onion, if you wish, before adding the eggs.

Enjoy some hush puppies. Mash leftover starch vegetables; add egg, leftover egg yolk or egg substitute, and crumbs to thicken; and deep-fry like hush puppies for "veggie puppies."

Make vegetable hash. Cut up leftover mixed vegetables such as corn, peppers, potatoes, peas, and beans, and then fry in a skillet with onion, garlic, and other seasonings of choice.

Keeping Track of Stored Leftovers

Date all leftovers in the refrigerator. This way you won't end up throwing them away because you don't know how long they have been stored. Tape an 8- by 11-inch sheet of fairly stiff plastic to the inside of a cupboard door. Cut little squares from a roll of masking tape and stick them on the plastic. When you need a date sticker, remove one of the squares and write the date on it. To save time, you could just write "5" for the fifth of that month or "25" for the twenty-fifth. There will really be no need for a month on refrigerator leftovers because, we hope, you won't have anything left over for that long. When the dish is empty, replace the date sticker on the heavy plastic to be reused; it's all marked and ready for the next leftover!

Put leftovers in the their place. Always put leftovers in the same area of your refrigerator, such as on the top shelf. Even consider marking the area "leftovers." This way, they'll never be overlooked or forgotten. One of my favorite hints is to put them in glass jars so that I can see what I have to work with when I'm holding a "combination-of-leftovers gourmet event."

LEMONS

Enjoy lemon-fresh water. Add a few slices of lemon to drinking water to perk it up or to bathwater to perk you up with the fresh scent. You can also add lemon juice to rinse water for your hair.

Remove bad smells. Rub your hands with pieces of lemon to remove odors like onions and garlic. Along the same lines, you can put lemon rinds down the garbage disposal to freshen it.

Freeze your lemons. Seal them in a sturdy plastic bag and freeze. When you need one, take it out of the bag and microwave it for a few minutes. Let it stand on the counter for 10 more minutes before using.

Substitute a lemon squeezer. Place a lemon half in a nutcracker and squeeze away.

LETTER WRITING

Ensure a special delivery. You may be tempted to forgo sending a thoughtful letter or get well card to someone staying in the hospital because you're concerned they may be home before the mail arrives. Don't worry—just put the patient's own return address on the card. Then, if the patient leaves the hospital before the card arrives, the card will follow the person home via the mail.

Improvise a scale. If you don't have a postal scale and think your letter weighs more than 1 ounce, here is a "Rube Goldberg" scale to weigh envelopes that really works. Balance a 1-foot ruler on a pencil, in the middle, at the 6-inch mark. Place the letter on the ruler, centered at 9 inches, and a stack of 5 quarters (which weighs 1 ounce) centered at 3 inches. The quarters' side will stay down if the letter is lighter than an ounce.

Make the most out of spare moments. You can write letters in secretary's notebooks whenever you are waiting someplace, such as at the beauty or barber shop, the doctor's office, or in the car when you pick up children. A tablet makes lap writing easy, and the people who care about you don't care if you don't use fancy stationery. When you are occupied, the waiting time seems shorter, and besides, you've used time that would have otherwise been wasted.

Keep a correspondence calendar. If you do a lot of letter writing, you can keep track of who owes whom a letter if you make a list of those to whom you frequently write. Then, note the date you've received a letter from a person in black ink and the date you answered the letter in red ink. You can tell at a glance if you owe a letter.

Give yourself a head start. When you receive a letter, use a highlighter to mark the parts of the letter that you need to answer or comment on. Then address an envelope to the sender immediately and put some stationery in it. If you can, take the envelope with you to places where you'll have waiting, a.k.a. letter writing, time. Just having the envelope stamped and addressed removes that stumbling block to writing for some people.

Keep envelopes addressed to people you write to frequently. That way you can insert newspaper clippings and cartoons that you think will interest that person. Then, when you are ready to write a letter, you'll have the clippings where they belong, ready to go. If you don't have time to write more than a short note, the clippings will show that at least you are often thinking about the recipient of your note.

Make a family newspaper. If your family is scattered throughout the country, put together a family newspaper, with each member contributing at least one article to it. Have one person in charge of gathering the information and getting it copied. Saving these newspapers in a scrapbook can provide a family history for generations to come.

The newspaper could be compiled at Thanksgiving time, with everyone writing what they are thankful for in the past year, and then mailed so each member receives a copy at Christmas time to reflect upon as the New Year approaches.

Share a diary. If you and your siblings are all too involved with children, church, PTA, and work to keep in touch throughout the year, keep a diary and send the information to each other at year's end. Knowing you are taking care of your letter writing at the same time is a good incentive for keeping a diary. If you have a computer, keeping a diary on disk and making printouts is easy.

Dare to share your doodles. Instead of writing, send pictures to small children. Cut them out of magazines and newspapers or hand draw them, even if they are stick people.

LIBRARY

Rely on a list. Keep a log of books checked out from the library, and then you'll not only see how many books your family has read in a month but also have a checklist to help you gather all of the books when it's time to return them. No more forgetting and paying overdue fees!

Brighten Your Lighting without Using More Energy

Lighting accounts for more than 16 percent of our electric bills, and most of us overlight our homes. The good news is that you can brighten your home and still save if you follow these handy tips.

♥ Use 25-watt reflector flood bulbs in high-intensity portable lamps. They'll give about the same light but use less energy than the 40-watt bulbs that usually come with these lamps.

♥ If you have "pole" or "spot" directional lamps, try using 50-watt reflector floodlights, which give about the same light as standard 100-watt bulbs but with half the wattage.

♥ When using night-light bulbs, get 4-watt bulbs with a clear finish instead of the usual 7-watt ones. They'll be almost as bright with half the energy use.

♥ Put photocell sensor units or timers on outdoor lights so that they will turn themselves off in daylight.

♥ Install dimmer switches or high-low switches when replacing light switches to reduce light intensity and save energy.

♥ When buying new lamps, get those with three-way switches so you can use high for reading and low when you don't need bright light.

♥ Fluorescent lights give out more lumens (light measurements), so use them whenever you can. New 20-watt deluxe warm white fluorescent can be used in makeup and grooming areas for a warmer light.

♥ Keep all lamps and lighting fixtures clean; dirt absorbs light.

♥ When decorating, save lighting energy by choosing light-colored walls, rugs, draperies and upholstery, which reflect light and so reduce the amount of artificial light needed.

LIGHT BULBS

Change the bulbs without burning your fingers. Take the new bulb out of the corrugated cardboard sleeve, and place the sleeve over the old light bulb to unscrew it. You'll avoid burned fingers, and the bulb ends up inside the sleeve ready for disposal!

Remove a broken bulb. First make absolutely sure the switch is turned off. Then insert an old-fashioned clothespin, not the spring type, so that the two prongs are inside the broken socket, and carefully unscrew it.

LINENS

Organize your linen closet by sets. Linen closets can become jumbled messes, especially when children make their own beds. To tame the chaos, organize bed linens into sets. Here's how. Fold one flat sheet in the middle, fold it in half and then in half again, making both folds the long way. Then fold a fitted sheet the same way, and lay it on top of the folded flat sheet. Add one or two pillowcases, each folded in half the long way also. Then roll them all together into one neat roll. Whoever is making a bed can grab only a roll instead of rummaging around and making a mess.

Launder lace carefully. Protect a lace tablecloth by laundering it in a mesh bag. Save yourself a lot of anguish and don't launder a crocheted tablecloth with long fringes in the washer, not even in a mesh bag. Believe me, the result will be the worst tangle you'll ever cuss at. Hand wash such items!

Drape-dry your tablecloths. Shaping a lace tablecloth after washing it is easy if you just drape it over the dining room table to dry. If it's starched, you'll need to pin it in place on a clean bedsheet using nonrust pins.

Caution: Water is an enemy of tabletops! Protect the table surface with a flannel-backed plastic cloth, a shower curtain, or a painter's drop cloth.

Use the "no-iron" ironing method. Here's how to iron a tablecloth, even a large Irish linen cloth, without really ironing it. First, place a large sheet on the floor. Then use nonrust straight pins to attach the wet tablecloth to the sheet, smoothing out wrinkles as you pin. Let the cloth dry while you read a book or do something else that's more fun than ironing a great big tablecloth.

Iron in the right spot. When ironing tablecloths on an ironing board, reverse the board so that you are ironing on the wider end. You can also iron a large tablecloth (and curtains or bed cover) on a bed.

Folding Tablecloths

Here's how to fold a tablecloth so that the creases look as neat as hotel banquet cloths.

1. Make the first fold down the middle with the right side out.
2. Then fold each half in half again, back toward and slightly beyond the center.

When the tablecloth is opened, the side creases will be alike, and you won't have a dust streak down the center. Having such even folds helps you center the cloth when you are putting it on the table.

Consider color fixes. Hopelessly stained or yellowed white linen damask cloths can be dyed commercially and given a new life. Or, if you're faced with an impossible-to-remove coffee stain on a white tablecloth, try dyeing the whole cloth with coffee to get a champagne-colored cloth. Here's how. Brew a big pot of strong coffee, pour it into a large plastic pail or tub, and then slosh the stained tablecloth around until the color is distributed evenly.

Repair your lacy linen tablecloths. Small cuts or slits in lacy tablecloths (and sheer or lacy curtains, too) can be repaired if you first place a piece of wax paper under the cut and then apply a little clear nail polish across the threads. After the nail polish dries, the mend should be nearly invisible.

Always clean linens before storing them. Spots and stains will set if left in the fabric. With fine linens, you'll save money in the long run if you have them professionally cleaned. Tell your dry cleaner what those spots and stains are so that they can be properly treated before cleaning.

Second guess the cedar strategy. If you store your fine linens in a cedar chest, the fumes from cedar oil may yellow them. Instead, store them in a dry place where they won't mildew or get musty-smelling.

Prevent white linens from yellowing. You can prevent yellowing of white linens that will be stored for a long time by wrapping them first in white tissue paper and then in blue tissue paper.

Keep them in the closet. Hang linens on hangers that you can cover with dry-cleaners' bags or garbage bags. Before putting tablecloths on the hangers, fold as described in "Folding Tablecloths" on page 289. An adjustable tension curtain rod installed in the back of a small closet will also hold table linens neatly and out of your way.

Stack them on the table. If you have a round table and several round tablecloths but very little storage space, store all of the tablecloths right on the table, two, three, or four deep. Put a plastic tablecloth under the one currently in use to keep the bottom layers clean. The best bonus of this is that all of your round tablecloths will be stored without wrinkles. You know how difficult it is to fold or hang a round cloth neatly!

For more linen care hints, see LAUNDRY and TABLECLOTHS.

LITTER

Control car litter. Save the small plastic bags from card shops and drug stores and keep them in a larger bag in the car so they'll always be handy to use as litter bags.

LUNCH

Freeze your juice. If you freeze individual containers of juice, they will thaw by lunchtime and keep the other lunch foods cool.

Protect delicate fruits. Place soft fruits, like peaches, plums, and grapes, in clean yogurt cups or other containers to keep them from getting squashed in your lunch bag.

Keep cold foods in recycled food containers. This strategy prevents them from sweating so much that the bag tears and, best of all, follows my Heloise philosophy of trying to reduce garbage output by reusing packaging as often as possible.

Make a handy money keeper. If you need to send lunch or milk money along with a very young child, poke a hole into the lid of a 35mm film canister, then poke both ends of a cord (that's long enough to go around your child's neck) through the hole. Knot the ends several times so that the cord won't come out of the hole. Put the money in the canister, attach it to the lid, and your child will have a safe lunch money "necklace."

Pack a sack of salad. Pack a green or chef's salad in a clean 16-ounce yogurt or 12-ounce cottage cheese carton and add a small glass jar containing salad dressing. (Baby food jars are perfect to save for this.) Just before you eat, pour the dressing over the salad, replace the lid so that you can toss the salad neatly, and enjoy.

Make some speedy sandwiches. Make sandwiches on grocery-buying day, assembly-line style, and freeze them. Make each sandwich with two slices of bread (sliced white, grain, whole wheat, or rye), lightly spread with margarine (not mayonnaise or mayonnaise-type salad dressing since it doesn't freeze), two slices of two different lunch meats (usually turkey types to reduce fat), and one slice of cheese. Place each sandwich in a plastic sandwich bag, and then return them to their original bread bag so that all know what kind of bread was used. Lunchmeats and cheeses are a surprise. Frozen sandwiches will thaw by lunchtime, taste fresher than those made daily, and help keep the other foods in the lunch box cool.

Keep the veggies crisp. Toss an ice cube or piece of wet paper towel into a zipper bag (or clean yogurt/margarine container) containing carrot and celery sticks to keep them fresh and moist.

Code leftovers at the office. One group of men wrote that they all keep lunch leftovers in the office refrigerator and color code them with a different color of plastic wrap for each day. Then they know which day the food came in and when it should be thrown away. I presume they write the day of the week on the box of wrap so that everyone knows the code!

MAGAZINES

 Recycle the stacks. Here's an idea to help your local library. Suggest they sell donated used magazines at 10 cents each. Volunteers sort and group magazines by type and stand them in boxes on a table with a locked coin box nearby. Payment is on the honor system; buyers drop a dime into the box if they decide to take one home. One Middle West library that did this grossed $4,800 in one year.

Organize your clippings. As you read a magazine, tear out the pages that you want to keep, and then store them in file folders or punch holes in the pages and store them in a ring binder. The information you want will be where you can find it. You can pitch the magazines to get rid of clutter.

Use your subscription number. Cut the address label from the last issue of the magazine and glue or tape it to the name and address space on the renewal or subscription card. Since your subscriber number and other identifying codes are on the label, there won't be any mistakes when you renew or cancel.

Avoid magazine overload. To avoid getting overwhelmed by saved stacks of magazines, scan the articles as soon as a magazine arrives. Cut or tear out everything of interest, and cut out and file coupons. Save the articles in a "to read" file and discard the rest of the magazine.

MAGNETS

Use the attraction. Keep a magnet in your sewing kit to help you find and pick up pins and needles quickly. Many husbands may say that the other way to find and pick up dropped pins is to walk around barefoot, especially in a sewing room!

MAGNIFYING GLASSES

Have one handy. Keep a small magnifying glass in the car to help you read maps. One of my readers wears one of those large magnifying glasses that you hang around your neck to do needlework when she travels. She can see a larger area of the map and doesn't get lost on vacation trips anymore.

Mail: Get Your Letter There Fast

The U.S. Postal Service handles more than a half billion pieces of mail daily and says properly addressing letters speeds up delivery.

♥ Print or type addresses clearly.

♥ "Attention" lines should be put above the street address, not in the lower left corner of the envelope.

♥ Street address lines should include directions such as North or South if part of the address, the complete street name (Avenue, Street, and Road), and a room or apartment number if applicable.

♥ A ZIP code is a must and should be on the same line as the city and state.

♥ Include the extra four numbers (ZIP + 4) if you know them.

♥ Always include a return address.

♥ When envelopes are included in a bill or correspondence, use them. They are coded to facilitate mail routing.

MAKEUP

Remove waterproof mascara the easy way. Apply mineral oil or petroleum jelly to the mascara, and then remove it with cotton balls, cotton pads, or a soft makeup sponge. Mineral oil is listed as an ingredient on many commercial makeup remover labels.

Hold steady. If you have trouble putting on eye makeup because your lids twitch, open your mouth to the biggest "O" you can make comfortably. Your face will stay put while you apply shadow, liner, and mascara to your eyes.

Use eye shadow for eyebrows. If eyebrow pencil looks too harsh and fake, stroke a thin flat makeup brush across eye shadow (light brown or gray), and then apply it to your eyebrows. Also, try light upward strokes of mascara to color eyebrows.

Cap it off! Before slipping a dress or sweater over your head, place a shower cap under your chin and up over your face, and then pull the garment on. Carry a shower cap in your purse when you go shopping so that you don't leave makeup on garments that you try on. Disposable shower caps found in hotels and motels are good for this purpose. Or, drape a large, square silky scarf over the top of your head, and you won't mess up your hair or makeup.

($) **Soften with sandpaper.** Gently rub a piece of fine sandpaper or an emery board across caked powder to loosen it. You can avoid caked powder by storing your powder puff upside down in the compact. If you store the powder puff makeup side down, oils from your skin could get absorbed into the puff and then into the face powder, which will harden it.

Make makeup last longer. Some makeup won't last more than 6 hours, no matter what type or application method. Here's what might help. Apply loose or pressed powder to your face, dab a lightly dampened sponge over it, and then apply foundation and blush. You can also dampen a sponge or cotton ball in astringent lotion instead of water to set the makeup.

MAPS

Map your new locale. When you move to a new city or are in a city you visit often, use a brightly colored pen to mark places you've visited on the map. It's a great memory jog if you want to try a great restaurant again or find that out-of-the way-shopping district. If there's room on the map, note the actual address, such as 1234 Maple Street, or draw a fine line to the margin and make notes there, such as Acme Book Store or Mary and Tom Smith's house.

MARBLE

Clean and polish. If you have a water ring on a marble surface, try rubbing the stain with a good marble-polishing powder, usually tin oxide (available from a hardware store, marble supplier, or funeral monument business). These companies are good sources for advice on polishing marble, too. Avoid trouble in the future by wiping up spills, even plain water, as soon as possible. And make sure you instruct your family members in proper care of marble countertops and floors. A few lessons will go a long way in keeping the marble looking great.

MARGARINE

See STAINS for hints on how to remove margarine stains from fabrics.

MARGARINE SQUEEZE-STYLE CONTAINERS

Put on the squeeze. Since mustard and margarine-style squeeze containers fit so well on the refrigerator door, wash them well after you empty them so that you can reuse them to hold syrups, ketchup, salad dressings, steak sauces, and anything else you want to squirt on your food. They're also terrific as dispensers for items you may buy in bulk, such as mayonnaise. Don't forget to write on the outside what's stored on the inside!

MATCHES

Don't go for the burn. Hold the match with a spring-type wooden clothespin when you light candles, a barbecue grill, or fireplace starters. No more singed fingertips!

MATTRESSES

Keep your mattress in place. If you have one of those mattresses quilted with shiny, satiny fabrics that often slips off the box springs, place a thin sheet of foam rubber between the mattress and the box spring and a second thin sheet of foam rubber on top of the mattress before you add the mattress pad and sheets. Sometimes, just placing foam on the corners of a mattress will hold the pad and sheets on. You can buy foam corners in catalogs and bedding stores. Some catalogs sell special nonskid sheets to place between the mattress and box spring.

Remember to turn. Turning a mattress every few months makes it last longer and prevents "dips" in the springs. But who can remember which way to flip the thing? The easiest method is to write the date you turn the mattress on some masking tape and tape it to a top corner of the box spring so you'll know at a glance when you should turn it again. Or, write a code on the corners of the mattress with permanent marker. For example, on one side of the mattress, mark J–M for January to March on the upper right corner and mark A–J for April to June on the diagonal corner. On the other side of the mattress, mark two diagonal corners again with J–S for July to September and O–D for October to December. When you change the sheets, just give the mattress a quick flip or turn every few months matching the code with the current month.

MEAT

Marinate without the mess. Put all the ingredients in a plastic bag large enough to accommodate the meat. Seal the bag, forcing out as much air as you can, and put it in the fridge (in a baking dish with sides if you're afraid of leaks). When you need to turn the meat to marinate the other side, simply turn the bag.

Go quick on the thaw. If you have a solid hunk of ground meat for meatloaf or meatballs, try this tip for thawing it quickly. Unwrap the frozen meat and carefully slice it with a sharp knife. Place the slivers in a bowl, and they will thaw in about an hour.

Make meatballs fast! To cook Swedish and Italian meatballs quickly, place them in a shallow baking dish and bake at 375°F for about 10 minutes (depending on size). You don't even have to turn them!

Substitute a crumb. Try crushed or blender-ground unsweetened dry cereal, dry oatmeal, instant mashed potatoes, or crushed soda cracker crumbs when you're out of bread or bread crumbs.

Menu Planning and Shopping Made Simple

Follow these tips to take the drudgery out of planning menus, making shopping lists, and buying groceries.

- ♥ Meal planning doesn't have to be a boring chore. If you make separate index cards for each dinner you prepare, menu planning becomes a simple matter of pulling out enough index cards for the number of meals you'll be shopping for.

- ♥ If you have a family computer, you can type in recipes and menus and organize the files according to seasonal availability of produce and other grocery items. Keep a master shopping list, too, but don't print out a new copy each time you go to the store. Just make checkmarks in a different color each week and you'll get three or four uses out of one printout. Keeping the list from week to week always means you'll have a record of what you bought so that you don't duplicate purchases. Revise your list every 3 months or so to make sure it suits your needs.

- ♥ Another ready-made grocery list is the sale page from the newspaper. Just circle the items you need, and jot down items that aren't in the ad in the margins. If you plan menus around groceries that are on sale, you'll see your savings add up. Sticking to your list also discourages impulse buying.

- ♥ When you just can't decide what to serve, look at frozen dinners to see combinations of meats, starches, and vegetables that you can duplicate with your own home cooking.

- ♥ Shop for one whole week to eliminate short but time-consuming treks to the store.

- ♥ Shop when the stores are empty, such as in early morning or in midafternoon before the office crowd heads home.

- ♥ With your grocery list in hand, head to just one or two stores. Bargain shopping is a good practice, but don't waste gas and time driving from store to store to save a dollar. Your time is just as valuable as your money.

Marinate with salad dressing. Need a quick marinade? Bottled Italian dressing or other vinegar-and-oil-style salad dressing will give flavor and tenderize meats and chicken without all the hassle of making your own marinade.

Know what's inside. When rewrapping meats for the freezer, cut the label off the original grocery package and tape it to the newly wrapped one. The label has all the information—type of meat, date of purchase, nutrition information, and weight. No more guessing at what is in the package.

Snip your steak in several spots. Of course, you already knew that the fatty edges of steaks and chops must be snipped in two or three places before frying and broiling to prevent their curling up into a difficult-to-serve cup-o-chop or steak cup. One might argue that when the meat curls up into a cup it holds sauces better, but if it's curled up, it won't brown and cook properly.

MEDICINE

Label meds with the malady. Mark containers with the malady for which they were prescribed as soon as you bring them home. For example, write "migraines," "allergies," or "high blood pressure" on the label for quick reference since many medications have similar names. While you should always take all of the medication as prescribed for an illness and should not have leftovers, some prescriptions are for ongoing problems (such as seasonal allergies), and you may forget what the tongue-twister chemical name drug was prescribed for.

Caution: If you forget what a certain medicine is for, don't take it! Call your pharmacist and ask if he can look up the computerized records for you and tell you what it's for and how it should be taken if the instructions are not printed on the container or you've misplaced the accompanying paper instruction sheet.

Clock it. Buy a "Will be back at" clock from an office supply store. Then when you take medicine, set it for the next time a dose is due. Hang it where you will surely see it, and you won't miss a dose.

Open pill containers with ease. When the cap's directions say "Squeeze at arrows while turning" and your fingers can't seem to manage, put a nut-cracker to the cap. The extra pressure and "torque" makes opening safety caps a snap.

Swallow pills easily. While most pills and capsules have slick coatings that help you swallow them, some are uncoated. If you have trouble swallowing such a pill, roll it in a bit of butter or margarine, just enough to help it slip down when you swallow.

Caution: Check with your doctor or pharmacist first to make sure that the butter or margarine won't interfere with your body's absorption of that medicine. Also, although it may be tempting to cut pills or capsules to make them smaller and easier to take, don't do it unless your pharmacist

Cleaning Out Old Meds

Make it a habit to clean out your medicine cabinet at least once a year—perhaps on your birthday or during the Spring Forward or Fall Back switches between standard and daylight saving time. Follow these guidelines to help you decide whether to keep or toss medications.

- ♥ Check labels for expiration dates. If the medication is expired, throw it out. If there is no date, discard any medicine that's over 2 years old.

- ♥ Discard cracked, smashed, or discolored tablets or capsules that have become soft or stuck together.

- ♥ Discard aspirin tablets that smell of vinegar.

- ♥ Discard any liquid medicine that has separated.

- ♥ If the prescription label has come off, you can't be sure about contents, dosage, or age, so discard it.

- ♥ Keep all medicines in a cool, dry place. The warm, steamy bathroom medicine chest is not good for storage; try a linen closet. But don't keep medicines near mothballs or insect repellent whose vapors can be absorbed by medicine.

or doctor approves. Some medicines are made for "time-release," and you could be changing the way they work.

Keep using your containers. If your pharmacist allows, take your prescription bottles back for refills instead of getting a new bottle each time. Less plastic in landfills!

MEDICINE CABINETS

Dowel the door. Dowel pins (round wooden sticks sold at hardware stores for less than $1) can be placed in the mirror track of sliding-door medicine chests to prevent young children from opening the doors.

MELONS

Scoop those seeds. To deseed a melon, try an ice-cream scoop!

MEMORY BOOKS

Capture a memory in writing. When couples celebrate 25th or 50th wedding anniversaries and don't want gifts, friends can write a personal letter to the couple relating a fond memory that they shared, their first meeting, or the like. Put all the letters in a decorated binder for many happy hours of reminiscing.

See also ALBUMS AND SCRAPBOOKS.

MICROWAVES

Microwave users depend on their microwaves for many different uses—from boiling water to cooking whole meals. Try out these hints for getting the most out of this handy appliance.

Choose containers carefully. Milk or creamy mixtures and some cereals boil up quickly and tend to overflow, so allow plenty of headroom by choosing a large bowl or glass measuring cup. Containers should be two to three times the volume of the ingredients to avoid messy boil overs.

Cover food while cooking. If you use waxed paper to cover food containers while microwaving, crumple the paper slightly and it won't blow off.

Making Meringue

Need a little magic to make meringue perfect? Follow these steps, and you'll be on the road to heavenly meringue.

1. Wash beaters and bowls thoroughly. Beaters and bowls must be sparkling clean and free from all grease and oil. Use only metal or glass bowls. Plastic bowls, even clean ones, may have a greasy film that prevents foaming.

2. Separate eggs carefully, making sure there isn't any yolk in the whites. Even a drop of yolk will prevent the whites from foaming properly. (It's the fat in the yolks that causes the problem.) It may help to separate eggs while they are cold.

3. After separating the egg whites, let them set for about ½ hour so that they come to room temperature. They will produce greater volume when they are at room temperature than if they were beaten while cold.

   Note: Many recipes instruct you to add ⅛ teaspoon of cream of tartar for each egg white before beating.

4. Beat with a rotary beater, whisk, or electric mixer at high speed just until foamy. Gradually begin adding sugar, about 1 tablespoon at a time, beating as you slowly sprinkle the sugar in.

   Note: Confectioners' sugar dissolves more easily than granulated. Always move the beaters or the bowl as you beat the egg whites so that all of the egg and sugar reaches the beaters.

5. Continue to beat at high speed until the sugar is dissolved. To test to see if all of the sugar is dissolved, rub a little of the mixture between your fingers. If you feel grittiness, beat some more. Whites should stand in soft or stiff peaks, depending on the recipe directions.

Test to be sure. Curious as to whether or not your dish is microwave safe? Place the dish in the microwave and place a glass measuring cup with 1 cup of water next to it. Heat on full power for 1 minute, then check the temperature of the dish. If the dish is cool and the water is very warm, the dish is safe. If the dish is slightly warm, it can still be used, but only for very short-term warming. If the dish is hot, it's not for microwave cooking. When you heat water in a mug for tea or instant coffee and the handle becomes too hot to hold, the mug is probably not recommended for a microwave oven. You can boil water, as I do, in a microwave-safe glass measuring cup. The handle doesn't get hot even when the water is still boiling in the measuring cup.

Identify microwave cookware. Identify your microwave-safe cookware with an indelible mark (use pens for marking glassware) so that everyone in the family knows which containers are safe. Then, when you place the container in the microwave oven, make it a habit to center the mark at "12 o'clock" so that if you have to give it ¼ or ½ turns during cooking, you'll know how much of a turn you've made.

Get on a roll. Heating bread products such as rolls and pastries too long makes them tough and dry. Microwaving them for just a few seconds, about 15, is usually enough. To prevent soggy bottoms on sweet rolls or pastries, place them on a paper towel or paper plate (real paper, not foam); you can use the plate several times.

Let off some steam. Pierce potatoes with a fork before you microwave them. The holes let out steam as the potato cooks. If potatoes aren't pierced, they can explode and possibly cause eye injury or burns if they pop when you are opening the door.

Pop that kernel right. Popcorn should be cooked only in microwave-safe containers or prepackaged microwave bags. Kernels can scorch and cause a fire inside the oven if improper containers are used. Reheating popcorn in the microwave is a fire hazard.

 Be safe instead of sorry. Never warm baby bottles in the microwave. Bottles can feel cool to the touch on the outside, but the fluid inside can be hot enough to scald a baby's throat. And cook eggs on the stove instead of the microwave because eggs in the shell can explode due to steam buildup and can damage the oven. Avoid reheating on foam meat trays or foam fast food containers; both will melt at high temperatures.

Take care while boiling water. When you boil water for cocoa, tea, or instant coffee in a microwave-safe cup or mug, be aware that stirring or dropping in a tea bag, powder, or crystals can cause the water to bubble over the edge of the cup if the microwaves are still active in the water. The water is less likely to bubble over if you wait a few seconds before making your beverage.

Remember the staple! Be careful not to run the microwave with the tea bag in it. I know of one case where a metal staple in a tea bag ruined the microwave.

Savor the seasonings. Add most seasonings as usual to microwave recipes. However, don't sprinkle salt on food; the crystals reflect the microwaves and cause uneven cooking. Dissolve salt in liquid, and mix it into the food. Better yet, add it just before serving. Pepper becomes more intense when microwaved, so use it sparingly. Add more after cooking if you wish.

Make aroma potpourri. Want your house to smell as wonderful as the aroma from baking fruit pies? Add 2 teaspoons of pumpkin pie spice to 1 cup of water in a microwave-safe dish. Microwave on high until it boils, then cook for 3 more minutes. For a delicious roast turkey scent, cook 2 teaspoons of thyme or sage in water the same way. You can use your imagination to create a tempting aroma with any spice you like.

Keep a lid on it. If you cook with lids on your microwave dishes, always remove them carefully by first tilting them with the open side away from your face; otherwise escaping steam can quickly burn skin. Be sure to position your hands so that they are not burned by steam or spillovers. Be especially cautious when you've put plastic wrap over a dish or container; always open the wrap so that steam escapes away from your face or, for that matter, away from anyone who is watching you cook.

Do a little everyday maintenance. As you do with other appliances, it's important to wipe up spills when they occur. The microwave surface is easy to clean. If soil doesn't just wipe off, try heating a bowl of water in the microwave. The steam will soften the spills, so you can wipe the surface clean. Wipe around the door seal, door surface, and frame frequently to maintain a good seal.

 Steam it clean. If your microwave needs a serious cleaning, put 2 tablespoons of either lemon juice or baking soda in a cup of water in a 4-cup bowl that's microwave-safe. Let the mixture boil in the microwave for about 5 minutes so that steam condenses on the inside walls of the oven. Then wipe off the walls, the inside of the door, and the door seals.

MILDEW

Prevent it from day one. Air conditioners and dehumidifiers are the best solutions in damp climates. Leaving a light on in the bathroom or closet helps. Commercial products such as silica gel or activated alumina, found in hardware stores, work well in enclosed spaces such as closets. These chemicals absorb moisture from the air. Follow package directions exactly, and keep all antimildew products away from children and pets.

Remove it from outdoor furniture. Plastic-mesh outdoor furniture can be difficult to clean. Try either of these two quick fixes. Be sure to allow furniture to dry completely before folding or storing it to help prevent more mildew growth.

- ⊛ Mix 1 cup of bleach with 1 gallon of water and test the solution on an inconspicuous area to make sure there will be no fabric color changes. If it is safe, apply the solution to the fabric and scrub it with a soft brush or rag. Be sure to rinse well.
- ⊛ If the bleach solution is not safe, vinegar may remove the mildew. Wash the furniture with white vinegar and rinse well.
  Hint: Always dry furniture completely to help prevent more mildew growth.

See STAINS for hints on how to remove mildew stains from fabrics.

MILK

See STAINS for hints on how to remove milk stains from fabrics.

MILK SUBSTITUTE

Make sure you've "got milk." Mix nondairy creamer with a little water to complete a recipe when you're out of milk and can't borrow some from a friendly neighbor.

MINIBLINDS

Think more creatively. Dust miniblinds with a new, clean, 2-inch paintbrush. You'll be done in no time.

MIRRORS

Make your own cleaner. Mix 2 ounces of nonsudsing ammonia, 2 ounces of rubbing alcohol, and a couple of drops of blue food coloring (optional) with 12 ounces of water in a spray bottle that has been clearly labeled with the ingredients. The food coloring helps you quickly distinguish window cleaner from other cleaning liquids. To remove hair spray from a mirror, clean the mirror with rubbing alcohol on a soft cloth.

See also BATHROOMS.

MITTENS

Get stylish with stitching. There are lots of great ways to decorate mittens so they're easily identifiable. Stitch or embroider the owner's initials on them or "R" and "L" for right and left. You can also add favorite-color buttons or bows.

MOSS

Take the slip off the bricks. To remove moss from bricks, sprinkle a solution of half water and half bleach onto the moss.

Caution: Always test in an inconspicuous spot in case the bleach discolors and damages the brick.

MOVING

Know before you go. To get information about the new city before you actually make the move, subscribe to the Sunday or daily newspaper to find out about the area. Write to the chamber of commerce to find out about special events and happenings. You'll also be able to acquaint yourself with stores, politics, and other facts before you get to the new city. Some chambers of commerce offer newcomer welcome packets or visitor information packets that are useful to "permanent visitors," too.

Reuse packing materials. Wrap dishes and breakables one at a time in clean dish towels, bath towels, washcloths, sheets, pillowcases, and clothing. You won't be wasting paper, packing peanuts, or Bubble Wrap.

Keep in touch. Type your new address and phone number in columns with 2-inch margins and fold on lines above and below each address segment so that you can tear off these new-address segments for friends.

Celebrate moving-in day. Christen your new home by tying a big bow on the front door and cutting it as you cross the threshold for the first time. Be sure to take a photo for your moving-day scrapbook. Later in the evening, have a family party with cookies, punch, and lots of conversation. Remember that talk about the ups and downs of the day may be more a "refreshment" than the cookies and punch, especially if you have children!

See also VIDEO CAMERAS AND CAMCORDERS.

$ Keep down moving costs. When contracting with a moving company, find out if charges are different for weekday and weekend and if they charge overtime rates after a certain number of hours. It may be better to schedule 2 days instead of 1 with overtime.

Have the hardware handy. To avoid confusing (or losing) which hardware belongs with which furniture when you disassemble it, gather all the nuts, bolts, screws, and brackets in a sturdy envelope or bag. Attach the envelope or bag securely (with tape or string) to the underside of the furniture so that it's ready when you reassemble the furniture at your destination. You could also label and gather all the bags of hardware in one box with reassembly tools so you'll have everything you need at hand.

Protect flooring with plastic. Protect carpets from dirt with plastic drop cloths. (You can reuse them later for painting.) You can protect varnished or new flooring from scratches with old flannel-backed plastic tablecloths, bedspreads, and rugs.

Caution: Be sure that the floor "protection" won't be a skidding or tripping hazard.

Get wired in before moving day. Contact the phone company in your new city to get a phone book. Then call utility and cable companies to find out what information and fees are necessary to get hooked up in your new location. You can look up service people to install appliances or make improvements. You can check out the chain department stores and know which credit cards will be useful and which to cancel. And take your old phone book with you when you move, just in case you leave a few loose ends to tie up. The old phone book will also list your old neighbors' street address numbers, too, which will be invaluable when you want to send them greetings at holiday time!

Leave something behind. Be kind to the next tenant or homeowner. Leave an envelope with helpful information such as utility companies, cable TV channels, garbage pickup days, the local pizza or other food delivery number, a roll of toilet tissue, paper towels and soap, and any manuals for the appliances you leave behind.

MUFFINS

Shoehorn 'em out. Use a shoehorn to lift the muffins out of baking tins without tearing the muffins. The shoehorn can go right into the dishwasher. Of course, keep that shoehorn for kitchen use only!

Get an oil change. If you're out of cooking spray for greasing muffin tins, pour about ¼ cup of vegetable oil in one of the muffin cups, then dip a waded-up paper towel into the oil. Rub the other cups with the towel, re-oiling it as you go.

MUSHROOMS

Store and savor. Don't wash mushrooms before you put them into the fridge; instead, make sure they're dry and then put them into a paper (not plastic) bag. Paper bags let them "breathe" so that they stay fresh longer; plastic bags or wrap makes mushrooms slimy.

Slice and dice. After washing mushrooms, cut off stems level with the mushroom cap and then place each mushroom in the egg slicer stem side up. Each slice will be of an equal thickness. If the mushrooms are firm enough, you may even be able to turn the mushrooms in the slicer and slice them again to get smaller pieces.

NAPKINS

 Find a white sale. Instead of paper table napkins or cloth ones that need ironing and show food stains, substitute small, cheap washcloths or fingertip towels for family dining.

NECKTIES

Protect them from pasta. Many men tuck their neckties into their shirts when they eat anything messy or covered with sauce. Businessmen traveling by plane often tuck in their ties because a slight bump or all-out turbulence could cause a major food spill and ruin a favorite tie.

NEEDLEWORK

 Give it the finishing touch. Your needlework or craft artwork deserves to have the spot of honor in your home, so be sure to frame it beautifully. Many large framing shops have do-it-yourself frame components that can help you save money. For a casual piece of needlework, use an embroidery hoop, unfinished or painted, to frame and hang a finished project.

Keep things at hand. Tie your needle threader and embroidery scissors

Caring for Neckties

Neckties are an expensive investment, so it's important to clean and store them with care. These tips are easy to remember and will keep those snazzy ties in tip-top shape.

- ♥ Undo the tie before removing it. Sliding the knot or leaving a tie tied may cause it to lose its shape.

- ♥ Take care when applying cologne or aftershave, because the fragrance's alcohol may fade colors in the tie.

- ♥ Hang ties to keep them from wrinkling. The best way to store ties may be to drape them over a dry cleaner's pants hanger—the kind with a paper tube.

- ♥ If you must press a tie, do it on the back side to avoid shine on the fabric.

- ♥ If you get a spot or stain, just blot it off and take the tie to a dry cleaner. Tell the dry cleaner what the stain is so that there's a better chance of getting it removed.

- ♥ Don't use club soda or water on ties. They can leave water spots, especially on silk ties.

on a string, yarn, or old shoelace, and you won't be as quick to lose them under your canvas or in the chair cushions. (If you haven't done needlework for a long time, new threader designs make using thread or yarn easier than you could ever imagine.)

Make a stand-in hoop. Tack, staple, or masking tape smaller embroidery work to an old sturdy picture frame if you don't have a hoop or embroidery frame to work on.

Solicit free advice and inspiration. Most needlework and craft stores offer free advice and demonstrations to help you get started in needlework and other craft hobbies. Ask about classes for adults and children.

Travel with ease. Replace scissors in your needlework travel kit with a pair of fingernail clippers since scissors are no longer allowed on most flights. Clippers will snip the threads just as well as scissors.

NEIGHBORHOOD SWAP MEETS

 Find treasure right next door. Lots of neighbors join for a garage sale, but how about trying a swap meet for books, records, tapes, or even children's clothing? Aside from saving money and letting you swap trash for treasure, it's a friendly, get-acquainted thing to do!

NEWSPAPERS

Such handy items, I have uses for newspapers and their bags, and even a hint for their bills. Read on, please.

Newspaper Bags

 Put 'em to good use. When the weather is stormy, you may find your newspaper slipped into a clear newspaper sleeve. These bags are great for a variety of uses. You can store tissue sewing patterns in them once you've cut apart the sheets and found the sheets won't fit neatly back into the pattern envelope.

Make a padded hanger. If you need a padded wire hanger in a jiffy, wrap several bags around a hanger to help prevent wrinkles.

Check out my favorite bag hint. The most ingenious hint of all is to slip newspaper bags on ceiling fan blades when you paint to keep off the splatters!

Newspaper Bills

Keep track of paid weeks. If you pay in advance, as many people do, highlight the paid-for weeks on your calendar so you can tell when the next bill will be due. A good calendar for this is the bookmark-style ones we get from various businesses at Christmas time.

Newspaper Clippings

Corral those clippings. When you cut out columns, recipes, and stories from the newspaper, tape or glue the clippings with rubber cement to the pages of a school composition book. Highlight the line that tells you the subject so you can quickly find what you're looking for when you page through the book.

NIGHT-LIGHTS

See clearly now. Plug a night-light in at the bathroom vanity level and you won't have to startle your eyes switching on the regular light if you get up at night. You could even get an automatic, light-sensor type. It remembers to turn itself on at dusk!

NUTS

Get cracking. Freeze Brazil nuts before cracking them, and you'll have an easier time removing the nut meats. You can do the same with pecans. If you still have trouble, try placing the pecans in a microwave-safe bowl and adding enough water to cover; heat on "High" in the microwave for about 3 minutes. Take the pecans out of the water and let them cool. The shells should crack easily.

See also ALMONDS and PEANUT BUTTER.

OATMEAL

Perk up the flavor. Perk up a bowl of oatmeal by adding chopped fruit (fresh or dried), nuts, chocolate or butterscotch chips, or crumbs from the bottom of a cereal box. Or you can add any of these old favorites to recapture the taste of your youth: brown sugar, cinnamon, raisins, applesauce, honey, or molasses.

Add oatmeal to yogurt. Add dry oatmeal to your fruited yogurt for extra fiber and a fuller feeling. It won't look particularly pretty, but it tastes just as good as granola, especially if you add a few chopped nuts.

Make a beauty mask. Mix a little water with some oatmeal until it's a smooth paste. Spread the mixture on your face, keeping it away from the delicate skin around your eyes. Allow it to dry and rinse it off with warm water. Your face will be clean, refreshed, and smooth.

OIL BOTTLES

Avoid a mess. Slip a plastic sandwich bag over the bottom of the bottle, leaving the sides open around the bottle to catch drips that run down the sides. You'll have a clean shelf!

OLIVE OIL

Store it properly. Olive oil keeps longer if you store the bottle in a cool, dark place that's protected from light. While it doesn't need refrigeration, you can store it in the refrigerator. Refrigeration makes olive oil thick and cloudy, but bringing it back to room temperature will lighten it again.

OLIVES

Perk up a party. Drop a clove of garlic into a jar of olives and add a drop or two of olive oil. Let set for a couple of days in the fridge and the olives will be tasty and shiny.

ONIONS

Slice a single slice. When you want only one slice of onion for a burger or other sandwich, there's no need to peel the whole onion. Slice through the middle of the onion, cut off one slice, put the two parts back together, then wrap or seal in a plastic bag and refrigerate.

Peel without crying. Chopping or slicing onions releases a gas that reacts chemically with the water in your eyes to form sulfuric acid. (Saying the name of the gas almost makes you cry, too—propanethiol S-oxide.) Tears are your defense against the acid irritant, and some people are innately more irritated by onion gas than others. The good news is that the more onions you cut the greater your tolerance. If you seldom cut onions, you're likely to cry more. Trying placing onions in the freezer for 30 to 45 minutes before slicing them, but don't leave them in the freezer too long or they will get mushy. (If you do forget and freeze them, you can still cook with them later.)

Use dried onions for cooking. If you only cook with onions occasionally, buy dried onions. You'll find them in the spice department of most supermarkets. You can even brown dried onions for casseroles and other recipes that require them. Just watch them carefully because once they start to brown, they can burn to black in a few seconds.

ORGANIZING

Keep recipes and hints right where they belong. Tape that special tuna casserole recipe to the tuna can or that special cleaning hint to the thing that needs cleaning, and they will be handy when and where you need them.

Make and keep New Year's resolutions. One reader sent in her system that is similar to business goal setting. Instead of making resolutions and then forgetting about them, she decides what her resolutions are, plans a definite date on which to start them, and decides a definite time in which to accomplish them. For example, what date will she start her diet? If she will plant a garden, what date will she buy seedlings, when might she put them outside, and so on. Then, the most important step is to mark all the dates on the next year's calendar so that she's reminded of what she wants to do and when.

Make Your Own Dried Orange Peel

It's easy to make your own dried and grated orange or lemon peel. Just grab a couple of oranges or lemons from the grocery store and follow these five quick steps. You'll have a ready supply of home-made spice in a jiffy.

1. Peel the orange or lemon. Scrape as much of the white off the peel as possible.

2. Cut the peel into small pieces, and place them on paper towels.

3. Cover the peels with a paper towel to protect from dust.

4. Let the peels sit for 4 to 5 days. The top of your refrigerator is a good place to dry things such as flower petals, peels, and seeds, because it's usually warmer there and the stuff is less likely to be disturbed.

5. Once the peels are dry, store them in the refrigerator or freezer in self-sealing plastic bags. Grate as needed.

 Make lists and never forget. Most of the well-organized people I know make lists. They use calendars, notebooks, bulletin boards, or whatever works to keep track of the things they need to do. Writing it all down means never having to say "I'm sorry, I forgot."

Record everything in a small notebook. Keep a small 3- by 5-inch memo book in your purse or pocket and write down whatever you need to remember. For example, if someone at a meeting asks you a question, you'll remember to call back with the answer if you have written the question and the person's phone number in the notebook. You can scribble the names of people you have just met or bits of information that you might need in the future into the notebook, and then you won't forget names and facts. Label these notebooks with the dates they were carried, such as June–

December 2003, and then keep them so that you'll have all sorts of phone numbers and information handy when you need it.

Make a to-do notebook. Spiral spelling test notebooks sold in school supplies sections are good for to-do lists. They are about half the width of a secretary's notebook and are lined and numbered. If you have access to a heavy-duty paper cutter, you can cut a secretary's notebook in half lengthwise to make a to-do list notebook.

Be flexible with index cards. Instead of a memo book, you can buy a spiral pack of 3- by 5-inch index cards and use it like the memo book. The advantage to using index cards is that you can remove the cards from the spiral pack and file them in an index card file box.

Remember names more easily. Believe me, if you have trouble remembering the names of people you meet at business functions, keeping a little memo book is a wonderful aid. Writing down information puts it more firmly into your brain's filing cabinet, and if your brain is not recording that day, you can look up your notes anytime. I've even taken out my notebook in the restroom and written down the names of the people seated at my lunch table so that they will get engraved on a brain cell somewhere in my head.

Use business cards as a memory jog. When you are given business cards at various functions, write the function, the date, and any other tips that identify the owner of the business card on the back of the card. Otherwise, you end up with a pile of business cards in a desk drawer that don't mean a thing to you.

Start your calendar early in the year. Keep track of birthdays and anniversaries by writing all the important days at the beginning of the year in your calendar. Then remember to check the calendar at the beginning and middle of each month to make sure you'll purchase cards or gifts in time.

Send timely greetings. Some people buy greeting cards and address them in bunches every 4 months or so, and then put the pack of cards into their bill-paying organizers (the accordion-fold envelopes that have space for each month) so they are ready to go at the beginning of the month when the bills are paid.

OVENS

Let's face it, if 10 is the highest rating on your Fun Things to Do Chart, cleaning the oven is rated a -93 (at best), but someone's gotta do it. Your oven has to be cleaned, if only to prevent oven grease fires or the unpleasantness of filling your oven and house with smoke and spoiling the flavor of whatever you're cooking. There's one more reason to keep the oven clean: If the oven and its thermostat are covered with baked-on grease, the thermostat may not accurately determine the oven's temperature.

Cleaning Continuous-Cleaning and Self-Cleaning Ovens

Know the difference between the two types. Continuous-cleaning ovens and self-cleaning ovens have made the dreaded chore of oven cleaning much less horrible. Many people are confused, however, by the difference between continuous-cleaning and self-cleaning ovens. A continuous-cleaning oven gradually reduces oven soil on a specially treated surface to a presentable clean condition during normal baking or broiling. Each time you cook, the oven burns off dirt and grease. You'll need to clean up large spills to keep the oven looking good. A self-cleaning oven provides for the removal of soil during a separate high-heat cycle. This means that you have to set the cycle for cleaning when needed.

Be sure to vent when cleaning ovens. Always turn on the vent or open a window to protect yourself from fumes when cleaning your oven, and always keep children and pets away from such cleaning projects!

Clean with ordinary dish detergent and water. Never use any kind of oven cleaning aid in a continuous-cleaning or self-cleaning oven because it will remove the oven's finish. Once that happens, the oven will no longer clean itself. Do all wiping up with ordinary dish detergent and water or window cleaner. Wipe clean with warm water.

Wipe up ash with a sponge or paper towel. In self-cleaning ovens, use a plain water-dampened sponge or paper towel to wipe up the ash that remains in the bottom of the oven after the cleaning process has finished.

Decide how to clean the racks. If you choose to clean the oven racks in a self-cleaning oven cycle, the racks will become discolored and have a dull finish. If the appearance of the oven racks is of no importance to you, you can clean them in the oven. Despite your best efforts, racks may not come clean in some ovens. To clean them take them outside, if possible, and put them in a large heavy-duty plastic trash bag. *Caution:* Keep them away from pets and children. Spray them with an oven cleaner or ammonia and close the bag tightly. You can also clean your racks in the bathtub with this method, but make doubly sure the bag is sealed tightly and that the rack ends don't scratch the tub surface. Keep the racks in the bag overnight. The next day, spray them off with a hose and use a steel wool pad to get any hard-to-remove grease spots off. Rinse well before placing the racks back in the oven.

Don't get creative. Many people try to experiment with cleaning other greasy kitchen things in the oven during the self-cleaning cycle. Remember that these ovens get as high as 500°F and sustain that temperature for more than an hour. A friend of mine tried to clean greasy barbecue grill lava briquettes during the cycle. The result was an oven full of flaming grease to contend with. Fortunately for her, the rush of air into the oven when she opened the oven door (to spray the fire with a kitchen extinguisher) put out the fire. When you are dealing with extreme temperatures and strong chemicals, follow the directions given for them to the letter, and don't get too creative. You may get results you haven't bargained for!

Cleaning Standard Ovens

Follow directions carefully. Manufacturers recommend cleaning standard ovens with commercial oven cleaners. You must be very careful using these cleaners because most of them contain lye and nitrogen compounds, which can cause burns. When you use oven cleaners, be sure to wear rubber gloves and have plenty of circulating fresh air. The fumes are dangerous to inhale so keep children and pets away from the area. To be on the safe side, protect yourself by wearing a face mask or at least eyeglasses.

Stay away from the oven's components. Don't spray commercial oven cleaners near any electrical connections, heating elements, or the thermostat. Try not to spray them on an unprotected oven light bulb that's hot from being lit, because the bulb may shatter.

 Try baking soda for a less-toxic alternative. If your oven isn't too grimy, try baking soda. Sprinkle some on a damp cloth and scrub the oven. Wipe with warm water.

 Wipe up fresh spills. Clean up any spill as it happens. It is easier to clean one layer of gunk than several old, hard-as-asphalt layers.

Sprinkle some salt on burnt food. You can get most of the burned food off if you pour some salt on the spill while the oven's still hot. Allow the oven to cool and wipe up the spill.

 Scrape and squeegee. Scrape oven-cleaner goop from the oven walls with a short-handled window squeegee. When all the goop is on the center bottom of the oven, scoop it onto a piece of newspaper or brown paper bag and then discard in the garbage. Then wipe down the inside of the oven with a wet sponge or rag.

Let the light shine in. Wipe the oven's glass window with ammonia and let it set for a few minutes. Then scrape away goop with a plastic ice scraper, such as those for removing ice from auto windshields.

PACKING

Pad with peanuts. Pad "care packages" and other gifts with real peanuts in the shell instead of foam ones; because they are edible it's really like you're sending along an extra gift!

Reuse foam peanuts. You can sprinkle them with a favorite perfume and place them in potpourri jars to deodorize a room; stuff them into plastic newspaper bags and use them to stuff into clothing for mailing or travel (for arms, put the bag into the suit coat arm and fill with "peanuts"); toss them into the bottom of a pot for drainage beneath your plants; or use them to replace the plastic pellet stuffing that gets mashed in pet pillows or beanbag chairs.

PADDING

Make space with scraps. Buy carpet samples and place them upside down on work surfaces to protect the surfaces from damage. This is an especially good hint to use on a clothes washer or dryer since these appliances are at a good back-saver height for many chores, including grooming a small pet.

For more on padding, see BLANKETS.

PAINTING, AROUND THE HOUSE

If you've had the advantage of learning to paint by watching a pro (or at least a semipro), you can probably paint around the house with a minimum of smears, drips, and mess-ups. Unfortunately, most of us learn how to paint by trial and error . . . and mostly error. Ultimately, we learn how to prepare a surface before we paint, which part or area to paint first, and how to clean up instead of having to throw away our painting clothes and equipment. The tips below will help both novices and semipro painters do it all better, more easily, and cheaper.

Timing

Think spring. It's the ideal time to paint a house's exterior. Do it as soon as the weather turns warm enough, but before the temperature gets too hot. When the heat is blistering, paint dries too quickly and leaves marks where strokes were overlapped. Spring usually puts us in the mood to redecorate anyway. When flowers start blooming and nature renews itself, we want to make our whole environment fresh and new.

Plan ahead and get some advice. Before you rush out to the paint store, do a little planning so that you'll have some idea about the color you want and the equipment you'll need. Get advice from the salesperson in the paint department. For example, some paints and varnishes are better applied with man-made bristle brushes, but others are better with natural bristles. Edges of brushes are made feathered or blunt, and each bristle tip works best with specific types of paint or varnish.

Choose your equipment wisely. A variety of rollers and paint pads are available, and it goes without saying that using the correct implement to spread the paint will ensure the best results. Information printed on the paint or varnish can will tell you what sort of applicator to use and give you general instructions about painting. Always check the label to find out if the paint or varnish you are buying is appropriate for the surface you want to cover, whether it is wood, stucco, masonry, or metal. Certain paints are better for certain wear areas, such as porch paints for walk-on surfaces, enamels for woodwork, and flat for walls.

Selecting Color

Start with a picture. Take a photograph of the outside of your house, and then look it over and determine what you don't like about it. Study the photograph to see if your house looks top heavy, small, or dumpy.

- ❈ *If your house is small and you want it to look larger,* paint the trim, walls, and shutters a light color. If you are reroofing, add a light-colored roof.
- ❈ *If your house looks too narrow and tall,* paint the upper story a darker shade than the lower story.
- ❈ *To make a house look less dumpy and awkward,* use a dark color on the roof and the side walls. The dark color outlines and limits the shape of the house against the landscape and sky and helps in making it look less chunky or short.
- ❈ *If your trim looks unattractive,* paint it the same color as the house, and it will be less conspicuous.

Keep whites white. It's sad but true, sometimes white paint yellows with age. To keep this from happening to you, stir a drop of black paint into your gallon of white. Your white paint will stay white!

Preparing to Paint

Pretreat water stains on the ceiling. You can't paint over water stains or mildew on walls or ceilings. You'll need to pretreat the spot by either applying a commercial spray product from paint or hardware stores or by applying shellac, letting it dry, and then painting over the area.

Clean first. Paint does not adhere well to dirty surfaces. If paint is applied to dirty surfaces, it is likely to peel, crack, or blister off the walls. First, scrape off all loose, peeling paint. Then scrub the surface well with a detergent solution and a broom or long-handled brush. Rinse well. You can use a garden hose to wash down exterior walls.

Remove mildew. What may look like fuzzy patches of black dirt is actually mildew, and it is a problem in shady areas on house exteriors. If your house has mildew, wash it with a mixture of 1 quart of bleach to every gallon of nonammonia detergent solution. After cleaning, let surfaces dry thoroughly before painting.

Caution: Please be careful with the bleach and don't let it get on something that it could whiten or streak. You might want to drape plastic drop cloths over the shrubbery and flower beds; if you are using bleach, remove any fabric awnings and lawn furniture cushions from the splash areas.

Check for dampness. Paint will not bind to a surface that is wet from morning dew or a prime coat that is not thoroughly dry. And without proper bonding, paint will peel.

Evaluate your paint. Wrinkling occurs when too much paint is applied or when the paint is too thick. You can correct wrinkling easily by sanding the surface and brushing on paint of a lighter consistency. See the paint can for thinning directions.

Treat old paint. It's not always necessary to remove the old paint when you are preparing old wood surfaces for paint. Seal all knots with thinned shellac and sand when dry. If the knot is loose, tighten it with wood caulking. After the caulking has dried, coat the spot with shellac and then sand the area smooth.

Don't dent with a disc. Don't use revolving disc sanders to remove paint from wood siding. They tend to gouge the surface.

Don't seal the door space. When painting the outside of your house, drape newspapers over the tops of doors and then close them. You won't paint the doors shut.

Put socks on the ladder. To avoid marring a paint job when leaning a ladder against clapboard siding, cover the top ends of the ladder with heavy, woolen socks. The paint will remain unblemished.

Prepare the panes. Windowpanes intimidate even the most ambitious home improvement buffs. Believe me, you can paint the wooden strips around windowpanes without getting paint on the glass and having to endure a pain-in-the-neck cleanup job. Cut newspapers into long 1-inch strips, then dip each strip in clear water. Gently pull the strips between your thumb and forefinger to get some of the water out and then stick the strips onto the windowpanes up close to the woodwork.

Because the strips dry out, you can do only two panes at a time, but if you don't have to painstakingly dab at narrow wood strips, you can really lay that paint on fast. Lift the paper strips off after you paint and wipe remaining water off the glass with a paper towel wrapped around the tip of your finger. Smearing petroleum jelly on the windowpane itself also works (its easy to remove any paint that happens to drip onto the glass), or you can use masking tape to tape around the window frame on the glass (but be sure to remove it as soon as the paint dries so that the goo doesn't adhere to the glass).

Protect the hardware. It's always best to take off hardware before painting, but if you can't, coat the hardware with petroleum jelly before painting. Paint splats will wipe right off. You can wrap doorknobs with aluminum foil or enclose them in plastic sandwich bags to protect them from paint smears.

Using a Ladder Safely

Place it correctly. To safely position a ladder so that it won't fall forward or backward, the distance from the ladder's base to the wall or tree should be one fourth of the ladder's extended length.

Lock the doors. If you are going to work on a ladder in front of a closed door, lock the door so that you won't be knocked over if someone inadvertently tries to open it.

Avoid paint showers. Paint cans tumbling and splashing around on your kids and pets or anyone else beneath your ladder is funny only in cartoons. To avoid paint showers from just a nudge to your ladder while you are working, securely tack the lid from a 2- or 3-pound coffee or shortening can to the bucket shelf of your ladder, rim side up. After filling the can with as much paint as you think is safe, set it into the plastic lid. The grip will hold well enough to hold the paint can against most wobblings. You can even move the ladder with the paint can in place if you're reasonably careful. Of course, nothing will help if you and the ladder tip over; so its best to keep the kids and pets out of the way.

Painting 101

Spare the label. Paint labels contain so much valuable information about paint (how to thin it, how to get it off clothing, etc.) that it is really a good idea to keep the can from becoming covered with drips. Here are two fool-proof tricks to try. Stretch a strong rubber band around the can lengthwise and use it to wipe your brush. All the drips will stay inside the can, where they belong. Or, using an ice pick, punch holes in the rim of the paint can, and the paint will drip through the holes back into the can.

Use a separate container. If you are working outside and want to keep dirt, leaves, and insects out of your main paint supply, pour as much paint as you'll use into a coffee can or other container. Keep the remainder covered.

Get at hard-to-reach places. Places like abutted door frames often can't be reached with a paintbrush. Try a wedge-shaped makeup sponge instead. Dampen it slightly, dip it in paint and poke it into hard-to-get-at spots.

Paint cabinets inside out. When you're painting cabinets, paint the insides first, then the tops, bottoms, and sides of doors before you paint the door fronts. This keeps you from having to reach over already painted areas and smearing the paint and yourself.

Keep painting this side up. You won't have drips on drawer fronts if you remove the drawers and paint the fronts when the surface is "face up."

Paint with a partner. If you're painting a chain-link fence, pour paint into a paint tray and dip a roller or sponge into it to paint. Wear rubber gloves if you paint with a sponge, and speed up the job by having another person sponge painting the other side of the fence. This really gets the job done in a hurry, and the bonus is that you can visit while you work and make time pass even faster!

Mask the jacks. When you paint around a phone jack, do not get paint inside the jack box; it could block a proper phone connection and make a repair by the phone company necessary. Instead, place masking tape around the wall jack before painting to protect it.

Ease your knees. If you're painting floor moldings, sit cross-legged on a skateboard and wheel yourself around the room instead of sitting and sliding across the floor as you paint.

Use a box. When painting small items that might get messy, place them inside a large cardboard box. Paint the exposed surfaces first, and then turn the items to expose other surfaces for painting. If you happen to be spray painting, using a box helps to eliminate ugly spots on grass or concrete, and it also keeps the paint mist from "attacking" shoes and clothing.

Use a cotton swab. If you have small chips or scratches on paint that you need to touch up, try a cotton swab instead of a paintbrush. The bonus is, you can just throw it out when you're finished painting—no brush to clean.

Rely on a reused tarp. If you've bought everything for painting but the plastic paint tarps, old plastic tablecloths, plastic shower curtains, and even old draperies or furniture throws make good substitute paint tarps. Fabric won't protect anything from liquid paint spills, but it will protect surfaces from spray paint mist.

Protect yourself from fumes and flying paint. If you have allergies, you may be bothered by the fumes from spray paints and varnishes. Wear a surgical mask to keep the paint fumes and mist out of your nose, bronchial tubes, and lungs. This may be a good idea even if you're not allergic to paint. I know people who wear surgical masks when they mow their lawns or spray insecticides in their gardens. I think your health is always more important than appearances or the few dimes it costs you to buy protective masks and goggles. Also, this is the perfect time to wear your old glasses, so that when you're painting ceilings, paint doesn't splatter in your eye.

Cleaning Up

Clean spray paint nozzles. As soon as you finish painting, and before paint has a chance to dry and clog the nozzles of spray paint cans, pop the nozzles into a small glass jar and cover them with lacquer thinner.

Clean equipment with ease. You don't have to completely clean up your paint roller, brushes, and pan between coats. After you apply the first coat, store your roller, brushes, edger, and other equipment in the paint tray and then put the whole thing into a plastic bag. Leftover paint and the applicators will stay pliable and fresh until you are ready to start the second coat a few hours later or the next day. Wrapped in foil or plastic, paintbrushes can be stored for a longer period of time.

To clean a paint roller, start by rolling it as dry as possible, first on the newly painted surface and then on several sheets of newspaper. Then remove the roller from its support and clean it with water, solvent, or whatever is suggested for the type of paint you've used.

Clean up paint trays. If you line your paint tray with a plastic bag before pouring in your paint, cleanup won't be a chore. After you've finished, you can toss used rags, paper towels, or disposable paint applicators into the tray, then turn the plastic bag clean side out as you remove it from the tray. You'll have messy rags wrapped up and a clean tray. You can also press a sheet of aluminum foil onto the tray before pouring the paint into it, and when you're finished, wrap up your paint rags and so on in the foil when you discard it.

Care for oil paints and paintbrushes. Soaking a new oil paintbrush in linseed oil for a day before it's used will make the brush last longer and easier to clean. Also, adding a capful of fabric softener to a quart of water and then soaking the paintbrushes in it will do the same trick.

Once used, if you clean oil paintbrushes by just poking them into a can of solvent or turpentine and letting them soak, you'll find that the bristles get squash-bent tips. But if you take an empty coffee can with a plastic lid and suspend the brushes from the plastic lid so that the bristles don't rest on the bottom of the can, you'll be able to reuse those brushes. You need to make two slits in the center of the plastic lid to form an X, then push the brush handle up through the X and replace the lid, which will protect the brushes and prevent the solvent from evaporating. Similarly, if you pour the solvent for cleaning your paintbrushes into a heavy-duty clear plastic bag and then put the brushes into the bag, you can work the solvent into the bristles throughout the plastic without messing up your hands.

What's more, you can reuse the paint thinner left over from cleaning brushes. Here's how. Pour paint thinner into an empty coffee can. Then, after you've cleaned your brushes in it, cover the can tightly, put it in a safe place out of the reach of children or pets, and let it rest for several days. Paint from the brushes will settle to the bottom as sediment. Drain off the "clean" thinner into another can and store for reuse.

Finally, if you happen to get oil-based paint on your work clothes, pour a little turpentine on the spot and rub it with a soft toothbrush. Then wet a bar of body soap and rub this into the spot, brushing gently with a toothbrush. After you have washed the garment with your regular detergent, the spot should be gone.

Caution: Turpentine is flammable. Always do this away from any flames (don't smoke!) and in a well-ventilated place.

Clean your skin safely. Remove paint from your skin by rubbing it with mineral oil. Once it's removed, wash with soap and water.

Storing Paint

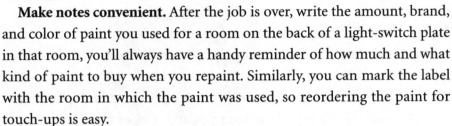

Make notes convenient. After the job is over, write the amount, brand, and color of paint you used for a room on the back of a light-switch plate in that room, you'll always have a handy reminder of how much and what kind of paint to buy when you repaint. Similarly, you can mark the label with the room in which the paint was used, so reordering the paint for touch-ups is easy.

Minimize the air. You can keep paint in an opened can from drying out if you make a pattern from the lid from wax paper. (Don't use plastic wrap.) Lay the wax paper directly on the paint, then put the lid on. The paper really will keep the either oil-based or water-based paints fresh for months! The paper is easy to remove and can be reused if you wish.

Another method for keeping air exposure to a minimum is to store a partly used paint can upside down to keep a "skin" from forming on the paint surface. But, before you turn that can upside down, be sure the lid is on tight, or you won't have any paint to store because it will be flowing all over the work surface.

Find alternate storage. If, for some reason (such as losing the lid), you can't store paint in its original can, you can store it in a gallon-size plastic milk jug. Be sure to label the jug with a marker, noting the color, number, and store where you bought it. When you need to touch up, shake the jug well, pour a dab or two of paint into a throw-away margarine tub, and touch up the spot.

Note how much is left over. If you mark the label on the can with the level of remaining paint before you seal the lid for storage, you'll know how much paint is left inside without having to open the can the next time you want to use it. You can use a marker or just dab a paint-level mark with your paintbrush.

Get rid of the lumps. If you have leftover paint that has lumps or shreds of paint skin in it, strain it through window screening to delump it before use. You can also use an old pair of panty hose stretched across the can.

See STAINS for hints on how to remove paint from fabrics.

PAINTINGS

Leave it to the pros. Valuable oil paintings should be cleaned by professionals. Have your painting appraised if you aren't sure about its value.

Dust carefully. Remove accumulated dust with a soft, clean paintbrush. Commercial cleaners from art-supply stores will remove residues from grease or smoke.

Caution: Don't dust paintings with a vacuum. It can pull chips off. Also, rags can catch on raised peaks in the paint and remove paint sections.

Make an easel easily. If you know a budding Rembrandt who could use an easel for his painting projects, you can make a child-size artist's easel easily with an old wooden chair. Place two C-clamps (available at hardware and home stores) at the front of the chair or nail a small piece of wood across the front of the seat of the chair to hold a sturdy board on which you can tack the drawing paper. An old barstool with a back could make a taller easel.

PANCAKES AND WAFFLES

Make fun shapes. When you are making pancakes, take a cake decorating tube (or pour with a spoon if you are handy) and make faces or names on pancakes, then flip them over. Or, instead of pouring one large round pancake, make squiggles, critters (one larger plus one smaller circle for the head, two ear dots and a tail), or large initials of the pancake lovers. This is such a fun treat for kids!

Try an alternate topping. Heat up some chunky-style applesauce with a teaspoon or two of cinnamon and spoon it on. Yum! And it adds the nutrition of fruit instead of just sugar from syrup!

Keep them warm. Keep pancakes and waffles in a bun warmer until the whole batch is cooked, then you can serve them all at once and the chief pancake-cooker won't end up eating alone!

Freeze the leftovers. Make bigger-than-needed batches of waffles and prepare as usual, but cook the extras until almost done; they will finish

Substitute for Syrup

Here's a good recipe to keep on hand in case you should run out of syrup with half a batch of batter yet to go. Mix 1 cup of brown sugar and ¾ cup of water in a saucepan. Bring the mixture to a boil, and let it simmer for about 15 minutes. (Don't let it boil again or overcook.) Add a teaspoon or so of maple flavoring to suit your taste.

cooking later. Cool the waffles on racks, separate them with waxed paper or a cut-up cereal box liner, put them in a freezer-safe bag or container, and pop in freezer. To serve, heat in microwave for about a minute and a half. Some folks like to toast leftover waffles. Enjoy!

Serve them neatly to kids. Avoid sticky syrup messes. Cut up the pancakes before serving and add the syrup yourself. You can also serve pancakes in soup bowls instead of plates.

PANS

Remove burned-on gunk. When a pot or pan is black from frying, sprinkle a small amount (1 or 2 teaspoons) of automatic dishwasher detergent in the pot with a little water. Then the put the pot on the stove, let it come to boil, and turn the burner off. After it's cool enough to handle, wash and rinse well. Avoid scrubbing frying pans; make it a habit that when you take the food out, you pour in enough warm water (and a few drops of liquid dishwashing detergent, if there's lots of grease) to cover the bottom about an inch. Then, allow the water to boil while the burner cools down on electric stoves or allow to boil a minute or so before you turn off a gas stove. The pan will clean itself and cool while you eat. Wash as usual.

PANTS

Replace elastic waistbands. If the waistband elastic of stitched waistband pants gets stretched out before the pants are worn, you can replace it easily. Start by removing the four lines of stitching through the waistband, cut a small slit at one of the side seams and then pull out the old elastic. Then measure your waist and cut a piece of the new nonroll elastic about 2 inches smaller than your waist measurement (do not pull the elastic tightly while measuring it). Next, attach a small safety pin to the end of the elastic to feed it through, and insert the new elastic all the way through the waist casing. Finally, stitch the two ends of elastic together to sew the opening shut. You may want to add a lengthwise stitch to both side seams to keep the elastic in place. That's all there is to it!

Plan for patches. When you hem children's pants, save the bottoms that you cut off. Then you can use the fabric whenever you need a patch.

PANTY HOSE

Create a tracking system. Before putting the panty hose of the day into the laundry, mark the waistband tag with a check if they have no runs, an X if they have a run but still can be worn under slacks, and turn inside out the ones that can no longer be worn. Old pantyhose can be recycled for many uses, including the one that follows.

 Make hair bands and ponytail holders. Cut across the leg of old pantyhose to make rings, roll the rings up, and you have a ponytail holder that won't break and damage your hair like rubber bands will. Cut off the panty and the foot, tie the ends of the legs together, and you have a stretchy headband or hair band.

PAPER TOWELS

 Creatively use the cores. Use the cores of paper towel rolls to hold extension or appliance cords (write on the outside to identify the cord size or type), Christmas lights, or small plastic grocery bags. Or you could flatten them and insert sharp knives to protect points of knives and your fingers. I like to wrap ribbon around the outside to keep it untangled and neat. You could tape two or three together for a boot tree.

Pack your glasses. When moving, pack your glassware and other breakables with paper towels. They are clean, won't leave newsprint marks like some newspapers, and, best of all, can be used again when you clean up the new home.

PARTIES

Trust me. It's possible to have fun at your own party, even if you are doing everything yourself. Basically, the key is to do as much as possible ahead of time and, above all, make a list of things to do and what to serve so that you don't have to clutter your mind with details on the day of the party. One of the best tips that I can give for enjoying your own party is to make sure that you get at least 15 to 20 minutes of rest at some point on party day. It's hard to smile when your feet are killing you, you are exhausted, and you are wishing that you had never even thought of having a party in the first place. Also, if some of your guests are helping you serve, lists enable them to help you more easily. With that in mind, here are some helpful tips for putting memorable party plans in place.

Party Planning

Test for messes. To avoid possible messes, pretest the capacity of serving pieces by filling them with water measured according to the anticipated recipe amount.

Trade favors with a friend. If you can't afford to pay for help with a party, make a trade-off deal with a friend in similar circumstances.

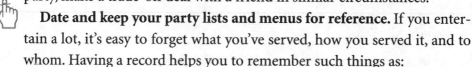 **Date and keep your party lists and menus for reference.** If you entertain a lot, it's easy to forget what you've served, how you served it, and to whom. Having a record helps you to remember such things as:

⊛ What amounts of food you prepared for how many people, and if you ran out or had too many leftovers.

⊛ How much longer you had to bake four casseroles than it usually takes to bake one in your oven.

⊛ If you served shrimp to Eunice and then found out that she is so allergic to them that she stops breathing. (By the way, it's not bad manners to ask a guest, "Do you have any allergies?" when they respond to your invitation.)

⊛ If Albert is totally wild about your kumquats au gratin you should serve them again.

(If at all possible, always invite one guest who really loves all food. It's good for your ego.)

Plan the traffic flow. At a buffet dinner where guests will fill their plates and then seat themselves at different tables, you want to make sure the guests move smoothly to their places without asking where to sit. If you want to be traditional, simply make up place cards. If you have seating at two tables in two different rooms and don't want to suggest who is to eat with whom, try this: Use two sets of china and linen colors and designate "blue cornflowers" to the "blue table" and "green bamboo" to the "beige table." Then, set the plates for the table farthest from the buffet service at the top of the plate pile.

Make punch. Freeze fruit juice punch in gallon milk jugs or cartons. Remove it from the freezer several hours ahead of time to thaw to a "mush" and then add cold ginger ale when ready to serve. (If you can't get the mush out of the plastic milk jug, just take a serrated metal knife and saw off the top section.)

Commonsense Catering

If you are having your party catered, book the caterer as soon as you know when you're entertaining. Whether you are having the party in your home or elsewhere, don't assume anything. Have all details about food, beverages, and serving spelled out in the contract so that on party day nobody says, "I assumed you were doing that." This is especially important if you are having food brought into your home. Make a list that addresses the following details, and make sure to get the entire agreement in writing.

♥ All food on the menu, from entrees to nuts and mints, and if serving dishes for these items will be yours or the caterer's

♥ All beverages, including soft drinks, wine, mixers, coffee, ice, coolers, and glasses or cups in which to serve them

♥ All tableware, including napkins, plates, cups, flatware—disposable or not

♥ Table linens and centerpiece

♥ Time the food will be served

♥ Fees for bartending and food service

♥ Price per person and variations of the price if you furnish the wine, a special dessert, or cheeses or whatever else you will take responsibility for

♥ Whether or not you get to keep the leftovers or if the caterer gets to take them with him or her

Put out signs. Whether the party is for adults or children, identify the house with a "you are here" sign, ribbons, or a bunch of inflated balloons tied to a porch, mailbox, or whatever will hold them without breaking them. Inside the house, place small signs directing people to bathrooms so that they won't always have to ask directions. Put a sign on the bathroom door, too.

Appoint a door-keeper. If your house is the kind that keeps you from hearing the doorbell or if your doorbell rings too softly to be heard above the chatter, either assign a friend to stay near the door to let guests in or put a sign on the door telling them to "walk in" or "go around to the back patio, because we can't hear the bell." Put up signs with arrows directing guests to the backyard gate.

Caution: If you and your guests are all out in your backyard, it's a good idea to lock your front door so that you don't get any unwelcome guests in the house.

Breaking the Ice

Bring in the music. If you can afford to hire a musician who knows how to entertain at your type of party, music really does soothe the savage breast and stranger guest. A guitar player from the church choir can lead Christmas carols in your home as well as in church; a restaurant fiddler can serenade guests in a home as well as in a restaurant. Such musicians need not perform more than an hour or so, because your guests can't converse well in a home if music is too loud. If you have a lot of musicians in your circle of friends, even amateur ones, ask them all to bring their instruments and jam for about an hour at your party.

Inspire a little friendly competition. If you have a pool table, have a tournament and award silly prizes. Or if you have yard space, and it's a casual party, set up a horseshoe game, badminton net, or a croquet set. Again, offer silly prizes to winners.

Don't expect swimmers. If you have a swimming pool party, don't be offended if only a few people actually swim. For reasons that I can't figure out, people tend to stand around and admire pools at pool parties but seldom actually bring their suits and swim.

Make fortune balloons instead of fortune cookies. On small pieces of

The 2-Week Party Countdown

If you are doing the cooking, plan your menu 2 weeks before a big party, and make a two-part shopping list. Here's how.

List nonperishables to buy ahead of time. Remember things such as bottled beverages, canned and bottled food items, spices, and paper plates and napkins if you'll be using them. Buying these things as soon as you know you'll need them eases the last-minute scramble before the party and ensures you'll have exactly the products you need. It's a good idea to order special cuts of meat ahead of time, too, even if your supermarket "always has that," because Murphy's Law will prevail. The day before your party will be the first day that your supermarket doesn't have those brands and items.

Make a second shopping list of perishable items. Plan to shop the day before or on the day of the party for things like salad veggies, coffee cream, and baked goods.

Post a copy of your menu on the refrigerator door. It's the best way to make sure you serve everything.

Review your lists. On the day before your party, review your lists to make sure you have everything, check out your serving trays and bowls to make sure they are clean, make some tentative arrangements on the table, make sure that you have enough trivets to protect your table from hot dishes and that the centerpiece fits, and check out your table linens to see if they need ironing (or, with some permanent-press, a spin in the dryer with a damp towel) to make them look right. Cut, chop, slice, marinate, cook, and do anything else to the food that can be done the day before.

Buy perishables. If you haven't bought your perishables, do it in the morning of your party when you are still calm; cook what needs cooking; set up what needs setting up; take a break for yourself.

Clean until you're comfortable. We all have different standards for cleaning before a party. Some people clean every nook and cranny with a toothbrush, while others think top cleaning is good enough and focus on the food and fun.

paper, write out "fortunes" that pertain to the particular group of people you've invited and then put the papers into balloons before inflating them and tying them securely. Let each person pop a balloon to find a prediction. This could be especially fun at a New Year's Eve party, where you could make predictions for the upcoming year.

Mix people up. For a Valentine's Day party, cut inexpensive valentines in half with different zigzag cuts for each one, and then have guests find their matching halves to meet each other or to be dinner or bridge partners. Similarly, you can cut cartoons from newspapers and use them the same way suggested for valentines.

Prepare some party favors. Cut paper-towel tubes in half. Cut colored tissue paper 6 inches longer than the tube; wrap paper around the tube with 3 inches on each end. Gather one end and tie with ribbon. Fill the tube with candy or small trinkets, then gather and close the other end with ribbon. One reader made these favors with her children and took them to nursing homes at Christmas time. (If you do this, fill some of the favors with sugar-free candy and mark them, then those who can't have regular sugar will get a treat, too.) The favors are fun for birthday and school parties, too.

For more party-related ideas, see CAKES, COOLERS, and SHOWERS.

PASTA

End boil-overs and pasta stuck to the bottom of the pan. Grease the pot (or spray with cooking spray) before putting the water in to boil. Also spray the colander so that draining pasta won't stick to it.

Keep it covered. Add a pinch of salt and a bit of olive oil when you first boil the water, and then add the pasta. When the water begins to boil again, cover the pot with its lid and turn off the burner, leaving the pan on the same burner for the recommended cooking time without the heat. After the cooking time has passed, remove the lid and drain the pasta. You'll save energy and keep from heating up the kitchen at the same time!

PASTRY BRUSHES

Keep them in the freezer. Most of my readers write that they don't wash pastry brushes. After using a brush, they wrap it in foil or put it in a resealable plastic bag and keep it in the freezer. It only takes a few minutes to thaw when you need it again. However, if you want to wash the brush, soak it in hot water and dishwashing soap immediately after it's used, rinse well, and dry before storing it. Some brushes can be run through the dishwasher cycle.

PATCHES

Sew military or scout patches on straight. Instead of pinning them before sewing, keep them in place with tape. Tape three sides of the patch to the fabric and start sewing on the remaining fourth side, untaping one side at a time as you go.

Peach Sauce

This jelled sauce makes a nice substitute for holiday cranberry sauce.

1	large can peaches
½	cup sugar
½	teaspoon ground nutmeg
1	box lemon gelatin

Drain canned peaches, saving the syrup. Puree the peaches in the blender. To the drained peach syrup, add enough water to make one cup of liquid. Pour into a saucepan and add sugar and nutmeg. Bring mixture to boil and let boil for about 1 minute.

Empty the box of gelatin into a bowl and stir in the hot liquid mixture until the gelatin is dissolved. Add pureed peaches and pour into a mold. Chill until set.

Note: If you are limiting your sugar intake, substitute sugar-free gelatin and peaches in light syrup or simply omit the sugar in this recipe.

PEANUT BUTTER

Soften natural-style peanut butter. When you buy natural peanut butter, the oil is usually separated and floating. Place the jar on its side for a day or so; it will be easier and less messy to mix in the oil if it's not all on top. (If you remove the oil to save fat or calories, you'll end up with very hard and dry, nearly inedible peanut butter so it's better to leave the oil in and count the calories into your daily total. Peanut oil is one of the "good" oils anyway!) Store this peanut butter in the fridge to keep the oil mixed in. If the peanut butter becomes hard, put what you'll use in a microwave-safe dish and zap it for a few seconds to make it spreadable again.

PENCILS AND PENCIL ERASERS

Stop the smudges. Rub the eraser with a few strokes of an emery board or fingernail file and it won't smudge your paper anymore.

Make a locker pencil holder. Magnetic plastic flashlight cases will stick to the inside of a school locker door and hold pencils and pens so there's no more hunting for them in the bottom of the locker. The cases can also hold pencils in truck cabs.

Put pencil "leftovers" to good use. Donate them to your church or any other organization; then it's no loss when they "walk away" after people fill out forms.

Make them easier to hold. To help people with arthritis or other finger problems get a better grip, poke the pencil through a tubed foam hair curler or through a small rubber ball.

PERSONAL RECORDS

Know what's needed for tax filing. You will need all 1099 forms (dividends and interest income) and W-2 forms, cancelled checks and checkbook registers, receipts for charitable contributions, deductible expenses receipts, property-tax receipts, records of mortgage interest paid, and brokerage confirmations and statements.

If you're self-employed, you need a bookkeeping system that records your expenses and stores your receipts according to the various tax-deduction categories (income, repairs, travel, dues and publications, meals and entertainment, etc.) as listed on the tax form to save time in tax preparation.

Make an emergency file. In it, include a copy of will and trust agreements; doctor and hospital information; family records (births, marriage, divorce, social security, military service, and citizenship); insurance-policy information (numbers, agent, and beneficiaries); funeral information (preferences, location of cemetery plots, and deeds); safe-deposit box information (key and location and person authorized to open it); bank account information (number and locations); debts (your own and owed to you); all pension and retirement plans; financial and legal advisors' names and phone numbers; brokerage accounts (with brokers' name and phone number); all business records; and all charge accounts.

Keep irreplaceable documents in a safe-deposit box. But make sure to keep copies for your home records. Remember that a safe-deposit box can be sealed when a person dies so that important information may not be available when it's most needed, such as to find out about funeral preferences and wills.

Determine what to pitch and when. Keep all paperwork on major purchases and any investments. Be sure to keep copies of tax returns as well as all receipts, canceled checks, and other necessary tax records. Bank statements should be kept for at least a year. I pare them down to checks I might need for the Internal Revenue Service (IRS) or other reasons and bunch all statements together and keep them for 3 years, just in case the IRS calls.

As a general rule, most canceled checks more than 6 years old can be tossed. Statements and canceled checks from utility, telephone, and water companies should be saved for at least 6 months unless you need them for a specific reason or just want to keep them to compare costs from year to year. Save checks for home improvements and other deductible costs.

See also TAXES.

PERSPIRATION

See STAINS for hints on how to remove perspiration stains from fabrics.

PEST CONTROL

It doesn't matter where you live, hot climate or cold, you're bound to find household pests. They are difficult to eliminate, but you can keep control of them using the following tried-and-true methods.

Roaches

Try my boric acid roach extermination formula. Whenever my roach recipe is published, I get an avalanche of mail from people who forgot to clip it from their newspapers. So here it is—you'll never have to clip it again. Gather together these ingredients, 8 ounces of powdered boric acid, ½ cup of flour, ⅛ cup of sugar, ½ of a small onion (chopped), ¼ cup of shortening or bacon drippings, and enough water to form a soft dough.

1. Mix boric acid, flour and onion. Next, cream shortening and sugar and add flour mixture to this. Blend well and then add enough water to form a soft dough.
2. Shape into small balls and put around the house in areas prone to roaches. If you place balls in open sandwich bags, they'll keep longer without drying out. When dough balls become hard, replace them with fresh ones.

Caution: Keep out of reach of children and pets; large amounts of boric acid can be toxic. If your child or pet does swallow some, immediately call your local poison control center for instructions.

Try a dry mix variation. I prefer to make this dry mixture that is easy to apply. Mix powdered boric acid with an equal or larger amount of flour, cornmeal, or sugar. For example: 4 ounces of boric acid mixed with 4 to 8 ounces flour, cornmeal, or sugar.

Place the boric acid balls or the powdered mixture throughout the house. Put them under your kitchen and bathroom sinks, near the pipes; under the dishwasher, refrigerator, and stove; where you store paper grocery bags and paper goods. Remove your wall plates and sprinkle the mixture behind the outlets. Put some in the garage. Place some under your deck. Put some under your water heater and in the closet.

In short, sprinkle this powder or place dough balls in the out-of-the-way places where roaches like to hide. After they walk through it, they groom themselves and become poisoned.

Go here to buy boric acid. You can buy small quantities of powdered boric acid (4, 8, or 12 ounces) at drugstores, pharmacies, or grocery stores.

To buy larger quantities, look in the telephone book yellow pages under "Chemical Distributors," some of which sell boric acid. (Most commercial products for killing roaches contain boric acid.)

Beware the brown bags. I understand that the small brown German roaches often lay their eggs in the grocery store brown paper sack stacks, and when they hatch, the babies feed on the glue that holds the sack together. Therefore, wherever you store stacks of brown paper grocery sacks, you are likely to have roach infestation.

Weevils

Keep them from the cupboards. While weevils don't cause as much worry as roaches, they are just as unwanted in the kitchen. In fact, once weevils have taken up residency in your cupboards, you'll have to take some pretty drastic measures to get rid of them. I've learned that there are 18 different species of weevils, each having its own food preference. Some parts of the country have flying as well as crawling insect invaders, with the corresponding different species. As noted in the food storage section, storing flour, cornmeal, grits, and other grains in jars or sealed plastic bags or containers prevents weevils from migrating from one food package to another.

Try my three-part weevil elimination plan. (Warning: This process is a chore if ever there was one!) First, take everything out of your cabinets and destroy every visibly infested box or bag. You may feel that this is wasteful, but in the long run it's cheaper than continually throwing out infested food. Be sure to check every single box of staples, including flour, meals, cereals, dried fruits, spices, dry pet food, pasta products, dry beans, peas, etc.

Next, take the boxes in which you have not seen any weevils and put them into the freezer for 4 days at zero-degree temperature or in an oven at 150° to 160°F for 30 minutes. Do not skip this step. Freezing or heating will destroy the weevil eggs, which you cannot see and which will hatch and reinfest your cupboards if they are not destroyed.

The third step is to scrub shelves with hot, sudsy water using a stiff bristled brush, paying special attention to cracks, crevices, and undersides of shelves, where weevils or eggs are likely to be hidden, ready to reinfest everything after you've cleaned up. Before returning anything to your cabinets, spray shelves, crevices, and cabinet walls with an insecticide that says it kills weevils or whatever unwelcome insects have established a village in your cabinets. Allow cabinet doors to remain closed for 3 to 4 hours. The alternative to spraying cabinets is to close up the kitchen, cover all food, get children and pets out of the house and use a fogger type of insecticide according to the directions given on the can.

After doing all of the above, put everything into sealable containers before returning foods to the shelves. Glass or clear plastic containers will allow you to see if foods are reinfested and prevent weevils from migrating to other parts of the cabinets.

Buy small amounts. My best advice is to buy small quantities of staples—enough for a few weeks—and get into the habit of freezing them before using. Open each food package when you get home from the store and return any infested items (with sales slip) without delay.

Put them on ice. Newly bought starchy foods should go into the freezer for at least 7 days. Alternately, just storing such foods in the freezer or refrigerator is another way to control weevils because freezing kills larvae.

Keep them at bay with bay leaves. Sticking a few dried bay leaves into the containers of flour, cornmeal, and so forth helps repel weevils. Some say that putting a few sticks of unwrapped spearmint gum on cupboard shelves or sprinkling black pepper where staples are kept discourages weevils, roaches, and other bugs.

Rodents

Use steel (wool). Instead of dangerous poisons, stuff all the cracks around gas and water pipes with steel wool to keep the varmints out.

Use the lids. Make sure all food is stored in covered containers, especially bulk pet food. Garbage should be kept in sturdy cans with tight-fitting lids.

Pitch the boxes. Cardboard boxes and cartons are favorite mouse nesting areas. Remove as many boxes as possible from closets and other storage areas.

Know when to call in the experts. Even with protective measures, you may still find signs of rodents in your home or hear them go bump in the night. Rodenticides are effective, but some can cause the rodents to die slowly within your walls, where they will decompose and smell until the remains mummify. If your problem is greater than just an occasional mouse passing through, you may need to call in a professional exterminator.

PETS

Speaking as one animal lover to another (and you must be one if you are reading this section), my best Heloise advice is if you can't properly care for a pet, don't get one. And if you don't plan to breed your pet, have it spayed or neutered. That good advice aside, here are other hints you should know about choosing a pet and making sure that it is well cared for.

Choosing a Pet

Find out how big the breed of dog you choose will be when mature. Remember that cute little puppies really do grow up. If you live in a house with a big, fenced-in yard, you can have any dog or pet you choose that is allowed by your city's zoning laws. But if you live in a small apartment, you may want to choose small, quiet pets that don't need as much tail-wagging space.

Add up the costs of pet ownership before you get one. Pets need immunizations and grooming in addition to food, water, love, and attention. Animals that will not be bred need to be spayed or neutered. If you can't afford a private veterinarian, call your local Humane Society to find clinics with less expensive services for neutering, spaying, and immunizations. (By the way, it's simply not true that female animals need to have a litter before spaying and that spayed or neutered animals automatically get fat and lazy. Ask your vet!)

Remember that pets shouldn't be given as gifts the way stuffed animals are given. Experts say that choosing your own pet helps to establish a binding relationship with the animal, so it's a good idea to make getting a pet a family decision so that everyone feels a sense of responsibility for the pet's care.

Don't forget your local animal shelter. It's sad to think about the numbers of stray animals that have to be euthanized because nobody wants them.

How to Select the Perfect Puppy

Puppies are so cute, it's hard to pick just one to take home to your family. Here are a few ideas.

♥ Shyness usually occurs when pups live with their litter for more than 12 weeks or when a timid pup gets trampled into a subordinate position. Shy dogs hold back while the others bark and run around and may be afraid of noise or people. Such a dog may become frightened and attack a person. Also, some owners cause shyness in an otherwise lovable pup by excessively authoritative training or abuse.

♥ Look for a curious and somewhat assertive puppy who is not afraid of strangers. Pups need to be handled properly at an early age so that they won't be frightened.

Note: If you have a shy adult dog, try giving it loving gentle care; talk to it in a soothing way. In time it may grow out of its fear and be as good a pet as any other.

Feeding

Use disposable dinnerware. Shallow carton-bottoms from canned goods can serve as tray place mats for pet-food dishes. Cat-food can "trays," for example, can be replaced each week as you buy your supply. If you don't want to toss out the "tray" each week, you can cover it with adhesive plastic; it is easily wiped and looks nice.

Prepare for easy cleanup. If your cat or dog leaves a few morsels of moist food in the dish and you find them "cemented" to the bottom of the bowl at the end of the day, try spraying food dishes with cooking spray. The food washes off easily and the pets get some extra oil for their coats. They may even lick off the food bits if they like the spray taste, like butter-flavored spray!

Keep thirst at bay. Drop a few ice cubes into your pet's water dish on hot days to keep it fresh and cool.

Treating Injuries

Consider a muzzle. Even the gentlest pet may snap at anyone when it is in pain. You may want to make a muzzle by lightly tying the pet's jaws closed with a soft rag or old panty hose leg.

Never give a pet medicines of any kind unless prescribed by a vet. "People" medicines can be poisonous to animals.

Know the numbers. Keep your vet's or your local animal emergency facility's number handy at the phone and know the emergency facility location so you can easily find it, even when you may be unnerved by the animal's distress.

Beat heatstroke. This is the greatest danger in summer. If your pet is staggering, vomiting, panting loudly, and looking bleary-eyed, put him in a shady place, sponge him with cool water or even submerse him and cool him down as quickly as possible, especially his head. Then call the vet for further instructions. Never leave a pet in a car; it can become an oven in just a few minutes.

Evaluate the injury. Since animals can't talk, you have to be a detective to find out if they are in pain. Some symptoms of pain are lameness, stiff

STEP ♥ BY ♥ STEP

Finding Lost Pets

Here are a few hints to help find a lost pet.

1. Contact local veterinarians and animal organizations, especially shelters, and give them flyers describing your pet. It helps to have recent photos of the pet and to be able to show his or her distinguishing scars or marks.

2. Tell your neighbors about the loss and post signs in the neighborhood describing your pet and giving a phone number to call.

3. Put signs on both sides of your car describing your pet and giving your phone number.

neck, reluctance to get up or lie down, and tense abdominal muscles. See the vet!

And remember that minor injuries, even those that don't bleed a lot and don't need stitches, still need cleaning with soap and water or hydrogen peroxide, followed by mild antiseptic and a bandage. If the wound swells or shows other signs of infection, call your vet; antibiotics may be needed. Some pets won't leave a bandage alone and may need a special collar to prevent their reaching a bandage with their mouths. Again, consult your vet.

Seek vet care for heavy bleeding. Press a clean rag or gauze over the wound, and hold it firmly to slow the bleeding until you can get to the vet. Tourniquets can cause damage to tissues; don't attempt to use one.

Make a splint. If you suspect a broken bone, you may be able to put a splint on a limb. A small animal can be placed on a board or large, firm section of cardboard carton. Or, you can wrap a pet in a blanket or large towel.

Use bandage alternatives. Tape usually won't work, especially for dogs; they pull bandages off their legs and elsewhere. Here are some other hints for keeping them on. Slip an elastic wrist sweatband or an elasticized terry ponytail holder (for a small animal) over the bandage to hold it in place (be sure it's snug but not too tight). Use the leg from a child's knit footed sleeper to cover a neck sore. Cut enough sleeper leg on the upper side of the ankle elastic to gather (about 3 or 4 inches) and cut just above the heel on the lower side of the elastic, then place the gathered "leg" on the animal's neck with most gathers toward the animal's shoulders.

Evaluate vomiting. As upsetting as it may be to see your pet appear to be sick, it's important to know that vomiting may or may not be a danger signal. When you have two dogs or two cats, the dominant one may eat so fast that it may vomit, especially if the animal exercises a lot after eating. Cats frequently vomit due to hair balls. Get a laxative from the vet to alleviate this problem.

If there are no other signs of illness, home treatment for vomiting includes stopping all food and water until the vomiting stops. A small amount of chicken or beef broth given every few hours can help prevent dehydration. Strained meat baby food can be added. Also, a bland diet of

Pets

A beauty operator and owner of a "weenie dog" attached a magnet to the low-slung dog's collar, so that as the dog walked around the shop hairpins were neatly collected. She said the dog was down on the floor anyway so it could earn its keep and save its owner the chore of bending down and crawling around to pick up hairpins. What a great and hilarious idea! Most of us have dogs that just go around gathering dust in the house and twigs in their hair when they roam the outdoors!

boiled rice and well-cooked, drained hamburger meat may be good. If the pet does well, it can go back to its regular diet after a few days.

Caution: If the illness persists, take the pet to the veterinarian. Vomiting can be a symptom of such diseases as kidney failure in dogs and feline distemper in cats. Very young pets that don't respond within a day or two should be taken to the vet.

Protecting Pets from Harm

Never leave your pet unattended in a car . You may think that it's not hot when it's only 85°F and you're parked in the shade, but even with the windows slightly opened, in less than 30 minutes the temperature inside the car can get as high as 120°F, causing heatstroke and possibly death. Please, when you go out, leave your pet home!

Protect kittens and puppies from their own curiosity. Prevent them from licking electric connections that could electrocute them; from falling into swimming pools, where they can drown; and from chewing and swallowing dangerous small objects or eating poisonous plants, such as Dieffenbachia, mistletoe berries, and poinsettia.

Plan to safeguard pets at night. Cats allowed to roam at night and even dogs trained to heel without being on a leash should wear reflective collars or have reflective tape stuck to their collars to alert motorists.

Seek expert advice. When you need pet health advice, see a veterinarian, not a pet store owner, who is in business to sell animals and pet food and isn't likely to know much about nutrition, disease, and pet problems. One of the easiest ways you can find a veterinarian is by asking your friends for recommendations. Plan to have your pet examined once or twice a year and given immunizations as the vet suggests. As with people, health problems should be found and treated before they become serious.

Consider the weather. Warm weather decreases animals' appetites. The heat may cause some dogs to be less active, and therefore they will eat less. Kittens shouldn't be allowed to fast too long; give them frequent, small feedings on hot days.

Give grass the green light. Many animals actually like to graze on grass. It's okay for your dog or cat to eat grass; it's their version of salad.

Keep puppies away from other dogs' droppings. Infected feces transmit a serious disease called parvovirus, which kills 75 percent of puppies under 5 months of age who get it. Older dogs are more or less immune. All dogs should be vaccinated to prevent this disease.

Administer medicines safely and wisely. To give liquid medications to a frisky, objecting dog, avoid a mess by putting the dog into the bathtub at medication time.

To give a dog a pill, insert the pill far back into his mouth, close the mouth quickly and tap his nose with your finger or gently blow on the pet's face. This causes the dog to lick and then swallow. Stroking a dog's throat will also make it swallow a pill.

Try a treat. To entice your pet to take a pill on his own, you can bury pills in cream cheese, peanut butter, cheese, or liverwurst—whatever he thinks is a treat.

Wrap them up. Cats and lap-size dogs can be wrapped and held securely in a towel before pills are popped into their mouths. Towel wrapping also works well if you have to apply ointments to eyes or ears of small pets.

Make medicine fun. When you start giving a dog heartworm pills, handle the pill as you do his other treats. Have him do a trick for it and then give him the heartworm pill as a reward. (This is just the opposite of the way you medicate children, who should never be taught that medicine is "candy.")

Hair and Grooming

Get to the root of the problem. In addition to regular seasonal shedding, some pets have "stress shedding" that can result from changes in routine, visits to the vet or boarding kennel, new visitors in the house, and other stressors. If the condition persists for a long time after the stressful situation has gone, have the pet examined by a vet to make sure it's just stress, not disease.

Make hair removal a snap. Try a damp sponge, a damp hand, or transparent tape wrapped around your hand with sticky side out on clothing, rugs, or furniture. If you want to remove hair from the furniture quickly, rub the "hairy" area with a clean sneaker that has a ribbed bottom.

Be prepared—everywhere you go. Keep tape or a clothes brush in your car so that you can do a last minute de-fuzz before going to a party.

Check air conditioner and furnace filters frequently during shedding season. Hair blocks them and can also go through to the mechanism, causing damage.

Spin it off. If you have trouble getting all the pet hair off in the laundry, try spinning bedding in the dryer on the fluff (no heat) cycle to remove the pet hair before you launder it. Sometimes, you may not even need to launder it after the hair is off!

Tick-proof your pet. It's especially important to protect your animals from ticks in areas of the country where Lyme disease, which is spread by ticks, is prevalent. For short-haired dogs and cats, try using a lint removal roller, the kind made from sticky masking tape. It will pick up nymphal ticks that are no larger than a tiny speck. If you find a tick on your pet, remove it with tweezers as soon as possible and then flush it down the toilet without touching it.

Make a mark. If your pet has no identifying marks (all black or all white cats, for example), dab on some colored paint or nail polish or snip out a patch of fur on its back or leg so that your pet won't get mixed up with a "twin" when left at the vet or boarding kennel. Collars can slip off and mix-ups can occur, even when people are careful. Be sure to point out to the vet or kennel person that you have marked your pet. Some cities have facilities to tattoo an owner's social security number on a pet. Inquire at your vet if this interests you.

Collar them wisely. S-clips on vaccination tags are hard to pry open

Appropriate Pet Dental Care

While pets have good natural defenses against tooth decay, plaque, and tartar buildup after years of soft food diets, veterinarians estimate that 90 percent of all cats and dogs suffer from some type of dental disease by the age of 6.

Crisp foods and leather chew sticks help, but they don't clean teeth at the gum line, where tartar and plaque buildup encourage the growth of bacteria that can lead to generalized infection, even heart disease. For your pet's sake, prevent periodontal disease. Here are the symptoms that should tell you your pet needs to see a veterinarian about dental problems.

♥ Persistent bad breath

♥ Tartar formation (creamy-brown spots on teeth)

♥ Inflamed gum line

♥ Bleeding or receding gums

♥ Loose, infected, or missing teeth

A veterinarian will treat periodontal disease by cleaning your pet's teeth to remove tartar and plaque. The veterinarian will then recommend regular brushing, along with periodic checkups.

when you want to replace old tags with new ones. Instead, bend the S-clips and slip them onto round metal key rings, then put the key rings on the collar and next year's change will be easier. Use the smallest possible key ring to prevent it from getting caught on fences if your dog is a jumper or if it's on a cat. Be careful not to lose the tags if you remove the collar to bathe or flea-spray the pet.

Traveling with Your Pet

Consider your companion's needs. Like some people, some pets are not good travelers and are best left with a sitter or in a boarding kennel. If the trip is short, perhaps a neighbor could look in on your pet while you are gone. Often older pets fare better when kept at home in familiar surroundings instead of in a kennel.

Investigate your options. Your vet or local Humane Society can recommend safe, well-run kennels in which to board your pet.

Select the right pet carrier. Ideally, the carrier should have opaque sides, several venting holes on all sides, a grille door, and be durable, with enough space to allow your pet to stand, sit or lie down. A secure door handle is a must. You'll find a large selection at pet-supply stores. Most domestic airlines sell pet carriers that meet travel standards.

Caution: Zinc nuts used to secure some types of dog cages can be toxic to dogs if swallowed. If the cage you've bought has zinc nuts, substitute stainless steel or nylon nuts, often sold for car license plates in automobile supply stores.

Plan for paperwork. You will need a veterinarian's exam to get the legal documents needed for transporting animals interstate and internationally. In addition to examining your animal to determine general health, the veterinarian should provide any inoculations your pet requires, such as for rabies, distemper, infectious hepatitis, and leptospirosis.

Ask for trip-specific medications. A veterinarian can prescribe a sedative or tranquilizer for jittery traveling pets, but you should never give your human medicines to pets. Some human medications can, at the least, make them ill and, at worst, damage the pet's internal organs or poison him.

Stop along the way. Traveling is easier if you take along familiar food and water, stop frequently to give your pets water and exercise, and check ahead to make sure the hotel or motel you've reserved will accept pets.

Keep everyone safe in the car. It's not safe to have pets crawling on your lap or around your feet while driving. As a habit, dogs should wear harnesses that attach to seat belts (such items are available in pet stores). Cats, because they tend to move erratically, should be in carriers. It saves them from getting injured by closing doors and getting lost if they make a panicked leap from the car when you make a rest stop. Finally, if you're planning to make a cross-country journey, make sure you first expose your pets to car travel gradually with some short trips beforehand.

Put two ID collars on your pet when traveling. This is a great idea, just in case one falls off. And please include an area code and phone number of someone who can be reached if your lost pet is found.

For more pet care tips, see CATS, DOGS, FISH, FLEAS, and STAINS.

PHONES AND PHONE BOOKS

Amplify the great outdoors. If you have one, place a baby monitor near the phone when you go outdoors for an "intercom-outercom."

Keep your phone clean—easily. Put a coiled telephone cord on a long wooden spoon handle, pushing the coils close together; wash them with household cleaner on a cloth or sponge and rinse with a clean sponge. To keep your phone clean and germ-free, wipe it with an alcohol-soaked paper towel often. Most of us don't think about cleaning a phone, but it does need a wipe every now and then. I know mine does.

Reuse your phone book. There are many wonderful uses for an old phone book. Here are a few of my favorites.

- ⊛ Recycle old phone books in your garden compost pile. Use pages to hold potato peels and other vegetable scraps that you routinely compost. (Paper is compost, too.)
- ⊛ Also, layer seven or eight pages in the bottom of the bird cage so that you can just remove them one at a time as they get soiled.
- ⊛ Stack two or three old phone books and join them with duct tape or

a fabric cover to make a child's booster seat. If you may need to use the books again, join them with lots of rubber bands.

⊗ Keep the current phone book(s) under your desk for a footrest.

⊗ Use pages for packing material.

⊗ Give an old book to relatives and friends who live near but not in your city so that they can refer to businesses they need.

⊗ Keep one in the car trunk to check addresses or phone numbers.

 Hang up your phone book. If you have a closet near the phone and want to keep your phone book neatly out of the way, slip a couple of wire coat hangers into the middle of the book(s) and hang it in the closet.

Personalize your phone book. Write the out-of-town numbers you call on the phone book page where you would normally find them if they were local numbers; they'll be easy to find. Along the same lines, either highlight or make a red check mark by the phone numbers you have used so that it's easier to find them the next time you look.

PHOTOGRAPHS

Handle with care. Handle photos and negatives by the edges to avoid fingerprints. Also, don't write on the front of photos. Instead, to make identifying them easy, lightly write either on the page of the album or on the back of the photo with a soft-lead pencil or felt-tip pen. Ballpoint pens can leave indentations.

Choose the right album. Photos are best mounted in a photo album with acid-free archival paper, held in place with triangle photo corners, not tape, glue, or rubber cement. Magnetic or self-adhesive page albums are not considered good storage for photos.

Use expert services. I get lots of questions about restoring old photographs. To get copies of one-of-a-kind photos, especially very old ones that you're afraid to let anyone work on, take them to a professional photo shop that makes copies with a color-laser copier. The results are great!

Foil-proof the mail. To safeguard against loss in case the envelope opens or tears, stick mailing-address labels on the backs of precious family photos before mailing them.

Store the negatives. Keep negatives in a dark, dry place separately from the pictures in case of accidents. Special storage envelopes that help keep out humidity are available. To organize negatives, starting with each roll of film you have developed, write a number (for example, 1) on the back of each of the photographs. Put all the negatives from the film role in an envelope and number it "1" as well. The next roll of film developed would be number 2; repeat the same steps. Be sure to add the date of the photos and names of the people in them.

Display family photos proudly. Make a memory wall of family happenings and milestones, such as the first days of school, weddings, and new babies. When there are several children, make composite collages for each one in a larger frame instead of a frame for each.

See also FILM.

PIANOS

Clean the ivories. Clean ivory with a mixture of mild soap and water, wiping the keys with a slightly damp cloth. Take care not to soak them, just wipe. Rinse well with a damp, clean cloth and dry thoroughly. Never use wax or abrasive cleaners on ivory.

Prevent the keys from yellowing. Ivory yellows naturally over time, but some say leaving the lid open so that the keys get daylight will slow down the process.

Replace the keys. It is possible to replace the keyboard with new plastic keys without affecting the quality of the sound, but if your piano is an antique, plastic keys will devalue it for some collectors. It may be a better idea to sell an antique piano with yellow keys to someone who loves it "as is" and use the money to get a new one with white keys if that's important to you.

PICKLES

Make pickle relish. When life gives you too many leftover jars of pickles, make pickle relish. Take the one or two pickles left in each jar and put them through a food processor, and you'll have a delicious relish for hot dogs and hamburgers.

Put the juice to good use. Add some of the flavored vinegar from pickle jars to salad dressing for a zingy new taste.

PICNICS

 Make your own picnic trays. Cut cardboard box bottoms about 2 inches deep. A cardboard tray holds your drink and plate, keeps plates from sliding, and keeps bread, chips, and other food from falling to the ground, which is especially helpful for children.

Pack knives safely. Put a paring knife in a toothbrush holder, or flatten an empty paper-towel roll and tape the end shut to hold a larger knife.

PIES

Keep the crust from browning too fast. Cover the edge of the crust with an aluminum foil strip while it bakes.

Make a reusable crust cover. Cut out the center of a foil pie pan to within an inch or so of the edge so that you are left with the rim of the pan; this is a time- and aluminum-foil saver and a recycling idea, especially if you bake a lot of pies.

PILLOWS

Fluff and freshen. Place bed pillows in the dryer with a fabric-softener sheet, and tumble on the air cycle for 20 minutes to fluff them up and give them a fresh, clean smell.

Make pillow shams do double duty. Use the decorative shams to store extra bed pillows or rolled-up blankets and quilts. Or stuff them with saved-up foam dryer softener sheets, leftover foam rug backing, pillow stuffing, shredded old panty hose, and other soft materials, then stitch them shut.

PILLS

See MEDICINE.

PINECONES

Burn them in the fireplace. You can burn pinecones in the fireplace, but be careful. They can pop and send out sprays of sparks, so keep the fireplace screen in place and never leave the fire unattended while pinecones are burning in it.

PIZZAS

Cut more than pizza. Pizza cutters are remarkably useful tools. You can use them to cut brownies or pan cookies or slice dough for noodles, cookies, and pastry.

Prevent the dough from sticking to the pan. After spraying the pan with cooking spray, sprinkle a tablespoon of cornmeal on the pan before placing dough on it.

PLACE MATS

Remove spaghetti sauce stains from vinyl place mats. Soak place mats in an enzyme stain-remover bleach mixed with a little detergent and warm water. Follow the box directions for amounts. After soaking, scrub the spots with a brush and rinse thoroughly. If stains still remain, put the place mats outside on a hot, sunny day and let the sun bleach them out.

Renew limp straw place mats. Wet place mats, lay them on a flat surface. Push down and flatten all edges, then liberally spray them with spray starch. When they dry, they should look good as new.

PLANTS

Wash before using again. Always clean plant pots thoroughly before reusing to avoid spreading plant diseases. Wash pots in hot water with a squirt or two of regular dishwashing detergent, and then let them soak for several hours in a solution of 1 part chlorine bleach to 8 parts water. Rinse well and dry, then reuse.

Choose big and hearty plants. Sometimes, people who don't have a green thumb find it easier to maintain big plants than small ones because they don't need as frequent watering or repotting.

Prop drooping plants. The following household items are marvelous tools to reuse to prop up drooping plants. You can use balloon sticks, plastic forks, the name-card holders from florist's arrangements, or "trellises" made by bending wire coat hangers into a round loop and burying the hook-end.

Water plants while you're away. Very delicate plants may need TLC from a neighbor or friend while you are gone, but most plants will last a week or two without their owners. The most basic method is to create a temporary terrarium. Water the plants well, then cover the entire pot with a plastic bag, tucking it around the bottom. They should stay moist for at least a week.

Make plant straws. Here's another way to water plants while you're away. Place a couple of bath towels in the bottom of the bathtub, followed by the plant pots and one large or several small buckets of water on the towels (Be sure that the water buckets sit higher than the plant pots.) Next, snip cotton string lengths to reach from the inside bottom of the water bucket to the top of the plant pot soil. Then gently push one string end into the soil to hold it in place and put the other end at the bottom of the water bucket. When you fill the buckets with water, the plants will be able to draw a drink with this method.

Protect them from wind damage. This tip works best for clay pots with large, single drain holes. Hammer a large (3-inch) nail into the railing where each pot belongs. Then place each pot over a nail so that it fits through the drain hole. This idea might also work on a wood deck to prevent pots from being nudged over by passing pets.

PLASTIC

Remove melted plastic from pots and pans. Try heating the part in a warm oven, then scraping the plastic off before washing in hot soapy water. Is there anyone with an old-style toaster who hasn't melted a plastic bread bag onto the toaster? I love the new, cool-sided appliances!

Put plastic caps from fabric softener or liquid detergent to good use. Keep them at your kitchen sink to hold soap scraps and a small sponge ready to scrub anything; use them to hold makeup—one lid holds five tubes of lipstick, for example, as well as makeup brushes, and other small items; put them to work at the workbench where they are handy sorters for screws and nuts; or use them in your hobby room as a good container for mixing small amounts of craft paints.

 Make your own coasters. Any size lid that fits under a glass makes a good coaster. My readers have decorated them in many creative ways.

- ⊛ Punch holes around the perimeter with a paper hole-punch, and then crochet a "frame" linking the "frame" to the holes; or instead of crochet, just make a yarn overcast stitch border in colors that match the room.
- ⊛ Cut out colorful pictures and cover the paper with clear adhesive-backed plastic, then push the picture into the lid.
- ⊛ Cut plastic needlepoint mesh or buy mesh rounds, then needlepoint designs or solid colors and push the rounds into plastic lids for really absorbent coasters.
- ⊛ Cut rounds of leftover fabric, carpet, or felt, and push them into the lids.

 Make mesh bags into scrubbers. Tie a mesh bag in a ball, and use it to scrub pots, pans, car windshields, bathtubs, and more. Or, use them to dry and store plant bulbs, pool and tub toys, and picnic supplies.

STORAGE SOLUTIONS

Grocery Store Bags

Bags from the grocery store seem to multiply like rabbits. Here's how to corral them in your closet.

- ♥ Hold empty plastic bags together with a terry-cloth elastic wristband, the kind tennis players wear.
- ♥ Bend the ends of a hanger all the way up and hang it on a hook, then slip the handles of plastic bags on the hanger ends for neat and orderly storage.
- ♥ Separate different types of plastic bags to save time digging through a pile. Put grocery bags in a grocery bag; newspaper bags in a newspaper bag, and so on.

Reuse your strawberry baskets. Use them as handy baskets during the holidays by weaving ribbon through the holes and attaching other decorations with glue. They can also hold soap and scouring pads in the kitchen and store perfume, nail-polish bottles, sample cosmetics, and small medicine containers in the bathroom. Place them over a damp area in carpet so it can dry without being stepped on. Or use them to hold packets of sauce mix and spices in a cupboard. (Double them to make them stronger.)

Put picnicware in the dishwasher. Instead of throwing away plastic "silverware," put it in a mesh bag and secure it to the top rack of the dishwasher. It will come out clean and ready to use again.

Wash your straws. Put several together and secure them to a dinner knife with a rubber band, then wash in the dishwasher. They'll come out clean and can be reused many times. Soaking straws used for milk in cold water helps get them clean.

Clean food containers easily. Leftovers can make plasticware greasy, sticky, and just plain yucky. Spray them with laundry prewash spray, let stand awhile, and then scrub with a brush and full-strength dishwashing liquid. Rinse thoroughly and enjoy using again.

Keep containers stain-free. Spaghetti sauce or chili stains plastic containers. To prevent this, line them with plastic wrap before pouring in the food after it has cooled.

Use plastic wrap with ease. Wrap stuck to the roll? Apply a piece of transparent tape vertically at the edge of the wrap and then lift. You'll pull the wrap free. If you want to keep it from tangling, store plastic wrap in the freezer or fridge.

PLATES

Especially when you're serving dishes that get cold quickly, such as quiche or spaghetti, it helps to warm the plates first. Here's how.

Use your oven. If you have a gas stove, you'll find that the pilot light will heat your dishes if you put them into the oven for several minutes before serving.

Run them through your dishwasher. It's quick to run them through the rinse cycle of your dishwasher. Then just towel them dry.

Try your microwave. Your microwave will heat plates, too, but remember, not all dishes are microwave safe. For a quick test from the Association of Home Appliance Manufacturers that will help you determine whether or not a dish is safe, see "Test to be sure" on page 302.

PLUMBING

Here's a simple plumbing tip that can save all sorts of mess. Teach everyone in the house where the main cutoff valve is and how to use it, as well as the various sink, toilet, and washer cutoffs so that all family members, housekeepers, and baby-sitters know how to stop a flood before they are up to their ankles in water. That tip aside, here's how to handle some other types of plumbing situations you might encounter.

Drippy and Noisy Faucets

Just turn until the water goes off. You don't have to turn faucet handles off until they feel tight. Any further turning compresses the gaskets, which will make the faucets leak.

Sleep through the drips. If you have a drippy faucet disrupting your sleep in the middle of the night, tie a 2-foot-long piece of string around the faucet so that the drips can run down the string from the nozzle into the drain without making any noise. If you don't have string, wet a small towel or washcloth and drape or wrap it around the faucet any old way that makes it catch the drips silently.

Stop a squealing faucet. If your faucet squeals (a sound as penetrating as a fingernail on a blackboard), the stem's metal threads and the faucet's threads are grinding against each other. Take the handle and stem off, then coat both sets of threads with petroleum jelly. You won't have goose bumps every time the faucet is turned. The handle will be easier to turn, too.

Clean the faucet aerators. Unscrew the aerator, take the screen out, and rinse it. If it is totally clogged with mineral deposits and hard water buildup, you can soak the aerator screen in vinegar to remove that, and then put the entire mechanism back together.

Clogged Drains

Prevent clogged drains in the first place. Use the following procedure once a month. Make a homestyle noncorrosive drain cleaner by mixing 1 cup of baking soda, 1 cup of table salt, and ½ cup of cream of tartar in a small bowl. Stir thoroughly. Store this cleaner in a clean, covered jar. (You will have 2½ cups of drain cleaner.) To use this drain cleaner, pour ¼ cup of it into a drain, then immediately add 1 cup of boiling water. Wait 10 seconds, then flush with cold water for at least 20 seconds.

Caution: Label the container so that this white powder isn't mistaken for food, and don't store it where food is stored.

Keep kitchen and bathroom drains clear of hair and clogged grease. Try this weekly. Pour 1 cup of baking soda into the drain, followed by 1 cup of vinegar. As the soda and vinegar foam, flush the drain with very hot water.

Boil a pan of water. If the drain is only slightly clogged, it can sometimes be cleaned by flushing boiling water down into it. A solution of 1 pound of washing soda in 3 gallons of boiling water can be poured down the drain. Commercial drain cleaners can also be used. However, commercial drain cleaners should always be used with caution because some may damage drain pipes and the finish around the drain. Washing soda is in the same family as baking soda, but it works wonders on grease. It is usually shelved with laundry detergents at the grocery store.

Pay attention to slow drains. While it seems that drains get clogged at the most inconvenient times, the fact is that drains warn us ahead of time. The problem is that we tend to ignore a slow drain until it's too late. It's so easy to ignore unseen gunk, isn't it? Prevention is the best idea.

Pull out the plunger. If you have a completely clogged drain, try a "plumber's friend," also known as a plunger. Plungers get better suction if their rubber caps are covered with water. To keep from spattering the walls, yourself, the sink countertop, and just about anything in a radius of 5 feet, when you are plunging a small sink make a tent from a bath towel over your arm, the plunger, and the splatters. Some sinks and all tubs have overflow openings. If you plug this opening when you use the plunger, you'll get better suction and force.

Try a wire coat hanger. If the plumber's friend doesn't unclog the clog, you can try dislodging it with a straightened wire coat hanger, bent at one end to form a small hook.

Caution: Never use drain cleaners in completely clogged drains; if the plumber's friend and a coat hanger can't do the job, call the plumber!

Flush the clog out. When floor drains, such as those in shower stalls and basements, are clogged and the clog isn't close to the opening, try to unclog the drain with water pressure from a garden hose. With the hose attached to a faucet, feed it into the drain as deeply as it will go; close up the open spaces around the hose by tightly jamming rags into the opening. Then turn on the water full blast for a few minutes.

Noisy Pipes

Measure the pressure. Isn't it awful when your plumbing "sings"? Sometimes it's the water pressure that makes pipes screech, whine, and even vibrate and bang against the walls in extreme cases. If the water pressure in your house is at or higher than 70 to 80 pounds per square inch, you may have to install a pressure-reducing valve to silence your protesting pipes. To measure the average water pressure in your home, you need to attach a pressure gauge to the cold-water faucet nearest the main shutoff valve. Since you probably don't own such a device, if this problem is annoying enough, you may want to call a plumber to fix it.

Make upfront plans with the plumber. Like all of us, plumbers have busy schedules, so it's best not to wait until he's already at your house for a plumbing repair to tell the plumber about the water pressure problem. Instead let him know upfront when you make the appointment that you want this checked. "By the way, will you check . . ." is not a good way to get things done. The plumber may have a tight schedule and only enough time to fix whatever it is you called about in the first place.

Stop the banging. If a noisy water pipe is banging against a wall, try wedging a wood block between the pipe and the wall. If you are handy, you can clamp the pipe to the block for more stability.

Frozen Pipes

Protect the pipes. In cold weather, protecting the water pipes is a must. The amount of protection can range from foam pipe wraps, which you buy in the hardware store, to covering pipes with straw when you live in rural areas. The idea is to protect pipes from the cold wind and temperatures so that they don't freeze and then burst.

Know what's best. Some people let faucets dribble to keep the water flowing and less likely to freeze, but in areas where water pressure is low, having everyone's water running, even at a dribble, can hamper fire fighting with inadequate water pressure. Find out what is the appropriate way to protect pipes from freezing in your community by calling a county Cooperative Extension Agent or watching for the TV and newspaper stories that are inevitable when a freeze is predicted.

Thaw a frozen pipe. Heat the pipe starting at the tap end. If you start in the middle, steam from melting ice can burst the pipe. Open the tap so that melting ice and steam can run off. In a pinch, you can use a hair dryer to thaw frozen pipes.

Toilet Tank and Bowl

Don't flush a clogged toilet if there is only a little water in it. Flushing will cause it to overflow. Get out the old plumber's friend, and if there isn't enough water to cover the rubber cup, get water from another source and pour it over the plunger cup to make the suction better. Some people poke an unbent hanger down the commode, but if you do this, it may scratch the bowl and then the scratches will stain. A real plumber's "snake" from the hardware store is probably better to use. If the plumber's friend or snake doesn't work, call the plumber. The clog may be farther down into the drain and need to be "rooted" out with a motorized device.

Check the tank. If you aren't getting enough water from the tank to flush the bowl clean, check the tank's water level. If the water level in the tank isn't within 1½ inches of the top of the overflow tube, you need to bend the float arm up slightly so that more water will be allowed to enter the tank.

Read the cleaner label. Many automatic toilet bowl cleaners that you drop into the tank contain strong bleach, which ultimately "eats up" the soft parts of the flush mechanism. Read labels before you buy!

Water Heaters

Drain it monthly. If you live in a hard-water area, you need to drain your water heater monthly to get rid of the mineral deposits that collect on the bottom and that eventually prevent the heater from functioning properly. Directions should have come with your water heater, or ask the plumber who installed it for instructions.

POISON IVY

Know the enemy. A tall climbing vine clinging to trees and fences, poison ivy's leaves are composed of three leaflets that vary in shape. Leaves are red in the spring but turn to shiny green later.

Get rid of it. Wearing rubber gloves, pull up small vines. Seal them in plastic bags and discard. Wash gloves in soap and water afterward. Kill larger vines by cutting plants at ground level.

Wash up quickly. You have about 10 minutes after exposure to poison ivy to avoid a skin reaction. Wash affected area thoroughly under running water. Some sources say wash without soap because soap removes the natural protective oils of your skin and can increase the penetration of the irritant. Other sources say to wash with soap. Everyone agrees on washing thoroughly and quickly.

POPCORN

Add extra flavor. Try sprinkling popcorn with various seasoned salts, salt-free herb blends, dry salad-dressing mixes, taco or chili seasoning mixes, grated hard cheeses like Parmesan or Romano, or the powdered cheese from macaroni-and-cheese dinners.

Pop it in the microwave. Regular paper bags can catch fire at the temperature needed to pop corn, and regular bowls and casseroles aren't shaped properly to concentrate the heat needed for kernels to pop.

Microwave corn poppers are cone shaped to concentrate the heat and will give you best results.

Make no-mess popcorn balls. Form the popcorn balls around lollipops. No more sticky-fingered party guests! Be sure to tell the children there's a surprise in the center so that they don't bite too enthusiastically on the hard core and chip a tooth!

Create popcorn cups. For edible party munchy holders, shape popcorn ball mix over the bottoms and side of glasses well-greased with margarine. After mixture hardens, remove "cups" and fill with nuts or other treats.

See also CAKES.

Save your teeth. Popcorn is a good low-cal snack, but it's a good idea to remove the unpopped kernels so that you don't damage your teeth while crunching away. When you make a batch at night, save some for workday or school lunches. Put the cooled popcorn in a large resealable plastic bag and cut a small hole in the corner of the bag. Give the bag a good shake and all the unpopped kernels will fall out of the hole. Then, when you or a child grabs a handful of popcorn, you're not likely to break a tooth on an unpopped kernel.

POSTCARDS

Overcome letter-phobia. If you never get around to writing letters, remember that it's the thought that counts and friends would enjoy knowing you think of them even if you don't have time to write the "minutes" of your life since your last meeting with them. Keep postcards on hand so you can send off quick notes, comments to politicians, and even "hints" to Heloise. P.S.: You can also FAX hints to me: (210) HELOISE or send me an e-mail at Heloise@Heloise.com.

Make your own. Cut postcards to size from poster board or shirt cardboards. You can place colorful stickers on the shiny side of the paper and write on the dull side just as if it's a regular postcard. Draw a line down the middle with address on the right and message on the left. Just remember that a postcard should not exceed 4½-inches by 6-inches to be sent by the lower postcard postage rate.

Use them as page markers. You don't have to forget the pretty pictures and pleasant memories that greeting cards bring. Old greeting cards, post-cards and even photos can be page markers in recipe books. Each time you open the book, you'll get pleasant thoughts!

POSTERS

Hang posters without damaging the walls. Apply pieces of double-stick tape to the backs of posters and attach the posters to the walls. If there is any residue left on the wall when the posters are removed, you can wipe it away with your finger.

POTATOES

Savor the skin. Instead of wasting the vitamins in potato skins by peeling them, scrub with a plastic pot scrubber. Ideally, cooking them whole with skins on retains the most nutrients. Potatoes are high in vitamin C and potassium, low in sodium, and a good source of fiber and complex carbohydrates. A medium-sized potato has only about 100 calories. It's the stuff you pile on top that breaks the diet.

Bake them in the microwave. To avoid rubbery, hockey puck potatoes, place potatoes on a large microwave-safe dinner plate (the plate you'll eat from if it's dinner for one) and slice each twice to allow moisture to escape. Put a little water on the plate, cover with microwave-safe bowl, and then microwave on high for about 4 to 7 minutes per potato (depends on size and your oven wattage) or as directed by your oven's directions.

As for toppings, I like low-fat yogurt and some parsley. Or you could make a spread with ½ cup of butter or margarine, 2 teaspoons of salt, ½ teaspoon of black pepper, and 2 teaspoons of finely chopped fresh chives. If you should ever tire of sour cream, chives, bacon bits, or yogurt, try spaghetti sauce, a sprinkle of oregano, and grated mozzarella cheese or Parmesan for a potato meal.

Match your potato to its purpose. Today's supermarkets are usually brimming with so many varieties of potatoes, it's important to choose just the right one to fit the dish you have in mind. Overall, you should pick those that aren't soft, bruised, cracked, wrinkled, sprouting "eyes," or greenish-looking. Keep in mind this quick rundown on some of the more popular varieties.

❀ Russet Burbank potatoes are large, oblong, with dark, rough skin. They cook up fluffy and make great mashed potatoes and french fries. Idaho Russets are baking favorites.

❀ California and white rose are all-purpose long, oblong potatoes, with thin, smooth skin. They're best for roasting, boiling, steaming, and pan frying.

❀ Round reds or whites are sold immediately after harvesting and without being stored. They are called "new potatoes."

Store spuds safely. Keep potatoes in a dark, dry place that's relatively cool, about 40° to 50°F. Don't put them in the fridge; the cold makes the starch change to sugar and changes the taste and texture. Also, don't store potatoes with onions; moisture from potatoes can cause onions to sprout.

Reinvent your leftovers. Add grated cheese to leftover mashed potatoes, shape into patties, and then fry them in margarine for breakfast or other meals.

Try a quick-fix when you've overcooked. If you've overcooked your potatoes, don't despair. Poke three or four extra potatoes with holes and pop them into the microwave. Then peel them, add them to the overcooked potatoes, whip them a bit, and make mashed potatoes.

POT HOLDERS

 Make some yourself. Cut circles or squares from old towels and blue jean legs (leftover when you turn jeans into shorts) and sew them together for sturdy, heat-protecting pot holders.

POTS AND PANS

I'm willing to bet that scrubbing pots and pans is a chore you'd like to get over as quickly as possible. Here are some of my favorite hints to help.

Aluminum

Clean the aluminum. Put about 3 tablespoons of cream of tartar and about 1 quart of water in the gunky pot. Bring the mixture to a boil and let it continue to boil for about 10 minutes. Wash and rinse the pot well.

Keep them shiny. Aluminum pans can be kept shiny by filling them to the brim with water, adding 2 tablespoons of cream of tartar, and then letting the water boil. The shine comes back in a few minutes.

Clean while you cook. To clean a stained aluminum pot like magic, try cooking tomato sauce in it. The acid brings back the aluminum shine and gets rid of most dark stains. If you have no plans to cook with tomato sauce, you can also clean aluminum pots by adding 2 tablespoons of white vinegar to boiling water.

Care for it wisely. Never use any type of ammonia or bleach-based cleaner on aluminum; it will cause pitting.

Cast-Iron Cookware

Most serious cooks say that cast iron is the best cookware you can use. It may take a little more work to take care of cast iron, but it's worth it. I have several cast-iron pots and skillets that have been passed on to me from my mother. They are more than 60 years old but still cook better than any other skillets I've used.

Season your skillets. It really doesn't take that long to season a cast-iron skillet. Seasoning should be done at least once a year so that your skillet can last you a lifetime and beyond. It works. Consider how many of us have inherited iron skillets from our mothers and grandmothers.

First wash it with sudsy water, then rinse with hot water and dry well. Slather on a thick layer of unsalted vegetable shortening over the inside and outside of both the pot and lid. Cover the pot with the lid, set it on a cookie sheet, and bake it in an oven at 250°F for 1½ hours. Swab the grease around occasionally with a dry cloth or paper towel to keep the surface of the pot evenly coated.

After baking the pot, allow it to cool, then wipe out any excess grease. Buff to a sheen with a dry, clean cloth or paper towel.

Reseason if rusty. If you have an old cast-iron skillet that has become rusty, all you need to do is reseason it. First remove all the rust by using a nylon scrubber, then wash and dry. Season as described above. You can season and reseason a cast-iron skillet by using it to deep fry. You'll be boiling the oil into it.

STEP ♥ BY ♥ STEP

Cleaning Stainless Steel

This method is only for stainless-steel pots and pans, not for aluminum pots or pans. Very stubborn gunk may take more than one application.

1. Place the pot in the oven to slightly warm it.
2. Spread a plastic trash bag over some newspaper on the counter and place the pot in it.
3. Generously spray the pot or pan with oven cleaner and allow to set for 5 to 10 minutes.
4. Rinse off oven cleaner; wash in hot, soapy water; rinse well.

Never soak in soapy water. As soon as you have finished using your cast-iron and it has cooled, wash it quickly in soap and hot water, using a mild dishwashing liquid, or run lots of hot water on it and scrub with a nylon net scrubber. Dry the pan thoroughly to prevent rust.

Remove food particles with a nylon scrubber. Never use a harsh cleanser or metal scouring pads on cast-iron cookware. They will scratch the surface.

Store it safely. Rinse the pan after washing, then place it on the burner on medium high for a few seconds to dry it. Don't keep it on the burner long; if it starts smoking, the seasoning will be removed. When completely dry, rub the pan with a light coating of vegetable oil before storing. Place a heavy grocery bag (or paper plate or coffee filters) above and below the pan if you're stacking it in a cupboard.

Burn off the grease. Every now and then, you need to clean the grease that gets burned onto your iron skillet and sticks to the bottom and sides like asphalt on a road. Many people simply put the iron skillet into the fire of a barbecue grill after they've finished cooking so that the grease just burns off as the coals burn down and go out. The skillet needs to stay in the hot fire for about an hour.

Caution: Don't touch the skillet until you are absolutely sure it has burned off and cooled. And don't try to cool it with cold water; it will crack the iron. After it's cool, reseason the skillet as noted in this section.

Buy them used. If you haven't been lucky enough to inherit a good cast-iron skillet, go to an antique store, flea market, or garage sale, where you can find one that has been cooked in and seasoned for years and years.

Nonstick Pans

Never use metal. Nonstick surfaces scratch easily, so you should never use metal utensils when you cook with them. Even when the tags say you can use metal utensils, it's still better to use plastic or wood to save the surfaces from scars. As with anything else, if you take care of your nonstick cookware, it will last a long time.

Be gentle. Nonstick surfaces are very easy to keep clean; just soak them in hot, sudsy water and clean with a nylon scrubber. Don't ever use abrasive cleaners, and especially don't use steel wool. If you have a heavily soiled or discolored nonstick pan, just fill the pan with water and add 2 tablespoons of bleach or dishwasher detergent. Simmer the solution in the pan to loosen the crusty stuff. Don't let this boil dry!

Never let nonstick pots and pans burn dry. The fumes can contain a poison that is especially hazardous to babies and small animals and deadly to pet birds.

Enamelware

Avoid abrasives. Enamelware is usually made with a metal base. The outside and inside may be coated with porcelain enamel, or the outside may have an epoxy enamel, acrylic enamel, or polyurethane finish. This cookware washes well in the dishwasher, but it must never be scoured with powders or steel wool. Porcelain enamels may be scratch-resistant, but you shouldn't use any abrasives until you check the manufacturer's directions carefully. Soak pans with burned-on food in water and then scrub with nylon scrubbers.

Glass Cookware

Use commercial cleaners. These products are available for ceramic and glass cookware and ceramic tops on ranges.

Caution: Never scrub glass cookware with a highly abrasive cleanser or a steel wool pad, because it can eventually weaken the glass to the point where it will crack if used at too high a temperature.

Soak them in hot water. You can get burned-on foods off by soaking the cookware in hot, sudsy water. If you've burned starchy or sugary foods, try adding baking soda to the soak; scrub with more baking soda and a nylon scrubber.

Remove the grease and stains. Burned-on grease can be removed with ammonia. Coffee and tea stains will come out if soaked in a solution of 2 tablespoons of bleach per cup of water or 2 tablespoons of automatic dishwasher detergent to a pot of warm water.

Remove the mineral deposits. Mineral deposits on range-top cookware will come off if you boil full-strength vinegar in the pot for about 15 minutes. (Pour this used vinegar down your kitchen drain to clean and sweeten it.)

POUND CAKE

Treat yourself to topping. Heat about ½ cup of preserves and 1 tablespoon of flavored liqueur in a small saucepan and dribble it over a slice of pound cake for a yummy dessert.

PRESCRIPTIONS

See MEDICINE.

PREWASH SPRAY

See LAUNDRY.

PRICE STICKERS

Remove the label residue. Apply either a prewash spray or vegetable oil (mineral oil and baby oils work well, too) before removing with a nylon scrubber.

PRODUCE

Anyone who gardens knows how to buy produce, because watching things grow teaches you to observe what's old and what's fresh. For example, broccoli with little yellow flowers trying to poke through the green heads is older than broccoli that has no flowers. The same goes for asparagus, which also flowers when it's mature.

You can tell how long asparagus, lettuce, and other vegetables that have obvious cut ends have been in the store just by looking at the cut end. Is it a fresh cut or is it brown and, in the case of asparagus, somewhat dry? And when you see delicate leaves on the ends of carrots or radishes, you know they didn't just get off the turnip truck yesterday; they are sprouting and, therefore, old.

But even if you've never gardened, buying the best fruits and vegetables is an easy skill to acquire. To help you know what is best and why, I've compiled the following information from my own experience, but I checked with the experts, too.

Buying Fruits and Berries

Many fruits and berries used to be luxury foods, available only if you grew them in your own backyard or lived in areas of the country where they were grown. Otherwise, if they were available at all, the costs were out of sight.

The kiwi is a good example. Not only were these fuzzy brown, yummy fruits rare in markets, they were so expensive that few people would even try them. One small kiwi (and all are relatively small) used to cost more than $1 each. Now that kiwis are grown commercially and shipped throughout the United States, they can even be found as specials priced reasonably for just about anyone's fruit salad.

It takes time and trial and error to learn how to select the best of those fruits, berries, and melons that are relatively new to supermarket displays. Here are hints to help you.

Avocados: Most avocados used to be sold very firm and took a long while to ripen; now many are ready to use when bought, but because they are so ripe they are often bruised at the market.

To quick-ripen avocados in half the natural time, put the avocado into a brown paper bag with a tomato and then put the bag in the warmest part of the house. The natural ethylene gas from the avocado and tomato plus warmth speeds up ripening.

Avocados don't ripen in the fridge, and refrigeration will make the flesh turn black. To test for ripeness, put the avocado in the palm of your hand. A Florida avocado is ready to serve if it yields to slight pressure. Let a California avocado ripen one more day after this test. Florida avocados are usually twice as big as California ones and have a lower calorie count. California avocados have a more nutlike flavor and a richer, creamier flesh. According to some avocado fans, the difference between California and Florida avocados is like that between ice cream and ice milk, with the Florida product being the ice milk.

Cut avocados turn dark when exposed to air. Sprinkle the surface with fresh lemon or lime juice and use it as soon as possible. If you use only half of an avocado, leave the pit in the unused half. Here in Texas, we put the pit into avocado dip when we refrigerate it to prevent darkening. You can freeze pureed but not whole or cut avocados.

Gooseberries: These look like green grapes and can be eaten raw, but they are usually made into jam or pies and are seldom seen in stores.

Guavas: Available from December to February, guavas are light green or yellow. They are plum-shaped; the flesh is white to dark pink. Unless tree ripened, they are tart. They are usually made into jelly.

Kiwis (or kiwifruit): These sweet fruits are available from May through November when grown in California and from November through May when imported from New Zealand. Buy fairly firm kiwis and ripen them at room temperature for about a week. A kiwi that is about as soft as a ripe plum is ready to eat. If a kiwi is in this stage at the store, it may be bruised and ready to deteriorate.

Some people like to sprinkle kiwi, after it's been peeled and sliced into rounds, with lime juice and eat it as is; others use it for chocolate fondue, and it is also glazed for topping pastries. If you like yogurt, then kiwi and any kind of berries or vanilla-flavored low-fat yogurt is a tasty and fairly low-calorie dessert.

Kumquats: They peak from December to May, are very tart, and contain a lot of seeds. Few people like to eat them raw, and they are usually used for marmalade. Buy firm, orange fruit and store it in the fridge. Don't buy green kumquats; they won't ripen to an acceptable flavor.

Loquats: They peak from mid-March to May and are usually too expensive to be more than just a "taste" item. They look like small, fuzzy apricots and have three or four pits.

Lychees (lychee nuts): You are not likely to find these in regular supermarkets because they're very expensive. They are about as big as a golf ball and have a rough, tough inedible skin that fades from strawberry color to dusty pink after it is picked. The light green flesh surrounds an inedible nut. The edible part of one lychee is about the same as two or three grapes. Both fresh and dried lychees are sold in Asian communities as gifts.

Produce Shopping Rules

Here are my general rules for hassle-free produce buying.

- ♥ Buy in season (grocery ads and specials will indicate this).
- ♥ Buy the best quality you can afford, but avoid overpriced out-of-season foods.
- ♥ Don't buy too-ripe or too-green produce because, in most cases, flavor will never reach its peak.
- ♥ Don't press your thumb into produce, because such bruising causes a lot of waste and spoilage that the rest of us shoppers end up paying for.
- ♥ Be wary of oversize fruits, which may not taste as good as they look, except for Bing cherries and blueberries, where bigger is better.

Mangoes: In season from January through September, they peak in May, June, and July. Ranging in size from a few ounces to 4 pounds, several types of mangoes are available in the United States. Some mangoes are fibrous and stringy, but three types are recommended: the Haden (yellow-skinned with a red cheek when ripe); the Kent (large, green-skinned, with reddish cheek); and the Keitt (large, green, with or without red cheek). Flat, kidney-shaped mangoes are usually fibrous and sour.

Tree-ripened mangoes are the sweetest, and imported mangoes are usually ready to eat when bought at the market. Florida mangoes are picked hard and need a week at room temperature to ripen. Buy unbruised fruit. You can peel and slice mangoes and serve them alone or in fruit salad.

Papayas: In season year-round, papayas are usually light green when harvested; they ripen to a golden yellow. The flesh is yellow or orange pink.

Buy firm, pale green or pale yellow fruit and ripen it at room temperature. It's better not to refrigerate papayas.

Passion fruit: About as big as an egg, its inedible skin is usually purple but can be red and gold; the flesh is yellow. I used to pluck them from the trees in Hawaii when I was a child and eat them until I was stuffed.

Persimmons: Domestic persimmons are available from October to January; Chilean ones are sold in the spring. Ripe persimmons are shiny, acorn-shaped, and deep orange. (A second type has more of a tomato shape and can be eaten when firm.)

Eating an unripened persimmon can cause you to pucker more than you'll ever know or want to remember. The old wives' tale about freezing unripe persimmons so that they will be ripe and edible when they thaw is true. Buy firm, colorful persimmons and ripen them for several days at room temperature. When the skin is shriveled (blistered skin is not yet ripe) and has lost its color, the fruit can be eaten. The skin can be eaten.

Pineapples: Available year-round, pineapples are jetted in from Hawaii or shipped from Latin America. Generally, Hawaiian pineapples are the sweetest and juiciest because Latin American pineapples are picked while too green to have reached their full sugar content. The tags will tell you where the pineapples have been grown. Buy the largest pineapple in the display that is firm and shows some color.

Pomegranates: Although some have yellow skin, most commercially grown pomegranates have red, leathery skin. The flesh is made up of juicy red kernel clusters, and each kernel has a seed that is optionally edible. They peak in October and November and need no refrigeration, although fridge storage will help them last longer.

It's interesting to know that the Egyptians used pomegranate juice for ink and dyeing fabric—a warning not to dribble any of the juice on your clothing!

Prickly pears: These are the fruit of the cactus and are not actually pears, although they are more or less pear-shaped. Although most are deep red, some are pale yellow, orange, or pink. Buy large fruit, ripen at room temperature, then refrigerate.

You have to be determined to eat prickly pear because its skin is covered with barbs and the pulp has lots of seeds, which are edible but very hard to chew. Most prickly pear in the market has been singed to remove the barbs. To eat it, cut off the top and bottom and then cut it from end to end so that you can peel off the inedible skin. You will be rewarded by a tasty, juicy fruit.

Star fruit (carambolas): Star fruit peak from September to January. They look like five-pointed starfish, and most come from Hawaii and the Caribbean islands, although some are grown in the United States. The deeper the yellow color of the fruit's waxy-looking edible skin, the less tart the fruit. They can be eaten raw, used in jams and jellies, and included in fruit punches.

Watermelons: They peak from June through August. The only way to be certain of a watermelon's ripeness is to cut a plug or to buy one that is cut in half or quarters. Sometimes, melons that have been displayed in very hot sun at roadside stands will be sun damaged—almost mushy, as if cooked. (This is also true of tomatoes.) Ask to have the watermelon plugged so you can see what's inside.

Buying Vegetables

It's no secret that I love vegetables and only rarely eat meat. Veggies— raw, steamed, or stir-fried—please the eye as well as the palate, and, as medical research is showing, the nutrients and fiber from vegetables and grains may be our best ally against numerous diseases, including cancer of the colon, a disease almost unknown in parts of the world where people eat an abundance of fruits, vegetables, and grain and very little meat. Dietary fiber intake is becoming important in the control of diabetes as well. Plus, if you are trying to lose weight, veggies fill you up without filling you with lots of calories, unless you smother them in sauces or butter.

Modern farming and shipping give us a variety of vegetables throughout the year, and like fruit, many vegetables that we can buy at any supermarket were almost or totally unknown by our grandmothers and even our mothers.

Combinations of vegetables are available in the frozen-food sections, but fresh vegetables are becoming more popular because they are so readily available and priced so reasonably these days.

Here are some tips to help you get your money's worth when you buy vegetables, which, until recently, were not always available in supermarkets. Unless otherwise noted the vegetables listed are available year-round and should be kept refrigerated.

Anise (sweet fennel): Usually out of season in hot weather, anise has fernlike green foliage that looks a bit like fresh dill weed. The greens can be chopped and used for seasoning. Buy fresh, green foliage and crisp-looking bulbs for a sweet licorice flavor.

Broccoli: Broccoli should be firm, green, and not yellow or budded with yellow flowers. Some broccoli has a slightly purple cast to the buds, and this is a mark of quality.

Celeriac (knob celery): Used as a cooked vegetable or raw in salads, celeriac is usually sold in bunches with three knobs and green tops attached. Larger knobs tend to be woody; buy smaller ones. If the greens are fresh, they can be used for soup. It's easy to peel after cooking. If served raw, you'll need to sprinkle it with lemon juice because it discolors when cut.

Kale: A curly-leafed member of the cabbage family, kale tastes much like cabbage when it's cooked. Buy crisp, dark green or slightly blue leaves. Wilted, limp, or yellow leaves are old. When you see pink, purple, or white-hearted kale, it's ornamental and usually too expensive to eat.

Kohlrabi: This looks like pale green beets but grows above the ground. Buy kohlrabi that is the same size as beets to avoid getting a woody, over-mature one. It should look crisp; if the leaves are wilted or yellow, don't buy it. The leaves, if green and fresh, can be cooked like spinach. Kohlrabi is served raw or cooked.

Mustard greens: Although these are popular in the South, they aren't often eaten in the rest of the United States. Buy dark or light green leaves, which may have a bronze cast. If limp and yellow, they are old; don't buy them. They are wonderful when cooked and seasoned the old-fashioned way, which is to cook the living heck out of them after adding salt, pepper, bacon drippings, or bits of ham.

Chinese mustard greens have white stems, green leaves, and a slightly bitter flavor. They are usually stir-fried or used in soups.

Okra: This native African vegetable is like the little girl in the nursery rhyme: When she was good, she was very, very good, but when she was bad, she was horrid. When okra is overcooked it is really horrid—it's gluey and slimy.

Buy velvety, small (less than 2½ inches—bigger ones are woody and stringy) pods, then bake, boil, or fry them in various ways. Okra is popular in Cajun dishes, and in the South it's often fried after being rolled in corn-meal. If you cook it in water, especially in an aluminum pot, add lemon juice to prevent discoloration of the okra and the pot.

Chinese okra (sing gwa) is dark green and about an inch in diameter and about 12 inches long. It is often used with seafood dishes.

Peppers: Either sweet or hot, peppers come in many sizes, shapes, and colors. Immature peppers are green; mature peppers can be red, yellow, orange, and purple. Generally speaking, the redder the pepper, the sweeter the flavor and shorter the storage time. To tell the difference between hot and sweet peppers, you need to know their names. For example, chili, jalapeño, cayenne, pulla, and serrano are hot peppers. Bell and California wonders are sweet peppers.

Hint: Wear rubber gloves when handling hot peppers; they can really ir-ritate your skin. Some people say it's the seeds that are hot, and some say it's the veins in serrano peppers that are hottest. Whatever's the hottest, wear rubber gloves (the thickest possible) to protect your hands. And don't ever rub your eyes.

Swiss chard: Sold in bunches, chard should have crisp green leaves, not wilted ones that are turning yellow. Popular for cooking, even when over-cooked, Swiss chard will keep its texture and color and won't get dull and slimy like spinach. Bok choy is an Oriental type of Swiss chard.

Using Vegetables

Don't clean them too soon. Don't wash vegetables until they will be used; the extra moisture causes spoilage.

Eat them while they're fresh. Eating fresh vegetables as soon as possible ensures getting maximum food value from them. Store vegetables in the crisper drawer of your refrigerator.

See also FOOD STORAGE AND SAFETY.

Freeze nature's bounty. If you have a garden or access to large quantities of certain vegetables, you may want to freeze the surplus. Except for green peppers or onions for seasoning, most vegetables need to be blanched (put in boiling water for several minutes) before freezing to prevent deterioration.

Tomatoes have a high water content and tend to collapse when thawing, losing their juice. Many people freeze surplus garden tomatoes anyway. Once frozen, they are easy to peel. Hold them under running water for a minute or so and the peel comes off. Frozen tomatoes are easy to pop (still frozen) into soups, stews, and sauces.

Potatoes must be cooked before freezing.

Lettuce, cabbage, onions, celery, and carrot sticks lose crispness when frozen, becoming limp and tough. You won't want to thaw and eat them raw, but they're fine for soups, stews, and casseroles.

Ask the USDA. The U.S. Department of Agriculture (USDA) offers many fine booklets on canning, preserving, and freezing. Call the USDA's local office or your local Cooperative Extension Agent. You can find the number in the government section (blue in some cities, but not all) of your phone book under the federal government listings for the USDA or under your state listings for your local county Cooperative Extension Agent.

Have a chopping helper. Buy a brightly colored plastic dustpan to hold chopped vegetables for the wok. Then you can push them from the cutting board into the dustpan and from dustpan into wok without "flying veggies" all over the floor. Be sure to mark it "Vegetable Dustpan" so that it doesn't end up collecting dirt on the floor!

See also APPLES AND APPLESAUCE, ASPARAGUS, BANANAS, BEANS, BROCCOLI, CANDIED FRUIT, CELERY, CORN, FOOD STORAGE AND SAFETY, GRAPES, JACK-O'-LANTERNS, JAMS AND JELLIES, JUICE, MELONS, ONIONS, POTATOES, QUINCE, RHUBARB, SALAD, SHALLOTS, SQUASH, STRAWBERRIES, STUFFED PEPPERS, and SUPERMARKETS.

PUMP-SPRAY BOTTLES

Put them to good use. There are dozens and dozens of good uses for pump-spray bottles, so never throw a good one out without considering how you might be able to reuse it. Just make sure that you wash it thoroughly, allow to dry, and always label with contents.

Put preelectric shave liquid in it. This is especially helpful for someone whose hands or fingers are disabled so that pouring liquids is difficult. Or you can use it to store homemade cleaning solutions, such as vinegar and water or ammonia and water.

Use it for oil. If the pump spray is from an edible product or is a new bottle and so is safe for food, you can put oil in it to spray on pots and pans and also on your breaded chops before turning them over so they don't stick as easily. Or spray oil on a salad for diet portions. You can also spray flavored vinegars on salads to avoid dribbling too much.

Fill it with water. Finally, don't forget your own refreshment. If you take a spray bottle of plain water with you to the zoo or other hot place, you'll have a handy spritz to cool yourself and companions when needed. If you're on a picnic and have a cooler, keep the spritzing bottle in the cooler and really get refreshed!

PUNCH

Ice a nice punch. When you're using punch or store-bought eggnog, pour half into ice-cube trays and freeze so that you can cool the rest of it at serving time without watering it down.

PURSES

Change purses without forgetting the essentials. Keep a drawer or box just for your purse items and dump them in when you come home. Then you won't have to search through several purses looking for scattered bits and pieces when you're in the A.M. rush.

Another timesaving idea is to keep all of your bits and pieces (cosmetics, pen, pins, sewing kit, medications, etc.) in a plastic zipper pencil case (the kind you can put into ring binders) or just a plastic zipper bag. They'll be in one place when you switch purses.

QUICHE

 Jazz up the crust. Add grated cheese, chopped almonds, or ground pecans to the crust recipe.

Replace the bacon. If you aren't eating bacon, substitute imitation bacon bits for flavor.

QUILTS

 Pare it down. Worn parts of quilts can be cut off and the remaining good parts can be finished with a new border to make lap robes, child-size bedcovers, hot-dish holders, or, if the design is suitable, a vest or skirt.

 Repair with old clothing. Repair old quilts with fabric from old clothing that's faded like the rest of the quilt. The patch won't be so obvious.

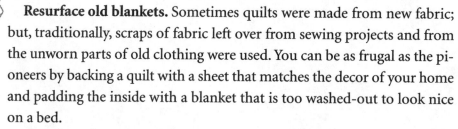 **Resurface old blankets.** Sometimes quilts were made from new fabric; but, traditionally, scraps of fabric left over from sewing projects and from the unworn parts of old clothing were used. You can be as frugal as the pioneers by backing a quilt with a sheet that matches the decor of your home and padding the inside with a blanket that is too washed-out to look nice on a bed.

Consider it American art. Quilts are as appropriate for wall hangings as

European tapestries. To make a colorful wall hanging, attach wooden rings to a quilt or attach matching cloth tabs and hang it from a wide wooden rod. Or just drape the quilt over a bracketed wall-hung rod.

Enjoy the tradition. Host a quilt shower and revive the "quilting bee," the tradition of relatives of the bride getting together to make quilts for her hope chest. If the bride and groom's friends and relatives sew, ask each to make a square, perhaps with a special appliqué or embroidered design that recalls special times of their lives, and join the squares for a keepsake wedding present.

QUINCE

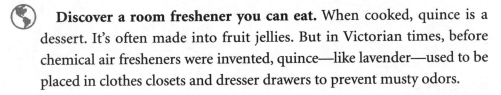 **Discover a room freshener you can eat.** When cooked, quince is a dessert. It's often made into fruit jellies. But in Victorian times, before chemical air fresheners were invented, quince—like lavender—used to be placed in clothes closets and dresser drawers to prevent musty odors.

RABBITS

Don't consider them Easter gifts. Rabbits are cute, trainable pets, but they should never be given to very young children as Easter surprises to be discarded when children tire of them. Remember, they are domestic animals, unable to fend for themselves. They won't live if they are just dropped off in the wild. If you buy a rabbit from a reliable pet shop, get books on its care.

Create the right environment. Rabbits can be trained to use a litter box and so are good, quiet apartment pets. They need a cage large enough to be comfortable, and they need to be played with to get enough exercise. They are affectionate; stroke them on the head and back like you do a cat.

Carry them carefully. Never pick a rabbit up by the ears or scruff of the neck; don't pull its tail. When carrying rabbits, support their backs by holding them by the hind legs; rabbits have been known to injure their spinal cords or even break legs when kicking and squirming.

Keep them safe and healthy. As with all animals, do not allow small children to handle rabbits without supervision. Consult a veterinarian if you think the animal has been injured or is ill.

See also PETS.

RAIN GAUGE

Make a mark for easy reading. Mark your rain gauge with red nail polish or red tape at the 1-, 2-, and 3-inch levels so that you can see them more easily when you want to check how much you have watered from a hose or how much nature has watered from the sky.

Add color, too. Put a drop of red food coloring into the gauge whenever it's emptied to help see the levels from your window without going outside.

RAISINS

Prevent them from sinking in baked goods. Mix the raisins with the dry ingredients before both are added to the wet ingredients mixture. The flour will help suspend them.

Chop them up. If you cut each raisin in half with a pair of kitchen shears, they'll be lighter in weight and won't sink. The bonus here is that the flavor is spread better throughout the batter.

REBATES

Help others with your rebate dollars. Save all your rebate money and donate it to charity at the end of the year.

RECIPES

Hold your cards at eye level. While cooking, tape or tack photo pages with clear plastic pockets to the inside of your kitchen cabinet doors. When you plan a guest menu, insert the cards into the pockets, and they'll be easy to see.

Keep special recipe ingredients off-limits. To make sure roommates or family don't eat specially bought ingredients before you get a chance to prepare the recipe, have a code such as marking the package with a red X or writing a note on it. Then everyone knows which foods are off-limits.

Preserve your family favorites. Either clearly write favorite family recipes in notebooks or type them and make duplicates to be pasted in notebooks, and then give the collection of old favorites to children and grandchildren. P.S.: If giving them to grandchildren, you could leave

♡

Recipe for Family Life

I've had to reprint this popular recipe, which was sent to me by Francesca Ugolini, a young girl from Corpus Christi.

Loving Family Life Recipe (for 2 or more people)

$2\frac{1}{2}$ cups love
$\frac{1}{4}$ cup peace
9   tablespoons faith
6   tablespoons trust
$1\frac{1}{4}$ cups caring
7   tablespoons forgiveness
5   teaspoons sharing

Mix all ingredients together gently. The result is a happy family full of love, peace, faith, trust, caring, forgiveness, and sharing.

Note: My editor says there's a part of the directions missing. It's "Don't ever put any of these ingredients in hot water!"

---

enough space so that both parents' childhood favorites could be placed in the notebook.

Find your favorites in cookbooks. Note on an index card the name and page of the cookbook in which you can find favorite recipes then file in the recipe box under the appropriate category. You'll save time paging through a whole cookbook collection to find the recipe you want.

Record recipes given on TV. It's easy to miss some of the ingredients or instructions for recipes given on TV even when you're not interrupted by a phone call. Keep a tape in the VCR, and tape the recipe presentation. You can copy it at your leisure and make notes on "how-to."

Consider keeping recipe binders. Instead of amassing piles of clippings, buy an inexpensive binder and polypropylene sheet protectors (from office supply stores) or a binder-style photo album with magnetic pages and tabbed dividers to separate recipe categories (breads, meats, leftover uses, low-cal foods, sugarless desserts, vegetarian dishes, Italian, etc.). They'll even hold the pictures with newspaper/magazine recipes. As you collect more, add more refill pages. And, if you keep the binder near your reading chair, you can file each recipe as you clip it—no more messy piles of clippings! These books make nice gifts, too.

File recipes in a loaf pan. Tape recipes with nonyellowing transparent tape to index cards and file the cards in a loaf-size plastic bread container, which holds more than ordinary file boxes.

RECORDS

Find new uses for old favorites. Make flower pots from old vinyl records by melting them into shape over clay pots in the oven. To keep the melted shape symmetrical, make a plug out of aluminum foil and force it though the hole in the record and the hole in the clay pot below.

"Unwarp" your tunes. Sometimes when old records get warped, you can

Know What Can Be Recycled

Use this cheat sheet to help recycle and keep materials out of landfills.

Paper	Newsprint, corrugated cardboard, computer paper, and office stationery
Plastic	1- and 2-liter soda bottles, milk jugs, vinyl siding, antifreeze containers, motor oil and other auto fluids in hard plastic, hard plastic dish and laundry detergent bottles, ketchup and condiment bottles in hard plastic, shampoo bottles, baby wipes containers, Clorox and other bleach bottles, salad oil bottles, and most hard plastic containers
Glass	Clear, brown, or green glass bottles and containers (no need to remove labels)
Metals	Aluminum and tin cans, clean aluminum foil, clean aluminum food trays, and aluminum siding

place them on top of a television set where it's warm and dry, and then weigh them down with several books. Leave them there for a few days. You may not be able to salvage all of them, but this does work for some records, and so it's worth a try.

RECYCLING

Get the information you need. The Plastics Industry introduced a coding system in 1988 in which a three-sided triangular arrow with a number from one to seven is stamped on the bottom of most plastic containers shows how to separate plastics for community recycling programs. Look under "solid waste" or "waste management" in the white or blue pages of the phone book for the phone number of your state, city, or county recycling agency then call to find out what kinds of plastics are recycled in your community.

If you want to do your part to keep beverage bottles and cans out of landfills but your city has no recycling program, call the Environmental Defense Fund's toll-free hotline to get information about recycling programs in your area.

Donate your magazines, office paper, computer sheets, greeting cards, boxes, jars, paper rolls, and sewing scraps. Call local preschools, day care centers, nursing homes, and disabled persons' craft centers to find out if they can use such things. I get letters from preschool and other teachers telling me that with budget cutbacks, school art classes can use many items for their projects.

REFRIGERATORS

Sometimes we take our appliances for granted, but can you imagine life without a refrigerator or freezer? Like our other appliances, refrigerators and freezers have lives of their own. And, if we are to keep them in good shape, we have to take time to properly care for them.

Cleaning and Defrosting

Clean the gasket regularly. To remove mildew from the refrigerator gasket, wash it with mild soap and hot water. Do not wash with bleach; it can cause the gasket to become brittle and crack. The trick is to keep it clean with frequent washing. Badly mildewed gaskets may have to be replaced.

Keep a proper seal. A brittle or torn gasket won't provide the seal needed for proper refrigerator temperature. Close a dollar bill in the door. If it slips out easily, you probably need a new refrigerator gasket.

Avoid cleaning greasy residue from the top. Cover the top of the fridge with plastic wrap; clean by removing wrap and replacing it with clean wrap.

Don't forget the floor. Pull out the refrigerator/freezer at least three or four times a year so that you can scrub the floor and vacuum the condenser coils at the back and bottom of the appliance. Newer refrigerators may have the back coils enclosed within their walls, but they still need to be cleaned underneath.

If you don't do this regularly, get ready for a shock the first time a repair person moves your appliance from its usual spot. Accumulated dust and dirt can interfere with the air circulation around, and therefore the self-cooling system of, the coils and motor. You can also use your vacuum cleaner to pull the dust off from the bottom front of the refrigerator coils.

For in-between cleanings, simply attach an old stocking or nylon net to the end of a yardstick or broom handle with a rubber band. Carefully slip it under the refrigerator and move the stick from side to side.

Avoid dangerous situations. First and foremost, unplug the refrigerator before doing any major cleaning. Never poke at ice with an ice pick because you could puncture the coils.

Time it right. The best time to clean the interior is the day the trash is being picked up and before you go grocery shopping.

Consider the water temperature. When you wash and rinse frost-free or automatic-defrost refrigerator parts, you can use hot, sudsy water and hot rinse water on metal and porcelain parts, but since plastic and glass can crack from sudden changes in temperature, use lukewarm water for washing and rinsing these parts.

Use soft scents only. Wipe out your refrigerator with detergent, borax, or baking soda solution, then rinse and wipe dry. Don't use strongly scented detergents for washing plastic refrigerator or freezer parts because they may retain the odors.

Follow the ¼-inch rule. Defrost refrigerators or freezing compartments when frost buildup is about ¼-inch thick. Cooling efficiency decreases when frost buildup is greater than ¼ inch, and energy use increases because the engine runs more.

Keep food frozen while the freezer defrosts. Keep the food you've removed from the freezer in a cooler or in a laundry basket lined with newspapers. Cover the laundry basket with more newspapers and put ice cubes on top. Or line your kitchen sink with newspapers. Place the frozen food there and top it with newspapers to help insulate it.

Prevent frost buildup. Don't overload refrigerators, and open the door as seldom as possible, especially in hot weather.

Storing Food in the Refrigerator

Keep food covered. Covering all cooked foods and liquids not only prevents spills and transfer of odors to other foods but helps prevent humidity buildup.

Use clear containers. I like to save various sizes of jars and buy clear plastic containers on sale to use for storing my leftovers; it helps everyone see what's there. I try to keep leftovers in the front and always on the same shelf so that I can have easy access to them and they don't get lost when somebody does the refrigerator shuffle. (The refrigerator shuffle is a dance some people do during the TV commercial go-get-a-snack break.)

Assign specific spaces. I've developed a system of keeping certain things in the door shelves and using certain shelves like assigned parking spaces for specific foods. For example, the dairy products, such as milk, yogurt, and cheese, are kept on the top shelf, leftovers are kept on the second shelf, and so on.

Freshen the fridge after frightening food finds. If you find food way in the back of the refrigerator that's grown "hairy and green" and has left a terrible odor in the refrigerator, you can freshen the fridge by washing it with a mixture of 1 tablespoon of baking soda and water. For a wonderful aroma, add some lemon extract or a teaspoon of vanilla in clean water, then wipe the interior thoroughly.

Prevent stale smells. Always keep baking soda or a cup of fresh charcoal in the back of the refrigerator to keep it smelling fresh and clean. When you move and expect to have your refrigerator and freezer closed up for several days on a van or in storage, tossing in a handful of baking soda, charcoal, or unused ground coffee in a cloth bag (or knotted knee-high or panty hose leg) will prevent your being greeted by a musty odor the first time you open your appliance. (This is a favorite hint among military families, whose appliances are frequently in storage while they go to new stateside or overseas duty stations.)

REMOTE CONTROLS

Make a "command central." These days, some people have as many as three remote controls—stereo, VCR, and TV. To solve the problem of never being able to find some of them, take a suitably sized board, sand it smooth, and then put all your controls on one holder with strips of self-gripping fabric tape. If you attach the fuzzy strips to the board and the hooked ones to the controls, the controls will be unpleasant to carry around and will more likely be left on the board.

RHUBARB

 Enjoy this summer treat. But take care to only eat the stalk; the leaves are poisonous. Because rhubarb is bitter, it is either poached, stewed, or baked with sugar. To stew, cut up 1 pound of rhubarb into small pieces and place in a heavy pot with a couple of tablespoons of water and ½ to 1 cup of sugar. Simmer for about 20 minutes. You might want to add strawberries in the last few minutes of cooking. Remove from heat, cool, and then chill. Serve it plain or with ice cream on it.

ROACHES

See PESTS.

ROASTS

Grind up the leftovers. To get the last bits of meat out of the grinder, grind a slice of bread last to push the meat out. You can wash away the remaining bread.

Substitute an edible rack for a metal one. Place three or four whole stems of washed celery across the bottom of a roasting pan and place a roast or whole chicken on top. At serving time, garnish the meat with the celery.

ROCKING CHAIRS

Reduce the roaming. If your rocking chairs have a tendency to move along the floor as you rock in them, consider gluing velvet ribbon on the bottoms of the rockers along the entire length. Trim off excess. Allow the glue to dry completely before turning the chair right side up. Your rocker will stay put the next time you use it.

ROOF

Inspect your roof regularly. Early spring and late fall are the best times to inspect your roof so that all is ready for seasonal changes. If you have a shingle roof, look for loose shingles or shakes for curling, fraying, and tears at the edges. With tile or slate roofs, look for missing or cracked pieces.

Check the flashings around chimneys, vents, skylights, and other roof penetrations. They should be tight and in good condition. Call a professional contractor for a more thorough inspection if you have doubts.

Clean gutters and downspouts of leaves, sticks, and other debris. But make sure that you stay off the roof; walking on its surface can do a lot of damage. If you must get up on the roof to inspect, climb only on a firmly braced or tied-off ladder with rubber safety feet.

ROSES

Use a defensive cutting strategy. Hold stems with a spring clothespin to keep prickly thorns from sticking you.

Honor special occasions with rosebushes. A reader, whose husband always brought her roses when they were dating, wrote that after they were married and had more responsibilities, they couldn't afford them anymore. But, still romantic, her husband planted a rosebush for her on each major holiday so that now she has a yard with many different shades of roses and a heart filled with lots of happy holiday memories.

RUBBER BANDS

Make a rubber band ball. To keep rubber bands from being tangled in a drawer (if you don't use the time-honored method of looping them over a doorknob) loop them into a ball. The ball grows each day if your newspaper comes with a rubber band. The bonus for grandparents is that this ball can be a toy when the grandchildren come to visit.

RUBBER GLOVES

Find new uses for old gloves. Cut good fingertips off and put them into new gloves to reinforce fingertips; if the gloves are rubber, you can cut cuffs and parts of fingers in strips for rubber bands. Save the palm and back of the glove for traction when opening jars.

Enjoy a moisturizing glove treatment. Slather lotion or oil on your hands before wearing rubber gloves for washing dishes or general cleaning. The gloves will slide on and off more easily and your hands will get a good moisturizing treatment, especially if they'll be in hot water.

RUGS

Make them nonskid. Either buy rubber-mesh pads for this purpose and place them under the rug, or tack a piece of old rubber-backed drapes (or other flat rubber sheet) to the backside. Put a rubber tub mat under the bathroom rug to keep it from slipping.

Brighten dull colors. Dull colors may not indicate that your carpet has

Care for Oriental Carpets Correctly

Here are some hints for caring for these precious antiques.

- ♥ Don't use steam cleaners; they remove the wool's natural oils and prematurely age the rug.

- ♥ Blot; don't rub spills. Get a professional cleaner for dried stains. You can dilute the spill with cool water, continuing to blot until the rug seems clean. Don't ever soak unstained parts, and always dry the rug thoroughly using absorbent towels on top and underneath the stain.

- ♥ Never put house plants on rugs; moisture will condense beneath the pot causing mildew damage to the rug.

- ♥ Old-fashioned beating breaks the foundation of the carpet.

- ♥ Sweep fringes with a broom instead of vacuuming, which can tear them. Broom-sweeping brings out the wool's sheen and removes dirt.

- ♥ Padding reduces wear and prevents slipping. You can get special pads to prevent slippage of Oriental rugs placed over carpeting.

- ♥ Turn rugs annually to prevent wear paths and equalize light exposure.

faded; it may just be dirty. One home remedy is to vacuum to remove dust, then, taking care not to saturate the backing, sponge the rug with a wet rag that has been dipped in a mixture of 1 quart of white vinegar and 3 quarts of boiling water. Allow to dry completely.

Get the best padding you can afford. When buying new carpets, you can sometimes reduce costs if you get top quality thick padding instead of higher end carpets. However, when considering the overall cost, remember that installation and padding may or may not be included in the price.

Identify hand-loomed Oriental rugs. When you see an Oriental rug that appears to fade gradually toward one end and both ends are not finished or fringed exactly the same way, it's likely to be hand-loomed the traditional way. Fringes or threads at the top of the loom are tied differently from those at the bottom. Because the yarn is dyed in hanks with natural dyes, the first yarn used (from the outside layers of the hank) will be darker hued than the inner layers; the top of the rug, which was woven first, will be darker than the bottom edge.

Camouflage the worn spots. To cover worn areas, buy waterproof colored markers to match the worn spots and just color the carpet backing that's showing through. This works especially well with dark-colored patterned carpets like Orientals.

See also CARPETS.

RUST

See STAINS for hints on how to remove iron rust stains from fabrics.

SACHETS

Get them for free. Take the perfumed sample paper inserts from magazines and tuck them into your lingerie drawers, clothing or linen closets, or with your stationery and greeting cards for free sachets.

Tuck a few in closets. Store scented soaps (wrapped) tucked amid the towels in your linen closet for a fresh-from-the-store scent. After the scent fades, use the soap for your bath where getting it wet will reactivate some of the scent.

SAFETY PINS

Hide one in the hem just in case. Safety pins are so useful. They can hold up a torn hem, close up a blouse with a popped button, and hold your eyeglasses together when the screw falls out! My dry cleaner always pins tags to the garments so when I remove the tag, I pin the safety pin to the hem of that garment. That way I always have a safety pin handy for emergencies.

SALAD

Prepare it in advance to save time. To prevent soggy salad, put the desired dressing in the bottom of the salad bowl, and then layer in tomatoes and vegetables. Last, add the lettuce or spinach leaves. Place the prepared salad in the refrigerator and toss just before serving.

Make your own salad bar. To encourage your family to eat healthy, nutritious fare, make salads more inviting by offering a family salad bar. You'll need to accept the reality that not everyone likes the same ingredients in a salad, so offer sliced mushrooms, carrots, beets, celery, chopped green onions, olives, garbanzo beans, kidney beans, sprouts, radishes, and more

---

QUICK REFERENCE

Know Your Salad Greens

You can find many kinds of greens alongside the iceberg lettuce in grocery stores. You can combine these tasty greens for delicious salads. It's best to rinse lettuce right before you use it, so avoid washing lettuce and placing it back in the refrigerator. Here's a quick rundown of some of the greens you'll find on store shelves and in convenient family-size fresh packs.

Boston lettuce has green outer leaves with yellow-green inner leaves. Its buttery flavor is best enhanced by a mild salad dressing.

Bibb lettuce has soft, green broad leaves. Its delicate taste is also best enhanced by a mild dressing.

Red leaf lettuce is usually a large head of frilly green leaves with reddish tips. It also has a delicate taste and is best with a subtle dressing.

Curly endive is a chicory and has a somewhat bitter flavor. Its leaves are large, lacy, and fringed. The outer leaves are darker in color and have a stronger taste. Mix with some milder greens and a strong-flavored salad dressing.

Watercress leaves are small and dark green with crisp stems. Its strong peppery taste is good when teamed with other pungent greens.

Belgian endive has a long, small, firm head. Its leaves are creamy white and have a hint of yellow at the tips. It's crisp, has a pleasantly bitter taste, and is best mixed with stronger-flavored greens.

in the cups of muffin tins, served beside a large bowl of greens and several salad dressings. Let family members customize their salads, and you'll be surprised at how youngsters will try new things if other siblings seem to be enjoying them. Cover the muffin tins with plastic wrap after dinner to store leftovers in the refrigerator for the next day or two.

Keep salad fixings fresh. Some vegetables, such as celery, radishes, and carrot shreds, will keep fresher for the next day if you put a wet, but not drippy, paper towel on top before the wrap.

Stop the gushing. To prevent bottled salad oil from gushing out too fast, instead of removing the entire seal when you first remove the cap, cut a slit or punch a hole in the seal. It will be easier to measure or sprinkle.

Clean salad for a crowd. When you tear up romaine lettuce for a crowd or dinner party, wash it and put it in a large, clean pillowcase and then spin it dry in the clothes washer spin cycle. You won't bruise the romaine, and it's fast and neat! Your friends may get a kick out of this entertaining process.

Do a real salad toss. Tear greens into a large, plastic bowl with a tight-fitting lid, add dressing, and give the bowl a few shakes. No more tossing with bulky wooden utensils and no more "bruising" on tender lettuce leaves!

SALT

Avoid lumps (and it's not the dry rice tip). If you don't want to keep rice or crushed crackers inside the salt shaker to keep it free-flowing in humid weather, upend a small, clear jelly glass over the shaker. The jelly glass "dome" will keep the salt dry and ready to shake.

Remove excess salt from hot soup. Add sliced raw potato to absorb the salt. You can remove the potato slices when they begin to soften if you don't want to eat them.

Reduce salt in canned foods. Pour off the liquid from canned vegetables to reduce the sodium content by one-third. If you rinse the vegetables with water, you'll decrease the sodium content even more. This hint is good also for canned tuna and shrimp; be sure to rinse shrimp very gently to prevent breakage.

Make a salt substitute. Mix 5 teaspoons of onion powder; 1 tablespoon each of garlic powder, paprika, and dry mustard; 1 teaspoon of thyme; ½ teaspoon of white pepper; and ½ teaspoon of celery seed. Combine the spices, and store the mixture in a clean, empty spice jar in a cool, dry place.

SAP

Zap the sap. If dripping tree sap has stained or gunked up your wooden deck or patio, carefully scrape off as much sap as you can with a paint scraper and remove the remaining residue with turpentine. The turpentine will also remove any paint or water sealer from the wood, too, so you'll have to repaint or reseal once you've removed all of the sap. If the sap is on your car, you may be able to get it off chrome parts with turpentine but for painted surfaces, contact your car dealer's service department for advice. Service departments have specific products that work with different auto paint finishes.

SAW BLADES

Safely stow saw blades. An old record rack will hold saw blades safely and will help protect the cutting edges from getting damaged.

SCALES

Glue on a new covering. If your home scale is looking a bit worn and the footpad edges are curling up, replace the covering with an adhesive-backed floor tile. You can trim the edges and cut out the area for the dial; just make sure you recalibrate the scale to 0. If you already have vinyl tile in your bathroom, you can make your scale match the flooring and be less conspicuous. And don't we all want the scale to be less conspicuous on those days when we've indulged in munchies?

SCARVES

Keep scarves free of fold lines. Hang scarves over a pants hanger—the kind designed to hold several pairs on different rods. Or sew plastic rings about the size of a quarter (available from craft shops or drapery stores) across the bottom of quilted or crochet-covered hangers, positioning the rings about 3 inches apart. Thread scarves through the rings to store them.

Make your own scarf slide. When rings don't fit any longer (or even if they still do), use them as scarf slides. Just slip the ends of a scarf into the ring, slide the ring into position, and adjust the drape of the scarf.

SCORCH MARKS

See STAINS for hints on how to remove scorch marks from fabrics.

SCREENS

Fight wire with wire. If you need to repair a wire screen, cut a piece of wire mesh from an old screen and sew it over the hole with some fishing line or plastic thread. Most hardware stores sell screen-repair kits if you don't want to attempt something on your own. If you only have a small hole in your screen, you may be able to seal it with clear fingernail polish.

Don't dread cleaning screens. Washing screens doesn't have to be an all-day chore if you approach it with an assembly-line mentality. Remove the screens from your doors or windows and place them up against a tree, fence, or sawhorses. Using a scrub brush, wash each screen with a mixture of 1 cup of ammonia to 1 gallon of water, making sure to clean the tracks, too! After scrubbing the screens, rinse them well with water (a hose works great) and dry them in sunshine.

SCREWDRIVERS

Make an a-peeling substitute. Need a Phillips screwdriver in a hurry, but don't have one handy? Try a metal potato peeler!

See also TOOLS.

SEASHELLS

Don't throw away beach souvenirs. Put seashells into a large, clear jar and use it as a paperweight or door stop. If you're handy, make a large shell-filled vase into a lamp.

Keep Fido from digging. Cover the soil of potted plants with seashells to hold in moisture and make them less attractive to digging pets.

Decorate! Those large, flat shells you picked up on your vacation make good soap dishes.

Make them pretty as a picture. Arrange and glue shells on an old picture frame, and then frame a picture or mirror with it. If you have some spare time, you can even practice saying, "Boutiques at the seashore sell seashell-framed shiny mirrors." (Bet you can't say that 10 times fast!)

SEAT CUSHIONS

Stop them from slipping. Try putting a thin sheet of foam rubber or a rubber sink or bathtub mat between the sofa or chair cushion and the springs.

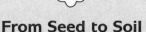

From Seed to Soil

Starting plants from seed is economical and a lot of fun, but transplanting tiny seedlings takes some care. Here are three quick ways to get seedlings out of their containers whole and undamaged at planting time.

1. Start your seedlings in paper cups. You can tear away the cup at planting time and place the intact soil and seedling right in the planting hole.

2. If you cut both ends out of juice cans, set them on a tray and plant seeds in them. At planting time, you just gently push all the dirt and roots out of the juice can at the same time and into the planting hole.

3. Start seedlings in egg cartons, but place a section of eggshell in the bottom of each cup so removal is a snap. Place the eggshell full of soil right in the planting hole; if you can, crack the shell a bit to help speed its decomposition in the ground.

SEEDS AND SEEDLINGS

Give seeds the big chill. The butter compartment of your refrigerator is just the right temperateure for storing seed packages. Seeds will still germinate several years after the date shown on the package if they are kept in the refrigerator in a zipper-lock bag to keep out moisture.

Test for germination. If you find old seeds in packages, try sprinkling a few between two damp paper towels. If they're still viable, they'll sprout in a couple of days if you keep the paper towels slightly damp and in a warm spot.

SEWING

Here are some sewing tips that I think you can use, whether or not you make garments "from scratch."

Hand-Sewing

Avoid knots. You'll get fewer knots and tangles in your thread if you keep your thread shorter than 20 inches for hand-sewing.

Have needles on hand. If you're hand-sewing or mending and find that your thread keeps fraying, choose a needle with a larger hole. Packages of assorted needle sizes are available for about $1.00 in variety or fabric stores.

Try a new needle. If you're pulling or puckering the fabric as you're hand-sewing, try a new needle. Old needles can become bent, dull, or point-damaged over time. The oils from your hands can remove the slick finish from the needle as well, making it harder to pull the needle through the fabric. Most seamstresses use a new needle every time they start a new project. Since needles cost only a few pennies, treat yourself to a new needle, and you'll be rewarded with easier sewing.

Treat yourself to new thread. You won't save time or money by using old thread from wooden spools because it's likely to break more easily as you sew. Wooden spools haven't been used for years and have become collector's items. Stop by a fabric store and pick up a few basic colors of thread to have on hand.

Be magnetic! Place a magnetic strip in the bottom of your pin box. Even if you drop the whole box of pins, you won't have to pick them up because they'll still be attached to the magnet.

Substitute embroidery floss. Embroidery floss is a good substitute for regular thread when you are mending. If you use all six strands of floss, you'll have a stronger repair (especially if you're sewing on buttons). Floss comes in hundreds of colors, so if you match the floss to your fabric the repairs can be invisible.

Use fabric glues with caution. If you use those wonderful timesavers such as glue stick, liquid seam sealant, and basting tape, be aware that they can damage your sewing machine if you don't follow directions exactly. One important rule is to always let glues dry completely before stitching over them.

Clean in the tight spots. A well-washed and -dried mascara brush is great for cleaning around the bobbin case of your sewing machine. The twisted brush can fit into those tight places to pick up lint.

Grab a fabric-softener sheet. Your needle will glide through fabric more easily if you stick it through a fabric-softener sheet a few times. Thread the needle and knot the thread before doing this.

Give patches the slip. If you're sewing patches on your child's school or scout uniform pocket, slip a piece of cardboard into the pocket to keep from sewing the pocket to the shirt. To position the patch properly, place it on the garment and then staple it before sewing or use fabric glue to glue the patch in position; let the glue dry and then hand-sew around the perimeter of the patch.

Threading Needles

Angle it! If you cut thread on an angle instead of straight across, you'll have an easier time threading the needle.

Thread needles with ease. Can't thread the needle? Dab a tiny bit of clear nail polish on the tip of the thread, allow it to dry, and the thread tip will glide right through the needle's eye.

Spray a little starch. Dampen the end of the thread with a bit of starch when you thread your sewing machine, and the thread will glide right through the eye of the needle.

Use white paper for better visibility. If you need a little help trying to thread your sewing machine needle, place a small piece of white paper behind the needle. You'll instantly see the eye and can guide the thread right towards it.

Thread needles in bulk. Instead of threading just one needle, thread two or three before you start to hem a garment. Then when you run out of thread, you can pick up another threaded needle without stopping and breaking your work rhythm.

Sewing Supplies

Organizing your sewing supplies really saves time. If you can find things quickly and easily, even mending can become less tedious. Here are some tried-and-true storage hints.

♥ After you have pinned and cut all the necessary pattern pieces, place the pinned fabric, instructions, and all notions needed for that particular project in a plastic grocery bag that has handles. Drawstring hotel laundry bags are good storage bags, too. You can either hang each project on a hanger or lay it flat until you have time to complete the sewing. This is a great way to keep things organized if you tend to cut several projects at a time.

♥ You can store sewing machine bobbins in an empty prescription bottle that has been thoroughly washed. Colors are easy to find when the bobbins are stacked and kept together.

♥ A fishing-tackle box is the perfect organizer for storing sewing notions. It has compartments of different sizes, and the arrangement of the compartments is very suitable for scissors, needle threaders, buttons, and more.

♥ To keep your spools of thread in view, drive headless nails at an angle into a peg board or on the right size of a board for your needs. Hang the board over your sewing machine, and you will be able to select the color you need quickly without having to hunt for it.

♥ Use a bar of soap as a pincushion. Keep the wrapper on and put the pins and needles in. It not only holds a lot of needles but also lubricates the pins, making them slide more easily into fabric.

♥ Make your own travel mending kit. Wrap small amounts of different-color threads around a piece of cardboard. Add a needle threader and a small pair of scissors, and you'll be ready to make repairs at a moment's notice.

Hemming

Knot every few inches. The whole skirt hem doesn't have to fall when one hemming thread breaks! When you're hemming a skirt or fixing a hem, knot the thread every few inches. The knots prevent the hem from opening up entirely if the thread breaks.

Undo misplaced hem tape. If you accidently put iron-on hem tape on the wrong side of the fabric, try this. Place a damp cloth over the tape, hold a warm iron on it for at least 10 seconds, then pull off the tape while it's still warm. It may take several tries. If residue remains, hold a steam iron above the area and the residue should disappear into the fabric. Wash as the care label directs.

Hem suede or leather the right way. These garments are hemmed with acrylic latex glue (water based and clear drying) made especially for leather and suede. You'll find the glue at leather shops and craft stores.

Making Clothing

Press pattern pieces before pinning. Press the pattern with a dry iron before pinning it to the material so that the pieces will lie flat on the fabric. You'll get a much more accurate cut than if you used the wrinkled patterns pieces directly from the pattern envelope.

Make perfect collar points. If you sew, you know that turning collars and cuffs properly is the key to a professional look. When turning the points of collars and cuffs, trim the seam close to the point as usual, then turn the collar right side out. Thread a needle and make a rather large knot so it won't pull through the point. Place your needle as close as possible to the stitching of the collar point. (Place the needle on the interfaced side, being careful not to catch any material on either side.)

Pull the thread through until you get to the knot, and then tug on the thread until the entire collar or cuff point has "surfaced." Cut the thread as close to the point as possible; the knot will stay buried inside the fabric. This nifty trick gives a crisp point every time.

Machine Sewing

Bag it! When sewing, you can avoid the mess of thread clippings and fabric snips on the floor if you tape a plastic kitchen-size trash bag to the side of the sewing machine or the front of your sewing surface. As you cut and snip, drop the scraps into the bag. Cleanup is automatic.

Bring out the vacuum. Use the dusting attachment on your vacuum cleaner to suck the lint and fuzz out of your sewing machine. (Be sure to remove the spool of thread, bobbin, and face plate first.) It's amazing how much lint accumulates out of sight. Lint buildup can affect the working parts on your machine and interrupt stitching, so be sure to clean the machine often.

 Be prepared with your numbers. When you're ready to go shopping for parts or attachments for your sewing machine, write the name and model number of the machine on a small piece of paper and immediately put it in your wallet. Many parts (including lights, belts, and bobbins) are specific to a certain model, so having the model number ready will save you a trip home for your product booklet.

SHAKERS

 Add a pinch of this and a dash of that. Keep large shakers of flour and sugar on the kitchen counter to avoid hauling out canisters when you need just a teaspoon or so of either one.

SHALLOTS

 Use shallots for best flavor. Shallots are members of the onion family, but their flavor is somewhere between onion and garlic. Substituting regular onions or garlic for shallots won't give you the same flavor in a recipe as shallots do. When using shallots, follow the recipe directions to mince and brown them quickly; they often become bitter if they are overcooked.

SHEEPSKIN RUGS

 Take them to the cleaners. Since it's almost impossible to know what type of tanning process was used on these skins, it's best to take them to a reputable dry cleaner where special cleaning processes and chemicals can be used.

Note: White sheepskins tend to yellow after they are cleaned.

SHELVES

Make sure they're level. When you install shelf brackets and measure both ends of the shelf from the floor up to the proposed hanging height, imperfections in construction and flooring may throw your measurements off. Instead, measure to the desired height on one end of the shelf, and then use a carpenter's level to mark the shelf line on the wall, making sure that the bubble is in the center of the level before you extend the line.

Forget shelf paper for heavy-duty use. Heavy pots and pans can quickly tear shelf paper, so try vinyl floor tiles instead. They're easy to install. Cut them to fit, and then peel off the backing. Maintenance is a snap, too; just wipe clean.

Substitute and save money. Buy wallpaper remnants instead of shelf paper and cut it down to fit your needs.

Zip through it with a saw. If you have a kitchen full of cabinets to line with shelf paper and you find that your shelf paper is too wide for the job, remove the excess by cutting through the whole roll with a handsaw.

Create more storage space. Rectangular plastic dishpans can double your shelf storage capacity if you fill and stack them. Print the contents of the dishpan on tape or labels instead of writing directly on the dishpans (just in case you want to change the contents). Or use small plastic mesh baskets in your cupboards. A rectangular plastic laundry basket can hold shoes on the closet floor, too!

SHOE BAGS

Get organized throughout the house. Those compartmentalized shoe bags are terrific. You already know that they're great for organizing shoes and save space when they're hanging on the closet door or from a sturdy hanger. But did you also know that they also hold socks and undies, school supplies, knitting and crocheting supplies, toys, rolled T-shirts and polo shirts, panty hose and tights, and just about anything that takes up drawer space or makes it jumbled. You'll want more than one in a closet!

SHOES AND SHOEHORNS

Clean off heel marks with prewash spray. To clean heel marks off white and colored shoes, apply prewash spray. It may take a bit of scrubbing, but it works if the shoes are just marked and the leather hasn't been scratched or scraped.

Get coordinated. Replace plain white laces in white tennis shoes with colored ribbon or cord to match your outfit.

Be nice and dry. Stuff wet shoes with old panty hose to help keep their shape while they dry. Or put them on the floor next to the hot-air exhaust

Proper Care for Leather Shoes

Leather shoes are expensive, so you'll want to keep them looking their best by following these few steps. Even though shoes look terrific right out of the box, it's easy to scuff or stain them because the gloss sprayed on new shoes does not protect like polish. Get in the habit of polishing new shoes before you wear them.

♥ Use a sponge and saddle soap at least once monthly to remove dust and grime. Follow with good-quality paste or cream to moisturize the leather; never use liquid polish on leather.

♥ Use a soft cloth to apply polish and allow it to dry. Buff the shoes with a brush in long easy strokes, and then buff in a circular motion with a soft cloth to remove excess polish and deepen the shine. Clean or get new brushes and shine cloths every 6 months.

♥ Strip off polish buildup every eight shines with leather balm to prevent cracking.

♥ Dress the heel edge with black dressing product to lock out moisture (which can lead to cracks).

of the refrigerator to hasten drying if shoes can't be tossed into the clothes dryer.

Fix heels damaged from driving. A good cleaning and polishing may remove scuff marks from floor mat damage. To remove scrapes, heat a curling iron to warm (not hot) and gently press it against the scraped area. The "ironing" will remove wrinkles so that you can smooth the leather and glue it back into place. You can avoid the problem altogether by keeping a pair of slip-on shoes in the car to wear while driving.

Fix scratches with felt-tip markers. Scrapes and scratches on brightly colored shoes can be touched up quickly with colored felt-tip markers. They come in many shades to match almost any color. Be sure to test the color in an inconspicuous spot.

Stop squeaks with talcum. Moisture in the soles is the usual cause of squeaky shoes, so try shaking some talcum powder in the shoes before and after each wearing. Or, turn over each shoe and nail a couple of short tacks in the bottom of the sole on either side of the metal arch support. Do not push the tacks all the way through the sole or the tacks will puncture your foot. If the talcum and tacks don't take care of the problem, take the shoe to a shoe-repair shop for advice.

Give suede shoes the brush-off. Brush suede shoes weekly with a stiff bristled brush to remove dirt. A gum eraser can remove light stains; heavier stains need cleaning professionally. Apply water and stain-preventing spray after cleaning and brushing.

Make shoes last by taking care of them. When putting on shoes, untie, unbuckle, or use a shoehorn to avoid ruining the shoe's "mouth." Shoe trees help shoes keep their shape. Let shoes rest in ventilated areas between wearings to dry out; don't store them in their original boxes because there isn't any air circulation. Clean and polish shoes regularly; once they're scuffed and shabby, it may be difficult to revive them.

Replace heels often. Replace heels when one-fourth of the heel is worn off. Before I store my good leather boots at winter's end, I like to have them professionally cleaned and shined at my shoe repair shop.

Stop the slip. To stop a stray strap from slipping, put a piece of moleskin on the inside of the heel strap where it hits your heel or try sticking a piece of thin foam rubber weather stripping on the strap. Either material can be trimmed to fit a heel strap and should help to keep it in place.

Make your own shoehorn. Cut a plastic margarine tub lid to the right shape and it will bend around your heel better than a real shoehorn. In a pinch, the tongue end of a man's belt can be an emergency shoehorn.

SHOPPING

Be careful with credit. Compare grace periods, annual fees, and interest rates. If you have a lot of cards, protecting them by joining a credit card protection service may be a good idea, but if you have only one or two cards, you can easily report loss or theft yourself.

Caution: Never sign up with a registry by phone; there are fraudulent protection services that ask for your card numbers but instead of protecting you they make unauthorized charges on your card.

10 Ways to Cut Grocery Spending

1. **Use what you have.** Plan meals from your cupboard using ingredients you already have so that you can use up these foods and free up money to spend on this month's sale items.

2. **Know the score.** Before you decide on your menu, check grocery ads to see what's on sale.

3. **Plan all three meals for the day.** But don't feel bound by tradition—if you like pancakes for supper or lunch and soup or sandwiches for breakfast, it's okay.

4. **Change your eating habits.** U.S. government studies show that nutritious foods are less expensive than junk foods.

5. **Experiment with substitutes.** If beans are on special and the recipe calls for peas, use the beans; both are green. Rice and noodles are interchangeable. Chicken or turkey can substitute for beef in some recipes; you can doctor them up with seasonings or soup mix.

6. **Avoid convenience foods when you can.** They cost more, and many are overpackaged, adding to our overtrashed landfills. Also, many are high in fat and salt content.

7. **Be creative with leftovers.** If you cook enough rice or noodles for two meals, you can use the leftovers in a casserole another day. Bake double the number of potatoes you need for one day and use the leftovers for stuffed baked potatoes another day, saving baking energy.

8. **Be flexible.** Change your menu to accommodate specials and remember that sometimes buying after the promotion of specialty foods can be a good buy, especially in January when overstocked gourmet foods and condiments get marked down.

9. **Avoid impulse buying.** Steer clear of too many shopping trips where you "pop into the store to pick up a few things."

10. **Make budget-stretching a game not a burdensome chore.** Shop more economically each week and make notes of your savings so that you can take pride in your efforts.

Create a co-op. If your city has vegetable or farmer's markets where you can save money by buying produce in bulk, get together with five or six friends and buy bulk produce weekly, dividing purchases and their cost for substantial savings. You'll get a taste of veggies that you might not otherwise have tried, too. In some co-ops, each person takes a turn each week to shop and divide the produce; in others they make it a fun, get-together day for several of the co-op people to shop together.

If you enjoy this form of shopping, you might want to consider applying it to other areas of your life. For example, if several people in your neighborhood are shopping for stereo equipment at the same time, try to buy as a group. Some group members research audio magazines in the library to find out which brands are best quality and how to combine the various components-speakers, CD player, receiver, etc., and others scout local stores to compare prices. Then, all go to a dealer together and try to negotiate a group discount. Even if you don't get a discount, you'll surely get the best researched buy on your equipment.

Read the fine print on all warranties and service contracts. Always read the fine print and if you are trying to decide between two similar items, take the one with the most extensive warranty. If you decide to buy a service contract, find out how long the contract will be valid, whether repairs will be done in your home or at a service center, whether a dealer or repair center will do repairs, and, if repairs are done by a third party service center, if your contract be honored if the third party goes out of business. Also, will the contracts still be valid if you buy the item under your name and give it away as a gift?

Organize your shopping trips. You'll save time as well as money and gas. For example, you can buy several weeks' worth of supplies on double-coupon days or when your favorite brands are on sale. When I run errands all day, I put a plastic laundry basket in the trunk of my car and put my packages in the basket. Small bags don't get lost, and I carry in the basket with all the bags in one trip when I get home.

Shop with friends. If you have friends who meet for a weekly card game, tennis, or whatever, do your shopping together on that day and take turns driving. One car going for weekly groceries sure beats several when it comes to saving gas, and you have the added bonus of pleasant company.

You and your friends also can buy in bulk and then split for extra economy.

Carry a cooler. Put an inexpensive foam cooler in the car, and you can put frozen foods in it when you grocery shop. Then you don't have to worry if you need to make extra stops en route home and you won't have to pass up a good buy on milk or meat. Ice cream will be in better shape, too.

Know how much you need. Most of us use certain products more frequently than others. It helps to know how much of a product you use over a period of time so that you can stock up without overstocking when there's a sale.

Date products as they are put to use. That way you'll know how long it takes to use them up. For example, if you find that you use about six tubes of toothpaste and 11 bottles of shampoo in one year, you can safely buy those amounts of toothpaste and shampoo.

I don't date food items that I will consume in short periods of time, but I do date such items as a large jar of jelly, aluminum foil, instant and regular coffee, salt, and pepper.

Look all around. Higher-priced items in the store are usually placed at eye level; you'll save money if you look up, down, and sideways at all the brands of the product you want.

Always compare weights and volume, not just the size of the package. A box or jar may be bigger but still contain the same contents. Also, the giant economy size may not cost less per ounce, pound, etc. Many people carry small calculators to assist their supermarket math, and some stores have price per ounce or piece actually posted on the shelf.

Computerize your shopping list. After you've listed every possible thing you could or would buy at the supermarket, save the list in your computer and make a printout when needed. You'll never have to waste time making up a new shopping list again. Keep the list on your fridge door and highlight items to be bought.

Avoid shuffling through your coupons. Instead, make a note on your shopping list which items have coupons and also the best-buy amount off with brand name.

Use self-stick notes. For short lists, write your needs on a self-stick note, and attach it to the fridge. When you go shopping, you can stick it on your dashboard or an envelope holding your coupons, and then you can stick your list on the handlebar of the shopping cart so that your hands are free.

See also "Menu Planning and Shopping Made Simple" on page 297 and SUPERMARKETS.

SHORTENING

Measure without the mess. An easy way to measure solid shortening or lard is to use the displacement method. For instance, if you need ½ cup of shortening, fill a one-cup measuring cup with ½ cup of water, then add solid shortening until water level reaches one cup. Drain off the water and the shortening comes right out without scraping.

Substitute with oil. When you substitute vegetable oil for butter or lard in recipes other than baking bread and desserts, you may need to experiment with your recipes. As a rule you use one-third less oil. For example, 2 teaspoons of vegetable oil replaces 1 tablespoon of solid shortening. Remember that while a good vegetable oil may be low in cholesterol, it's still fat.

SHOULDER PADS

Stick them under a strap. Tuck shoulder pads under bra straps when you don't have time to sew them in. If you have the "teeth" section of self-gripping fabric tape and the pads are of a soft fabric, you may be able to secure the pads in place by putting a strip of the tape over both the strap and shoulder pad.

Try double-sided tape. If you don't like self-gripping fabric tape or pin-on shoulder pads, try sticking the double-sided tape safe for walls on the pads and inserting them. The tape is good for emergency hem repair, too.

Reuse old shoulder pads. Instead of throwing away the stuffing from unwanted shoulder pads, stuffed pillows, children's toy animals, or soft-sculpture crafts, make knee pads for gardening or cleaning. Simply hold the pads on your knees with the tops of old socks. Or, if you feel more ambitious, sew them into work pants knees. Another idea: Insert shoulder pads in bras for "push-up pads" or "enhancers."

SHOWER CAPS

Find new uses for hotel "freebies." The next time you're in a hotel, take the shower caps home with you. Use them to cover leftover food in bowls or round 35mm slide carousels to keep them dust-free and to keep the slides in place. (Place an identifying index card under the cap so you know what's inside.)

SHOWER CURTAINS

Clean them safely. To remove water spots, spray full-strength vinegar to both sides of the curtain, and leave it on for at least 30 minutes. Scrub persistent spots with a brush.

Remove mildew. Machine launder with warm water and ½ to 1 cup liquid chlorine bleach, regular detergent, and a couple of white bath towels. Run through a whole cycle. Toss in the dryer for a few minutes to remove wrinkles and rehang immediately after removing from the dryer.

Repair hanging holes. When the hanging holes tear, take a handheld hole puncher and punch a hole about a half-inch from the torn one.

For a more permanent mend, if you have clear plastic mending tape handy, it helps to reinforce the area with it before you punch the hole either in the same place or a half-inch from the torn place. Fold the tape over the top so it reinforces on both sides.

Prevent water spots on a clear plastic curtain. Either get a second shower rod and curtain as a splash guard for a clear plastic one or put a thin film of lemon-oil furniture polish on to prevent the "gunk" from sticking.

Grease the rings. If your family (Not you, of course, because you are more careful!) tears the shower curtain because it doesn't slide shut easily, it could be due to the rings sticking on the curtain rod. Grease them with petroleum jelly.

Trick the tieback. When the adhesive hook that comes with some shower curtains won't stick to the tile, substitute a rubber suction cup to hold the tieback. It's easy to remove and replace when you clean the tiles.

SHOWERS

We're not talking about bathroom showers here. This section is on party showers—bridal and baby.

Bridal Shower Ideas

Since many newlyweds already have fully equipped apartments and are in enough of a quandary about what to do with "his and hers" everything, personal items or pantry food items may be more appreciated than such traditional shower and wedding gifts as toasters, blenders, and silver. Shower invitations can say that it will be a "kitchen," "pantry," or "personal" shower. Many showers now include the groom, too. Often the bridesmaids pitch in together to buy some item for the couple that none of them could afford to buy alone. Here are some unique gift ideas.

Books, craft supplies: If the couple has hobbies or special interests, buy books and items related to them. If you buy cookbooks, add some of the spices used in the recipes to the top of the package as a decoration.

A honeymoon kit: Include headache pills, antacids, adhesive bandages, a small tube of antiseptic or spray that can be used on sunburn if the couple is going to the shore, hand cream, tweezers and clippers for hangnails and splinters, and maybe a couple of granola bars for emergency middle-of-the-night hunger pangs.

A home-warming kit: Gather scissors, gauze, tape, cotton, thermometer, heating pad, hot water bottle, upset-stomach remedies, pain relievers, and other accessories for a home first-aid cabinet, including a first-aid book.

A fix-it kit: Include a hammer, set of screwdrivers, pliers, nails, and picture hooks. You can also add a gas can, oil or silicon spray, garden hose, and any other home-aid items.

A cupboard kit: Add grocery staples and boxed mixes such as cake mix, corn bread mix, meat helper mix, pastas, basic spices, flavorings and colorings, and other food items that are nice to keep on hand. You can also include casserole dishes or baking pans and wooden spoons or spatulas to go with the mixes.

A personal shower: This kind of shower is ideal for the nondomestic bride (and groom). Consider giving a few trousseau items to the bride, such as a negligee, lacy underwear, favorite bath product or cologne, and leisure clothing. For the groom, a robe, wallet, pocket knife, or shirt might be ideal.

A life-saving kit: Every newlywed's new home should be equipped with a fire extinguisher. Include a carbon monoxide detector and a smoke detector, too, for added home security.

Toys: For this gift, include games such as word games, banking games, board games, and puzzles. (Remember the saying that "you can tell the age of the boys by the price of their toys"?)

A recipe kit: Put together a recipe box with your favorite recipes, and if you're the mother of the bride or groom, her or his favorite recipes. You can ask each shower guest to bring her favorite recipes to add to the box. Also, if it's a kitchen shower, favorite recipes could be accompanied by non-perishable ingredients and the proper pan, cookie cutter, or other utensil needed to prepare the recipe.

You could "theme" the kits so that you provide the staples and spices for making Italian, Cajun, Tex-Mex, or other ethnic foods. Tuck in a few store coupons with food kits.

A picnic kit: Fill a picnic cooler with disposable plates, cups, napkins, and flatware and some munchies, ranging from bean dip and a six-pack to caviar and champagne, depending upon the taste of the couple.

A sewing kit: A supply of different-color thread, a sewing box or basket, measuring tape, mending tape (fusible, iron-on), scissors, needles, straight and safety pins, a few assorted buttons, snaps, hooks, fabric glue, pincushion, and anything else that catches your eye at the store will help a couple keep themselves and their clothing out of tatters and tears. (If you like, ask each shower guest to put a spool of colored thread on the gift as a decoration.)

A happy memory quilt: If the shower guests sew, each can bring a quilt square embroidered with the guest's name, so that all the squares can be sewn together for a treasured keepsake.

A reality kit: Include a bucket, broom, mop, cleaning supplies, sponges, and other facts of life. You can also attach small kitchen items (potato peelers, can opener, wooden spoons) to a clothesline and then put them into a laundry basket; as the line is pulled out, so are the utensils.

A Heloise kit: A copy of this book and some of my favorite "do-alls," such as white vinegar, lemon juice, salt, candles, baking soda, dental floss, and any of the other ordinary items used in my hints to do many extraordinary things.

A "kitchen maid": For fun, make a "kitchen maid" gift for a bridal shower. The main part of the "maid" is an ironing board. Tie a pretty apron around the middle of the ironing board to form the waist and put a dishtowel in the apron pocket. Attach a toilet plunger to one side for an arm and a bowl brush to the other side for another arm. A mop, attached to the back with the mop end over the top of the ironing board, will be the hair. For an extra touch, add a colander for a hat. Two scrubbies can be eyes. And a small sponge for the nose and a nail brush for the mouth. Add a dustpan for the feet and a few personal final touches and you have the fun favorite "kitchen maid."

A gift-for-every-month kit: One reader had each of 12 guests draw slips of paper printed with the months of the year. Guests would bring gifts useful during certain months and marked the gift for that month. For example, March gifts were spring-cleaning needs; April included Easter goodies; May was vegetable seeds and gardening tools; October included Halloween goodies and a leaf rake. Another reader included a sample list of the couple's likes and dislikes in hobbies and home-entertainment choices when she sent the invitations. Guests had fun picking out such shower gifts as adult board games, craft and hobby kits, and gave gift certificates for videotape rentals, local home delivery restaurants, videotaping of the wedding ceremony, and other "couple" instead of "bridal" shower gifts.

Capturing the Memories

Make a copy of the guest list. List names and addresses to help the honoree send out thank-you notes. Leave about three lines of space so that a description of the gift can be noted after the name as the gifts are opened.

Draw door prizes. Have each guest write her name, address, and the gift on a slip of paper or index card to be used for a door-prize drawing at the shower and by the honoree for writing thank-you notes after the shower. Index cards can be put into a permanent address file for Christmas cards.

Inscribe some index cards. Have each guest write her name, address, and her hint for a happy, successful marriage on an index card, which can be read by the bride during the shower and, as noted above, kept in a permanent address file. Reviewing friends' hints for a happy marriage in the address file is a sure cure for the monotony of addressing Christmas cards.

Take instant pictures. Snapshots taken during the shower can be put into an album for the honoree.

Present photo albums. Mothers of the bride and groom could assemble photo albums of precious shots from birth to adulthood and present them to the couple, or friends could call the mothers and ask for the photos so that they can assemble them. (This is a good idea for a baby shower, too. Everyone wants to know "who the baby looks like," and so such an album can be a reference after the baby is born.)

Start a guest book. Have shower (and wedding) guests sign a guest book, which the couple can later use in their home. The custom of guest books comes and goes, but anyone who's been married a long time and has kept one through the years knows how nice it is to remember good times, not to mention how nice it is to be able to find the answer to "What was Harry's first wife's name?"

Collect autographs. Set out a plain tablecloth with laundry pens or liquid embroidery/fabric paint nearby so that guests can sign it and then give it to the honoree. Or create a lasting memory by having guests autograph a wooden rolling pin, tray, or cutting board with a felt-tip marker; later, you can shellac it and present it to the couple.

Have the wedding invitation matted and framed professionally. This makes an especially memorable gift. Or, if the couple has written their own vows or if they have a special poem or biblical text read at the wedding, have the words done in calligraphy and framed for a keepsake gift. We were lucky enough to receive three of our wedding invitations mounted, matted, and framed, and it's such a delight I have one in each area of the house.

There is one exceptionally beautiful one hung in my bathroom, and each morning when I brush my teeth I look at it and smile.

Craft a gift-bow bouquet. Cut a hole in the center of a paper plate and, as each gift is opened, poke the ribbons through the hole, leaving the bows on top. By the end of the gift opening, the bride will have a bouquet to save or to throw as she chooses.

Baby Shower Ideas

A baby shower tree: Attach coupons for "Three Hours of Baby-Sitting in Your Home or Mine," interspersed with store discount coupons for baby supplies, to a small, squatty end of a tree branch that has been spray painted white and weighted in a flower pot so that it won't tip. Multicolored bows can be attached in between the coupons so that this table centerpiece can be a decoration in baby's room after the shower and after all the coupons have been redeemed and used.

A hospital kit for Mom: Include toiletries, comb, brush, instant "dry" shampoo, regular shampoo, lotion, mascara, lip gloss, and a bag of change so that Mom can use a pay telephone or vending machines once she's up and about in the hospital or birthing center. A nice bed jacket, robe, or nightgown is a help, too. Make sure these open conveniently in the front if Mom plans to breastfeed. Breast pads could be included in this kit if you feel very practical.

A beauty certificate: Consider treating the mother-to-be to a manicure or pedicure. This gift is ideal for those last months of pregnancy when a mom-to-be can't even see her feet, much less give them a pedicure. Along the same lines, consider a certificate for a haircut by a hairdresser who makes house calls if your city has these services. Very new mothers often need such a boost in the first week or two after the baby comes and may have trouble getting out of the house, especially if they are breastfeeding.

A frozen casserole shower: Food that's ready to thaw, heat, and eat is a blessing to new mothers, especially those with other children at home. Just make sure to put the food in disposable containers so that there's no chore of returning dishes.

A gift certificate for a cleaning service day: This gift is to be used when the mom-to-be gets a frantic "nesting" urge to "have everything nice and clean for the baby" or a few weeks after the baby is born, when the house has been neglected for more important things—like enjoying the baby.

Long-Distance Bridal and Baby Showers

Being separated by miles doesn't necessarily mean families and friends can't have the traditional showers that mean so much to brides and moms-to-be. The shower tradition just needs to be carried out in some untraditional ways. Here's how to hold a shower for someone far from home.

Make it a surprise! Tell the honoree to call home (or elsewhere) at a specific time and day. When the call comes through, have all the guests shout "surprise" and then take turns wishing the bride or mom-to-be good thoughts and love. If you don't want to make it a surprise shower, just tell the honoree that you will be having a long-distance shower and that you will call her at a certain time on that day.

Describe the gifts. While the honoree is on the phone, have each guest describe the gift brought to the shower. These gifts need not be wrapped; just have cards attached to them for identification. The host can just pack up all the gifts and send them to the honoree.

SIDING

Clean aluminum house siding. Mix ½ cup of ordinary, mild, nonabrasive laundry detergent to each gallon of water used. To clean, apply detergent solution with a soft bristle brush and rub gently. (Rubbing too hard will take the shine off.) Reduce streaking by washing the house from the bottom up and rinsing as you go. To remove stubborn stains, contact the siding manufacturer or a local siding installer for instructions. (To find out if the manufacturer has a toll-free number, dial (800) 555-1212 and ask the operator.)

SILVER

Polish with paste. Rub with a paste of baking soda and water.

Never store silver in plastic wrap or thin plastic bags. Thin plastic can melt in the heat of an attic and adhere to the silver.

Treat antique silver with extra care. Also, instant silver polish and the instant cleaning method of detergent water in an aluminum foil-lined pan is not safe for antique silver. It can remove all the oxidation that fills darkened parts of the design and make the silver look too white to be old.

Wash it up. Sometimes, if tarnish isn't too bad, you can wash enough of it off for respectability with regular liquid hand-dishwashing detergent squirted full-strength on a sponge. Rinse well and shine with a soft towel.

Don't wait for special occasions! Sterling silver cries out to be used instead of being hidden in drawers. The tiny scratches that occur naturally when it's used produce what is called the "patina."

Sterling silver, except for knives with cemented handles, can be washed in dishwashers. Silver plate, on the other hand, which is normally treated just like sterling, should not be washed in the dishwasher.

Steer clear of sulfur foods. Silver gets tarnished faster when it is exposed to eggs, salad dressing, and other foods that contain sulfur. Salt will corrode silver. Infrequently used items can be wrapped in silver cloth (cloth treated with silver nitrate) or thick plastic bags. Do not wrap silver with rubber bands—the rubber can discolor the silver.

See also TABLEWARE and UTENSILS.

SINKS

Prevent clogged drains. Before draining foods in the sink, place a paper towel (preferably reuse one that has already dried your hands) over the drain; after the liquid drains through it, remove the towel and food bits and toss. No bits down the drain!

Transform a pedestal sink. When your bathroom has a pedestal sink there's no countertop to put cosmetics, hair curlers, etc. Place a clear acrylic cutting board or an appropriately sized tray of a coordinating bathroom color across the basin—you get a wide, sturdy temporary counter, and you can lift away everything on it at once when you need to use the sink.

SKIN

Cleanse and Soothe

Try any of my skin-care tips, and I know you'll look and feel better in no time flat!

Testing Your Skin for Sensitivity at Home

This test may seem like a lot of trouble, but think about how you'd feel if you soaked in an herbal bath and your whole body reacted to an allergen! I have an allergy-prone friend who spent 3 days itching from an expensive spa herbal bath. It was anything but a relaxing experience! Here's what to do:

1. Apply a small dot of the test material, about the size of a match head, to a ½-inch square or circle of unmedicated gauze adhesive bandage. Mix dry materials like herbs with a couple of drops of water or mineral oil. Mineral oil is good because it doesn't evaporate.

2. Place the patch on a hair-free area of the skin like the inside of your arm or elbow or your back. Leave it there for 48 hours without getting it wet.

3. If the test area burns, itches, aches, or feels even a little bit irritated, remove the patch immediately and flush the area with water. If the irritation continues, get a nonprescription cortisone ointment from your pharmacist or see your doctor. If you are sensitive to the material, you will probably have a reaction in 2 to 48 hours after putting the patch in place. If you have no reaction, such as redness, swelling, pimples, blisters, or itching, the material is safe for you.

Freshen and soothe. Add pulp-free aloe vera juice to water in a spray bottle and spritz your arms, legs, back, and face for a quick cool-off and moisturizer. This feels especially good at the beach!

Try witch hazel. This old-fashioned barbershop aftershave is an inexpensive and effective skin freshener, and it's especially nice in the summer if it's been refrigerated. Apply with a cotton ball and allow it to dry before applying makeup.

Cleanse without making a mess. Using a washcloth to wash off makeup and skin remedies instead of cotton balls or other throwaway pads is one way to decrease your trash output! Every little bit counts!

Take advantage of inexpensive oils. Baby oil or just plain mineral oil costs less than expensive lotions and potions and can be applied harmlessly to soften skin or remove makeup. The oils are especially useful if you react to food dyes, lanolin, perfumes, and other ingredients found in many commercial creams. These oils can also be put into your bath water when you soak, but they can make the tub slippery.

Avoid "shower shock." Store your favorite body lotion within the tub or stall area, then after bathing, towel dry yourself lightly and apply the moisturizer before opening the shower curtain or doors. The oil will keep you warm when you do open the door, and you'll benefit more because moisturizers capture and retain water for the skin.

Make a milk bath. Swirl a package of powdered nonfat dry milk or pour

Six Kitchen Remedies for Irritated Skin

Try these easy remedies for whatever itches you.

1. Rub dry, irritated skin gently with juices from a peach or cucumber at night.

2. Apply mashed avocado to skin, leave on for a few minutes, and rinse off gently to clean and condition it.

3. Apply buttermilk as a soothing lotion to cleanse and soften.

4. Add ½ cup of baking soda to tepid water for a soothing soak for dry, irritated skin.

5. Apply cornstarch to prickly heat rash.

6. A paste of baking soda and water, vinegar, or yogurt can soothe minor sunburn.

Caution: If your skin is very red or blistered, see a doctor.

a quart of regular low-fat milk into a tubful of warm water and soak. (This also soothes sunburn.)

Experiment with sea salt. Add ½ pound of sea salt to warm water for a super skin-cleansing bath.

Soothe with vinegar. Add about 2 cups of apple cider vinegar to a tub of warm water to sooth sunburned, itchy skin. Some people prefer to splash the cider on their bodies before sitting down in the water; others just add it to the water before soaking.

Make an oatmeal skin scrubber. Dangle a cloth bag of oatmeal (2 cups or so) on the faucet as the tub fills and then rub your skin with the bag after it's moistened by the water flow. Or, just add oatmeal to the water, then soak in it. This also is a sunburn or itchy skin soother.

Take an herbal bath. Many herbs, alone or combined, can be put into a cloth or net bag, tossed into the tub or hung on the faucet as the tub fills so that you can have a soothing herbal bath straight from your garden. Soothing herbs include rosemary, chamomile, any mint variety, comfrey, rose petals, lavender, yarrow, or camphor. About ½ cup of dry or fresh herbs is the usual amount, depending upon how much "flavoring" you want.

Caution: If you have allergies to plants, do a skin test before soaking your whole body in herbs or herbal combinations.

Replenishing the Moisture

Heating systems dry out the air and can make our skins feel tight and dry even when we apply lotions and oils. You don't need to buy an expensive humidifier to put moisture into the air of your home. Instead, try the following hints first.

Simmer an 8-quart pot of water on the stove for a few hours. Add some potpourri or spices to put a pleasant fragrance in the house, too. Place pretty containers of water around the house to evaporate moisture into the air, but remember to keep them filled!

Let houseplants help rehydrate the air. Ferns, bamboo, begonias, zebra plants, and coleus are among those liking lots of moisture, and they grow fast, too. Put the pots in a shallow tray filled with pebbles or moss and

Sneeze Stopper

A reader sent this rhyme that she says helps her to stifle sneezes in crowded company.

When you feel that warning tickle,
And your nose begins to prickle,
Open your mouth and take
Two or three quick breaths to make
That sneezy feeling disappear.
I hope it works for you, my dear.
But if you find it's not your day,
That sneeze will come out anyway!

water to help keep moisture in the plants and in the air. Keep plants well watered and mist them frequently.

Mist your face with a spritz. Use a spray bottle several times a day. If you can't spritz, dab on water with a cotton ball or makeup square. It's refreshing as well as moisturizing for your face.

Let dishes air dry in the dishwasher. You'll save energy and put moisture into the air at the same time. Stop the dishwasher after the final rinse and open the door. Hold your face where it will be moistened by escaping steam, but caution, not where the steam is hot; it can burn.

Avoid overheating. Keeping the house a few degrees cooler saves on utility bills and energy use and also prevents the air from becoming too dry.

Moisturize skin from within. Drink five, six, or more glasses of water daily. Keep a pretty glass on your desk, counter or wherever you'll most likely see it as a reminder to drink water.

SLEEP

See Z-Z-Z-ZS.

SLEEPING BAGS

 Always check care labels first. It's important to know what the manufacturer recommends for cleaning instructions. Most sleeping bags can be laundered or dry-cleaned and should be repaired before cleaning.

If the instructions say that the bag can home laundered, set the washer on a slow speed and high water level. A suds cycle should remove heavy soil and a second rinse should thoroughly remove detergent from the filling. Tumble dry to fluff up batting. Fluff down-filled bags by throwing in a clean pair of sneakers or tennis balls.

Find an arrangement that pleases everyone. Often at slumber parties, cousin or grandma visits and when children bunk on the floor in sleeping bags, nobody wants to sleep on the "outside" and everyone wants to sleep in the middle or next to one child or other. The solution is simple. Place the sleeping bags in a circle with all the pillows in the center so that the children and their sleeping bags are spokes on a wheel. Everyone is sleeping next to a "buddy," can hear all conversations, and has plenty of foot room.

SLEEVES

See CLOTHES.

SLIDING GLASS DOORS

Make a mark for safety. If you are lucky enough to have a family that keeps these doors so clean that people can't tell if they are open or closed, the quick-fix way to signal they're closed is to place a stick-on note at eye level. Permanent markers can be decals, stickers, auto window decals, or tub safety decals.

SLIPS

See CLOTHES.

SOAP AND SOAP DISHES

Avoid the mess and goo. Put three rubber bands around the soap dish lengthwise. Rest the soap on the rubber bands and it will dry without the messy goo.

Enjoy your fancy soaps—now! When a reader wrote for advice on preventing guests from using decorative soaps and towels, an overwhelming 94 percent of the responses from other readers agreed with my advice to just use them; they recalled cleaning out attics full of new, "too good to use" things after loved ones had died. My mother also always advised using your decorative or "good" china, silver, linens (and fancy guest towels and soap), etc. She always said that if you don't use your "good" things, somebody else will after you're gone; you may as well enjoy them. One reader, who lost everything in a house fire, now enjoys using everything and never cares if they get broken or "used up." Best Advice: *Carpe Diem* (Seize the Day)!

Make a pressed bar. A tried and true hint is to moisten an old soap sliver and a new bar until they are sticky and press them together, blending the edges. Let it dry, and you have a bigger new bar.

Make liquid soap. For this project, you'll need to separate hand from deodorant soap (they don't mix well for this project). First, cut your soap into slivers and soak overnight to soften (optional step). Next, place all soap slivers into a blender with some hot water. Blend on "grate" setting. Add more water to thin out the liquid to the consistency you prefer, and blend a bit more. When you're satisfied with the consistency, pour the liquid into a pump-style soap bottle for bathroom or kitchen.

Note: The plus is that your blender gets a good washing, too!

SOCKS

Make some nonskid slipper socks. Draw stripes (or designs or names of sock-owners) on the bottom of socks with a craft pen used to decorate T-shirts. The raised design will keep you off the skids. If you're considering giving some homemade slipper socks around the holidays, don't waste paper. Instead, buy red socks and substitute them for Christmas wrap, then write gift recipient's name on the sock bottoms and insert the gift. (If there is just one gift, put the second sock inside with the gift.) Tie the sock shut with yarn or crinkle-tie.

Prevent laundry loss. Sometimes socks flip over the edge of the washing machine basket during the wash cycle and can be found later between the drum and basket. Some find their way into the drain, believe it or not. Ask your family members to pin their socks together as they take them off so they will stay together through washer and dryer and be less likely to escape.

Repurpose lonely socks. Single socks have many uses. Among them, you can slip your glass of iced tea or canned beverage in a sock, roll the top down and you'll have dry hands and no puddles under the glass. Or slip an old sock over a yardstick or ruler so that you can clean crevices such as beneath the fridge, washer, or dryer.

You might also want to keep an old sock or two in your car so you can use it to wipe sticky fingers, an oily dipstick, or fog from your windshield. You can also tie it to the steering wheel when fuel is low to remind you to get gas on the next trip.

Secure a second use for socks. When the toes of your socks are completely worn out, consider cutting off the foot so you can use the cuffs. Some handy uses include covering a crawling baby's knees (they add protection even when baby's wearing long pants); covering a gardener's knees, or closing up the opening at pants or sleeves cuffs so insects don't get in as easily; wearing them as leg or knee warmers; sewing them on to child's jacket sleeve to lengthen it; or putting them on over mitten tops and jacket sleeve bottoms to keep snow out of children's jacket sleeves.

Use a separating strategy for color-blind men. Men's navy blue, black, and dark brown socks tend to look all the same in a drawer, even if you're not color-blind. It helps if you buy small plastic baskets and then put navy socks in a light blue basket, dark brown socks in a tan one, and black socks in a white one.

Save time when sock sorting. Black and dark-navy sock colors and styles can look the same when you're matching them. Instead of pinning them in pairs or holding them together with a plastic hook, buy paint pens at a craft store. Match up the socks and label each pair of black socks with a letter and each pair of navy socks with a number. You'll find mates at a glance. If several family members have similar socks, write with different pen colors.

SODA

Maintain the fizz in 2-liter bottles. Put the cap on loosely, then squeeze the plastic bottle until the remaining liquid comes right up to the neck or as close as possible. Then, while holding it there, tighten the cap. With almost no air in the bottle, the contents keep more of their fizz. This works except for the last few ounces.

Make some flavored ice. When 2- or 3-liter bottles go flat, don't discard the soda. Instead, pour it into ice cube trays and you'll have flavored cubes for your drinks that don't dilute!

SOFA

Know the right dimensions. When you measure the space for the sofa to make sure it will fit, don't forget to measure doorways, too. I know of one couple that had to return a sofa that just wouldn't fit through the doorway!

Secure straying sectionals. Hook sections together by attaching screen-door hooks to the underside frames. Attach the eye of the hook on the outside frame of one section and the hook on the outside frame of the adjoining section and then hook 'em up so you won't lose friends in the cracks. You can also keep your sectional sofa from coming apart by using large metal hose clamps around the sections' legs.

SOUP

Get the fat out. Store soup stock in the fridge so after the fat rises to the top and hardens it's easier to lift off. You can also put the soup in a container with a tight lid and turn it upside down in the fridge; once the fat is hard, you can just pour the broth off the top.

Add an instant thickener. The next time you want to add a bit of body to your homemade soup, consider mixing in a scoop of mashed potatoes. Potatoes tend to take salt from dishes, so check to see if more is needed after they are added.

Keep oyster crackers crisp. Pour the tiny crackers into a well-washed and dried plastic quart- or gallon-size jug and put the lid on. You'll have airtight storage for retaining freshness and a handy pouring container, too.

Season your soup stock. Make your own soup stock from leftover necks and backs of poultry (or bones cut off steaks and chops) and lots of herbs and seasonings. Then freeze the stock in cubes, store the cubes in a sealed bag, and you can toss a cube of stock into dishes you want to season. The bonus is that you can make it salt-free or low-fat if you have special diet needs.

SPEAKERS

 Make the most of their magnetism. Old stereo speakers are great magnets. When you finish a task that involves nails, you can drag them around and they will pick up what you've dropped. This is especially good when you've been nailing outdoors where nails in the grass could ruin a lawn mower blade.

Put them at the right level. Most manufacturers say that lower-priced speakers sound better if located off the floor and away from corners—at "ear level."

SPICES AND SPICE BOTTLES

 Use your empty spice bottles. Fill empty spice bottles with cinnamon sugar for toast or flour to sprinkle on meats before frying, use as a toothpick holder, store glitter for crafts in it, or put embroidery thread in it and feed through holes to prevent tangling.

Give them the sniff test. Spices don't spoil, but they do lose potency over time. If they don't have full aroma, toss them out.

Stay away from the heat. Store spices in cupboard or rack away from the stove, oven, and sunny windows.

Keep out moisture when cooking. When adding spices to food, avoid allowing the upside down spice container to absorb heat and moisture from cooking food—instead, measure into a spoon or your hand. Spice cans won't get messy, hard-to-close powder-caked tops with this method.

SPLINTERS

 Remove them with glue. Apply a thin layer of white glue over the splinter, spread it around the area and let it dry. Then peel off the glue and out comes the splinter.

SPRAY BOTTLES

Use it all up. Get out the last 2 inches in the spray bottle by dropping in some marbles to raise the liquid level back to where the spray pump works.

Prevent clogs in the spray nozzle. After using hair spray, spray starch, or other aerosol cans or pump-spray containers, remove the sprayer and run clear water through it so that it's clog-free and ready when you need it the next time.

SQUASH

Treat summer squash tenderly. Summer squash is harvested before full maturity and while the rind and seeds are still tender and edible and its flesh is tender and string-free. Select smaller and firm squashes; if either end is soft or if the squash is rubbery, it's old; don't buy it. The most popular summer squashes are green zucchini, straight- and crook-neck yellows and flat, discus-shaped white squash. Store them in the refrigerator.

Savor hearty winter squash. Most winter squash have hard rinds (avoid

Last-Ditch Stain Remover Formula

Here is my favorite last-ditch stain remover for white and bleachable clothes (no silk, rayon, etc.). I use it when all else has failed and I have nothing to lose because I can't wear the garment anyway with the spot on it.

You'll need 1 gallon of hot water, 1 cup of powdered dishwasher detergent, and ½ cup of household liquid chlorine bleach. Mix well in a plastic, enamel, or stainless steel container. (This solution should not be used in an aluminum container or come in contact with aluminum because it will discolor it.)

Place the stained garment in the solution. Let it soak in this solution for 5 to 10 minutes. If any stain remains, soak longer, then wash as usual.

those with soft spots on the rind) and may be kept for 3 to 6 months in a cool dry place, but not in the refrigerator unless cut. The most common winter squashes are acorn (dark green or orange and green and shaped like an acorn—what else?), buttercup (oval and dark green with whitish stripes), turban (brightly colored with rounded lumps on one end), butternut (long, tubular and creamy brown in color), hubbard, (one of the largest squashes, bumpy all over and in various colors), and spaghetti (smooth yellow outside and stringy spaghetti-textured inside).

SQUEAKS

Silence the squeaks. Petroleum jelly applied to moving parts may help. It's safe around pets so you can use it on that squeaky exercise wheel in your hamster or gerbil cage.

STAINLESS STEEL

Remove water spots. Rub the area with a clean, soft cloth dampened with white vinegar. Wipe dry to avoid spots.

See also UTENSILS.

STAINS

I think everyone has one blouse, shirt, dress, and so on, that seems to attract stains whenever it's worn. For some reason, when that bad-luck garment is worn, all ballpoint pens seem to be gooey and nonretractable, all chairs have strange stain makers deposited on them no matter where you sit, and, when you wear these spot grabbers to a restaurant, suddenly all waiters have accidents, all soup spoons have holes in them, and you're sure to fall victim to "flying lettuce" or "hyperactive noodles." Naturally, the "flying lettuce" will have a vinegar and oil dressing and the "hyperactive noodles" will have a tomato sauce so that they will splat a super stain upon your hapless spot grabber. But then, who told you life would be stainless?

There is hope! Our friends at the International Fabricare Institute have sent me the following hints for the care and removal of stains from clothing, and I've found others that work. Here's some first aid for stain removal.

Don't wait! Treat spills and stains immediately. The longer a spot remains, the more difficult it will be to remove. Blot up spills with clean, white, absorbent materials (towels, napkins, tissues, etc.). Work from the outer edge of the spot toward the center to prevent rings.

Launder promptly. If the clothing is washable, spray the stain with a prewash stain remover spray, then wash it using a mild detergent. Repeat the process if the stain still remains.

Never iron over a stain. The heat from the iron will set the stain, thus making it almost impossible to remove. A stained article shouldn't be placed in the dryer either.

Point out problems to the professionals. If you take your clothing to a dry cleaner, be sure to call attention to spots and stains, so that they can be prespotted. It helps if you can remember the cause of the stain because the dry cleaner can more easily determine the appropriate remover to use.

Never store clothing away unless it is clean. Although worn clothing may look clean, it still needs to be washed so "mystery stains" (usually brown or yellow spots) won't appear after the clothing has been washed. These stains are most likely caused by beverages that contain sugar, such as coffee, fruit juice, and tea. They are relatively easy to remove when they are fresh but become more difficult to remove as they age. They are almost impossible to remove after they have completely set.

Here are hints for some specific sources of pesky stains.

Baby formula: If formula stains are not removed after washing with detergent and bleach, try this. Pour lemon juice on the stain and place it in the sunshine for as long as it takes. Sometimes it will work in as little as 15 minutes. If it doesn't get the stain completely out, repeat the process.

Or try this. For white, bleachable articles, place the following ingredients in an enamel, plastic, or stainless-steel container (no aluminum): 1 gallon hot water, 1 cup dishwasher detergent, and ¼ cup liquid chlorine bleach; stir until dissolved. Put in the stained garments and let them soak for about 15 to 30 minutes. Rinse and wash as usual.

Ballpoint pen ink: Prewash sprays will work on some ink stains. Rubbing alcohol will remove most ballpoint pen ink, but be sure it is safe for the fabric. (Test it on a part of the garment that isn't normally seen, such as a shirt or blouse tail.)

Blood: Although bloodstains are difficult to remove unless you get to them immediately, I have found that unseasoned meat tenderizer works well on fresh stains. Rinse with cold water first, then pour on some meat tenderizer. Let it stay on the stain for a few minutes and then wash the clothing as usual.

Try washing the stained article with a detergent containing enzymes, found on the supermarket shelf with all other detergents or bleaches. Enzyme detergents won't damage colored fabrics and work best on wine, coffee, tea, chocolate, and dairy stains.

You can also bleach the stained article with 3.5 percent hydrogen peroxide, but use caution, as this may bleach color also. Wash and rinse the article with cool water.

Candle wax: Using the dull edge of a knife, scrape off as much of the hardened wax as possible. Place paper towels on either side of the wax-stained area of the fabric and iron on a low to medium setting; the wax will be absorbed into the towels. Change the towels often, as they become soiled.

If any stain remains, apply liquid detergent and water, and then rinse or wash as usual. Dry-cleaning fluid may be necessary to remove any dye from the wax.

Chewing gum: Apply an ice cube to the gum to harden it, or place the garment in the freezer. Then scrape the gum off with the dull edge of a knife or spoon until all the gum is removed. Apply an enzyme detergent as a prewash spray to the back of the stain, rub in well, and wash as usual.

Chocolate: Soak the garment for 30 minutes in cold water. Rub some detergent into the stain while still wet. Bleach will remove it, but use it only with colorfast clothing.

Cleaning-fluid rings: Sometimes these can be steamed out if the garment is held over a teakettle.

Caution: Steam can burn; put the garment, not your hands, over the steam spout.

Cosmetics: A bar of white hand soap does a great job. Wet the stain and rub the soap into it. If the stain remains, use regular liquid detergent. Gently work it into the stain and then wash the garment as usual.

Finger marks on felt: Try rubbing the finger marks with the finest sand-paper you can find. Rub gently with the felt's nap until the marks don't show.

Fruit juices: Soak for about 30 minutes in cold water. Rub some detergent into the stain while it's still wet. Wash as usual. If this treatment doesn't work and the garment is bleach-safe, apply hydrogen peroxide, and then rinse well.

Glue: For school glue, apply water and blot. Mix 1 teaspoon of a colorless, mild detergent or dish-washing liquid in 1 cup of lukewarm water and apply to the stain. Rinse with water, and blot until dry.

Grass: Apply an enzyme detergent and blot. Rinse with water or mix 1 tablespoon of clear household ammonia with ½ cup of water and apply to stain, then blot and rinse. Or mix ⅓ cup of white vinegar with ⅔ cup of water. Apply to stain and blot until dry. Wash as usual.

If the material is white and bleach-safe, use bleach according to the bottle directions.

Grease: A quick remedy for grease stains that occur when cooking is to apply some talcum powder or cornstarch to the stain. Apply just enough to cover the grease. You'll see the powder get thick as the grease is absorbed. Wipe it off and put fresh powder on, let stand awhile, and wipe it off again.

Place the stain facedown on paper towels and go over the back with full-strength liquid detergent or dry-cleaning solvent (don't mix these), using a clean, white cloth. Mechanics' hand cleaner may also be used to remove the spot. Launder as usual.

Iron rust: Moisten the stain with water, apply lemon juice, and then rinse. You may have to repeat the treatment several times to get the stain out.

Caution: It may be wise to test lemon juice on an inconspicuous place on the garment to make sure it won't bleach certain colors. Of course, if you can't wear the garment with the rust stain, it probably doesn't matter if it gets a bleach spot!

Ketchup or chili sauce: Blot up as much of the stain as you can using a white cloth and cold water. Use an enzyme detergent as a presoak and launder as usual.

Hydrogen peroxide can be used on bleach-safe fabrics. Rinse with cold water after bleaching.

Lipstick: Before washing, treat the stain with a prewash spray or rubbing alcohol and blot the spot with a clean, white cloth or paper towel. Keep applying the spray, always using a clean section on the cloth, or change the paper towel when you blot the spot.

You can also try wetting the article, then rubbing the stain with a bar of face soap. Wash as usual.

Margarine or butter: Mix 1 teaspoonful of a colorless, mild detergent or dish-washing liquid in a cup of lukewarm water. Apply to stain and blot until dry. Or blot with a mixture of ⅓ cup of white vinegar and ⅔ cup of water. Rinse with water and blot until dry. If all else fails, apply some dry-cleaning solvent and blot. Launder as usual.

Mildew: Apply white vinegar or salt and lemon juice to the garment to kill the mildew. Then place the clothing in the sun. Wash as usual. Bleach will also kill mildew; follow directions on the bleach bottle.

Milk: Soak article in warm water, using an enzyme detergent as a pre-soak product.

Paint, oil-based: A bit of turpentine or paint thinner can remove this if the fabric is color-safe; rinse well. Be sure to follow directions on the can of turpentine or thinner. Rub with a detergent paste, and wash as usual.

Paint, water-based: You will need to get to this stain as soon as possible; after this has set it cannot be removed. Rinse the stain well in warm water and wash as usual.

Perspiration: The International Fabricate Institute says that applying a large amount of deodorant and using cold "hard" water (high mineral, low alkaline water) when washing the garment can cause this problem.

Many deodorants and antiperspirants contain aluminum salts. When combined with laundry detergent and cold water, the salts cannot be easily dissolved and therefore remain on the fabric. Therefore, before washing the garment, rinse the area with plain water, then wash with the rest of your laundry in either warm or hot water with good suds.

To remove fresh perspiration stains, apply diluted ammonia to the stains and rinse with water. For old stains, try applying white vinegar and rinse with water.

Pet urine: You'll get the best result if you get to the stain immediately.

Blot up as much liquid as possible with absorbent white paper towels. Change the towels frequently, until the carpeting seems dry. Then sponge a little white distilled vinegar on the stain to neutralize the urine. The vinegar also helps to stop discoloration of the carpet.

Blot the vinegar right away so it doesn't go through the carpet backing. Rinse by dabbing with water. Then mix 2 tablespoons of mild liquid dishwashing detergent to 1 cup of water. Apply this sparingly. Blot up any excess.

The final cleaning step is to rinse the stained area with clear water to remove all the detergent. Then, blot up as much of the wetness you can. Place an old white towel over the wet area, then walk around on the towel. As it gets wet, change to a dry part of the towel. Keep doing this until the area seems pretty dry.

Finally, place a dry towel over the area and weight it down. The towel will absorb any leftover moisture from the carpet and make it dry more quickly. Leave the towel on overnight. When it's dry in the morning, fluff up the carpet nap with your fingers.

Scorch marks: Persistent marks can be bleached with hydrogen peroxide if the fabric is bleach-safe; then rinse well.

Urine stains on mattresses: Blot up as much as possible if the stain is still wet. Use upholstery shampoo on the stain and rub the spot from its outer edge to its center to avoid making it any larger. Spray with a dry fabric air freshener to prevent a musty or urine odor. If possible, put the mattress out in the sunshine to help air it.

Note: Urine stains may cause permanent dye removal from fibers.

Water on velvet: Hold the fabric over steam spouting from a teakettle for a few minutes; then shake off steam moisture until the garment is dry; then brush up the nap.

Wine: First, blot up or rinse all liquid. Rinse in cool water. Bear in mind that many times the dye from wine is difficult to remove and sometimes even impossible.

Homestyle Sugar Starch

When regular spray starch won't hold up frail fabrics, try the old-fashioned method Great-Grandma used for her lacy doilies.

1. Mix ¼ cup of water and ¾ cup of sugar in a small pan. Stir the mixture over low heat (don't boil) until clear, not sugary. Shut off the heat and let cool.

2. Wet the collar and cuffs of a blouse (or lacy doily) with water. Roll it in a towel to remove excess moisture and dip it into the mixture. Squeeze out excess starch, then shape the collar and cuffs. (People used to dry small round crocheted lace doilies over a bowl after starching this way; you get a lace bowl.)

3. Allow to dry and iron on a warm setting. (Lace doilies don't need ironing when you use this starch; just smooth out and shape while wet on a clean, flat surface.)

Try this: Mix 1 teaspoon of a colorless, mild detergent or dish-washing liquid in 1 cup of lukewarm water, and blot. Then blot with a mixture of ⅓ cup of white vinegar and ⅔ cup of water. Then mix 1 tablespoon of clear household ammonia with ½ cup of water. Rinse thoroughly with water and blot until dry. After treating the stain, launder as usual.

STATIC CLING

Slip on a little lotion. When your slip and skirt have a life of their own and it's embarrassing you, rub a little hand lotion on your hands and then rub your hands over your slip.

STICKERS

Make children's fun last longer. Have children put stickers on waxed paper so that they can be repositioned many times before the child decides how to stick them permanently in a scrap book.

Finding Space in a Small Apartment

Even if your apartment's bursting at the seams with stuff, you may be able to make some breathing room with these hints.

1. Store seldom-used items in empty suitcases.

2. Stash boxes under the bed.

3. Fold winter blankets and store them between the mattress and box spring.

4. Buy a large plastic garbage can, fill it with stored items, invert the lid, and top it off with a round piece of plywood. Cover with a tablecloth, and you have a lamp table/storage unit for any room.

5. Put shoes in shoe bags to free the closet floor for other things.

6. Stack storage boxes or add shelves to closet shelves.

7. Have a system of making a proper place for everything and putting everything back in its place; clutter takes up space.

Remove them easily. Remove stickers and sticky residue from wood paneling by rubbing with mineral oil on a cloth or paper towel. Let oil set a while and repeat if necessary.

You can also remove sticky residue from labels with prewash spray. Apply, let set, and then rub off with a nylon scrubber. For hard-to-remove bumper stickers, use this same method with spray lubricant instead.

STORAGE

 Color code creatively. Use colored stick-on dots to keep track of books, records, and video tapes according to categories so that you don't have to shuffle through them each time you search for something.

Books can be coded according to fiction, biography, etc.; records according to jazz, country and western, etc.; videotapes according to comedy, drama, homemade family films, and home-taped favorite shows or movies.

STRAWBERRIES

Use super-slicing strategies. After pinching off the green "hat" of the strawberry with a metal gadget made for this purpose, slice it with an egg slicer. No stains on your fingers and uniform slices, too!

STUFFED PEPPERS

Keep the stuffing in while they cook. If you bake stuffed peppers in a well-greased muffin tin, the peppers stay upright and look more appetizing when served.

SUGAR

Add some color. Add a few drops of food coloring to a cup of granulated sugar in a glass bowl. Mix well until the coloring is distributed evenly. Darken the color by adding a drop or two more of the food coloring. Let dry and store in a sprinkle-top bottle for decorating cookies and cakes.

Soften sugar. In a microwave safe container, microwave for a minute or so to soften. Another method is to place a slice of fresh bread or piece of fresh apple into the sugar canister or box, seal, and it will soften after a while.

Store sugar in an empty milk jug. An empty, clean, plastic milk jug keeps sugar from attracting bugs and from getting hard and lumpy, is easier to handle than a bag, lets you see how much is left, and, best of all, is free for the recycling!

See also BROWN SUGAR.

SUNBLOCK

Use the highest protection formulas. For best protection, you need a good sunblock with a sun-protection factor (SPF) suitable for your skin. SPF numbers are based on the time it takes unprotected skin to turn pink.

Letter of Laughter

Sugar

A reader wrote that when she told a young bride to "put the brown sugar in a container with a tight-fitting lid and put a slice of bread on top to keep the brown sugar from going hard," the bride said it didn't work. When the reader visited the bride, she saw why. The sugar was in the canister, and a piece of bread was lying on top of the tightly closed jar.

It's not only what you say, it's how you say it!

The highest number is the greatest protection. Read labels for your type of skin.

Apply it right when nobody nice can help you. Apply sunblock to your back or other unreachable spots with a sponge-type dish-washing mop with a long handle.

SUPERMARKETS

 Avoid products with excess packaging. Instead, look for those in recyclable packaging. When buying vegetables, look for the most food in the least packaging: for example, a pound of peas in a plastic bag generates less waste than two 8-ounce boxes of peas that have paper wrappers since both types of packaging will end up in a landfill. Also, consider buying canned vegetables if you can recycle the cans and don't mind the extra sodium and fewer vitamins in canned veggies.

Finally, avoid packaged microwaveable foods in which special bags or separate trays or dishes are used for cooking; these are just marketing gimmicks. If you use these quickie products, look for those where you can serve right out of the package.

Package produce with ease. Instead of wrestling a bulky head of leaf lettuce into the bag, put your hand into the bag as if it were a glove. Then with your "bagged" hand, grasp the bottom end of the lettuce and invert the bag up and over the head. No more shop-torn salads!

Recycle all packaging materials that you can. Many supermarkets collect plastic bags, paper bags, and bottles, and many cities have recycling programs, but nobody can come into a consumer's home to get recyclables! You have to sort and deliver!

Take your own bag to the supermarket. This is a great way to reduce the number of bags you take home. You can also recycle grocery bags you do take home so that you don't have to actually buy bags. At home, plastic grocery bags are good for garbage, storage, and all sorts of uses. Paper bags hold newspapers for recycling, absorb grease from fried foods, can be "racks" for cooling cookies, and on and on.

QUICK REFERENCE

Know Your Product-Dating Terms

Check dates on all items to get the most for your money.

Expiration Date: The last day the item should be used or eaten.

Freshness Date: Stamped on the item by the manufacturer to tell how long freshness is guaranteed, if the item is stale before that date, manufacturers usually refund your money.

Pack Date: Date the product was packaged or processed by the manufacturer. It does not tell how long the food will stay good, but only when it was processed.

Sell or Pull Date: The last day an item should be sold; after this date it should be removed from the grocery shelf.

Favor jugs over cartons. If you recycle milk containers, it's better to buy milk in polyethylene jugs than in cartons, which are made of paperboard coated with polyethylene; it's too costly to separate the coating from the carton paper, and so these are not often recycled.

Evaluate your egg cartons. When you buy eggs, look for molded pulp cartons (which are usually made from 100-percent recycled paper) instead of polystyrene cartons.

Check the inside. Recycled paper cereal and other boxes are usually grey or tan inside and some have the "Recycled" logo on the outside; nonrecycled boxes are white inside.

SWEATERS

Eliminate "pills." Gently and carefully remove "pills" with a tiny scissors or a commercial sweater shaver. Always brush or shave gently to avoid damaging the area around the "pill."

Remake old sweaters. Make mittens from an old sweater by tracing an old one on paper or putting it on the bottom of an old sweater. The bottom is a ready-made cuff. Cut and sew around the "hand" shape, double-stitching for extra security. You can also make leg warmers from sweater sleeves.

Safeguard against shrinkage. Before buying a sweater, check the label for shrinkage potential and if there is no such information, assume the sweater will shrink at least one size. Threads get stretched during the knitting process and that's why knit clothes shrink more than woven ones. Even some synthetics shrink one size like cotton, wool, and rayon do.

Never cut or tug snags. Try to pull the snag to the underside with a large sewing needle or crochet hook; this is best accomplished if you work from the inside of the garment. If the yarn is broken, try to fasten the broken ends on the inside of the sweater with a needle and transparent thread, which you can also use to close up a hole from the inside.

Store sweaters safely. Most knits are best folded for flat storage because if you hang them on hangers, they will usually stretch out of shape. If you wish to hang them, however, drape them over a cardboard tube-type hanger, like those cleaners use for pants, or slit a tube from gift wrap to cover the hanger. (If the cardboard tube is slippery, you can wrap it with old panty hose to provide some friction.)

SWEET SUBSTITUTES

Know the limits in replacing the sugar. You can't substitute corn syrup or honey for baking because sugar is a dry ingredient—it adds bulk as well as sweetness. If you substitute corn syrup for honey, you'll need to add a bit more because it isn't as sweet as honey.

Experiment with many flavors. If you have to limit your sugar intake, try to substitute other flavorings instead of adding sugar. For example, add cinnamon, vanilla, or other extracts to your coffee; add vanilla or fruit (dried or fresh) to plain nonfat yogurt; sprinkle cinnamon on baked apple or in applesauce; sprinkle pumpkin pie spice mixture on sweet potatoes with a sprinkle of butter substitute; and add chopped dried fruit to your cereal.

TABLECLOTHS

Put an end to tablecloth creases. Toss a tablecloth into the fluff cycle of the clothes dryer with a damp towel to get some of the creases and wrinkles out. After use, store the cloth for the next time on a coat hanger. To prevent a center fold, make a lengthwise slit in a cardboard tube from a gift wrap roll that you have cut to hanger width. Then put the tube on the hanger and the tablecloth over the tube.

Remove the wrinkles from flannel-backed vinyl. Put the tablecloth in the clothes dryer with a few damp towels, set dryer on the lowest setting, then check the tablecloth frequently until all wrinkles are removed. Allow to lay flat for cooling to avoid more wrinkles. You can also remove wrinkles by ironing at a warm setting with a steam iron on the flannel side. Never iron on the vinyl side.

Weight the corners. To keep tablecloths from blowing off of a picnic table, sew pockets on the corners to hold small rocks or just knot a rock into each corner.

Keep the tablecloth in place. If you fear that any young children may be tempted to play "magician" with the tablecloth during your next party, open the table as if to insert a leaf, poke about an inch of tablecloth into the crack with your finger, then close the table again. The tablecloth will stay put, and your real friends will understand the reason for the crease across the table. Or use place mats.

Be wary of plastic or foam-backed plastic tablecloths. Laying plain plastic or foam-backed plastic tablecloths directly on a wood-finish table can result in the plastic or foam sticking to the finish. Picking up plastic sheeting that has been on a table for a while can just pull up sections of varnish on some pieces. The only solution may be to refinish the furniture. You can try removing stuck-on foam with a plastic scrubbie or nylon net and vegetable oil.

Prevent stains. When a tablecloth is clean or brand new, spray it several times with soil-repellent spray—tough stains won't set in.

Identify the dimensions. Whether you hang your tablecloths on a hanger or fold them and store in a linen closet, save yourself aggravation. Attach a small piece of paper to each cloth with a safety pin, giving its dimensions and the size of table it fits along with any special information such as if it fits your table with one or two leaves or none.

See also LINENS.

TABLES

Fake a table extension. Place a thick pad on the table. Then on top, place a piece of plywood, 4 feet by 8 feet; top with another pad and cover with a tablecloth. You will be able to seat 10 or more people. Store the plywood under the bed in between dinner parties.

Create a card table buffet. Make a long buffet table from two or more card tables placed side-by-side. Keep them from separating by snugly standing their "feet," by twos, in cans.

Add a makeshift pad. An old mattress pad can provide good padding and protection for a table, but you'll still need to put a hot pad beneath oven dishes.

TABLEWARE

My personal philosophy is that you should use your good china, crystal, silverware, and so forth, as often as possible. Obviously, if you have small children in your household, I wouldn't recommend using them every day. Instead, set them on a shelf that you can reach and use them when you fix yourself a sandwich, a glass of tea, or the like. After all, as my mother used to always say, "If you don't use them, the second or third wife will."

Storing China, Crystal, and Serving Pieces

Keep them in boxes. Dishes and serving pieces that are stored in the back of lower kitchen cupboards will be easier to slide in and out if they are in boxes, small plastic storage baskets, or dishpans. You won't have to crawl into the cupboard to get them. The other advantage of having them in covered containers is that they will stay clean.

Store platters in drawers. If you have extra kitchen drawer space, try storing flat baking dishes and platters in drawers instead of on cupboard shelves. You can just pull them out easily when you need them.

Fight scratches with filters. Protect your china from chips and surface scratches by placing cushions between plates, cups, or other stacked pieces when you store them. Use coffee filters, paper or cloth napkins, paper towels, paper plates, cloth remnants cut into handkerchief-size pieces, clean hand- kerchiefs, or clean foam meat trays. If you have some spare time and want to spend some money, buy flannel, felt or nonwoven interfacing at fabric shops when it's on sale and make custom-size pads to place between china pieces.

Cover them in plastic. Store the padded stacks of pieces that you only use a few times a year in plastic bags or just cover them with plastic bags the way people cover kitchen appliances with ready-made covers. Store larger items in plastic bags closed with a twist-tie or in boxes to keep them clean. Silver items can be wrapped in tarnish-preventing cloth or bags, not with light plastic and rubber bands. However, a heavy plastic bag that you can close is sufficient.

Drape a tarp in the cupboard. Instead of wrapping each piece or stack of seldom-used china or crystal, you can lay a "tarp" or "drapery" of plastic wrap over a whole cupboard shelf of items. The construction of some cup- boards will allow you to tape a "window" of plastic wrap over the shelf face. This is especially effective for top cupboard shelves that seem to attract greasy dust like magnets.

Rotate your dishes. If you live alone, you may find that you only use the top one or two plates of a stack, while the bottom ones gather dust. Rotating your dishes occasionally will give them all a turn at being used and washed.

Maximize your dishwasher. When you don't have a full dishwasher load, you can fill up the space with seldom-used tableware so that it gets a bath between uses.

Alternate your rows of glassware. You don't have to stack glasses to save shelf space if you put them in rows, alternating one glass right side up and the next upside down. Alternate right side up and upside down with the rows, too, and you'll be surprised at how many more glasses can be put on a shelf. This method works very well with slanted water glasses and many shapes of stemware.

Tableware Tricks

Rub out dark scratches. If your china has dark scratches on it from being stacked, you may be able to remove these marks by rubbing them with baking soda and water on a damp sponge.

Make cracks vanish with milk. When a favorite dish or plate gets a slight crack, put it in a pan of milk, then bring to a boil and simmer for 45 minutes at low heat. In many cases, this method makes the crack disappear, and you can use your dish again.

Reclaim your ironstone china. Old ironstone china items that are crazed and stained from food and oven heating can sometimes be reclaimed if you soak them in liquid bleach, diluted by half with water. If you can't submerge an item, such as a platter, in bleach because it's too large, try wrapping paper towels around it before putting it into a plastic bag. Put the bagged item in a bathtub or sink where it will be safe from children and pets and then pour bleach over the paper toweling. The paper will keep the bleach on the platter's surfaces and edges, and you'll use less bleach than if you try to submerge a large item. Close up the bag and let the bleach do its job for 24 or more hours.

Most stains will come out with this method although some badly burned plates can't be recovered. You may have to do this in two steps, bleaching the top side of a platter or bowl the first time and then the bottom with the second application.

"Paint" stains away. In some cases, you can remove stains from china by "painting" the item with liquid dishwasher detergent and letting it sit for several hours or a day. A poultice of baking soda or powdered dish-washer detergent and water will also remove some stains.

See also STAINLESS STEEL, SILVER, and UTENSILS.

TAXES

Make a filing checklist. Make sure that it includes brokerage confirmations and statements, cancelled checks and checkbook registers, receipts for charitable contributions and deductible expenses, property-tax receipts, records of interest paid on your mortgage, 1099 forms (dividends and interest income), and W-2 forms.

TEA

Make your coffeemaker do double-duty. Measure the amount of water needed into the coffeemaker tank, put the appropriate number of tea bags in the carafe, turn it on, and presto—hot tea. You can make iced tea with the leftovers.

Note: Let the bags steep for at least 3 to 5 minutes for fullest flavor.

If you prefer loose tea, sprinkle tea leaves into a coffee filter in the brewing basket as you would ground coffee. Use the same amount of tea leaves that you would brew in a teapot, or experiment to get the perfect amount for strength and flavor.

Spice up your iced tea. Mix ½ teaspoon of ground cinnamon and 1 cup of orange juice. Pour the liquid into an ice cube tray and freeze. Add a cube to your glass of iced tea. Delicious!

Alternately, you can stir your tea (herbal or other) with a cinnamon stick. It can be reused for numerous cups of yummy, lightly spiced tea.

Avoid "fishing" in hot tea. Instead, wrap the tag around the pot or cup handle; cut an L-shaped slit in the tag, starting at the bottom edge and then when you make a cup of tea, open the slit and hook the tag on the cup lip.

Making a Tea Concentrate

Tea concentrate for a large crowd can be prepared ahead of time. Here's how to make 40 to 50 cups of tea.

1. Bring 1½ quarts of fresh cold water to a rapid boil.

2. Remove water from heat and immediately add ¼ pound of loose tea. Stir to immerse leaves and then cover. (Double this recipe for 80 to 90 cups.)

3. Let stand 5 minutes. Strain into a teapot until ready to use.

4. To serve this concentrate as hot tea, bring out a pot of boiling fresh water, right from the boiling kettle. Pour about 2 tablespoons of tea concentrate into each cup, and fill up with hot water. The strength of the tea depends upon the water-tea ratio.

 Cook with your tea ball. Put peppercorns, bay leaves, and other whole spices in a tea ball so that you don't have to fish them out of soup or stew to avoid biting into them.

Caution: Bay leaves (whole or in pieces) are special hazards because they can cause choking if they get stuck in the throat.

Remove mineral deposits from your teapot. Fill the teapot with full-strength vinegar, let it boil for a few minutes and let the teapot sit overnight. If the mineral deposit film is very thick, you may need to soak it for a couple of nights. In the morning, wash and rinse the pot. Avoid excess hard-water buildup in the future with regular cleanings.

Look for proper packaging, and store wisely. Tea bags hold dried tea leaves, but they do not protect the flavor unless they are individually wrapped and sealed in plastic or foil. Tea is a fragrant herb, and whether you buy loose tea or tea bags, always store tea in a container with a tightly fitting lid.

Check the bag-to-pound ratio. When you buy tea, the number of tea bags per pound tells you how strong the tea is. Most teas are sold with 200 bags to the pound. If you usually get one to two cups per bag from such a tea, then you may get four cups per bag from a tea that has less than 200 bags per pound. But you may need two bags for one cup if the tea has more than 200 bags per pound.

Make some tea ice for iced tea. Use leftover hot tea for iced tea, or freeze "tea cubes" to cool your next cup of hot tea or glass of iced tea.

Clear up cloudy tea. If you make a pitcher of iced tea and the tea becomes cloudy, add a small amount of boiling water and stir, and the tea will clear up. Teas sold especially for iced tea are less likely to get cloudy.

Savor some sun tea. Sun tea is an energy saver—yours and electrical power. It tastes better than regular brewed tea, too, and can be made with any kind of tea. Just put the appropriate number of tea bags (about the same number of bags for the amount of water as for hot tea) into a quart or gallon glass container, and fill with fresh, cool water. Put the container on a sunny patio or doorstep where it will be safe from curious pets and children. Depending upon the weather, you'll have tea by noon or certainly 4 P.M. tea time. Pour the tea over ice and add flavorings of choice.

If you are in a hurry, make "sun tea" in your microwave by heating water for less than 2 minutes in a glass jar or pitcher, then tossing in the appropriate number of tea bags. Let the tea steep on the kitchen counter for a couple of hours until it reaches the right strength. I once tried to speed this process along by simmering the tea bags in the pitcher in the microwave oven, but it was a mess because the bags broke and I had to strain the tea to use it. So, better let the tea steep naturally.

Caution: Wait 30 seconds before adding a teabag to just-microwaved water. There is a risk of the water bubbling up and burning you. Also, put the container on a stable surface where spillovers can be cleaned up easily.

Read the ingredients. When you are buying herb teas, read the labels to be sure what sorts of ingredients have been combined. You don't want to drink herbs that you're allergic to. Also, some of the properties of certain herb tea ingredients may have effects you haven't bargained for, especially if you drink excessive amounts.

For example, many herb teas contain caffeine, which you may be trying to avoid. Some contain chicory and other herbs that are mild laxatives and could cause distress if you drank too much. Some herbs, such as tonka beans and sweet clover, are coumarins, substances that prevent blood clotting, and could be dangerous to some people when consumed in excess (several pots daily).

TEA BALLS

See UTENSILS.

TELEPHONES AND TELEPHONE DIRECTORIES

Lighten it up. Sometimes people with arthritis or hand disabilities have problems handling thick phone books when their cities don't separate white and yellow pages into two books. To help out someone in this situation, carefully cut apart the white and yellow pages with a sharp knife. Reinforce the spines of both sections with heavy duty plastic tape such as that used to seal cartons, and then either tape the back and front pages from last year's directory to the coverless sides of the new half-books, or make covers from halves of a manila folder.

Use a highlighter. When you find a number that you've searched for in the phone book, highlight it so that it's easier to spot the next time you need it.

Clean the mouthpiece. A moist towelette will wipe an earpiece and mouthpiece clean with a whisk.

Make your own large-print directory. Big push button phones help elderly or visually impaired people dial phones, but phone books are a challenge. Make a phone book with a loose-leaf notebook filled with unlined note paper. Turn the pages sideways and, with a broad, black (or red for some people) marker, print names in large, block letters with numbers beneath.

Keep pad and pencil handy. Stick a pen or pencil to the side of your telephone with self-gripping "dots." Then remove several stick-on notes from a pad, and stick them on the front of the phone (just a few, too many will be too heavy to stick). You'll always have paper and pencil ready for messages and recording information.

Use a programmable phone. Not only can you program frequently called numbers of friends, relatives, businesses, and emergency aid numbers, but you can also program pizza delivery, weather, time, and other useful numbers.

Make group phone calls more pleasant. Having several people get on different extensions for group phone calls may weaken the signal and make hearing each other difficult. Speaker phones work better, plus with a speaker phone everyone gets to hear what the person on the other end of the line said, so he or she won't have to keep repeating, "I'm fine, thank you." Just make sure everyone speaks loudly and clearly.

When using a speaker phone with lots of people, it helps if you intro-

Telephone Installation

Installing your own phones with modular plugs and jacks means that you have to know the do's and don'ts. Here are a few from the Electronic Industries Association.

- ♥ Don't ever attempt to install telephone wiring if you wear a pacemaker.
- ♥ Don't place phone wire in any conduit or outlet box that contains electrical wiring or water pipes.
- ♥ Never place a telephone jack where it would let a person use the phone in the bathtub, shower, swimming pool, or anywhere else near water.
- ♥ Four-conductor telephone station wire used for house wiring is very low voltage, so you can safely hide it under carpets, between walls, over basement ceiling joists, and up and around doors and windows.
- ♥ Don't run any wire through places where it will be damp, excessively hot, pulled out by mistake, or subjected to abrasion. (Worn wires can cause interference.)

duce yourself by saying, "It's Jane" or "This is Bob" before you start to talk, so the people on the other end of the line don't have to keep asking, "Who said that?"

Rely on redial. Phones with redial or busy-dial functions will help you win radio phone-in prizes because it's faster to punch one button than to dial or punch a whole phone number's worth of buttons when you're trying to get through on a very busy line or to be the first caller. Being able to punch only one button also helps if you are trying to voice your opinion on radio and TV phone-in talk shows, which have super-busy lines.

TELEVISIONS

Keep a cheat sheet. When cable brings you so many different selections and it's a challenge to remember all the numbers, clip the list of stations and channels from your cable guide and tape it to the back of the remote control. You'll always have the right numbers in hand!

Clean the screen. Fuzzy television pictures don't always mean that something is wrong with your set. Before you call the service shop—and don't think this is silly—try cleaning your screen. Don't be too shocked at how much dirt a screen can collect! Wipe the screen with a damp, soft, clean cloth and then let it air dry.

Caution: Never apply liquid or aerosol cleaners to the screen, and unplug the set before any cleaning. If you have a projection television set, do not touch or attempt to clean the screen; you may damage it beyond repair. Call a service professional.

Analyze the antenna. High winds or birds landing hard on an outdoor antenna can put it out of line. If you notice a change in television reception, check to see if your antenna is bent or turned, or if its lead-in wires are worn or corroded. If they are, call a service professional. Installation and repairs of outdoor antennas should always be done by experts.

Eliminate the interference. You can get interference (static noises and lines) from too many electrical appliances plugged into one outlet, a CB radio in the neighborhood, a nearby high-voltage tower, or, in some cases, from placing a VCR on top of or beneath your TV, even if there's a wood shelf in between.

Keep tabs on your TV schedule. Punch a hole at the top, loop a string through the hole, then tape the other end of the string to the TV set each week when the new schedule comes out. When you look through your weekly TV schedule, use a highlighter to mark the shows you want to see during the week so that you won't miss them.

TERMITES

Examine the perimeter. Shrubs, fences, trellises, stacked firewood, and wooden decks that touch the house and the ground at the same time all provide traveling routes for termites from the ground to your house.

Keep water away from the house. Because termites seek water, make sure that all gutters drain away from the foundation and repair all plumbing leaks right away. Don't place wooden planters against the house. They are a double invitation to the termites—wood and water!

Call a professional. If you see any evidence of termites such as their tunnels; damaged wood steps, porches or decks; fine powder beneath wood furniture; holes along stud lines of your walls; or the termites themselves, call a professional exterminator. You won't save money ignoring them, and their damage can be very serious, especially if they eat their way into the supporting structure of your house.

TERRARIUM

Water them wisely. An ordinary basting bulb syringe will help you get the right amount of water into a terrarium, especially a bottle-necked one, without disturbing plants or messing up the sides.

TERRY-CLOTH TOWELS

Make pot holders. When the middles are worn and the ends still thick, make pot holders from the ends of terry-cloth towels, either by cutting circles and sewing them together to make a mitt or making long rectangular "casserole" pot holders.

Turn them into bibs. You can also make baby bibs from the good parts of old towels. Simply cut them to the right size.

Keep out drafts. Use old towels to keep cold air from entering your home. Roll them lengthwise to place on windowsills and door thresholds to block drafts and blot condensed moisture.

Use them as rags. Don't forget how great they are as rags. Old terry cloth is great for polishing engraved or patterned silver or brass. Put the polish on with an old sock and buff with an old towel, then pitch it all if you don't want to wash the rags.

THANKSGIVING

Celebrate with a Thanksgiving tree. If your family can get together at Thanksgiving but not for Christmas, have a Thanksgiving tree. "Plant" a medium-size tree branch in a coffee can weighted with rocks and sand and then put the can into a nice basket. Decorate the tree with bows, fall leaves and other Thanksgiving motif ornaments. Put presents under the tree and have Christmas in November!

See also PARTIES.

THERMOSTATS

 Consider programmable thermostats. If your heating needs vary through the day, for example, if you want heat when you wake up, but prefer to save heating bills by keeping your apartment or home cool at night and during the day when you're at work, you can save money on your utility bills by using programmable thermostats that will automatically adjust the temperature according to a set of instructions that you preset. Programmable thermostats are sold at electric supply stores and hardware stores.

THROW

Use your robe as a comfy throw. When you need a throw to keep cozy while napping, try snuggling under your robe if it's full length, but switch ends so that the "shoulders" are covering your feet and the lower robe portion is over your upper body where you need more "snuggle."

TIN

Keep it clean. Most tin utensils are solid tin. Tin-plated iron items will rust if the plating is worn away by polish. Because unpolished tin absorbs heat better than polished, most tin ware is not polished. Try rubbing rusty tin with 0000 steel wool that has been dipped in mineral or vegetable oil.

TIRES

Make a planter. Fill a tire with soil to make a planter for your ornamental plants. If you have four tires, build a pyramid planter with three in a cloverleaf pattern on the bottom and one top and center. (Place a piece of pegboard inside the top tire to keep soil in.)

Make a stand. Fill a tire with cement and insert a pipe in the center to hold a pole for tetherball, basketball, a mailbox stand, a temporary small flag pole, and such.

TISSUES AND TISSUE BOXES

 Reuse old tissue boxes. Place an empty tissue box near the clothes dryer to hold used dryer sheets and then toss the box and all away when it's full. (But don't throw away used foam dryer sheets. Instead, use them to stuff pillows, children's plush toys and cloth dolls, craft soft sculptures, and more.

Square tissue boxes make good holders for cotton balls near your makeup area, or you can use them to store knee-high stockings. If you store singles of the same color together, you'll have a dispenser!

Keep facial tissues dry on bathroom vanity counters. When you buy a new box, turn it upside down and stick a bulletin-board push pin in each bottom corner so that it has "feet" to keep it above water spills.

TOILETS

Loosen up lime deposits. Pour full-strength white vinegar in the bowl, let sit for several hours, and brush away. If that doesn't work, pour a bucket of water quickly into the bowl to empty it, then cover the lime marks with paper towels soaked in vinegar. Let stand for several hours and scrub with sturdy brush or plastic scrubbie.

Caution: Don't flush the paper towels down the toilet; toss them in the trash. Towel-strength paper can clog sewer or septic tank lines.

Test for leaks. My husband, who is a plumber, recommends this test: Add some food coloring to the commode tank—green or blue is best. Do not flush the commode for an hour, then check to see if any coloring has seeped into the toilet bowl. If so, you need to replace the tank ball.

Trick an enthused toddler. Sometimes a newly pottie-trained toddler will unfurl most of a roll of toilet paper just for fun. One mom found this solution. After placing the roll on the roller, squeeze it to bend the inner cardboard roll. This prevents a child from unrolling the whole roll at once.

See also PLUMBING.

TOMATO SAUCE

 Transform soup into sauce. Add your favorite spices to undiluted canned tomato soup and use it as a sauce in your favorite recipe.

TOOLS

Hammer safely. If you have to pound in a nail at a level that is below your knees, face away from the wall, standing or crouching near the nail. Pound in the nail by hammering toward the rear.

If a nail is too short to hold, press it through a piece of cardboard or index card. Hold the paper in one hand and the hammer in the other. Tear away the cardboard before you pound the last taps or tap the last pounds, whichever sounds right to you. The cardboard will protect the wall from "hits and misses," too. You can also place the nail between the teeth of a comb to hold it while you're hammering.

Use a nail punch. This tool should be used for the final hammer drives to prevent "scars" on the surface from "hits and misses." It's also helpful to use when you have to drive a nail into a crevice. A nail punch will get the nail all the way in.

Use the right size screwdriver. Screwdrivers come in different sizes. Using the right size will keep the screw head from being damaged.

Make a hole first. If you make a small hole with a nail first, it is easier to screw in a screw.

Wax the threads. If you soap or wax screw threads, the screw will go in more easily.

TOOTHBRUSHES AND TOOTHPASTE

Travel with a toothbrush holder. Keep lipstick, eye shadow and eye- or lip-liner pencils in plastic travel toothbrush holders and you won't loose them when you travel. Get different colored holders for eye pencils and lip pencils so you don't have to open them each time. They might be so handy that you decide to keep them in your purse all of the time for repairs.

Make yours unique. A mother of seven children wrote that she solved the confusion by giving each of the boys a different colored brush (always the same color). All girls get the same color brush but personalize their brushes with leftover, lonely pierced earrings attached at the end hole.

Give new life to old toothbrushes. Bacteria can multiply in old toothbrushes, and if bristles are bent or scraggly they don't clean properly and may cut your gums. Change toothbrushes about every 3 months. After a good rinse, old toothbrushes will clean nooks and crevices in furniture and appliances; apply shoe polish; scrub stains on laundry before washing; clean a garlic press, graters, and other kitchen utensils; and clean jewelry.

Keep plastic tubes rolled up. Try holding the toothpaste roll with a snack bag clip, a clothespin, or a clothespin-type hair barrette.

TOWELS

Identify your houseguest's towels. When you have a hideaway cabin, your friends and relatives usually end up hiding away with you. Keeping track of whose towel is whose gets to be a problem, especially if swimming is involved. Write the names of guests on wooden spring clothespins with a pencil and ask them to clip the pins to their washcloths and towels. They can hang their towels outdoors to dry between swims with the same ID clothespins. You can erase the names after they leave so that there's space for the next arrivals' names. If you feel "crafty" you can decorate the clothespins with flowers and bows, too.

Remove the stiffness. Usually stiff-as-a-board towels are due to detergent buildup or overloading the washer. Avoid the problem by using less detergent, hotter water, and fewer towels per wash load. Remove detergent buildup by washing towels in very hot water with baking soda, borax, or washing soda, then add a cup or so of vinegar to the rinse water. Repeat the "treatment" periodically to keep towels soft and fluffy.

TRASH

Keep bags at the bottom of the can. Toss the whole roll of plastic bags into the bottom of your trash can after it's been cleaned. Draw up the first bag, leaving it attached to the roll, open it and drape it around the top rim.

When the bag is full, tie it shut, lift it up, and tear the plastic bag off the roll as you grab the next bag. Then drape the new bag over the rim as before.

Make a trash can garter. Cut off the elastic from men's shorts or old panty hose and use it to hold plastic garbage bags in place in trash cans. Just put the bag in so that several inches go over the lip of the trash can and put the elastic over the bag like a garter. You can also tie together pieces of elastic from your sewing supplies.

Craft a mini-trash can. When there's no space for a small waste basket, such as near a dressing table, vanity or clothes dryer, substitute an empty square tissue box. You can throw the box out when it's full of used tissues, makeup pads, dryer lint, or any other small trash. And, it's free! Plastic-lined woven-tray baskets that come on florist-delivered plant or floral arrangements also make good small bathroom or bedroom wastebaskets; just line them with small plastic bags from the stores.

Prop up your bags with TV-tray legs. Make holders for plastic trash bags for collecting leaves and trash in the yard, storing cans for recycling and for any other time you need to have a bag held open. Fold the top of a plastic trash bag over the top of the tray legs and fasten with spring clothespins.

TRAVEL

Look for a house-sitting service. Most major cities have house-sitting services in which bonded people check your house daily; pick up newspapers, flyers, and mail; water your houseplants; feed your fish; and take care of your cat or dog. The fee you pay is worth it if you get peace of mind. Always ask for references and check them out when you hire a sitter service for anything.

Update your insurance. If you are going on an extended trip of several months, and you want to rent out your house or condominium, check with your insurance agent about your policy's coverage.

Unplug your garage door. If you have an automatic garage door, unplug it to avoid having the door opened by someone with an opener that's operating on your frequency. Most people who have automatic garage doors report occasional mysterious openings due to others nearby having the same-frequency openers.

Protect Your Home While You're Away

It's most important to make sure that your home doesn't look empty. Here are some hints on how to do that.

♥ Set a timer that automatically turns lights on and off in several rooms at various hours. A timer can also turn a radio off and on.

♥ Park your car halfway up the driveway to prevent thieves from parking vans or trucks near the house.

♥ Be sure to have a neighbor pick up your newspaper, mail, and other deliveries. (It's safer to have these things picked up than canceled, I'm told by the police. Canceling tells a lot of strangers that you'll be gone and for how long.)

♥ Have someone take your trash out on pickup day and have your lawn mowed or snow shoveled to maintain an occupied look. (Check out bonded and insured house-sitting services in your city. Some of these services are nationally franchised and provide people to water plants and care for pets, in addition to keeping your home looking occupied. The cost varies but is certainly worth it to keep you from worrying during your fun-time vacation.)

TURKEY

Avoid leftovers. During the holidays when turkeys are cheapest, have your butcher cut them in half from neck to feet, then freeze them. You can serve half a turkey with dressing, all the trimmings and give thanks all year-round for having saved money on main dish meat.

Save some for casseroles. Divide leftover cut-up meat into 2-cup portions (or other frequently needed amounts) and freeze in separate freezer-safe bags so that you can just grab a bag of ready-to-use turkey (or chicken or beef) when you're cooking. If you have leftover gravy, freeze it in 1- or 2-cup portions to go with the meat.

Letter of Laughter

Twins

When her granddaughter told her about the twin girls in her class, Grandma asked how she could tell them apart. "Well, one wears blue sneakers and the other wears red," the child replied. When asked if that was the only way, the girl added, "Well, if I call Elizabeth and she comes, that's Elizabeth." Surely another "out of the mouths of babes" story. Aren't children smart?

TWIST-TIES

Save your twist-ties. They have many handy uses. You can use them to temporarily mend eyeglasses, tie plants to stakes, make hooks for Christmas ornaments, organize loose keys, hold stitches when knitting, and tie up stored extension cords.

UMBRELLAS

Don't tote a wet one. This is one of those "Why didn't I think of this before" hints. Before leaving home to go shopping, tuck a plastic grocery bag in your purse or briefcase so that you can put your drippy umbrella into the bag. Slip the handles over your arm and proceed to wherever you are going without messing up your clothing or leaving your umbrella someplace where it will "walk off."

Fix it with floss. When material comes loose from an umbrella spoke, reattach it with dental floss. It's stronger than thread and waterproof, too.

Take your patio umbrella for a swim. Is your plastic patio umbrella covered with mildew? A reader wrote that she just put hers into the swimming pool, left it there a day or two, and all the mildew disappeared.

Caution: This "swim" treatment is not for canvas umbrellas. Canvas shouldn't be bleached. Also, be sure the pool has plenty of chlorine or you could cause an algae buildup in it.

UPHOLSTERY

Don't lose the directions. Always keep cleaning instructions in a safe place so that you can clean upholstery properly.

STEP ▾ BY ▾ STEP

Cleaning Fabric Upholstery

Vacuum pieces regularly to keep dirt and dust from getting ground in. Here's how to clean washable fabrics after first testing for color fastness.

1. Mix ¼ cup of high-suds laundry detergent with 1 quart of warm water in a blender.

2. Apply just the suds with a medium-bristled brush. Work the lather in small circles, overlapping as you go.

3. Wring out a towel in clean water and wipe the entire upholstered surface.

4. When dry, vacuum the furniture to remove any residue.

Call an expert. If there is no care label on your upholstered furniture, you may have to rely on professional advice when it gets soiled or stained. Care depends on the type of fabric and whether or not the fabric has coating materials on its reverse side.

Keep it zipped. Don't assume that when an upholstered item has zippered cushion covers that the covers can be removed for cleaning. For example, Haitian cotton is a common upholstery material, but while other fabrics can be hand washed, wrung out, and air dried, Haitian cotton is uncleanable. The fabric does not respond well to water, leaving yellow rings that can't be removed. A good rule of thumb is never remove cushion covers for separate cleaning.

Don't let it take a tumble. Any tumble cleaning method can destroy the backing, shrink, or otherwise damage upholstery fabric.

Shop smartly. If no care instructions are attached to the furniture when you buy it, ask for some. If you have doubts about care and can't get advice, it may be a good idea to choose other furniture brands that offer care advice—unless the price is so low that the furniture is "disposable" if soiled, which is very rare these days!

Cleaning Leather Upholstery

Always keep the instruction tags that come with leather upholstery. Different finishes require different care methods. Generally, you need to dust and vacuum often and clean spots or surface soil with a weak solution of only a few drops of mild dishwashing liquid dissolved in a gallon of water.

Caution: Never soak leather! After cleaning, rinse and dry well. Apply saddle soap or an oil made especially for leather, if the manufacturer advises it, to protect the leather from scratches and to prevent it from becoming brittle.

UTENSILS

Face 'em forward. If you keep cooking utensils in a kitchen drawer, you can identify them more easily by turning the handles to the back of the drawer.

Smooth rough edges. When the edges of plastic utensils get a bit rough or burred, file them down with a fresh emery board. You can cut away the rough edges of rubber and plastic scrapers with good kitchen shears. You'll replace your spatulas and turners less frequently and prevent scratching expensive nonstick pans.

Realize it's not just for eggs. To make chopped eggs easily, use an egg slicer and then place the slices crosswise and slice again. You can also use the egg slicer for fresh mushrooms. Placed stem up, two or three small ones can be sliced at a time. The slices will be thicker and more uniform than those produced by a food processor.

Shop at a medical supply store. Some surgical tools are marvels in the kitchen. For example, some of the best kitchen shears I know are blunt-ended surgical shears, available in medical supplies stores. You have to be careful because they are extremely sharp, but you'll also be able to disjoint a raw or cooked chicken faster than with a knife. These shears can also make quick snips in the fatty edges of steaks and chops, even after

Organize Kitchen Clutter

Install a pegboard, painted to match your decor, on your kitchen wall and hang slotted spoons, skimmers, whisks, strainers, and other utensils that are too large or bulky for kitchen drawers. It makes the kitchen look like it's inhabited by a professional chef, too!

they are already in the pan and starting to curl up because you forgot to snip.

Another all-purpose tool that you can buy at medical supplies stores is forceps. These pointy-nosed, handle-locking tools are actually a doctor's version of needle-nosed pliers. Forceps will retrieve things from small openings, such as drawstrings from pajamas, drape cords from the rods, or bobby pins or jewel stones from crevices; hold small objects like jewel stones or decals for placement while they are being glued; and help in a variety of crafts. They clamp on to things you'd usually use tweezers to grasp and hold them until you release the handles. They also can be used to fix jewelry clasps and bezels.

Let clothespins spring into action. Spring clothespins are helpful everywhere. They hold skirts on hangers and notes on curtains. In the kitchen, they pinch bags shut, hold coupons and recipe cards together, clip a recipe to a nearby object so it's easily read, clip a dish towel to your blouse when you need an apron and are in too much of a hurry to get one, clip a towel around a child's neck for an instant bib, and . . . need I say more? Keep a bunch in the kitchen clipped to any convenient object.

Use a tea ball. Use a tea or spice ball to hold the bouquet garni of spices when you make soup or stew. Nobody will ever bite into a stray whole pepper ball, and you won't have to fish around with your spaghetti grabber for those bay leaves lurking in the murky depths of pots.

VACUUMS

Protect your palms. If pushing and pulling your upright vacuum cleaner gives you a blister on the palm of your hand, wear an oven mitt. The padding keeps your hand safe.

VALENTINE'S DAY

Postmark it with love. To get your Valentine cards postmarked "Valentines," gather your cards, and make sure they are properly addressed and have correct postage. Put them in a large envelope along with a note to the postmaster requesting the special postmark. Mail to Postmaster of Valentines, Valentines, VA 23887-9998. Don't forget to include a Valentine addressed to yourself so that you'll know what the postmark looks like.

See CAKES for Valentine's Day cake ideas.

VAPORIZERS

Scent and moisten the air. Fill a vaporizer-humidifier to the full line with water, and add a little potpourri. As you mist the air, you'll also put a fragrance in it.

See also HUMIDIFIERS.

VASES

Let the beauty shine through. Use only distilled water for floral arrangements; you'll avoid accumulation of cloudy residue.

Soak away lime. If lime deposits build up, fill the vase with hot water and drop in a couple of denture tablets. Let them soak for a few hours, and then scrub with a bottle brush, rinse well, and let dry. Or soak the vase with vinegar for several hours; rinse and dry.

Note: Save the vinegar for other cleaning. It still has cleaning power left!

VEGETABLE CRISPER

Stash a sponge to suck up moisture. Place a dry sponge in the refrigerator vegetable crisper to absorb excess moisture and help keep veggies fresh.

Prevent soggy veggies. Use a container with a lid or a self-seal plastic bag, add a couple of sheets of paper toweling to absorb moisture and keep veggies from getting soggy, and then replace the towels as they get damp. This method is especially good for lettuce, cucumbers, and mushrooms.

VEGETABLES

See PRODUCE.

VEGETABLE SPRAY

See COOKING SPRAY.

VIDEO CAMERAS AND CAMCORDERS

These wonderful devices should never be left in intense heat. When used outdoors, they should never be pointed directly at a bright light source. Bright lights can cause permanent damage.

Also, never travel with a portable video camera that's not protected from shock and moisture by a hard case or custom-fitted shock bag. Check out the rain and thermal covers available from equipment stores. To avoid problems related to condensation, let the camera get adjusted to extreme changes in temperature before you try to operate it.

That said, here are some ideas for using your video camera like a pro.

Capture the action. Remember that the idea is to film moving people even if you have them standing together. You can use a still camera for "picket fences" of family members frozen in position.

Talk while you film. Like TV reporters, talk while you film with your video camera. Record your "Gee whiz!" feelings instead of just descriptions and straight information. If you record impressions "on site," you won't sound like a dull travelogue later and will better capture all those special moments.

Film a party and have guests tell their favorite jokes. Then, years later, you can decide if the jokes are still funny. Or have each guest tell a favorite guest-of-honor story.

Treat your taping sessions as if you were making a TV documentary. Start your party filming with preparty cooking and other preparations; finish with the cleanup. Start wedding films by showing the bride putting her makeup and veil on. If available, you could start a wedding film with some footage of the bride and groom that led to this important occasion. Have the camcorder scan the bridal pictures of the newspaper's wedding and engagement announcements page, leading to the announcement of the engagement or wedding.

Show the details. It may be an interesting visual twist to show "locknut A's" being joined to "toggle bolt Z's" when a child's bike is being assembled and then show the child learning to ride it. Or if you are using your camcorder to film antiques and family treasures, describe them while you are filming them, and have someone else show all sides and the manufacturer's marks on the bottom (if they are gadgets, demonstrate how they work). Add any anecdotes about the treasures as you go.

Borrow a book title. You can also have fun using your imagination and newspaper headlines or book jackets for titles of your home movies, even if they are only semiappropriate. For example, *A Tale of Two Cities* or *Europe on $5 a Day* could be the title for your vacation-trip film. "Hurricane Gilbert Leaves Path of Destruction" could be the title preceding your after-party shots or a film of children playing after they've totally emptied a toy box. *The Joy of Cooking* could be the title preceding a barbecue scene. "Classified" cut from the want-ad section could be the title for just about any tape.

VIDEOCASSETTE RECORDERS (VCRs)

Clean the tape heads. If the video picture is distorted or has tiny white flecks, the tape heads may need cleaning. Use the head cleaning system suggested by your VCR instruction book or the system below. When using a commercial tape cleaner, run the tape for only 10 to 15 seconds or whatever the exact time prescribed on that specific tape. Longer is not better. It will only tend to gum up the tape heads more.

Keep your head clean. Always check directions to find out what type of commercial cleaner kit should be used, a wet or a dry method. If you have no cleaning kit handy, record on a new tape for about 30 minutes, and then play the recorded part of the tape back several times to let the heads rub against it so that they clean themselves. The next time you clean the heads, repeat the process starting at the point where the tape is new and unused. After you have used all parts of this tape for cleaning, toss the tape.

Give VCRs breathing room. Never stack videotapes, TV schedule booklets, or anything else on the recorder. "Insulating" your recorder with stacked stuff keeps all the heat it generates inside and will ultimately cause deterioration and a service call. Your recorder needs "breathing space" to keep cool.

Check your connections. Many unnecessary service calls are made because of bad connections. If your VCR is connected to a defective cable converter box (which is, in turn, connected to the TV set), the VCR won't record properly even if it plays prerecorded tapes. Try connecting the VCR directly to the TV set. If it works properly, you'll know to call the cable company instead of your VCR repair service.

Remember to reset the clock. If you've had a power outage, remember to reset the videotape machine clock. Otherwise, any programs that you've set up to tape won't be taped.

Use quality tapes. Tape heads get clogged by oxide particles that chip or flake off from tapes. You can prevent clogging by using quality tapes, which are labeled "high grade" or "super high grade" and don't shed oxide easily. Discard tapes after about 100 hours of use, and clean tape heads regularly.

Don't miss a moment. When taping a show, set the "on" time for 5 minutes earlier than the show's start time and 5 minutes past the show's scheduled end to make sure you don't miss anything.

Keep a recap. Identify the shows that you've taped to save by clipping out the review from your newspaper's TV guide and then tape it onto the videotape cassette or its jacket with the clear plastic tape (¾" covers a review) that you can write on, and you'll know the theme and the stars. These reviews fit nicely on the tape/jacket side.

If you are taping a series or several shows on one tape, you can usually get three to four reviews on the wide edge. It doesn't matter if the transparent tape overlaps; you can write short notes or numbers on the tape if you need to identify parts 1, 2, and 3.

Avoid accidental erasures. To avoid taping over a show that someone wanted to watch, use self-stick notes on the tape jacket to record the date, show, and names of the people who want to watch it. Each watcher checks off his or her name and the last person removes the note, which signals to everyone that the tape is free for recording.

Shop Sensibly for a VCR

Here are some things to think about when buying a videocassette recorder.

Do you rent movies only? If all you use it is for playing rented movies, the most basic equipment is fine.

Do you record off of TV? If you like to record TV shows for future viewing, look for models that are easy to set up ahead of time for automatic taping.

Do you edit out commercials? If you record a lot of programs and want to cut out the commercials, having a remote control is a must.

Do you edit and dub? If you have invested in expensive video camera equipment, you'll need a more elaborate type of recorder that allows you to edit and dub tapes.

Zip it up. Take a tip from fast-food restaurants, which keep their cash registers clean by covering them with plastic. Put your remote control into a zippered plastic bag so the TV munchers can press the buttons without making them icky.

Program for the week. Check the TV listings at the beginning of the week, set your VCR to tape the shows you want taped, and then let the VCR remember the taping sessions that are so easy to forget. Use a highlighter to mark the programs in your TV schedule so you can see at a glance what you've chosen to tape.

See VIDEOCASSETTES below.

Five Hints for Videocassette Care

Keep these hints in mind to enjoy many hours of video viewing.

♥ Keep videotapes away from any heat source to prolong tape life and preserve recorded material. Store them vertically to protect them from dust and dampness.

♥ Fast-forward and rewind tapes at least once a year.

♥ Always take up tape slack before playing. Wind the cassette hub with your finger until it's tight. Run new tapes on fast forward before using to remove any slack.

♥ Never take tapes from cool to warm places just before playing them. If moisture condenses on the tape, it will stick to the video head.

♥ Don't leave tapes on top of a TV set. When the TV is turned on, the TV's magnetic field can erase the tape.

VIDEOCASSETTES

Always rewind. Videotapes are very fragile, thin plastic film, which tends to stretch, wrinkle, and break when improperly handled. Video rental stores ask you to rewind the tapes because inserting a cassette that has tape

Videotaping Your Slides

Have you dreamed of being the next big-name film editor? Here's how to get professional results when converting your slides to video.

1. Set the video camera on a tripod and project the slides onto a good screen. (Experiment until you get the distance just right.)

2. Working with another person, have one show and focus the slides while the other operates the video camera and says when it's okay. The video operator turns on the camera and counts to four, then turns the camera off while the slides are being changed. One person can add dialog by explaining the photo.

Note: This takes a little practice. It helps if your video camera has a freeze-frame feature. There are machines that transfer photos or slides onto videotape, too. Check out photo-equipment stores.

on both reels can cause the tape to misfeed and get mangled. (Some stores charge an extra fee to your account if you don't rewind!)

This applies to your home recording tapes, too. Rewind them and then fast-forward when you add to the tape. Storing tapes without rewinding them allows the tapes to stretch and sag, then misfeed when played.

$ **Rent midweek.** Many video shops have special prices for midweek rentals, and you're more likely to get popular movies at that time.

Let videos make moving easier. One family wrote to say that when they moved, they felt sad about leaving their home and neighbors. So they decided to take their fond memories with them by making a film of their home—inside and out—and of their neighbors talking to their children. It made the move easier for everyone.

Send video messages. When one reader's mother was in the hospital for several weeks and children weren't allowed in to visit, she made a videotape of her children for their grandmother. They talked to granny, told her stories, sang songs, and drew pictures and cards for her and held them up to the camera. Granny was gratefully teary-eyed, and the children were happy to do something nice for their grandmother. The bonus is that the tape is a treasured family keepsake.

Keep a video log. By the time movies are available in video rental stores, you may have forgotten what they were about. So, when the movie ads and reviews first appear in newspapers, cut them out, and file the clippings in a file box or envelope. (You can paste them to index cards if you feel ambitious.) Then take your file to the rental store to jog your memory to help make your selections.

Don't overuse daily viewing tapes. Since the recommended life of a tape is about 100 hours, you could get the most out of each tape if you tape daily programs for several viewings and then tape a "keeper" (a movie or documentary that won't be viewed frequently).

VINEGAR

Keep it handy. Keep vinegar in a clean squirt bottle so it's handy for pretreating stains before laundering, cleaning bathrooms, etc. This planet-friendly cleaner has so many valuable uses, I consider it an indispensable household item.

Make strawberry vinegar. Combine a bottle of white wine vinegar with ½ cup of fresh, washed, and dehulled strawberries. Cover the mixture and let it sit at room temperature for one week. You can remove the fruit or leave it in, but if you leave it, the vinegar will continue to mellow and become stronger. Use in recipes calling for fruit vinegars.

Letter of Laughter

Visitors

A reader reminded us about one of life's ironic rules. Nobody every drops in to visit you when you've just cleaned up your home, but someone always drops by when the place is a wreck!

WAFFLE IRONS

Stop the sticking. To temper a waffle iron, clean the surface well. Then take a slice of bread and grease both sides with unsalted fat (never salted fat). Lay the bread in the waffle iron and close the lid. As the bread browns, it greases all the small square surfaces. For a double waffle iron, temper with two pieces of bread. After removing the bread, crumple it and feed it to the birds.

For more on waffles, see PANCAKES AND WAFFLES.

WALLPAPER

A beautiful alternative to plain, painted walls, wallpaper can be tricky to maintain. Here are few of my favorite hints. Before attempting these, it's important to know if your wallpaper is washable or not. Check the packaging, if you still have it, or consult the manufacturer.

Cleaning Wallpaper

Use old-fashioned soap and water. Most washable wall coverings can be cleaned with mild liquid soap and cool water. Work from the bottom up, using as little water as possible. Work on small areas and overlap as you wash. Rinse with clear water and blot dry.

Consider the alternatives. Nonwashable wall coverings can sometimes be cleaned by rubbing gently with kneaded eraser, fresh white bread, or doughy wallpaper cleaners from hardware stores. If you use the commercial doughy cleaner, be sure to knead and turn it often so you use clean surfaces on the wall.

Spot-clean wallpaper before spots set. Blot grease spots with paper towels or facial tissue while you press lightly with a warm iron over the towels or tissue.

Caution: If possible, always get manufacturer's directions for cleaning your particular kind of wallpaper. Always test cleaning methods on an inconspicuous place before doing a whole wall or conspicuous place like the areas around light switches.

Remove grease spots. If the paper towel hint doesn't work, make a paste of baking soda and water and then apply the thick paste to the grease stain and let it dry. Brush the residue off with a soft brush or cloth. Try to avoid future grease on special places, such as behind the stove or beside the trash can, by putting clear adhesive plastic over the "grease magnet" area.

Decorating with Wallpaper

Calculate the cost. If you'd like to install new wallpaper, here's how to estimate the expense. Multiply the wall width by the wall height to get the number of square feet. Then add together the total square feet for all four walls. That's the absolute minimum amount of wallpaper you'll need. Keep in mind that you'll need to allow extra for pattern matching.

A single roll of American wallpaper usually covers 30 square feet, depending upon the pattern. A single roll of European wallpaper usually covers 23 square feet.

Take advantage of sales. If you are doing only one wall of a room, you may be able to take advantage of remnant sales, but be aware that sale wallpaper may be a closeout and if you underestimate your needs, you may not be able to buy more.

Select carefully. Wallpaper is expensive to replace but may last longer than paint in some rooms. It may last too long if the pattern is too busy; less-busy designs stay pleasing longer.

Use the leftovers. Cover books or shelves, wrap gifts, make decals for sliding glass doors, cut and laminate for placemats, or cut pictures out of wallpaper scraps and frame them.

Make some borders. If you like wallpaper, but don't want it all over your walls, make some into borders. Buy a double roll of striped wallpaper that matches your wall colors, and then cut the stripes individually into border strips. You can make wider borders by combining strips. You'll save even more if you catch a wallpaper remnant sale.

Substitute a border. When you can't find just the right wallpaper border or the right color, try buying heavy ribbon at a fabric store and putting it up with tacky glue.

Make wallpaper borders easy to apply. When putting a wallpaper border around a room at the ceiling, you can save climbing up and down a ladder and constant repositioning of the ladder if you line up all your chairs along the wall and cover them well with old sheets or drop cloths. Then you can step from one chair to the next as you work. If two people work on this project, one can walk in front of the other holding the wet strip of border while the second person applies the other end.

Cover your mistakes. When her dark blue print wallpaper dried, a reader was dismayed to see a strip of white in between each sheet where the paper strips had pulled away from each other. She solved the problem by painting right down the seam with a small brush and some stencil paint that matched the wallpaper. She did about 5 inches at a time and wiped excess paint from the wallpaper with a damp cloth as she worked. Stencil paint comes in many different shades so you can match just about any color when you need to make a quick repair.

Prime before painting. If you decide that you've had it with the wallpaper in your home, an easy option is to paint over it. Painting over paper is easier than removing existing paper and repairing the walls. Also, painting over heavily textured paper is very attractive since the texture shows through the paper. Before attempting to paint over wall paper, you need to apply a product that primes the paper before painting. It's sold at most paint stores.

See also DECORATING.

WALLS

Since they serve as the backdrop for all of your décor, the shape of your walls is key to your home's appearance. Read on for hints to keep them in tip-top shape.

Repairing Walls

Quick-patch nail holes. If you have small holes in white walls, fix them with white toothpaste or with moistened crushed aspirin that you push into the hole. You can also cover over the patch on colored walls with color-coordinated typewriter correction fluid.

Touch up with water paints. After patching nail holes in colored walls, use a dab of watercolor paints if you don't have leftover paint. You'll be amazed at how closely you can match colors with water paint.

Use cotton swabs for touch-ups. If you have leftover paint, touch up small spots with cotton swabs instead of a brush. You don't waste paint or have to clean a brush.

Extend drying time with vinegar. If you add 1 tablespoon of white vinegar (I know, vinegar again!) to the water when you are mixing patching plaster, the compound won't dry so quickly, and you'll be able to work more slowly.

Fill from the inside out. When you are filling wide cracks in plaster, it's best to fill from the inside out, pressing fresh plaster in with a putty knife or a trowel.

Loosen the plaster with a beer can opener. A beer can opener makes cutting loose plaster out of a wall before patching a large crack a snap. You can use the pointed end of the opener to undercut and widen the opening.

Restore worn-out screws. When a screw hole in the wall has worn grooves, stuff the hole with a cotton ball soaked in white glue, let it dry for 24 hours, and then put the new screw into the hole securely with a screwdriver.

Cleaning Walls

Clean methodically. Dust walls before washing and wash from the bottom up so that drips won't make their marks. Clean small areas at a time, then rinse and dry before moving to another area.

Use soaps and soft waters. You can safely wash most painted surfaces with soap or mild detergent and water or mild commercial household cleaners (when in doubt, spot test first). To soften soap waters and rinse waters, add 1 tablespoon of borax or a commercial water softener per quart of water.

Removing Incidental Artwork

Surely, your little angels would never do this, but children with crayons, pencils, and pens in hand seem to be drawn to white walls as if by magic. Here's how to repair the damage.

- ♥ Crayon can sometimes be sponged off with dry-cleaning solvent.
- ♥ Pencil marks and smudges can sometimes be removed with art gum or pencil erasers. (Always rub gently.)
- ♥ Ink may be removed by bleach, or commercial ink remover may work on wallpaper, but either one may also remove the color of the wallpaper; test first.

WASHCLOTHS

Travel with disposable cloths. Disposable cleaning cloths cut in half are just the right size for travel washcloths, especially in Europe where washcloths aren't usually provided in smaller hotels.

Keep one on hand for kids' messes. Washcloths dry quickly and, if left behind, are no loss. Keep a wet one in a zipper bag close at hand when traveling with children.

WASHING MACHINES

Try a vinegar rinse. To get rid of the residue left by detergents and minerals in hard water areas, fill the machine with hot water and pour in

1 quart of vinegar. (Yes, I know, vinegar again!) Run the machine through the entire cycle. The residue should vanish. Do this only occasionally, as overuse of vinegar can possibly hurt the inside of your washing machine.

Sprinkle salt on soap suds so suds swells subside. If you've added so much detergent to your wash that the washer starts belching suds, add salt. Then say that sentence fast five times before you scold the person who put too much detergent in the machine . . . even if the culprit is you.

WATCHES

Consider all the costs before you buy. Whether it's a designer watch or a $15 special, consider its guarantee of accuracy and the cost of upkeep,

Troubleshooting Washing Machines

These hints may save you a costly service call if your washer or dryer doesn't work. Sometimes it's as simple as a circuit breaker that has tripped, a loose plug, or a blown fuse. Before you call the service agent, check the following.

- Some washers will turn off automatically if the clothes aren't balanced. Rearrange them and push the button to start again.
- There's a button under the lid of the washing machine that stops the machine action when the lid is raised. Check to see if the lid is closed tightly.
- Check to see if there is a kink in any of the hoses or if the drain hose has become disconnected from the machine.
- Check if the water faucets are turned on.
- Make sure that the selector button is pushed in all of the way.
- Be sure that the plug is connected and a fuse hasn't blown.

such as batteries, and not the price tag alone. Battery-powered watches usually need a new battery, costing $5 to $10, about once a year. Before you buy, find out what type of battery is needed, how easily it's replaced, if stores in your area carry the batteries, and if you can replace them yourself. Some mainspring watches need cleaning and oiling annually. Check into the cost before you buy one.

Research repair costs. Local watch repair shops can repair watches powered by a mainspring and some battery-powered watches. However, some battery-powered watches must be returned to the manufacturer. It can be very expensive to have special parts made for antique watches. A friend paid over $200 to have a mainspring made for a family heirloom watch.

Know the terminology. "Water-resistant" means that the watch can be submerged in fresh water to 80 feet and in salt water to 75 feet without leakage or loss of accuracy. Some watches are no longer water-resistant after the case has been opened for battery replacement. "Shock resistant" means that a watch can be dropped from 3 feet onto a hard wood surface without being damaged. "Antimagnetic" means that the inside working parts of the watch are made from metals that will not magnetically attract each other and therefore work independently. "Jewels" refers to the usually synthetic gemstones that serve as bearings inside a mechanical watch.

Avoid metal allergies. If you've discovered you're allergic to your watch, or if the metal leaves a greenish-black mark on your wrist, either paint the back side of the watch with clear nail polish or cut corn pads to fit the back side and stick them on to protect your skin.

WATER

Save your humidity. If you use a dehumidifier in your basement, save the water it collects in old plastic jugs and use it to water plants.

Collect rainwater. Place 30-gallon plastic garbage cans at the end of rain gutters so they collect water for watering house and garden plants.

Let your air conditioner water the flowers. Have the water drainpipe from your air conditioner drain water into a flower bed. (You may need to check periodically to make sure the end of the pipe doesn't get clogged with mud or vines. If clogged, the water will back up to its source!)

Drink eight to ten glasses daily. Put eight to ten pennies on the kitchen counter and remove one each time you drink a glass of water.

Cover up water stains. The tricky thing about water stains on ceilings is that they will come back through paint. You need to seal the area first with a special sealant sold in paint stores for that purpose or with clear varnish. Make sure varnish dries before painting over it.

WAX

See CANDLES AND CANDLEHOLDERS.

QUICK REFERENCE

Buying Bottled Water: Know the Terms

Water, water, everywhere—here's how to know what to drink.

- ♥ "Natural sparkling" and "sparkling" waters are water that is bubbly because carbon dioxide (but no other chemicals) has been added to it. The word "natural," according to the FDA, has not been defined, so products labeled "natural" may not be different from other brands.

- ♥ "Spring" water comes from a spring and has no minerals added or removed.

- ♥ "Drinking" water comes from a water well and has no minerals added or removed.

- ♥ "Purified" water has all minerals and chemicals removed. It is generally not consumed as drinking water unless ordered by a doctor.

- ♥ "Distilled" water is recommended to prevent mineral buildup in some appliances such as steam irons. It still contains a minute amount of minerals.

> ## Five Steps to Water Conservation
>
> Water is such a precious commodity, especially where I live in Texas. I think it's so important to conserve water however we can.
>
> 1. Shower instead of taking a tub bath.
> 2. When brushing your teeth, turn the water off until it's time to rinse instead of letting it just run away down the drain.
> 3. Keep a container of cold water in the fridge to avoid wasting tap water by running it until it feels cool.
> 4. Wash only full dishwasher loads.
> 5. Either wait until you have a full load to run the clothes washer or adjust the water level to avoid waste.

WEDDINGS

 Make anniversaries easier to remember. When you buy a wedding gift, also buy a first-anniversary card. Then, when you get home, make it ready to mail at the appropriate time. Write the name on the envelope and pencil the date it should be mailed on the corner where the stamp will go.

Note: It's better not to write the address on the envelope because the couple might move.

Send a video chain letter. Make a copy of the wedding ceremony's videotape and send it via "chain letter" to all those who couldn't come to the wedding in person. Include a list of names and addresses to send with the tape that begins with the first person who received it and ends with the bridal couple. Also include instructions to send the tape to the next person on the list. When the tape returns to the bridal couple, they'll know everyone has seen it.

For wedding shower gift ideas, see SHOWERS.

WEEVILS

See PESTS.

WHIPPED CREAM AND WHIPPED TOPPINGS

Enhance a good thing. Add a sprinkle of allspice, cinnamon, or nutmeg and a drop of vanilla extract to whipped cream or topping to make it extra special.

Keep the bowl steady. The mixing bowl won't slip and slide across the counter when you're whipping cream if you place a damp washcloth under it before turning on the mixer.

WICKER

Wash it regularly. Start by brushing dust out of all cracks with an old toothbrush or scrub brush, or vacuum with brush attachment.

Next, with a soft brush, scrub wicker with a solution of 2 pints of cool water and 1 tablespoon of salt. Rinse with damp sponge. After furniture dries, rub with furniture polish and soft cloth.

Caution: Wipe excess polish off chairs with a second cloth to prevent damage to clothing of "sitters."

WINDOWS

Oh come on, don't say, "I don't do windows." Unless we hire other people to do them, we all have to do windows once in a while or we miss all the sunshine. For many of us, doing windows is a major project even if it's just to clean them. Some of the tips below go beyond the mere cleaning level but are minor repairs that can be done with simple tools.

Washing Windows and Shades

Pick an average day to do it. Always wash and dry windows on an average day, not on an extremely hot, sunny day, because the washing solution will dry too quickly and you'll end up with lots of streaks.

Make a homestyle cleaner. Add ¼ cup of nonsudsing ammonia to 1 gallon of water and wash away grime.

Dry with direction. My best window-washing hint is that when you dry windows, dry them on the outside from right to left, and on the inside, dry with the strokes up and down. That way, if there's a streak, you can tell whether it's on the inside or the outside of the window. It's easy to remember which is which because the up and down motion makes an "I," which stands for "inside."

Use the news. By far, the best and cheapest thing to use when drying windows is newspapers. You don't need to use paper towels or cloths that have lint on them. There seems to be something in the printer's ink that makes windows shine and sparkle, and it hasn't cost you an extra penny.

Remove water spots. To dissolve hard water deposits on windows, spray full-strength white vinegar on the window, let it set, and then wipe. Heavy deposits may require two or three applications and scrubbing with a stiff brush.

Try hosing down your house. You won't get the windows perfectly clean, but you will get some of the daily dust off, and the bonus is that you'll get a lot of cobwebs off the rest of the house. Do this on a hot day in your swimsuit and cool off at the same time. Get the children into the act and you'll end up with a day the whole family remembers! (Let the children use water pistols and you control the hose. Claim parent privilege!)

Keep window shades clean. If the shades are washable, take them down, unroll, and lay them on a flat surface. Dust with a clean cloth, and wash with mild detergent suds and warm water. Rinse well, wipe dry, and hang immediately.

If the shades are not washable, they should be cleaned by a professional cleaner; a clothing dry cleaner can recommend someone for you. Or, you can buy a dough-type wall cleaner at paint or wall-covering stores and follow the directions carefully. Always test cleaners on an inconspicuous place before doing a whole project.

Repairing Windows and Window Screens

Unstick a stuck window. Try to wedge a putty knife around all sides of the window so that you can spray furniture polish into the space. "Shake" the window to get as much furniture polish as possible down the sides. When it gives a bit, move the window up and down until you can open it all the way. Spray more furniture polish on the inside of the frame to get it lubricated well.

Another strategy is to get a block of wood and place it on the spot before you tap (not pound) the window sash with a hammer. If you hit the sash directly with the hammer, it will dent.

Remove cracked glass carefully. In order to do this without cutting yourself and having dangerous pieces of glass to clean up, crisscross both sides of the broken pane with many strips of masking tape before you tap it out with a hammer. The tape will hold most of the pieces together safely.

Repair small tears. Push the wire strands of a torn window screen back into place with an ice pick. If you can't completely close up the hole, sparingly brush clear nail polish or shellac across the remaining opening. After the sealer dries, reapply until the pinhole is invisibly sealed. Blot up any drips of sealer that run down the screen to make this a neat job.

A clean cut or tear in a window screen can be stitched together if you use a long needle and strong nylon thread, fishing line, or fine wire. As you zigzag-stitch back and forth across the cut, don't pull the thread or wire too tightly, because this will pucker the patch. After you are finished with the mend, apply clear nail polish to keep the thread or wire from pulling loose.

Patch large holes. If the screen has a large hole, cut a patch from a scrap of the same type of screening, and then zigzag the patch into place. Apply clear nail polish to the stitching to reinforce it.

You can heat-fuse a patch when you have to repair fiberglass screening. Just lay a fiberglass patch over the tear or hole and carefully run a hot iron around the edges. You'll need to put some foil over the screen and patch to keep the iron from touching it directly.

Other Hints Regarding Windows and Shades

Avoid drippy condensation in the winter. Wipe the moisture off the windows and be sure they are dry. With a couple of tissues, apply undiluted hair shampoo to the windowpanes. They may look cloudy at first but should clear up.

Hint: The best solution is to try to vent extra moisture from your home with kitchen and bath exhaust fans. Too much moisture for too long can cause wood framing to rot or warp and can make paint peel.

Install simple security measures. If you have wooden frame windows, drill a hole about 4 to 6 inches above each bottom window section in the inside framework. Insert a bolt into each hole. The windows can be opened only 4 to 6 inches, not enough space for a burglar to squeeze through, and you can remove the bolts when you want to fully open the windows.

Minimize indoor air pollution. When you install storm windows, weather stripping, caulking, and wall insulation, indoor pollutants (such as household and personal products, formaldehyde or asbestos in building materials, lead, pesticides, tobacco smoke, radon, molds, and gasses from heaters) can become concentrated because less outdoor air is entering your home. Some weatherizers such as caulk can emit pollutants of their own, too.

Therefore, before you weatherize, you should also take steps to minimize pollution from sources inside your home due to inadequate air flow, stuffy air, moisture condensation on cold surfaces, and mold and mildew growth. The good news is that sometimes when you seal up your home to prevent heat loss, you can also reduce indoor pollutant levels. For example, sealing foundation cracks can also prevent radon gas from getting into your home.

Reuse your window shades. Cut up old window shades for shelf and drawer liners; they are sturdy and free!

WINDSHIELD

Keep cleaning supplies on hand. Fill a spray bottle with equal parts of rubbing alcohol and water; spritz, and wipe clean with soft cloth or paper towels.

In the winter, when it gets so cold that your windshield washer fluid freezes inside your car, carry a small spray bottle filled with the stuff. Then you can spray the windshield while the wipers are running to clean it off before you drive.

Clean the inside of the windshield on the road. Squirt washer fluid from the automatic windshield washer on a paper towel or disposable towel and then wipe the inside of the windshield. If you can't reach the window cleaning mechanism while holding the paper towel, just lay the towel on the windshield before operating the cleaner; it should get enough of a squirt to do the job.

Note: The car should be stopped to do this, but then you knew that.

Remove windshield film with a homestyle cleaner. Mix 1 part vinegar or 1 part nonsudsy ammonia (not both) to 3 parts water and clean the windshield with it.

Stop "fingernail-on-the-blackboard" wiper blade squeaks. If blades are worn down, they will squeak and even scratch the windshield; replace them. If blades are in good condition, tree sap or road tar can cause squeaks, and washing with a good commercial cleaner should solve the problem.

WINE AND CHAMPAGNE

If you buy caviar, you'll probably buy champagne to enjoy with it (although some people like vodka with caviar). In France, all sparkling wine labeled "Champagne" can come, by law, only from the Champagne region. However, American vintners are not prevented from calling their sparkling wines "champagne." German sparkling wine is *Sekt*, and Italian is *spumante*.

Wine

Select the right wine. The rule of white wine with white meat and red wine with red meat may help you select wines for food but this rule isn't the final word because the characteristics of both recipes and wines differ greatly. For example, the heartier flavor in a poultry roast might be better enhanced by a dry, light-bodied red wine instead of the traditional white. Vinegar, citrus juice, and egg yolks can give wine an off taste. Artichokes, asparagus, onions, and pineapples also can have an unpleasant effect on certain wine flavors.

Examine the cork. When you see tiny crystal looking particles on the bottom of a wine cork, don't panic and think it's broken glass. Usually, these bits are malic acid crystals that have solidified and are evidence of an inferior, but not unwholesome, wine-making process.

Lay it down. Wine that doesn't require aging or that will be consumed soon can be stored standing up for a short time, but wine to be aged should be stored lying down to keep the cork damp and prevent air from reaching the wine. Also wine rests better in the dark. So, if you buy a case of wine for a party, just place the case on its side in a cool basement or other cool, dark place.

Store wine in a quiet place. Wine, especially aged varieties, don't like vibrations. So store the bottles away from laundry or other equipment that's likely to vibrate.

Take note of the temperature and humidity. Humidity keeps the corks from drying out and allowing wine to evaporate and spoil. The best humidity level for wine storage is 75 percent. Most wine experts say the ideal temperature for a wine cellar should be 55° to 60°F, with 45° to 70°F as the outer limits. Keeping the temperature constant is even more important than the exact temperature.

Keep it away from odors. Wine can "breathe" through the cork, so any odors absorbed during storage can affect the flavor.

Simple Ways to Make Your Own Wine Rack

Whether your taste is for sparkling or still (nonbubbly) wines, proper storage of wine will preserve the flavors you've spent your hard-earned money to buy.

♥ Construct a concrete-block "student" bookcase by layering blocks with sturdy boards and then stacking wine bottles, which have been inserted into mailing tubes, on the shelves.

♥ Stack clay tubular drain tiles against a cool cellar wall to hold wine bottles. The tiles can be supported on the sides of this "wine rack" if they are placed wall to wall or within a bookcase or other sturdy frame.

♥ Fit two sturdy pieces of wood, which have been fitted with grooves so that they are joined diagonally to form an X, into a square cabinet and then insert wine bottles in the spaces.

♥ Accordion-type wooden wine racks can also be installed in any type of cabinet or bookcase with doors to hold wine bottles on their sides and in the dark, as nature demands.

Minimize the air space in open bottles. Don't just cork a half-empty bottle of wine left over from a meal and put it into the fridge. Pour it into a clean, empty half-sized bottle that you keep for this purpose, then cork and store. Leaving air space between the cork and the wine speeds up deterioration of the wine. (This air space is called "ullage," if you're a Scrabble player or just like to astound your guests!)

See STAINS for hints on how to remove wine stains from fabrics.

Champagne

Catch identified flying objects. Place an oven mitt over a bottle's cork and bottleneck after you take off the foil and wire covering. Then, holding the bottle and mitt with one hand, release the cork with the other. Exploding corks will fly into the top of the mitt. It's not very glamorous, but beats hitting someone in the eye or taking potshots at the chandelier!

Sometimes running warm water over just the neck of the bottle will help. If you keep the bottle at a 45-degree angle during this procedure,

---

QUICK REFERENCE

Crack the Champagne Code

Here's some champagne measure language for you to use when you play guessing board games and to help you shop when you have a party.

A half-pint (1-2 glasses) is called a split

⅛ gallon (2-3 glasses) is a pint

¼ gallon (5 glasses) is a quart (a bottle)

2 quarts (10 glasses) is a magnum

4 quarts (21 glasses) is a jeroboam

6 quarts (31 glasses) is a rehoboam

8 quarts (41 glasses) is a methuselah

12 quarts (62 glasses) is a salmanasar

16 quarts (83 glasses) is a balthazar

20 quarts (104 glasses) is a nebuchadnezzar

---

more of the champagne's surface will be exposed to the atmosphere and therefore the champagne will be less likely to have pressure built up at the bottle neck and will be more likely to remain in the bottle until you can pour it and enjoy.

Buy champagne in smaller quantities. Champagne is meant to be drunk within a short period of time. Therefore, do not buy champagne to keep and store away for 5 or 10 years at a time. If you are buying champagne for the future, it's better to buy bottles of less than a magnum size. They last longer. Keep dated records of where and when you bought champagne and wine, then record any comments after you open and taste it.

See "Crack the Champagne Code" on page 499.

Do not store champagne in the refrigerator. This hint is most important since purists think that champagne can absorb odors from other foods in the refrigerator over a long period of time. In addition, the cork will eventually shrink in cold temperatures, allowing the bubbles to escape and the wine to go flat. Store it in a cool, dark place on its side. Then put it in the refrigerator or in a bucket of ice water 2 hours before serving.

WISHBONES

Quick-dry a roasted wishbone. If you have impatient Thanksgiving guests who can't wait to make their holiday wishes, try microwaving the wishbone for a few seconds to dry it immediately.

WOOD

Find a new use for bread boxes with a woody odor. I've had many letters about "woody" odors in these boxes that even get into the bread stored in them. We've tried every conceivable method to remove the woodsmell, without any luck at all. We use our box to store letters, and I'm sure there are other uses. The alternative is to return it to the store for a refund.

Reseason wooden spoons. After washing spoons in hot sudsy water, scrub if needed and rinse well. Wipe dry and allow to air-dry completely. Then heat some mineral oil (not vegetable oil, which can get rancid in wood) over medium heat and dip the spoons in it until they are completely coated. Drain on paper towels (save towels, place one layer of towels over newspapers) until they are cool enough to handle. Wipe them off and they are ready to use.

See also FURNITURE.

WOODSTOVES

Make sure it's maintained properly. If you have a woodstove in your vacation cabin or home, it needs an annual tune-up that includes chimney cleaning; thorough cleaning of the stove, including cleaning the secondary air chamber; installation of new door gaskets to keep the stove airtight; adjustment of the door latch and the thermostat; and polishing the griddle. These chores can be done by a certified woodstove professional or with a tune-up kit sold by stove manufacturers.

Remove creosote from the glass. In an old bowl, put some wood ashes and add enough vinegar to get the consistency of a light paste. Apply it to the window and allow to soak. Then use a wet cloth to remove the paste. The creosote should be gone.

XYLOPHONE

Mute your child's toy. When a child's xylophone makes a tinny noise that keeps your eardrums vibrating, get rid of the wooden sticks. Instead make new sticks by attaching a small rubber ball, like the kind on paddle-ball sets or from jacks, to a pencil or piece of doweling. You won't have a musical treat, but the sound will still be muted enough to avoid a really bad headache.

This reminds me of a joking "curse" a friend of mine used to place on people who annoyed her. It's "May all your children get drums for Christmas (or Chanukah)."

YARN

Sort with six-pack rings. Plastic six-pack rings will hold looped yarn strands or partial skeins of yarn so that they can be stored or carried neatly.

Save the scraps. Save small lengths of yarn from needlework and craft projects so that you can loop the yarn on gift tags and tie them on package ribbons. Don't forget to make the gift tags from the fronts of old greeting cards for total recycling!

YOGURT

Curb cravings. Add fruit, jam, vanilla, or other flavoring (about a ½ teaspoon per cup according to your taste) to plain, nonfat yogurt. Or try vanilla yogurt as a delicious low-cal and nutritious dressing for sliced fruit.

I have a dieting friend who adds plain cocoa, vanilla, and sweetener to nonfat yogurt when she has an attack of the munchies and finds that she's consumed all but her allocated calories of milk for that day. It's not ice cream or pudding, but it stops the cravings!

Make yogurt "cream cheese." Place a coffee filter in a strainer and empty a container of low-fat or nonfat yogurt into the filter. Place the strainer over a bowl and refrigerate overnight. By morning, the liquid will have separated from the solids. Mix with fruit, honey, wheat germ, vanilla, or a bit of sugar for flavoring; then, spread on whole-grain toast or bagel for a nutritious and tasty, low-cholesterol breakfast.

Corral things in one place. Use cleaned and empty yogurt containers to store small items like paper clips, thumbtacks, rubber bands, nails, screws, and pins.

Make perfect portions. Save the lids and cups of yogurt containers, wash well, and use for children's or dieter's individual ice-cream portion. It avoids the mess from large cartons and won't tempt the dieter to take more than allowed.

Pack 'em for picnics. Yogurt cups are free drinking cups for kids at picnics. Or personalize cups for family members and use in your bathrooms until the cup gets yucky—then dispose of it.

Use them as measuring cups. Small yogurt cups can be ½- or 1-cup measuring cups; quart-size could be a measure for a dog's daily serving of dry food.

Make lunch food squash-proof. When packing lunches, yogurt cups will hold chips, small cookies, grapes, and other fruits and goodies that get crushed in a lunch bag. No more squashed plums!

ZIPPERS

Free a boot flap zipper. When this happened to me, I cut a small slit in the leather just above the zipper, then slid the zipper to the top to free it and then back to the bottom.

Release zippers stuck on clothing. Rub the teeth with dry bar soap or candle and zip!

Replace a broken zipper pull. If the movable zipper part has a hole on either side, a small paper clip or safety pin can replace the pull tab.

Get a grip. When luggage, handbag, or other zippers are hard to grasp, attach a key chain (especially those brightly colored promotional key chains that accumulate in desk drawers), the remaining "dangles" of un-mated earrings, other pieces of costume jewelry, charms, or even a loop made from a piece of leather thong or shoelace.

ZUCCHINI

Freeze the inevitable surplus. Grate zucchini in a food processor and pack the pulp in freezer bags. Measure your portions so you can make zucchini bread or other recipes later in the year.

Z-Z-Z-Zs

Here are six things to do when you can't sleep.

Don't change your schedule. Keep regular hours and bedtime routines.

Avoid caffeine, cigarettes, and alcohol. Avoid caffeinated beverages for 6 to 8 hours before bedtime. If you smoke, be aware that nicotine is an even stronger stimulant than caffeine. Alcoholic beverages can hamper your falling asleep easily and sleeping soundly, once you doze off.

Nix the naps. Afternoon naps and sleeping too many hours at night can interfere with falling asleep.

Write it down. If worries and distractions keep you awake, make to-do lists for the next day so that you don't worry about forgetting something as you try to nod off. Keep a note pad and pen next to the bed so that you can jot down last minute thoughts on paper instead of keeping them inside your head where they keep you awake.

Eat moderately. Starving or stuffing yourself can keep you awake. You can't settle down if a too empty digestive system is rumbling or a too full one is stressed.

Drink a soothing liquid. Mother was right! A glass of warm milk at bedtime really does help—unless, of course, you are lactose intolerant and it won't digest! Then, a nice hot cup of herbal or decaffeinated spiced tea can soothe some people as much as the traditional warm milk.